ENCYCLOPEDIA OF
CIVIL WAR
BIOGRAPHIES

ENCYCLOPEDIA OF
CIVIL WAR
BIOGRAPHIES

VOLUME 2

SHARPE REFERENCE
an imprint of M.E. Sharpe, Inc.

SHARPE REFERENCE

Sharpe Reference is an imprint of cM.E. Sharpe INC.

cM.E. Sharpe INC.
80 Business Park Drive
Armonk, NY 10504

Library of Congress Cataloging-in-Publication Data

Encyclopedia of Civil War biographies / edited by James M. McPherson.
p. cm.
Includes index.
Summary: Presents brief biographical sketches of nearly 400
soldiers, politicians, reformers, and other figures associated with
the Civil War.
ISBN 0-7656-8021-1 (set : alk. paper)
1. United States—History—Civil War, 1861–1865 Biography
Encyclopedias. [1. United States—History—Civil War, 1861–1865
Biography.]   I. McPherson, James M.
E467.E53   2000
973.7′092′2—dc21   99-35226
[B]   CIP

Printed and bound in the United States of America

The paper used in this publication meets the minimum requirements of
American National Standard for Information Sciences—Permanence of
Paper for Printed Library Materials,
ANSI Z 39.48.1984.

BM (c) 10 9 8 7 6 5 4 3 2 1

For *cM.E. Sharpe* INC:
Vice President and Publisher: Evelyn M. Fazio
Senior Reference Editor: Andrew Gyory
Editorial Coordinator: Aud Thiessen
Cover Design: Lee Goldstein

For American Reference Publishing Inc.:
President: Richard Gottlieb
Editorial Director: Laura Mars
Editorial Assistants: Amy DiDomenico and Robin Williams

Contents

VOLUME 2

G 265

 Garfield, James Abram
 Garland, Augustus Hill
 Garnett, Richard Brooke
 Garrard, Kenner
 Geary, John White
 Getty, George Washington
 Gibbon, John
 Gibson, Randall Lee
 Gillem, Alvan Cullem
 Gillmore, Quincy Adams
 Goldsborough, Louis Malesherbes
 Gordon, George Washington
 Gordon, John Brown
 Grant, Lewis Addison
 Grant, Ulysses S.
 Greene, George Sears
 Greene, Samuel Dana
 Gregg, David McMurtrie
 Gregg, John Irvin
 Gregg, Maxcy
 Grierson, Benjamin Henry
 Griffin, Charles
 Griffin, Simon Goodell
 Griffing, Josephine Sophie White
 Grimes, Bryan
 Grimes, James Wilson
 Grimké, Angelina Emily
 Grimké, Thomas Smith
 Grover, Cuvier

H 319

 Halleck, Henry Wager
 Hamilton, Charles Smith
 Hamlin, Hannibal
 Hammond, William Alexander

Hampton, Wade
Hancock, Winfield Scott
Hardee, William J.
Harney, William Selby
Harper, Fletcher
Harris, Isham Green
Hartranft, John Frederick
Hartsuff, George Lucas
Hatch, Edward
Hatch, John Porter
Haupt, Herman
Hawkins, Rush Christopher
Hayes, Rutherford Birchard
Hays, Alexander
Hazen, William Babcock
Heintzelman, Samuel Peter
Helm, Ben Hardin
Herron, Francis Jay
Heth, Henry
Hill, Ambrose Powell
Hill, Benjamin Harvey
Hill, Daniel Harvey
Hoke, Robert Frederick
Hollins, George Nichols
Holmes, Oliver Wendell
Holmes, Theophilus Hunter
Hood, John Bell
Hooker, Joseph
Hovey, Alvin Peterson
Howard, Oliver Otis
Howe, Albion Paris
Howe, Samuel Gridley
Huger, Benjamin
Humphreys, Andrew Atkinson
Hunt, Henry Jackson
Hunter, David
Hunter, Robert Mercer Taliaferro
Hurlbut, Stephen Augustus

I 393
Ingalls, Rufus
Iverson, Alfred

J 395
Jackson, Claiborne Fox
Jackson, Thomas Jonathan
Jackson, William Hicks
Jeffers, William Nicholson
Jenkins, Micah
Johnson, Andrew
Johnson, Bradley Tyler
Johnson, Edward
Johnson, Richard W.
Johnston, Albert Sidney
Johnston, Joseph Eggleston
Johnston, William Preston
Jones, Catesby ap Roger
Jordan, Thomas
Julian, George Washington

K 427
Kautz, Albert
Kautz, August Valentine
Kearny, Philip
Keitt, Laurence Massillon
Kell, John McIntosh
Kemper, James Lawson
Kenly, John Reese
Kershaw, Joseph Brevard
Keyes, Erasmus Darwin
Kilpatrick, Hugh Judson
Kimball, Nathan
King, Rufus

L 443
Lander, Frederick West
Lane, James Henry
Lawton, Alexander Robert
Lee, Fitzhugh
Lee, George Washington Custis
Lee, Robert Edward
Lee, Samuel Phillips
Lee, Stephen D.
Lee, William Henry Fitzhugh
Lincoln, Abraham
Lincoln, Mary Todd
Livermore, Mary Ashton Rice
Logan, John Alexander
Longstreet, James
Loring, William Wing
Lovejoy, Owen
Lovell, Mansfield

Lowry, Reigart B.
Lyon, Nathaniel
Lytle, William Haines

M 491
Mackenzie, Ranald Slidell
Magoffin, Beriah
Magruder, John Bankhead
Mahan, Alfred Thayer
Mahone, William
Mallory, Stephen Russell
Mansfield, Joseph King Fenno
Marmaduke, John Sappington
Martindale, John Henry
Mason, James Murray
Maury, Dabney Herndon
Maury, Matthew Fontaine
McCann, William Penn
McClellan, George Brinton
McClernand, John Alexander
McCook, Alexander McDowell
McCook, Edward Moody
McCulloch, Ben
McDowell, Irwin
McLaws, Lafayette
McPherson, James Birdseye
Meade, George Gordon
Meade, Richard Worsam
Meagher, Thomas Francis
Meigs, Montgomery Cunningham
Memminger, Christopher Gustavus
Meredith, Solomon
Merritt, Wesley
Miles, Nelson Appleton
Milroy, Robert Huston
Mitchel, Ormsby McKnight
Morell, George Webb
Morgan, Charles Hale
Morgan, George Washington
Morgan, John Hunt
Morrill, Justin S.
Morrill, Lot Myrick
Morton, Oliver Hazard Perry Throck
Mosby, John Singleton
Mott, Gershom
Mower, Joseph Anthony

N 555
Naglee, Henry Morris
Negley, James Scott
Nelson, William
Newton, John
Nicolay, John George

G

GARFIELD, JAMES ABRAM, twentieth president of the United States, was born Nov. 19, 1831, in Bedford, Orange township, Cuyahoga Co., O. He was the youngest son of Abram and Eliza (Ballou) Garfield, the latter of French Huguenot stock, the former a descendant of Edward Garfield, who came to America from his birthplace in Wales in the same ship which brought over the famous Gov. Winthrop. His father purchased eighty acres of forest land and had begun the work of clearing it, but died in 1833, when young Garfield was only eighteen months old. The mother determined upon keeping her family together and undertook to run the farm, with the assistance of her eldest son Thomas, and as soon as young James was able to assist he also devoted himself to farm labor, and as he grew older did his full share of the work. He also chopped wood, and assisted in bringing money for the family necessities. At one time he had an opportunity to go on the Ohio canal and accept a place as driver at $12 a month. Here he nearly lost his life by falling overboard on a dark night, being rescued with great difficulty. This gave him enough of canalling and he went home, where he had a severe fit of sickness. On recovering from this he attended school as much as was practicable in his neighborhood, designing to fit himself for a teacher. He was now seventeen years old, and a friend induced him to go to Chester and attend the high school. At the end of the first session he returned home and worked until the second term began, when he went back to school, and at the close of that term thought himself competent to teach, and eagerly sought employment, but he was considered too young wherever he applied. Finally, he had the opportunity of taking a school with rather a bad reputation, near his home, and this he accepted, although the rowdyism of the big boys was likely to be, and was, a severe trial. He succeeded in conquering them and came out with the reputation of being the best schoolmaster who had ever taught there. In the spring of 1850 he returned to the seminary at Chester, and at about the same time appeared to experience religion and joined the Campbellites or Church of the Disciples. The next winter he taught in the village school at Warrensville, and later

studied at Hiram, Portage Co., O., where in three years' time he fitted himself to enter the junior class of Williams College. In the winter of 1855, during a vacation, he went to North Pownal, Vt., where he taught a writing-class, and here comes in an instance of the curious series of coincidences in connection with the name of Chester A. Arthur, afterward vice-president with, and successor to, James A. Garfield. To begin with, the ancestors of both were Welsh; the earliest ancestry of Garfield were born at Chester, in Wales; young Garfield received the most important part of his early education at Chester in Ohio, and Chester A. Arthur and himself both taught writing in the same little village in Vermont. On his second winter vacation Garfield visited Troy, and was offered a position in one of the schools at a salary much greater than he could hope to earn after graduation in Ohio, but he refused this proposition, desiring to continue his college life. He made his first political speech in support of the nomination of John C. Frémont, the standard-bearer of what was then, in 1855–56, the new republican party. In the latter year Garfield left Williams and entered Hiram College as a teacher of ancient languages and literature. The next year he was made president of the college, which office he continued to hold until 1859, when he was elected to represent

the counties of Portage and Summit in the Ohio state senate. He had already, in 1858, entered his name as a student in a law firm in Cleveland, and had carried on the study of law by himself while still performing his official functions at Hiram. In the senate he proved himself industrious in the committee work and also an able debater. It happened that when Garfield was at the academy at Chester, he made the acquaintance of Lucretia Rudolph, the daughter of a Maryland farmer, who was also a student, and a refined, intelligent, and affectionate girl. They were married in 1858. As secession began to make its appearance in 1860–61, Mr. Garfield contributed much to the direction of public sentiment and aided in preparing for the national defence. At this time he wrote to a friend: "I regard my life as given to my country, and I am only anxious to make as much of it as possible before the mortgage on it is foreclosed." On Aug. 14, 1861, Gov. Dennison offered Garfield the lieutenant-colonelcy of the 42d regiment. He accepted the commission and at once began to organize and

Garfield Res

discipline his command, of which, when it was ready for service, he was made colonel. In December he reported for duty to Gen. Buell, at Louisville, Ky., and was ordered in command of a brigade of four regiments of infantry to drive the Confederates under Gen. Humphrey Marshall from the valley of the Big Sandy river. In this he succeeded, defeating Marshall in the battle of Little Creek, and forcing him to retreat from the state. Garfield was now commissioned brigadier-general, placed in command of the 20th brigade, and was sent forward to join Gen. Grant, who was facing Albert Sidney Johnston *at Pittsburg Landing*. He reached the field of Shiloh with his brigade on the second day of the battle, aided in the final repulse of the enemy, and next day, with Sherman, took part in the attack on the enemy's rear-guard. The following year he joined the Army of the Cumberland, under Rosecrans whose chief-of-staff he became. In the meantime, in the autumn previous, he had served on a court of inquiry and on the court-martial which tried Gen. Fitz John Porter, and whose verdict was afterward reversed by a court of inquiry, comprising Maj.-Gen. Schofield, Maj.-Gen. Perry, and Maj.-Gen. Getty. In 1863 Garfield was ordered by Rosecrans to make a report with regard to the wisdom of a forward movement, and, as chief-of-staff, Garfield collated the written opinions of the seventeen generals in the Army of the Cumberland and summarized the substance of these opinions, accompanying them with arguments of his own, the report altogether inducing Rosecrans to move forward; contrary to the opinions of most of his generals, in the campaign which opened the way for the advance on Chattanooga. In the battle of Chickamauga, in which the Union forces were badly defeated, Garfield was sent, while the engagement was still active, to convey

Monument at Washington.

dispatches to Thomas, who, on being advised of the necessities of the situation, moved his wing of the army forward rapidly and succeeded in saving Rosecrans's flying forces. This occasion was the last appearance of Gen. Garfield on a field of battle. On Dec. 5, 1863, he resigned his commission, and went to take his seat in congress, being at once made a member of the military committee of the house, a position which he continued to hold until the close of the war. Garfield justly believed that his path of usefulness to the country lay in the direction of politics rather than that of military affairs. He soon became known in the house as a powerful speaker. His first speech of importance in the house of representatives was delivered Jan. 28, 1864, and was in favor of the confiscation of rebel property. In March, 1864, Garfield spoke on free commerce between the states, and Jan. 13, 1865, on a constitutional amendment abolishing slavery. In 1865 he was assigned to the committee on ways and means, and in March, 1866, made an elaborate speech on the public debt and specie payments. He also spoke on the revision of the tariff and against the inflation of the currency. December, 1867, he returned to the military committee as chairman, and during the reconstruction period he held that position. In January, 1868, Mr. Garfield in this connection delivered a speech in which he severely criticized the action of the president and the course of Maj.-Gen. Hancock, at that time military governor of Texas and Louisiana, and more particularly the latter's celebrated "Order No. 40," by which Hancock endeavored to restore judicial proceedings in the territory under his command through the courts which existed before the war, and through which, he believed, justice could be obtained for all the people with the least possible friction. Garfield sustained the motion to impeach President Johnson, and throughout his congressional career was a strict party debater and leader. In 1868 he made an argument on the currency and on taxing U.S. bonds. In the next congress he was chairman of the committee on banking and currency. He drafted several important bills, and in 1871–75 was made chairman of the committee on appropriations. In 1873 charges of corruption were made against Garfield in connection with the exposure of the "Credit Mobilier." These charges excited earnest discussion, even in his own congressional district, where he defended himself with great force and determination in personal speeches and in a pamphlet. He succeeded in regaining his re-nomination and re-election. The charges were renewed two years later, but again he succeeded, and in 1876 and 1878 opposition on this ground was practically at an end, but the "Credit Mobilier" investigation and the "Salary grab" resulted in a tidal wave for the democratic party in the election of 1874, and it was not until 1877, when Mr. Blaine, the republican leader of the house, was transferred to the senate, giving Garfield his opportunity, that the leadership descended to him without opposition. During the following years he spoke frequently on important measures, such as the Bland silver

bill, the protective tariff, and on the passage of appropriation bills without political riders. In 1880 he was elected by the Ohio legislature U.S. senator for six years from March 4, 1881. In the republican convention at Chicago, June, 1880, Mr. Garfield appeared in behalf of the claim of John Sherman to the nomination for the presidency. In the early part of the convention his advocacy of his friend seemed to be earnest and faithful, but as the difficulty of making a choice became more obvious, and the necessity for the selection of some one outside the familiar group of possible candidates presented itself, the confidence of the convention began to center in James A. Garfield as the only one whose nomination was feasible. Some accused him of selling out Sherman in his own interest, but many of those present afterward remarked the almost anguished expression of James A. Garfield, when delegation after delegation came over in response to the announcement of his name, and when at last the nomination was made, it is said that he was entirely unmanned by the unexpectedness of the honor and the exciting conditions under which he obtained it. The campaign was a vigorous one, during which the old "Credit Mobilier" charges were brought up—of course by the democrats—and tossed back and forth between the two excited parties. Dissensions in the democratic party in the state and city of New York and the alleged traitorous selling out of democratic votes for the presidency in exchange for republican help in the state and local offices were reasons commonly given and by very many believed, why Gen. Hancock was defeated and James A. Garfield elected. Immediately after his election Garfield found himself in the midst of internal dissensions in the republican party in the state of New York, there being formed two factions—the stalwarts, as they were called, of

which Senator Conkling must be considered the active leader, and the half-breeds, in whose interest Garfield appointed Mr. William H. Robertson, Conkling's chief political enemy in the state, as collector of the port of New York. The brief presidential career of Mr. Garfield was destined to end in tragedy. On July 2, 1881, the president had arranged to attend the commencement exercises of Williams College and also to make a somewhat extended trip through the New England states. He accordingly went to the station in Washington of the Baltimore and Potomac Railroad, accompanied by his secretary of state, James G. Blaine. The party passed through the door which opened into the ladies' room, where a few people were waiting, and among them was a man who afterward proved to be Charles Jules Guiteau. As the president, walking arm-in-arm with his secretary, passed this man, he turned, made a step in their direction and, drawing a heavy revolver from his pocket, pointed it carefully and fired deliberately at the president. The latter said nothing, but turned and with a surprised but not excited look gazed at Guiteau. Secretary Blaine sprang to one side. Guiteau recocked his revolver and deliberately fired again at the president, who fell to the floor, covered with blood. Guiteau fled, dropping his pistol as he went, but was immediately caught. Meanwhile the president neither stirred nor spoke. An ambulance was summoned and he was driven to the executive mansion, where he was at once attended by the best physicians in Washington. It was judged by them, and more particularly by Dr. Bliss, that his condition was so critical it would be highly dangerous to attempt to probe for the ball. To these physicians the death of the president seemed very near, but, as not altogether unfrequently happens, in this instance medical judgment was at fault. The president continued to linger, and at length it was determined to remove him to the seashore, and he was accordingly taken to Elberon, near Long Branch, where for a time the sea breezes seemed to assist nature in the efforts to restore him to health. For eighty days the condition of the wounded and suffering president continued to hold the sympathy, not only of the people of his own country, but of those of all civilized nations. Bulletins were constantly issued, and though these sometimes indicated grounds for hope, the dying man gradually became feebler, and wasting very slowly, day by day, on Monday, Sept. 19th, death relieved him from his sufferings. The remains of the late president were removed to Washington and placed in the rotunda of the capitol, where they lay in state until the 23d. At the foot of the coffin rested an immense wreath of white rosebuds ordered to be placed there by Queen Victoria, and bearing this inscription: "Queen Victoria to the memory of the late President Garfield. An expression of her sorrow and sympathy with Mrs. Garfield and the American nation." President Garfield was a very many-sided man. Brilliant and dashing as a political leader, possessing remarkable eloquence, gifted with a stalwart form and a fine, buoyant, animated face, he reminded one in some respects of Gambetta. There was no more able debater on the floor of the house during the period in which he was a representative. He was, as he himself conceded, a strong partisan, and was often misled by this narrowness of political vision to the detriment of himself and even of the party which he desired to serve. The curious tendency toward an emotional sort of religious fervor which characterized his youthful entrance into the Campbellite Church, represented one phase of his nature, its romantic and sensuous side. Garfield had, after leaving college, devoted himself to such reading and

study as would eventually make him a scholar of considerable breadth and force. He was fond of general literature, read French with facility and liked the work of the best French novelists. He was genial and companionable in society, but the tenacity of his friendship would seem to have been rather that belonging to membership in a party or a community, than to individual affection. The date of President Garfield's death is Sept. 19, 1881.

GARLAND, AUGUSTUS HILL, United States attorney-general, was born in Tipton county, Tenn., June 11, 1832. He received his education at St. Mary's College, Lebanon, Ky., and at St. Joseph's College, Bardstown, Ky., the latter being an institution famous for its learning. Mr. Garland studied law, was admitted to the bar in 1853, and practiced law in Washington, Ark., for three years, when he removed to Little Rock, Ark. He was admitted to practice as an attorney and counselor in the supreme court of the United States in 1860, and took the official oath of that day. He entered

political life as a whig, and was an elector on the Bell and Everett ticket. His first public position was that of delegate to the convention called by his state to consider her relations with the Federal Union after Mr. Lincoln's election. He was chosen as a Union delegate, but after the war began he favored secession ad voted for the secession ordinance. He was elected a member of the Confederate provisional congress, which assembled at Montgomery, Ala., in 1861, Arkansas being admitted as a state in May of that year; and he was also a member of the house of representatives of the first congress of the Confederate states, and then a member of the senate, where he remained until the end of the war. After the war he showed his desire to use his powers in assisting to restore the Federal relations, and received a full pardon from President Johnson in 1865, on condition that he would support the United States constitution, and obey the laws abolishing slavery. He undertook to renew his practice in the supreme court, but was not permitted to do so, according to act of congress passed on Jan. 24, 1865, requiring all attorneys and counselors to take the "Iron-clad" oath, prescribed by the act of July 2, 1862. Mr. Garland filed a brief in his own behalf, in a case he instituted to test the constitutionality of that act, employing as his counsel Reverdy Johnson and M.H. Carpenter. He argued the case himself in a masterly manner, for which he received high credit, and the decision was in his favor. He was elected to the United States senate in 1866, but was not permitted to take his seat. In 1874 he was for a time acting secretary of state for Arkansas when the carpet-bag rule was overthrown, and in the same year was elected governor of that state. He found the treasury bankrupt, and the financial standing of the state in the lowest possible condition. It was with much hard work

and a great deal of opposition that he finally succeeded in settling all differences, and placing matters on a firm financial basis. He was elected to the United States senate without opposition in 1876, succeeding Powell Clayton, becoming a member of the judiciary committee, and was re-elected without opposition, serving until 1885, when President Cleveland appointed him attorney-general of the United States, which position he retained until the close of that administration, when he returned to the practice of law. Senator Garland's steady perseverence and keen executive ability early ranked him with the best lawyers of his state, and promised him a famous future, which his subsequent brilliant and successful career has amply fulfilled. In society he was genial though unassuming, and his conversation was agreeably interspersed with a variety of anecdote and humor. He was a delegate to the Chicago convention of 1892, and supported the nomination of his former chief. *He died Jan. 26, 1899.*

GARNETT, RICHARD BROOKE, soldier, was born in Virginia, in *1817*. He was graduated at the U.S. Military Academy in 1841, and

entered the army as second lieutenant. He served in the Florida war and on the Texas frontier, becoming a captain on May 9, 1855. From 1856 until 1857 he was engaged in Kansas, and was also in the Utah expedition of 1858, resigning May 17, 1861, to join the Confederate army. He was in many of the battles in Virginia, and was afterward attached to Gen. Lee's army with the rank of brigadier-general, and fell at Gettysburg, July 3, 1863.

GARRARD, KENNER, soldier, was born at "Fairfield" in Bourbon county, Ky., Sept. 30, 1827, son of Jeptha Dudley and Sarah Bella (Ludlow) Garrard; grandson of James and Nancy (Lewis) Garrard; great-grandson of James Garrard, who was governor of Kentucky, and his wife Elizabeth Montjoy; and great-great-grandson of William Garrard, a native of England, who settled in Stafford county, Va., in the second quarter of the 18th century, and was married to Mary Lewis. His father was a Cincinnati, Ohio, lawyer; his mother, the daughter of Israel Ludlow, a founder and proprietor of that city. Kenner Garrard attended Harvard university, but withdrew at the end of his sophomore year to enter the U.S. military academy where he was graduated in 1851. From the 4th artillery he was transferred to the 1st dragoons in 1852. After routine duty for two years he was appointed cavalry instructor at Carlisle barracks, Pa. He was promoted 1st lieutenant in 1855 and was commissioned captain Feb. 27, 1861. In April 1861 he was captured at San Antonio by Texas insurgents, and paroled upon refusing to join the Confederacy. He was instructor in artillery, cavalry, and infantry tactics and commandant of cadets at the U.S. military academy during parole and, after his exchange in 1862, joined the army of the Potomac in the Rappahannock and Pennsylvania campaigns. As colonel of the 146th N.Y. volunteers, he participated in the battles of Fredericksburg, Chancellorsville, and Gettysburg. For "gallant and meritorious services" at Gettysburg, where he commanded the 3d brigade after the death of Gen. Weed, he was brevetted lieutenant-colonel in the regular army. *He was also promoted to brigadier-general of volunteers on July 23, 1863.* He was in the Rapidan campaign, and as commander of the 2d cavalry division in the Army of the Cumberland, participated in operations around Chattanooga, the Atlanta campaign and the battle of Nashville. In the siege of Spanish Fort, Mobile, Ala., he personally led a storming column in the capture of Ft. Blakeley. He was brevetted major-general of volunteers, Dec. 15, 1864, and brevetted major-general of the regular army, Mar. 13, 1865. He commanded the district of Mobile and was assistant inspector-general of the department of the Missouri until he resigned Nov. 9, 1866. Harvard awarded him the honorary degree of B.A. in 1865. His last years were spent in Cincinnati where he had charge of his mother's estate and was chairman of the city planning commission (1871–79), a member of the sewerage commission (1875–79), director of the Musical Festival Association (1875–78) and of the Harmonic Society of Cincinnati, and an active member of the Historical and Philosophical Society of Ohio. Garrard was a man of unusual force of character, a born leader although modest and unassuming, and, in civil life as well as in the army, an example and influence for the general good. He was unmarried and died in Cincinnati, May 15, 1879.

GEARY, JOHN WHITE, governor of Pennsylvania (1867–73), was born in Westmoreland county, Pa., Dec. 30, 1819, of Scotch-Irish ancestry. After receiving careful preliminary training under his father, a man of liberal education, who conducted an academy, young Geary entered Jefferson College at Canonsburg, Pa. *The death of his father compelled Geary to drop out of college before he graduated.* He taught school for a brief time and then made a special study of civil engineering and for several years was connected with the Alleghany Portage Railroad. At the opening of the war with Mexico in 1846 he raised a company in the mountain districts of Cambria county, denominated the "American Highlanders" and with it joined the 2d Pennsylvania regiment of which he became lieutenant-colonel. Owing to the disability of the colonel he led the regiment on the triumphant march of Gen. Scott to the Mexican capital. At the storming of Chapultepec Col. Geary was wounded, but remained with his command. By his coolness and bravery at the Belen gate, which guards the immediate defences of the city of Mexico, he won the approbation of his superior officers, and upon the surrender of the capital was assigned to the

command of the great citadel and given the commission of colonel. After the close of the war he went to California, and in 1849 President Polk appointed him postmaster of San Francisco and general mail agent for the Pacific coast with the power to establish post-offices and mail routes. Soon afterward he was elected first alcalde when under Mexican rule, and subsequently the first mayor of San Francisco. He exercised a strong influence in framing the first state constitution and was largely instrumental in securing the admission of California as a free state. Upon the death of his wife in 1853 Col. Geary left the Pacific coast and lived in retirement on his farm in western Pennsylvania, until July, 1856, when President Pierce appointed him governor of Kansas. By the exercise of vigilant and strong authority he managed to restrain both the pro-slavery and the anti-slavery factions of the territory and bring them within the bounds of law and order. He convened the courts, enforced the laws and restored confidence. But immediately upon the accession of James Buchanan to the presidency in March, 1857, Gov. Geary resigned, fearing the accession of the pro-slavery influence. One hour after hearing of the attack on Fort Sumter in 1861 he began to raise a regiment for the defence of the Union and soon after reported to Gen. Banks at Harper's Ferry, with a command of 1,500 men. At Bolivar Heights he received a wound in the knee. On March 8, 1862, he captured Leesburg, a few days later was made a brigadier-general, and at the battle of Cedar Mountain on Aug. 9th, he was twice wounded. Upon his recovery he was placed in command of the second division of the 12th army corps, which he led at Chancellorsville, Gettysburg, Wauhatchie and Lookout Mountain. He next commanded the second division of the 20th army corps on Sherman's march to the sea and was appointed military governor of Savannah on its capture Dec. 22, 1864. His military career was brilliant and successful and he won the highest encomiums from his superior officers. In 1866 he was elected governor of Pennsylvania as a republican by a large majority over Hiester Clymer, the democratic candidate. He served two terms and during that period the state debt was reduced ten millions of dollars. It was a period of unusual activity in business and great development of the industrial resources of the state. Under an act of assembly passed in 1868 Gov. Geary appointed a board of commissioners who adjudicated the claims and allowed small amounts to persons in the counties bordering on Maryland, who lost property during the Confederate invasion of Pennsylvania. In July, 1871, he sent a military force to Williamsport in command of Gen. Merrill to quell a serious disturbance of the peace in that city. As there was no bloodshed it became known as the "Sawdust War." Gov. Geary was first married to Margaret Ann Logan of Westmoreland county; one of their sons was killed in the battle of Wauhatchie and another was graduated from West Point in 1874. In 1858 he married Mrs. Mary C. Henderson of Cumberland county. He died suddenly at Harrisburg, Feb. 8, 1873, eighteen days after the expiration of his second term.

GETTY, GEORGE WASHINGTON, soldier, was born at Georgetown, D.C., Oct. 2, 1819, son of Robert and Margaret (Wilmot) Getty, and grandson of John Wilmot, of Annapolis, Md. He was graduated at the United States Military Academy, July 1, 1840, when he was assigned to the 4th artillery as a second lieutenant. He served in Michigan during the Canada border disturbances of 1840–41; was in garrison at various posts from 1841–46, and was promoted first lieutenant, Oct. 31, 1845. In the war with Mexico he was engaged in the battles of Contreras, Molino del Rey, Churubusco, Chapultepec, and at the assault and capture of the Mexican capital; receiving the brevet of captain for gallant and meritorious conduct in the battles of Contreras and Churubusco, Aug. 20, 1847. He served in Florida against the Seminole Indians, 1849–50; and in 1856–57; he also was engaged in suppressing the Kansas disturbances in 1857–58, and became captain in the 5th artillery. In the civil war he was in command of an artillery battalion at Cincinnati, O., from May to August, 1861; and he commanded the artillery in the engagements on the Potomac river, near Budd's Ferry, November and December, 1861. While in command of four batteries in the Peninsula campaign of 1862, he was engaged at Yorktown, Gaines's Mills, and Malvern Hill; and in the Maryland campaign he served at the battles of South Mountain and Antietam. On Sept. 25, 1862, he was commissioned brigadier-general of volunteers, and he took a prominent part in the Rappahannock campaign of the army of the Potomac, serving with distinction at the battle of Fredericksburg, Dec. 13, 1862, and in the siege of Suffolk, Va., Apr. 11 to May 3, 1863, being brevetted lieutenant-colonel for his services. In the Richmond campaign he was engaged in the battles of the Wilderness, where he was severely wounded: in the expedition to Ream's Station, and in the pursuit of Gen. Early to the Shenandoah valley, and received the brevet of colonel for his gallantry. He distinguished himself in the Shenandoah campaign, taking part in the engagements at Charlestown, Aug. 21, 1864; at Opequon, Sept. 19th; at Fisher's Hill, Sept. 22nd and 23rd; at Cedar Creek, Oct. 19th; and in the siege of Petersburg, and the battle of Sailor's Creek, and he was present at Lee's surrender. On Aug. 1, 1864, he was brevetted major-general of volunteers, and on Mar. 13, 1865, received the brevets of brigadier-general and major-general, United States army, for gallant and meritorious conduct. He served in command of the first division of the provisional corps in June and July, 1865; of the district of Baltimore, Md., August, 1865 to January, 1866; and of the district of the Rio Grande, Feb. 19 to Sept. 1, 1866, when he was mustered out of the volunteer service. He was commissioned colonel of the 37th infantry, July 28, 1866, and was transferred to the 3d artillery, January 1, 1871. He commanded the district of Texas till 1867, and the district of New Mexico till 1871. He was in command of the troops stationed along the Baltimore & Ohio railroad during the labor strikes of 1877, and was a member of the court of inquiry in the case of Gen. Fitz John Porter (1878–79). On July 17, 1882, he became colonel of the 4th artillery, and having reached the age limit, was retired from active service, Oct. 2, 1883. Gen. Getty died at Forest Glen, Md., *Oct. 1, 1901.*

GIBBON, JOHN, soldier, was born near Philadelphia, Pa., on Apr. 20, 1827. His parents removed to North Carolina, when he was twelve years old, and he was appointed to the West Point military academy from that state in 1842. He was graduated in 1847, and during the Mexican war served as second lieutenant in the 4th artillery. In 1848 and 1849 he saw much hard service in the campaign against the Seminoles, whom later he helped to remove to the west of the Mississippi. In September, 1850, he was made a first lieutenant, and from 1854 till 1859 was an instructor at West Point. In 1861 he was stationed in Utah, holding the rank of captain. Ordered East he served as chief of artillery to Gen. McDowell until May 2, 1862, when he was made a

brigadier-general of volunteers. He was wounded at Fredericksburg, while commanding a division, and received another wound at Gettysburg while in command of the second corps, and opposing Pickett's famous charge. During the winter of 1863–64 he commanded draft stations at Cleveland and Philadelphia. He was made a major-general of volunteers in the spring of 1864, and commanded the 2d division of the 2d corps in the campaign that began in the Wilderness, and ended at Petersburg, acquitting himself with especial bravery at Spottsylvania and Cold Harbor. In January, 1865, he took command of the 24th corps, and engaged in the pursuit of Gen. Lee to

Appomattox Court-House. In July, 1866, he was made colonel of the 36th U.S. infantry, and in 1869 was transferred to the 7th infantry. He commanded the district of Montana for several years, and in 1876 led the Yellowstone expedition against Sitting Bull. In 1877 he fought the Nez Perces at Big Hole Pass, Mon., where he was wounded. In July, 1885, he was promoted to the rank of brigadier-general, and assigned to the command of the department of the Columbia, suppressing with promptness and energy the anti-Chinese riots there. Later he was placed in charge of the department of the Pacific with headquarters at San Francisco. His career as a soldier was, throughout, a gallant, honorable and meritorious one. On Apr. 20, 1891, he was placed on the retired list of the army on account of age. *He died Feb. 6, 1896.*

GIBSON, RANDALL LEE, senator, was born at Spring Hill, Ky., Sept. 10, 1832. His paternal ancestors, the Gibsons and McKinleys, came from Scotland and settled in Virginia early in the eighteenth century. Randall Gibson, his grandfather, after whom Senator Gibson is named, was a soldier in the revolutionary war, and at the conclusion of that struggle crossed the mountains and established a home in Mississippi. He married Harriet McKinley, and was one of the founders of Jefferson college, in that state. Senator Gibson's maternal ancestors, the Harts and Prestons, were among the earliest settlers of Kentucky. R. L. Gibson passed the years of his boyhood at Lexington, Ky., and on his father's plantation in Terre Bonne parish, Louisiana. His education, begun in the famous Kentucky town near the home of Henry Clay, was completed at Yale College, where he was graduated in 1853, being the valedictorian of his class. Upon leaving college he read law, and receiving a diploma from the

University of Louisiana traveled extensively in Europe. Upon his return, which was just previous to the civil war, he became a planter in Louisiana. Senator Gibson's military career began with the opening of the war, when he was aide-de-camp on the staff of Gov. Moore of Louisiana, of which Hon. Thomas S. Manning, afterwards chief justice of the state and minister to Mexico, was also a member. Subsequently he commanded a regiment, brigade and division in the Confederate army, serving through all the campaigns of the army of the Tennessee, and receiving high commendation from Hood, Stephen D. Lee, Breckenridge, Hardee, and Dick Taylor. He led the Louisiana brigade in the memorable charge at Shiloh; was recommended for promotion for skill and gallantry on the field of Perryville; *was finally promoted to brigadier-general Jan. 11, 1864;* took a prominent part in the battles of Murfreesboro, Chickamauga, Atlanta, and the retreat from Nashville; and crowned his military career by a masterly defense of Spanish Fort. After the war Gen. Gibson practiced law in New Orleans with success, until his election to congress. He was a representative from the first district of Louisiana in the forty-third to forty-seventh congresses, was elected U.S. senator in 1882, and re-elected in 1888. During his sixteen years of service in the national legislature he has displayed rare ability and achieved remarkable success. His influence has been exerted wherever the interests of the people he represented could be advanced, as in the emancipation of Louisiana from the evils of national interference in her domestic concerns *(This was a code phrase for the retreat of the national government from efforts to enforce equal rights for blacks in the South.)*; the protection and preservation of the sugar industry; the establishment of the Mississippi river commission, and the improvement of the navigation of that river; the protection of the alluvial lands from overflow; the preservation of the national currency; the restoration of railroad land grants to the public domain; all international questions relating to treaties, and many other subjects of vital importance. Senator Gibson was always active in the great cause of education, and was an earnest advocate of all educational measures. It was through him that the Tulane University of Louisiana was established by the munificence of Mr. Paul Tulane. He was president of the board of administrators of that institution; an administrator of the Howard memorial library of New Orleans; trustee of the Peabody educational fund, and regent of the Smithsonian Institution. He married Mary Montgomery, daughter of R.W. Montgomery of New Orleans, La., a lady of rare gifts and accomplishments, who died in 1887, leaving three sons. *He died Dec. 15, 1892.*

GILLEM, ALVAN CULLEM, soldier, was born in Jackson county, Tenn., July 29, 1830. He was graduated from the U.S. military academy in 1851, took part in the Seminole war of 1851–52, and was promoted captain May 14, 1861. He served as brigade quartermaster at the commencement of the civil war, earned the brevet of major for gallantry at Mill Springs, and was in command of the siege artillery, and chief quartermaster of the army of the Ohio, in the Tennessee campaign. On May 13, 1862, he was appointed colonel of *the Union 10th Tennessee volunteers,* was provost marshal of

Nashville, commanded a brigade in the Tennessee operations of the early part of 1863, and then served as adjutant-general of Tennessee until the end of the war, being promoted brigadier-general of volunteers Aug. 17, 1863. He had charge of the forces guarding the Nashville and Northwestern railroad from June, 1863, until August, 1864, afterward commanded the expedition to eastern Tennessee, and won the brevet of colonel, U.S. army, for bravery at Marion, Va. He was elected vice-president of the convention of Jan. 9, 1865, to revise the constitution and reorganize the state government of Tennessee, and also served in the first legislature. He joined the expedition to North Carolina and took a prominent part in the capture of Salisbury, which secured him the brevet of major-general U.S. army. He became colonel in the regular army July 28, 1866, commanded the district of Mississippi 1867–68, served in Texas and California, and later held a command in the Modoc campaign. Gen. Gillem died near Nashville, Tenn., Dec. 2, 1875.

GILLMORE, QUINCY ADAMS, soldier, was born at Black River, Lorain county, O., Feb. 28, 1825, of mixed Scotch, Irish, and German extraction. His father was a New Englander, born, in 1790, on the farm which his father continued to cultivate for many years, but which was finally exchanged for a tract of 1,000 acres of western reserve land in Ohio. Young Gillmore happened to be born on the day when John Quincy Adams was elected to the presidency, and the latter being a favorite of his father, he testified his joy by naming the boy after the successful candidate. Young Quincy grew up amid the employment and the atmosphere of rural life, and took part in the regular work on the farm, obtaining, as was the case with most country boys, his education in the winter months. He was diligent in his studies and a willing hand at farm labor. He especially showed a taste for mathematics, and at the early age of twelve began to question his teachers in a part of the arithmetic they had never touched upon. His evident precocity induced his father to send him to the Norwalk academy, twenty-five miles away from his home, where he made great progress in study. At the age of seventeen his proficiency was remarkable, and was publicly recognized by his appointment as teacher in a district school, where he taught for three years, studying during two of the summers at the high school in Elyria, O. Having completed his school education,

young Gillmore determined to study law, but had hardly begun to read on this subject, when the opportunity came to him of entering West Point military academy as a cadet. He was

graduated in 1849 with all the honors, and the same year he married Mary O'Meagher; received the rank of second lieutenant of engineers, and was ordered to duty as an assistant on the fortifications at Hampton Roads. Here he remained three years, when he was sent back to West Point as instructor in the department of practical military enginery, and subsequently he was appointed treasurer and quartermaster of the academy. On July 1, 1856, he was promoted to a first lieutenancy in the corps of engineers, and was in charge of the engineer agency in New York city when the civil war broke out. In August, 1861, he was promoted to the captaincy in his own corps, and appointed engineer-in-chief of the Port Royal expedition under Brig.-Gen. T. W. Sherman *(Thomas W. Sherman—"the other Sherman")*. He was in charge of the troops engaged in the siege of Fort Pulaski, as acting brigadier-general, and the siege resulted in the surrender of the fort. In August, 1862, Gen. Gillmore was assigned to the command of a division of troops in Kentucky, and by the beginning of the following year was in command of the central division of that state. At the battle of Somerset, March 21, 1863, he defeated Gen. Pegram, for which success he was brevetted colonel in the regular army, and in the following June he was called to the department of the South, being placed at the head of the 10th army corps. Gen. Gillmore conducted the siege operations against Charleston, comprising the descent on Morris Island, the reduction and capture of Fort Wagner, and the bombardment and practical demolition of Fort Sumter from batteries two miles distant. Of the success of Gen. Gillmore in this siege, Gen. Halleck said: "He has overcome difficulties almost unknown in modern sieges; and, indeed, his operations on Morris Island constitute a new era in the science of engineering and gunnery." In 1864 the 10th

army corps, in command of Gen. Gillmore, was transferred to the James river, *and on May 12–16, with the heaviest fighting on May 16 of that year,* was engaged in the battle of Drury's Bluff. In July 1864, Gen. Gillmore was in command of two divisions of the 19th

army corps in the defence of Washington; and, while conducting the pursuit of Gen. Early, was severely wounded by a fall from his horse. From February until November, 1865, he was again in command of the department of the South. In December, 1865, he resigned his volunteer commission, and was assigned to duty as engineer-in-charge of the fortifications on Staten Island, N.Y., and the South Atlantic coast, embracing North and South Carolina, Georgia, and Florida. In June, 1868, he was promoted to be major of engineers, and in January, 1874, was made lieutenant-colonel. Gen. Gillmore received, at the conclusion of the civil war, the four highest brevets in the regular army: brevet lieutenant-colonel, brevet colonel, brevet brigadier-general, and brevet major-general, U.S. army. In 1876 Gen. Gillmore was one of the judges at the International Exhibition, held in Philadelphia, and made two special reports, viz., "Portland, Roman, and other cement and artificial stone," and "Brickmaking machinery, brick kilns, perforated and enameled bricks and pavements." Gen. Gillmore has published a number of important and valuable professional works, such as, "Siege and Reduction of Fort Pulaski, Ga." (1862); "Enginery and Artillery Operations Against the Defenses of Charleston, S.C." (1863); "Limes, Hydraulic Cements and Mortars" (1893); "Roads, Streets and Pavements" (1876); and "Béton-Coignet and other Artificial Stone" (1871). In 1881 Gen. Gillmore was president of the Mississippi river improvement commission and also chief engineer of all the defences on the Atlantic coast, from New York harbor to St. Augustine, Fla. Gen. Gillmore received from Rutgers college the degree of Ph.D. *He died April 7, 1888.*

GOLDSBOROUGH, LOUIS MALESHERBES

GOLDSBOROUGH, LOUIS MALESHERBES, rear-admiral U.S.N., was born in Washington, D.C., Feb. 18, 1805. His father, Charles Washington (1779–1843), was for many years chief clerk of the navy department. Louis was appointed a midshipman at seven years of age in 1812, but did not enter the service until 1816. He served first under Bainbridge, and

from 1817 until 1824 cruised in the Mediterranean and Pacific, mainly under Stewart. He was made lieutenant in 1825, and until 1827 studied in Paris. In 1827, while cruising in the Russian archipelago on the Porpoise, he led at night a boat expedition of volunteers, and recaptured the British Brig Comet, which had fallen into the hands of Greek pirates. In the conflict ninety of the pirates were killed. In 1833 he married the daughter of William Wirt, and for some time resided on a tract of land which his father-in-law had purchased in Florida. During the Seminole war he was commander of a company of volunteer cavalry, and later of an armed steamer. Shortly afterward he returned to the naval service, and in 1841 was made commander. In 1849 he served as a member of the commission that explored California and Oregon; was promoted to be captain in 1855, and from 1853 until 1857 was superintendent of the Naval Academy. In August, 1861, he was appointed flag-officer, and in the following month was assigned to the command of the North Atlantic squadron. In January, 1862, he sailed from Hampton Roads for the sounds of North Carolina, and on Feb. 8, 1862, co-operated with Gen. A.E. Burnside in the capture of Roanoke Island. For his services on this occasion he received a vote of thanks from congress. Subsequently, by various expeditions into the bays and rivers, he completed the conquest of the North Carolina coast. He then returned to Hampton Roads, and during the peninsular campaign co-operated with McClellan in the York and James rivers. In July, 1862, he was raised to the rank of rear-admiral, *and in that same month,* was, at his own request, relieved from the command of the North Atlantic squadron. Thereafter and until the close of the war he was engaged in preparing a code of regulations for the naval service, and a revision of the naval book of allowances. From 1865 until 1867 he was commander of the European squadron, and in 1873 was retired. At his death he was, length of service considered, the oldest officer in the navy. He died Feb. 20, 1877.

GORDON, GEORGE WASHINGTON, soldier, lawyer and educator, was born in Giles county, Tenn., Oct. 5, 1836, son of Andrew and Eliza K. Gordon, the former a native of Tennessee and the latter of Virginia. He spent the early years of his life chiefly in Mississippi and Texas. He received a collegiate education at the Western Military Institute in Nashville, receiving there about the same instruction and training as were given at West Point at that time, and was graduated in the class of 1859. He

280

practiced civil engineering until the civil war broke out, and then enlisted in the military service of the state of Tennessee, in the capacity of drill-master of the 11th infantry regiment. Soon thereafter he was transferred, with the other Tennessee troops, to the military service of the Confederate states, was promoted captain, lieutenant-colonel and colonel of his regiment, and in 1864 was made a brigadier-general, serving with that rank and with enviable distinction until the close of the war. His military career was marked by varying fortunes, thrilling adventures, narrow escapes, and wounds received in battle. Though captured three times-first near Tazewell, East Tenn., again at Murfreesboro, where he was dangerously wounded, and lastly at the bloody battle of Franklin, Tenn., he participated in every engagement fought by his command with the exception of that at Bentonville, N.C., being at that time a prisoner in Fort Warren in Boston harbor. He was held in confinement until *July, 1865,* several months after the close of the war, and then returned to Tennessee. He studied law at Lebanon, Tenn., and practiced the profession at Pulaski and Memphis until 1883,

when he was appointed one of the railroad commissioners of the state. In 1885 Gen. Gordon received an appointment in the interior department of the U.S. government and served four years in the Indian country in the several states and territories west of the Rocky mountains. This work ended, he continued the practice of his profession at Memphis until 1892, when he was elected superintendent of city schools. He was an eloquent and magnetic public speaker, and was in popular demand, especially at 4th of July celebrations, on memorial and reunion days, and at educational assemblies. Gen. Gordon was married, at Bartlett, Tenn., Sept. 5, 1876, to Ora S., daughter of Constantine and Susan A. Paine, and had no children, Mrs. Gordon having died a few weeks after marriage. *He died Aug. 19, 1911.*

GORDON, JOHN BROWN, thirty-fifth governor of Georgia (1886–90), and U.S. senator, was born in Upson county, Ga., July 6, 1832. His great-grandfather was one of seven brothers who emigrated from Scotland to North Carolina and Virginia, and who were all

revolutionary soldiers. His grandfather was a prominent citizen of Wilkes county, N.C., and his father was Rev. Zachariah H. Gordon. *Gordon attended the State University of Georgia, but did not graduate.* He read law and practiced a short time in Atlanta with his brother-in-law, L. E. Bleckley, afterward chief justice of Georgia, but soon gave up the profession to aid his father, who was mining coal in Georgia and Tennessee. He married, in 1853, Fanny, daughter of Congressman Hugh A. Haralson. He was mining when the war began, but enlisted at once, becoming in succession captain, major, lieutenant-colonel, colonel, brigadier-general, major-general, and lieutenant-general in command of one wing of the army of Virginia. He settled in Atlanta after the war. He was a member of the national Union convention at Philadelphia in 1866, delegate to the national democratic convention in 1868, and Seymour and Blair elector the same year. He declined the use of his name as a candidate for governor of Georgia, but was finally nominated, made the race against R. B. Bullock, and, according to the claim of his party, was elected and counted out by reconstruction machinery. He declined the use of his name as a candidate for U.S. senator in 1871, when Mr. Norwood was elected, and the same year went before the congressional committee to defend his state in the "Ku-Klux" investigation. He was delegate-at-large in the national democratic convention at Baltimore in 1872, opposing the nomination of Greeley; was elected U.S. senator in 1873, and re-elected in 1879. He resigned in 1880, and raised the money to build the Georgia Pacific railroad. He was elected governor of Georgia in 1886, and re-elected in 1888, and in 1890 was elected U.S. senator. Gen. Gordon was one of the illustrious generals of the Confederate armies, and won an international fame as a soldier. An English correspondent of the London "Times" declared him the rising genius of the South. He was second only to the great Lee. *An exaggeration. Gordon had indeed emerged as one of the Army of Northern Virginia's best corps commanders by the end of the war, but most historians would rank Stonewall Jackson, James Longstreet, and probably others ahead of him for the war as a whole.* He was five times desperately wounded. His devoted wife, who accompanied him during the entire war, and whose narrow escapes would equal any romance, by her care and faithful nursing saved his life when pierced by five bullets at Sharpsburg. He led the last charge at fateful Appomattox, taking the Federal breastworks and capturing artillery during this closing scene of the drama. After the war he gathered his wing of the army, and made the greatest speech of his life to his broken-hearted men, exhorting them to bear the trial, go home in peace, obey the laws, rebuild the country, and work for the weal and harmony of the republic. His seven years' service in the U.S. senate was brilliant and statesmanlike. He delivered powerful and eloquent speeches upon finance, civil service reform, and made a masterly defence of the South, exerting a conservative influence. In the Louisiana troubles he was chosen by the democrats in congress to draft an address to the people of Louisiana and the South, urging patient endurance and an appeal to a returning sense of justice to cure wrongs. He took masterful part in the debate, and a serious variance between him and Senator Conkling was adjusted by Senator Bayard and others. The farmers of Georgia thanked him for his efforts for agriculture. He aided Lamar in saving Mississippi from political misrule, and was empowered by Gov. Hampton to look after South Carolina's interest, having canvassed the state for its redemption with Hampton, and after the adjournment of congress secured the removal of troops from Carolina. For this he received the historic despatch: "South Carolina thanks you." His life-size portrait hangs in the state capitol. *This interpretation of Gordon's actions during the later years of Reconstruction reflects the Southern white view of that era, an interpretation that denigrated black participation in Southern politics and made heroes of the Ku Klux Klan—a view totally discredited today.* The ladies sent his little daughter, born in Washington, a silver urn, with Hampton's despatch on it, and to Mr. Gordon a superb silver service, each piece mounted with a gold palmetto tree. As governor his administration was faultless. The N.Y. "Sun" declared his first inaugural "worthy of Thomas Jefferson." His last election as U.S. senator was a marvelous political victory. Unopposed, until he antagonized the sub-treasury plan of the farmers' alliance, which had four-fifths of the legislature in its favor, he was elected after the most exciting contest of the time. In the wild enthusiasm succeeding his victory, he was borne by the multitude through the capitol to the streets, placed on a caisson and drawn about the city, amid shouts and rejoicing, while the whole state was ablaze with bonfires. Mr. Gordon was all his life a model of social worth, and an ardent Christian worker. *Gordon died in Atlanta on Jan. 9, 1904.*

GRANT, LEWIS ADDISON, lawyer and soldier, was born at Winhall, Bennington co., Vt., Jan. 17, 1829, son of James and Betsey (Wyman) Grant. At twenty years of age, the death of a brother left him an only son, with his aged parents entirely dependent upon him for support. He was admitted to the bar in May, 1855, and practiced law at Bellows Falls, Vt., until the outbreak of the civil war, when he entered the military service as major of the 5th Vermont volunteers, Aug. 15, 1861. On Sept. 25, 1861, he was promoted to lieutenant-colonel, and on Sept. 16, 1862, to colonel. In February, 1863, he took command of the second brigade, second division, 6th corps, the famous "Old Vermont brigade," and continued in command, except at short intervals, when in command of a division, until the close of the war. He was promoted to brigadier-general April 27, 1864, and to brevet major-general, to date from Oct. 19, 1864, the date of the battle of Cedar creek, where he commanded the second (Getty's) division, 6th corps, repulsed the enemy's advance and successfully held in check five divisions of Early's army. He took an active part in nearly all the battles of the army of the Potomac, and that of Cedar creek and Charlestown in the Shenandoah valley. It was his brigade which led the attack of the 6th corps which broke the enemy's lines at Petersburg, *April 2, 1865*, and his brigade that was selected to go to New York and put down the draft riot in the summer of 1863. He was twice wounded in battle, and was honorably discharged Aug. 24, 1865. Soon after the war he resumed law practice, at Des Moines, Ia., and actively engaged in other business. He helped to organize the New England Loan and Trust Co., and was its president seven years. In 1884 he removed to Minneapolis, Minn. In April, 1890, he was appointed assistant secretary of war by Pres. Harrison, and held the position until Dec. 15, 1893, part of the time being acting secretary. He was twice married: March 11, 1857, to S. Augusta Hartwell, of Harvard, Mass., who died Jan. 27, 1859; and Sept. 9, 1863, to Helen M. Pierce, of Hartland, Vt. He had two sons, Ulysses S. Grant, Ph.D., assistant state geologist, and J. Colfax Grant, U.S. district attorney in Chicago, and a daughter. *He died March 20, 1918.*

GRANT, ULYSSES S., soldier and eighteenth president of the United States, was born at Point Pleasant, Clermont county, O., Apr. 27, 1822. He was descended in the eighth generation from remote Scotch ancestry; Matthew Grant, the first of the American line, settling in Dorchester, Mass., in 1630. Two of the Grant family were soldiers in the old French and Indian wars, a generation before the war of the revolution, and were killed in battle near Crown Point on Lake Champlain. His grandfather was a soldier of the revolution, bore arms at the battle of Lexington, and, when the war was ended, settled in western Pennsylvania. The fever for western emigration reached him, and he penetrated the wilderness of Ohio, settling in Columbiana county, thence removing to Portage in the northern part of the state, where he bound his son Jesse, Gen. Grant's father, to a tanner to learn the trade. The trade was learned, and Jesse Grant removed to Point Pleasant, where he made his home. He married Hannah Simpson, and "Hiram Ulysses" was the first-born of six children. As a lad Ulysses assisted on the farm. He showed courage, resolution, and a faculty for leading, but no special intellectual promise. He received the ordinary education of the frontier: he went to school in winter, and at all other times worked on the farm. While yet a lad of only twelve years he was one day sent to the woods for a load of logs, to be placed on the trucks by the lumbermen. Young Grant found the logs, but no men. He loaded them unaided. On his return his father asked, "Why, my son, where are the men?" The answer was, "I don't know, and I don't care; I got the load without them." His fondness for horses, which became proverbial, was shown early in life. When he was not quite seven years old, he one day took out of the stable a three-year-old colt that had never been worked, harnessed him, drove him

to the woods for a load of wood, and came back in triumph; the journey having been accomplished with but a single line or rein, or perhaps a halter. In 1839, through the instrumentality of Thomas L. Hamer, member of congress, he was appointed to a cadetship at West Point. He entered at the age of seventeen. Congressman Hamer, under the impression that "Ulysses" was young Grant's first name, and that his middle name was probably that of his mother's family, inserted in the official appointment the name of "Ulysses S." Cadet Grant, at his entrée at West Point, called attention to the error, but the authorities did not deem it of sufficient importance to correct, and it was acquiesced in, and became the name by which he was ever after known. From the initials he got the name of "Uncle Sam" at West Point; in later life, "United States," and when he had become the people's hero, the letters stood, in the popular mind, for "Unconditional Surrender" Grant. As a student at West Point young Grant was proficient in mathematics, and in cavalry drill proved himself the best horseman in his class. He was graduated in 1843, standing number twenty-one in a class of thirty-nine, slightly below the general average of the class. It is a rule at West Point that the members of the graduating class are permitted to record their choice of arms and service. Grant elected to enter the dragoons, with second choice for infantry. He was assigned to the infantry as brevet second lieutenant, and sent to Jefferson Barracks, St. Louis, Mo. In May, 1844, he was sent to Louisiana, and in September, 1845, commissioned second lieutenant. The country was on the eve of war with Mexico, and the young officer was to have a speedier "baptism of fire" than most West Point graduates. He joined the army of occupation under Gen. Zachary Taylor the same month, and saw a great deal of service, being in all the battles of the Mexican war in which any one man could be. He first saw blood shed at Palo Alto on May 8, 1846; at Monterey he showed bold and skillful horsemanship by running the gauntlet of the enemy's bullets to carry a message for "more ammunition." He borrowed the Comanche Indian trick, of hanging from the horse's mane by his hands, with one heel as a clinger to the backbone, and made the journey without harm, forcing his horse through the streets and over the crossings at the highest speed. In the spring of 1847 he was made quartermaster of his regiment, and placed in charge of the wagons and pack-train for the march. At Vera Cruz he served with his regiment during the siege, until the capture of the place, March 29, 1847. At the battle of Molino del Rey, Sept. 8, 1847, he was with the first troops that entered the place. Seeing some of the enemy on top of a building, he took a few men, climbed to the roof, and forced the surrender of six Mexican officers, for which service he was brevetted first lieutenant. At the storming of Chapultepec he distinguished himself by conspicuous services, and received

the brevet of captain. During the advance on the City of Mexico, Capt. Grant observed a point of vantage in the belfry of a church. He called for volunteers, and with twelve men made a flank movement, gained the church, secured a forced admission from the priest, mounted a howitzer in the belfry and dropped some unexpected shots into the ranks of the enemy. For this service he was summoned into the presence of Gen. Worth, specially complimented and promoted to a full first lieutenancy. Lieut. Grant remained with the army in Mexico until the withdrawal of the troops in 1848, and then went with his regiment to Pascagoula, Miss. Many years afterward, when Grant had become famous, Gen. Scott said of him that he could only remember him "in the Mexican war as a young lieutenant of undaunted courage, but giving no promise of anything beyond ordinary abilities." At the close of the Mexican war, Grant was transferred, with his regiment, to Detroit, Mich. An opportunity offering, he secured leave of absence and married, in 1848, Julia T. Dent of St. Louis, a sister of one of his classmates at West Point. The "gold fever" broke out soon after his marriage, and the throngs of emigrants to California made the presence of troops necessary on the Pacific coast. On July 5, 1852, he sailed from New York with his regiment for California, via the Isthmus of Panama. While the troops under his command were crossing the isthmus, cholera broke out, and one-seventh of his command were carried off. His skill and devotion, united with rare common sense, saved the lives of many of his soldiers. He went to Benicia barracks, California, and thence to Fort Vancouver, Ore., a lonely outpost in the wilderness of the extreme Northwest. His life there was dreary, uneventful and dispiriting, and the evidence seems to show that he did not resist the natural temptations to conviviality so well as he might have done. The prospect for advancement in the army was gloomy. The promotions for services during the Mexican war, many of them obtained through political influence, had filled every vacancy existing, or that was likely to occur. In July, 1854, the year after he became a captain, he resigned from the army and went to St. Louis, his wife's former home. He had at this time a wife and two children, but his pay as an army officer could not support them. He had saved nothing, being in fact absolutely penniless, without any trade or profession. His father-in-law had given his wife a farm of sixty acres near St. Louis, and three negroes. The next six years of his life were years of poverty, obscurity and failure. The

returns from his farm were small. He raised wheat and potatoes, converted trees into cord-wood, cutting them down himself; then loading his cart, drove into St. Louis, and sold his wood by the cord. There were many who, after he became president, well remembered the short square figure, felt hat, coarse blouse, and trousers tucked into the boots of the man who once brought them their firewood. As a farmer, Grant was not successful. He took up bill-collecting, but this also resulted in failure. He tried for the position of county engineer, but failed to get the place. He tried auctioneering, and also made an experiment in the real estate business. The result was the same in all his ventures. Whether, because the years spent in the army had unfitted him for business life or not, at any rate his life thus far had proved a failure. He was shabbily dressed and thoroughly poverty-stricken. In the winter of 1859 he was actually wandering about the streets of St. Louis seeking work, and even offering to become a teamster to accompany quartermaster's stores to New Mexico. He finally went to Galena, Ill., and became a clerk at a nominal salary of $66 a month, in the store of his father and brother, who had a leather and saddlery business. He remained eleven months, but was regarded as "a dull, plodding man." A singular incident of his life in his father's store is narrated. Some village worthy inquired: "Who is that chap in there who is always hanging around Grant's tannery?" "The short fellow with the cigar in his mouth, do you mean?" "Yes, he's always smoking, and walks up and down without speaking to anybody." "Oh, that's Grant's brother." This was the conversation that took place in Galena, Ill., a few months before the opening of the civil war. The man was then known as "Grant's brother," but he who was at that time an obscure citizen, even in the primitive town of Galena, was soon to be the most famous living general in the world, with perhaps one exception, and nine years later was inaugurated president of the United States. His extraordinary career has probably no parallel in the history of our country, nor perhaps in any country. The day before Sumter was fired upon, Grant had, apparently, no future ahead of him beyond the leather business and life-long obscurity. But the first flash of a Confederate cannon changed his life in an instant. He went into the store, took off his coat, as was his custom, and read the morning's news. He got up, put on his coat, and said, in a quiet, but decisive way, "The government educated me for the army, and, although I have served through one war, I am still in debt to the government, and willing to discharge the obligation." Lincoln's first call for troops was made on Apr. 15, 1861. The telegraph flashed the call throughout the country. That evening the Galena court-house was packed with an excited crowd. Grant, being known as a West Pointer, as well as a Mexican soldier, was called upon to preside. In four days he was drilling a company of volunteers, then offered himself to Gov. Yates of Illinois, and was given the charge of mustering regiments. *Grant became colonel of the 21st Illinois, June 17, 1861,* and when the time came to move there was trouble about transportation. "I will furnish transportation," said he, quietly. He took the regiment out on foot and crossed into Missouri, where it served as part of the guard of important railroads under Gen. Pope's forces. His eleven years' service in the regular army brought him a commission

as brigadier-general of volunteers, to date from May 17, 1861. On May 24, 1861, he wrote to Adj. Gen. Thomas, commanding at Washington, D.C., tendering his services to the government. No answer was received. The letter was carelessly filed away and temporarily lost. Gov. Yates then placed Grant in command of the 21st Illinois volunteer infantry, and on July 3d he led it to Palmyra, Mo., and from there to guard the Hannibal and St. Joseph railroad. Subsequently he took command of the district of southeast Missouri, with headquarters at Cairo. His troops were soon increased by the accession of Gen. McClernand's brigade. Cairo, being at the confluence of the Ohio and Mississippi rivers, was the key of the West. The surrounding country was full of disaffection and disorder, and distrust prevailed. Kentucky, which professed to be a Union state, and had furnished many gallant soldiers for the starry banner, was used as a place of refuge for rebel marauders and free lances. Grant, with his clear military eye, saw the point which must be occupied to command the troublesome territory. He took possession Sept. 6, 1861, of Paducah, Ky., on the Ohio, near the mouth of the Tennessee, thus commanding a large region. The proclamation he issued is notable for its firmness, its loyalty to the government, and its terseness: "I am come among you, not as an enemy, but as your fellow-American; not to maltreat and annoy you, but to respect and enforce the rights of all loyal citizens. I am here to defend you against the common enemy, who has planted his guns on your soil and fired upon you, and to assert the authority and sovereignty of your government. I have nothing to do with opinions, and shall deal only with armed rebellion and its aiders and abettors. You can pursue your usual avocations without fear. The strong arm of the government is here to protect its friends and punish its enemies.

GRANT, ULYSSES S.

Whenever it is manifest that you are able to defend yourselves, maintain the authority of the government, and protect the rights of loyal citizens, I shall withdraw the forces under my command." The occupation of Paducah was a prompt action, taken without communicating with Frémont, then commander of the department of the Missouri. Grant felt that no time was to be lost. In every action he showed the quick decision of the born commander. This rare ability was recognized almost as promptly as it was displayed. One of the most interesting features of his history and that of the war—for they are in large part the same— is his rapid progress from post to post of danger and responsibility. Men seemed to feel as he approached each new difficulty that this was the man born for the occasion. Early in November he was ordered to make a demonstration in the direction of Belmont, a point on the west bank of the Mississippi, about eighteen miles below the junction of the Ohio with the Mississippi, the object being to prevent the crossing of hostile troops into Missouri. He received his orders Nov. 5th; moved 3,100 men on transports on the 6th; landed at Belmont on the 7th, and broke up and destroyed the camp, while under heavy fire, with raw troops. The Confederate force was double his own—7,000 against his 3,100. Their loss was 642, and his, *about 600*. His horse was shot under him, but he gained the battle. *By the usual criteria of determining victory, the Confederates won the battle of Belmont, for they drove Union troops away and regained control of the battlefield.* When Gen. Halleck assumed command of the department of the Missouri he placed Grant in command of the district of Cairo, which was enlarged so as to make one of the greatest in size in the country. It included the southern part of Illinois, Kentucky west of the Cumberland, and the southern portion of Missouri. There

came a grave military difficulty—Grant wanted to attack; Halleck preferred to hold back. However, in February, 1862, Grant gained a reluctant consent to a well-matured plan that he had been cherishing for a month past, and started off with 15,000 men, aided by Com. Foote with a gunboat fleet, to capture Forts Henry and Donelson, the former commanding the Tennessee river, and the latter the Cumberland, near the dividing line between Kentucky and Tennessee. The plan is stated to have been Grant's own. As the troops approached the first fort on Feb. 6th, they heard the booming of Foote's guns, and quickened their march as well as they could along the muddy roads. Grant feared lest the boats might have been driven off, and sent an officer forward, who soon came galloping back with news that the Union flag was flying above Fort Henry, which had just surrendered after a bombardment from Foote's gunboats. Most of the garrison escaped to reinforce Fort Donelson, eleven miles distant, although ninety men, including Gen. Tilghman and his staff, were captured. Grant lost no time in preparing to invest the second fort, and on the 12th began the siege with a command numbering 15,000, which was increased on the 14th to 27,000. The weather was bitterly cold, and the troops suffered greatly, yet they maintained a fierce attack for three successive days. Gens. Floyd, Pillow and Buckner, who were in command of the Confederate forces, regarding their defeat by this time as imminent, determined to cut their way through the Federal lines on Saturday, Feb. 15th, and retreat to Nashville. That morning Grant was on the flag-ship consulting with Foote. His quick mind comprehended that the Confederates had concentrated their forces, and that the time had come for a final, overpowering onslaught on the enemy's works. Some distance down the river was an isolated

288

hill, crowned with a heavy battery. From the hill shot and shell could be rained into the fort, and by skillful firing the Confederates could be placed in a hopeless position. Grant ordered Gen. Smith to take the hill. The order was obeyed. Night came on and both sides waited for the morning. Within the fort, Gen. Floyd, recognizing the approaching disaster, decided to leave, and turned his command over to Gen. Pillow. Pillow, finding matters getting hot, turned his authority over to Gen. Buckner. The two generals—Pillow and Buckner—*who attended West Point,* so feared "Grant's bulldog pertinacity," that in the early morning, previous to the order for the assault, Gen. Buckner sent a flag of truce and wanted terms. Grant gave the grim response, which has gone down in history: "No terms but unconditional and immediate surrender can be accepted: I propose to move immediately upon your works." Buckner surrendered 15,000 prisoners, and a vast quantity of military stores was taken. Of the Confederates, 2,500 men were killed or wounded, while Grant's loss was less than

2,041. *The Federal force on the last four days' fighting was 23,000–25,000.* The capture of Fort Donelson caused great delight all over the North. It was the first great success of the war, and created intense excitement throughout the country. The army of the Potomac honored the event by a salute of one hundred guns. At the South the effect was correspondingly depressing. The road was left open for the Federal armies to Nashville. The first great breach in the line of defence that had seemed so strong from the Mississippi to the Atlantic had been made. It was the beginning of Vicksburg and the destruction of the Confederate army west of the Alleghanies. The boldness of the assault, and the completeness of the victory, made Grant the hero of the people. The terms of his brief, stern demand on Buckner became household words everywhere. The president nominated him to the senate as major-general of volunteers, to date from Feb. 16, 1862, the date of the surrender, and the senate immediately confirmed him. Ten months before he was a

quiet citizen—clerking behind the counter of his father's leather and saddlery store in Galena. In the house of representatives members rose to their feet, and cheered loudly and continuously. While all this was going on Gen. Halleck, who never seemed to estimate Grant's work at its value, was writing to the war department, that after his victory Grant had not communicated with him. The result of this complaint was that Grant was suspended from his command. In less than three weeks after his victory he was virtually in arrest, and without command. Halleck's jealousy met with a rebuff, and he was finally obliged to write to Grant: "Instead of relieving you, I wish you, as soon as your new army is in the field, to assume immediate command, and lead it to new victories." This unexpected order was owing principally to the concentration of the Confederate armies near Corinth, Miss., and Grant was ordered to move up the Tennessee river toward the Confederate rendezvous, but not to attack. On the 17th of March he transferred his headquarters to Savannah, on the Tennessee river. The forces under his command numbered about 38,000 men, and were encamped on both sides of the river. He at once concentrated them on the west side, and in the vicinity of Pittsburg Landing. He was directed not to attack the enemy until the arrival of Gen. Buell's army of 40,000 men. While Grant was eagerly awaiting Buell's appearance, Gen. Albert S. Johnston attacked him at daybreak, and forced the Federal army to fall back in confusion nearly to the Landing, and pressed their advantage during the entire day. On the afternoon Buell arrived on the opposite side of the river, threw a division of his forces across, and immediately went into action. During the afternoon Johnston received a mortal wound, and Beauregard, succeeding to the command, threw his army against the centre

and left wing of the Federal troops. The assault was repulsed, and at nightfall the gunboats supporting Grant's troops bombarded the Confederate position. 5,000 of Grant's troops did not arrive on the field during the day, so that his command was outnumbered. Grant sought shelter that night in a hut; but the surgeons having made an amputating hospital of it, he found the sight so painful that he went out and slept under a tree. At daybreak he ordered an attack, and it was pushed with such vigor that the enemy was driven back nineteen miles toward Corinth. On that day Grant's sword scabbard was broken by a ball. The Federal loss was 1,754 killed, 8,408 wounded, 2,885 missing, a total of 13,047. The Confederates had a loss of 1,728 killed, 8,012 wounded, and 957 missing, a total of 10,699. On the 11th Gen. Halleck arrived, and took command in person with a force of 120,000 men. The Confederates were strongly entrenched. Grant was named second in command of all the Federal troops, but especially intrusted with the right wing and reserve. On Apr. 30th the order was given to advance against Corinth. Thirty days later, May 30th, when the Federal army entered the works they were found deserted with nothing but "Quaker" guns to mark the place where the Confederate army had been. During the time Halleck had been watching behind breastworks, Beauregard and his command had quietly slipped away. On June 21st Grant moved his headquarters to Memphis. July 11th Halleck was appointed general-in-chief of all the armies, and on the 17th set out for Washington, leaving Grant in command of the army of the Tennessee. On Oct. 25th following, he was made commander of the department of the Tennessee. He had meanwhile fought the battle of Iuka, Sept. 19th and 20th. He also during the winter fought the battles of Port Hudson,

Raymond, Jackson, Champion Hill, Big Black, and others. *Grant and his army were not at Port Hudson. The other battles named here were fought in May 1863.* It was his desire to capture Vicksburg, and he proposed the matter to Halleck, his superior officer, in October. After waiting in vain for orders he started without them Nov. 3d. He ordered Gen. Sherman to move down from Memphis to attack Vicksburg, and prepared to co-operate with him by land. On Dec. 20, 1862, Col. Murphy, who was in charge of supplies at Holly Springs, yielded the place to the enemy after a feeble defence. Murphy was dismissed from the service in disgrace. His conduct frustrated Grant's plans. The difficulty of protecting the long line of communication necessary for furnishing supplies caused Grant to abandon the land expedition he had planned against Vicksburg, and make his movement down the Mississippi. Sherman was at Milliken's Bend, twenty miles above Vicksburg with 32,000 men. On Jan. 29, 1863, Grant arrived at Young's Point above Vicksburg, and took command in person, his available force numbering 50,000. Adm. Porter's co-operating fleet of gunboats carried 280 guns and 800 men. Three plans were suggested for investing the city: First, to take the forces down by the west bank of the river below the big bend, and so co-operate with Gen. Banks, ascending the river from New Orleans. The high water in the river, and the flooded condition of the adjacent territory precluded this plan. Second, to construct a canal across the peninsula formed by the big bend, through which the fleet of gunboats and transports could pass without being subjected to the fire of the river batteries in front of the city, and which could be held open as a line of communication for supplies. Work was prosecuted with vigor, but the high water swept away the levees, flooded the camps, and at the

end of two months was abandoned. Third, to open a new channel by the way of Lake Providence, and divert the current of the Mississippi into the Red river, but the Mississippi chose to cut its own channels, and not be guided by any agency other than its own. It broke the banks and flooded an immense cotton-growing district. Another plan was then attempted on the eastern side of the river by cutting a passage into Moon lake, thence across into Coldwater river, whose waters finally reached the Yazoo. The experiments generally failed. About the middle of April Grant discovered the river falling rapidly, and determined on carrying out his original plan of marching his troops down the west side of the river from Milliken's Bend to New Carthage, then run the batteries of Vicksburg with the gunboats and transports. The movement was begun March 29th, by McClernand with his corps advancing. On the night of Apr. 16th, the transports laden with supplies ran the gauntlet of shot and shell, only one escaping uninjured. On Apr. 30th the advance of the army was ferried across the river at Bruensburg, thirty miles south of Vicksburg. Everything was put in readiness for the most speedy action. Each man carried his own supplies. Grant himself had no personal baggage, and crossed the river without even a horse, but succeeded in obtaining a sorry specimen after reaching the east side. At this juncture in affairs, Grant ordered Col. Grierson with a force of 1,700 to make a raid extending from La Grange on the northern borders of the state of Mississippi, through the middle portion of the state, until he reached Baton Rouge. At noon of May 2d, fifteen days after setting out, his command galloped into the streets of Baton Rouge, having accomplished all the work planned by Grant. On May 3d Grant entered Grand Gulf. His movement proved a complete surprise to Pemberton at Vicksburg with 52,000 men; with Gen. Joseph E. Johnston at Jackson, fifty miles east, having 43,000 men. *At this time Pemberton had about 40,000 men altogether, and Johnston only a few thousand. Grant had 44,000. Johnston subsequently built up his force to 30,000 men; by then Grant had been reinforced to a total of 70,000.* Grant determined to march between the two armies of the enemy and defeat them in detail, before they could unite against him. Three days' rations were issued to the soldiery, and he gave orders that they must last five days. On May 1st he defeated a portion of Pemberton's force at Port Gibson; on May 12th he routed a part of Johnston's army, and pushed on to Jackson, capturing it on the 14th. He turned about and moved rapidly toward Vicksburg, and attacked Pemberton at Champion Hill. From this time onward the advance was steady and the fighting constant. On the 18th of May the Federal forces closed up against the outworks of Vicksburg, and drove the Confederate forces behind their fortifications. Sherman took possession of Haines's Bluff; on the 21st a base of supplies had been established at Chickasaw Landing, and the army once more had full rations. On the 22d assaults were made at points along the enemy's lines, and the next day the siege was regularly begun. Vicksburg was fairly invested. By June 30th Grant had 220 guns in position. The operations were pressed day and night. With 71,000 troops he surrounded the city and kept a careful watch on Johnston, who was massing his forces to make an attack in the rear. There was mining and countermining, and the lines were pushed closer and closer. On the 3d of July a flag of truce brought into the Federal camp two Confederate officers, Col. Montgomery and Gen. Bowen, bearing a sealed communication from Pemberton to Grant. He proposed terms of capitulation by the appointment of commissioners, three on each side, adding that he was "fully able to maintain his position for an indefinite period." The answer given was as terse as that given to Gen. Buckner—"unconditional surrender." Grant, however, agreed to meet Pemberton at 3 o'clock P.M., and have a personal interview. The two generals met at the appointed hour, under a gigantic oak in McPherson's front. The oaktree disappeared within a few months through the vandalism of relic-hunters. Upon the spot where it stood a monument was afterward erected, bearing the inscription—"To the memory of the surrender of Vicksburg by Lieut.-Gen. J. C. Pemberton to Maj.-Gen. U. S. Grant, on the 3d of July, 1863." This in turn was so much defaced, that in 1866 it was displaced by a sixty-four pounder cannon, placed with the muzzle pointing upward, the whole being surrounded by a strong iron fence, for the prevention of vandalism against even cast steel guns. The terms of surrender were not finally agreed upon until the following morning. As completed, Pemberton's army was to be permitted to march out of the city as soon as paroled, the officers taking with them their regimental clothing, while staff, field and cavalry officers might retain one horse each, the rank and file to be allowed all their clothing, but no arms. The necessary amount of rations could be taken from stores in hand, with utensils for cooking; also necessary wagons for transportation. The sick and wounded should be cared for until able to travel. A special order was issued by Grant to his own army: "Instruct the commands to be orderly and quiet as these prisoners pass, and to make no offensive remarks." It took three hours for the Confederate army to march out and stack their arms. In the afternoon the National troops marched in and took possession after an active campaign of eighty days. Grant's loss in the campaign had been 8,575, of which 4,236 fell before Vicksburg, while the Confederate loss had been 12,000 in killed and wounded, and 8,000 by disease and straggling. The surrender brought in 31,600 prisoners, 172 cannon, eighty siege guns, 60,000 muskets, and a large amount of ammunition, together with an immense amount of other property, consisting of railroad engines, cars, steamboats, cotton, etc. It was also discovered that much property had been destroyed to prevent its capture. Seven hundred and ninety men refused to be paroled, and were held as prisoners of war. When Gen. Johnston was apprised of the fall of Vicksburg, he abandoned his attempts to harass the rear of Grant's army, and withdrew to Jackson. His position was there untenable, for Sherman had 100 guns planted on the adjoining hills. Johnston retreated, for to remain was disaster. Jackson was evacuated on the night of July 16th, Johnston retreating to Brandon, 100 miles east of Jackson and burning his bridges behind him. Port Hudson surrendered to Banks, and the Mississippi was open for commerce through its entire length, or, as President Lincoln expressed it, *"The Father of Waters again goes unvexed to the sea."* It was universally felt that Grant was the foremost man in the campaign. His name was on every tongue. He was at once appointed a major-general in the regular army to date from July 4, 1863, and a gold medal was given him by congress. He had in the Vicksburg campaign shown his capacity for handling

a large army, and conducting extensive movements. He had boldness of conception, unlimited resources of physical and mental power, a bulldog persistence of purpose that would not be moved by any obstacle, or conquered by any succession of partial defeats; total defeat with such a commander was not possible. Toward the last of August, Gen. Grant proceeded on a tour of inspection through his department. He reached New Orleans on Sept. 2d. As he was returning to his hotel from a review of Ord's corps, his horses became frightened, and Grant was accidentally thrown, striking violently on the pavement, and so severely injuring his hip as to confine him to

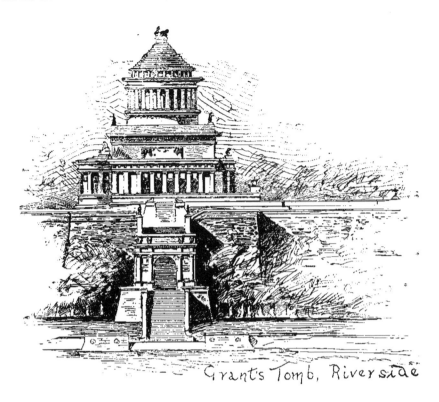

Grant's Tomb, Riverside

hospital care *for a few weeks and on crutches several more.* In October Secretary Stanton met him at Indianapolis, and together they proceeded to Louisville. Here on the 18th the secretary handed him the order of the president giving him the command of the "Military District of the Mississippi," comprising the departments of the Tennessee, the Ohio, and the Cumberland. This order gave Grant the military control of all the territory in possession of the government from the Mississippi river to the Alleghany mountains, and of four large armies under Sherman, Thomas, Burnside, and Hooker, numbering 150,000 effective men. Grant went at once to Chattanooga and took command in person. Five days later a three hours' battle was fought at Wauhatchie in Lookout Valley, resulting in a Federal victory, and the opening of a much-needed line of communication for supplies. The Confederates under Longstreet had a signal station on the top of Lookout Mountain, at an altitude of 2,000

feet and surmounted by a rugged and supposed impregnable dome of rocks, geographically described as "a perpendicular wall of limestone over which no wheel could pass." Grant ordered a concentration of forces near Chattanooga, and on Nov. 23d, one month after his arrival, began the series of battles embracing Chattanooga, Orchard Knob, Lookout Mountain, and Missionary Ridge. The conflicts extended over three days, and each was a desperate battle in itself. Grant had, all told, 60,000 men, but they were on half rations, the horses were technically considered "walking skeletons," and dying by thousands for want of forage. At the end of the three days' fight, the Confederates were routed and driven out of Tennessee; 6,442 prisoners were taken, with 40 pieces of artillery, and 7,000 stands of small arms. Nov. 28th Sherman was dispatched with a force to Knoxville to destroy supplies and bridge and railway communications. On March 1, 1864, Grant was nominated lieutenant-general, the grade having been revived by congress; was confirmed by the senate March 2d, and left Nashville in obedience to an order calling him to Washington, March 4th. His new commission was handed to him by the president on the 9th, and he was given formal command of all the armies of the United States on the 17th. Grant established himself at Culpeper, Va., with the army of the Potomac. The entire system of the military departments was rearranged, and organized into distinct armies which were to be concentrated on command, for moving simultaneously and operating vigorously and continuously Sherman was to move at the opening of the campaign, toward Atlanta, against Johnston. Banks had 56,000 men, and when he returned from the Red river expedition was to operate against Mobile. Sigel with 26,000 was to move down the valley of Virginia against Breckinridge; *Auger with 28,000* was to protect the department of Washington, which comprised an area of only a few miles; Butler with 47,000 was to ascend the James river and threaten Richmond; Burnside with 22,000 was to co-operate with the army of the Potomac, numbering 97,000, and Sheridan was to command the cavalry. The total effective strength of the National armies as reported to the adjutant-general of the army, on May 1, 1864, as present for duty, was 662,345. Those present for duty, equipped, numbered 533,477, a difference of nearly 129,000. President Lincoln had already designated the "present for duty" as a "paper army." To leave Washington uncovered would hazard the safety, not only of the capital, but possibly of the republic, and Grant determined to post himself between Washington and the Confederate army. The outlines of his plan were communicated only to his most important and most trusted commanders. They were not even divulged to the government. Orders were given the different commands to move forward on May 4th. Grant started by crossing the Rapidan on the nights of the 4th and 5th, the 5th, 6th and 7th witnessed the terrible scenes of the battle of the Wilderness between opposing forces aggregating 183,000 men. The "Wilderness" was a wild tract of country in Orange and Spottsylvania counties, Va., bordering on the Rapidan river. Lee showed superior generalship and had become so fully informed of Grant's movements that he advanced his own army, and for a time both armies were moving simultaneously toward each other. *At the end of three days Grant had lost just under 18,000 killed, wounded, and missing. Lee's loss was between 11,000 and 12,000.* Grant by strategic movements endeavored to outwit Lee, and a long series of battles resulted. On the 7th Lee moved back to Spottsylvania. Grant moved forward during the night. As he rode along by the lines of troops, he was recognized and wildly cheered. It was the first heavy fighting done by the army of the Potomac under his leadership, and the grim determination of his manner made them grim and determined to be worthy of their commander. Virginia became a mighty battle-ground. Spottsylvania, North Anna, Cold Harbor, Chickahominy followed, and by the time Grant had reached the James river he had lost an additional 39,000 of his troops. He made his headquarters at City Point, at the junction of the Appomattox with the James, and distant twenty miles from Richmond, and ten from Petersburg. Assaults were made on Petersburg June 15th, 16th, 17th and 18th, resulting in the capture of important outworks, and the possession of a line closer to Petersburg. Lee again confronted Grant at City Point, and the whole region witnessed heavy fighting. Sheridan had been busy with his cavalry making raids and destroying roads, bridges and inflicting other damage, and rejoined the army of the Potomac on June 20th. Gen. Early made a dash for Washington in July, drove the National troops out of Martinsburg, and crossed the upper Potomac. When the capital learned that he was advancing on its fortifications from the north, it was filled with the wildest consternation. Grant showed his appreciation of the danger and hurled the *6th corps* against the daring Confederate leader, and Early did not enter Washington. The city and the country also breathed more easily, for the capital had been saved, even in the very midst of the complications existing in and about Richmond and Petersburg. At a later date, Sept. 19th, Sheridan attacked Early at Winchester and completely routed him. He pursued him to Fisher's Hill and gained another victory. Grant was steadily making movements in all directions, especially toward investing Richmond and Petersburg, and studying to prevent Lee from detaching troops. All the available forces were working in obedience to his leadership. He ordered several movements against the two primal points, Richmond and Petersburg. Butler was ordered to advance Sept. 29th, and Fort Harrison with fifteen guns and several hundred prisoners was taken; the Confederates tried to recover the place next day, but every assault was repulsed with heavy loss. The other generals, each in his own department were grimly carrying out orders from headquarters, sometimes with heavy loss. On Oct. 19th Sheridan, while returning towards Winchester from Washington, suddenly heard the booming of cannon in the distance and knew that the enemy had attacked and were routing his forces. His "Winchester Ride," famed in song, turned the defeat into a victory. In the general complication of defeats and victories Grant was fearful lest Lee should suddenly abandon his works and fall back to

unite with Johnston's forces in an attempt to crush Sherman. This would prove a master stroke, and Grant enjoined sleepless vigilance on all his generals, and prompt reports of every movement. So passed the fall and winter away. On March 22, 1865, President Lincoln visited Gen. Grant at City Point, and on the 27th Sherman came. On the 29th Grant issued orders for a general advance. The advance was made from many points with varying successes. On the morning of Apr. 2d an assault was begun upon the lines around Petersburg. The Union forces began to close in upon the inner defences of the city. Richmond and Petersburg were evacuated that night, and the National forces entered and took possession on the morning of Apr. 3d. On the night *of Apr. 7th* Grant sent Lee a note, calling his attention to the hopelessness of further resistance, and asking the surrender of his army. Lee said he was not of Grant's opinion as to the hopelessness of further resistance, but asked what terms would be offered. Grant had found more difficulties than he had anticipated: a more skillful general in opposition, and a more stubborn soldiery than he had ever encountered before, yet he determined not to change his original plans, and he gave orders to press forward. *One day later,* Apr. 8th, Lee, at midnight, sent another note to Grant, saying he had not proposed the surrender of his army, but desired to know whether Grant's proposals would lead to peace, and suggested a meeting in person at ten o'clock on the following morning. Grant replied that the meeting would amount to nothing, as he had no authority to treat regarding peace. His mission was to make the South lay down its arms. The quicker this was done the better; thousands of lives would be saved, and millions of property preserved. Lee would not yield, and hostilities were immediately renewed. The next day Lee found himself hemmed in by cavalry and infantry. Grant received, while riding toward Appomattox Court House, a note, asking another interview in accordance with the suggestions contained in Grant's letter of the day before. Grant answered by offering to meet Lee at any place the latter might select. After some formalities they decided on meeting in the McClean house at Appomattox. *It was early in the afternoon when the interview began.* Little was said, for neither was in the habit of spending words. The decision was that the Confederate army surrender; all public property must be given up; the officers might retain their side arms, baggage, and horses; every man must be paroled; and every man who owned a horse might keep it to work on his farm. Terms so magnanimous were never before offered in the history of the world. The Federal army, when the news was heard, went wild. When Grant approached salutes were fired; shouts, and cheers, and yells indulged in. He immediately sent out an order, "The war is over; the rebels are again our countrymen, and the best sign of rejoicing after the victory will be to abstain from all demonstrations in the field." The army was paroled. Twenty thousand stragglers and deserters came in and surrendered. The war was at an end. On Apr. 10th Grant went to Washington, to arrange for disbanding the armies. Four days later Lincoln was assassinated, and Grant would probably have shared the same fate, had he not left Washington on his military business, and without the knowledge of the assassins. On the 17th Mosby and his guerrilla band surrendered. On the 18th Gen. Sherman received Johnston's surrender, but the terms did not please Grant, and he went to North Carolina to conduct further negotiations. On the 26th Johnston's army of 31,243 made full surrender, and received parole, Grant remaining at Raleigh, and leaving to Sherman the full credit

of the capture. On May 1st Morgan surrendered. *What this refers to is a mystery; no surrender took place on May 1.* On May 4th Taylor surrendered 10,000 in Alabama; on the same date the Confederate naval forces under Com. Farraud also surrendered; on the 9th President Johnson issued the proclamation of peace; and on the 10th Jefferson Davis was captured. As the news flashed over the country, other surrenders by detached commands rapidly followed; Kirby Smith, west of the Mississippi, laid down his arms on the 26th, and, when that had been done, there was not an armed enemy left in the states. Grant made Washington his headquarters. Wherever he went he was greeted with ovations; honors were heaped upon him from every hand, and he was universally hailed as the country's deliverer. After the incessant strain of four years' labor in the field, the war being ended and peace fully secured, Gen. Grant determined to get away as far as possible from everything suggestive of war. Consequently he devoted the months of June, July and August of the "peace year" to a recreation tour through the northern states and Canada. On his return he was welcomed by a demonstration that exceeded anything of a like nature that the city had witnessed before. The banquet and reception, and the manifestations of the people in their greetings were of the most extravagant kind. A special characteristic of Grant's determination to see fair play was shown in his action regarding Gen. Lee. Inasmuch as Lee's operations had been principally in Virginia, the U.S. court in that state had seen fit to summon the grand jury, and find various indictments against him, as well as other officers prominent in the civil war. Two months after the close of the war Lee made a written application to have extended to him the privileges given those included in the proclamation of amnesty issued by

President Johnson. The letter was referred to Grant, and he endorsed on it: "Respectfully forwarded through the secretary of war to the president, with the earnest recommendation that the application of Gen. Robert E. Lee for pardon and amnesty be granted him." President Johnson was bitter against all the defeated foes of the Union, and seemed by his every act to endeavor to wound their manly pride. When he began his embittered pressure on Lee, that general wrote a letter to Grant. Grant wrote to the president: "In my opinion, the officers and men paroled at Appomattox Court House cannot be tried for treason so long as they preserve the terms of their parole. . . . The action of Judge Underwood in Norfolk has already had an injurious effect, and I would ask that he be ordered to quash all indictments found against paroled prisoners of war, and to desist from further prosecution of them." He declared that in his position as commanding general he had a right to accord the terms, and the president was bound to respect the agreements entered into by him. He went so far as to threaten to resign his position in the army if such a gross breach of good faith should be perpetrated under the circumstances. He gained his point, but a chilled feeling between him and President Johnson grew into a daily increasing estrangement, which was never healed. Congress, as a reward for his military valor, created for him the grade of general. This was not enough, but corporations and societies presented him with swords, and private citizens urged him to accept residences. In December of the victorious year, after his tour in the North, he made a journey of inspection through the South. The result of his observations was embodied in a report to congress, and became the basis of important features in the drafting of the reconstruction laws. The civil war was scarcely getting its smoke cleared away when a Fenian disturbance broke out along the Canadian frontier, and threatened unpleasant disturbances in the country's relations with England. Various outbreaks had occurred at points along the border, but Grant made a visit to Buffalo in June, 1866, and such effective measures were taken that Fenianism not only ceased its menacing attitude, but went into retirement. *Not quite true; there were later Fenian attempts to invade Canada, though they turned out to be more farcical than serious.* Gen. Grant and President Johnson had radically different views regarding the management of the South after the close of the war, and President Johnson as ex-officio general-in-chief of the army, desiring to be rid of Grant, issued a special order sending him out of the country, to wit, on a special mission to Mexico. Grant, although not a lawyer, saw the trick. He declined the honor, giving as his reason that it was not a military, but a diplomatic mission, and he felt it his duty to decline a civil appointment. Grant afterward obtained, through congress, the entire control of affairs relating to the southern states, and in August, 1867, was appointed by President Johnson secretary of war ad interim while Secretary Stanton was under suspension. Grant protested against this action, and much dissension ensued, but he held the office until Jan. 4, 1868, when, the senate refusing to confirm the suspension of Stanton, Grant promptly retired, greatly to the president's annoyance. Although the two men were constantly opposed to each other in their views regarding the government of the nation, Grant's conduct was of so dignified a character that he daily grew in popularity with the people. At the Chicago convention, held May 20, 1868, he was nominated for the presidency on the first ballot, and when the election occurred in November, out of 294 electoral votes cast for president, Grant received 214, and Seymour, the democratic candidate, eighty—the former carrying twenty-six states against eight claimed by his rival. On March 4, 1869, the victorious general took the oath as chief executive of the United States. Grant had never had any political experience. In his early life his politics had been democratic, and his only presidential vote had been cast in 1856 for James Buchanan. In his presidential career he was indebted to his shrewd common sense for the excellence of much of his administration, while to his ignorance of human nature, outside of military life, will, by posterity, be charged his failures. In the selection of friends he was extremely cautious, giving his confidences to but very few. Many so-called friends made their way to him, but never succeeded in being cordially received. They either forced themselves, or were forced, upon him, and he, while frequently imposed upon, generally succeeded in ridding himself of their unpleasant companionship. In the hands of cunning and unscrupulous politicians he was powerless to defend himself, and such men used their influence most unfortunately for his reputation and the country when it served their purpose. During his first term of office occurred the Credit Mobilier scandal, in connection with the building of the Union Pacific railroad, but in all the investigations made in connection with the matter, no stain ever rested on Grant. There came another scandal, the "Back-pay" affair, where certain laws regarding salaries had been passed, retroactive in their character, but his manhood never wavered, and his personal integrity always remained unquestioned. Four years of a presidential life found him at its end in the same condition as at its beginning, calm, imperturbable, invariably silent, smoking a cigar whose rising smoke seemed never to be absent from him, and calmly regarding the silent workings of various political enemies, who declared they had "found a bigger man than old Grant." The lamented Horace Greeley was placed in the presidential contest of

1872 against Grant. Greeley, as the editor of the New York "Tribune," wielded an immense influence throughout the country, but while the people respected him as one of the ablest editors of the age, the fact was recognized that he was neither a statesman nor a military man—neither fitted for the senate or the camp. Grant carried thirty-one states, the largest vote ever given for any president. Greeley carried only six states, and died of a broken heart before his sixty-six electoral votes could be cast. Grant's second administration was mainly important for the passage of the "Resumption act," *an act to bring the greenback dollar to par with the gold dollar, which was accomplished on schedule by January 1, 1879,* and the detection and punishment of the ringleaders in the notorious "Whiskey ring," of which many were men of great personal influence, and with friends claiming to hold very important positions near the president himself. At the end of his second term, Grant, after yielding the presidential chair to his successor, decided to break loose from all ties connected with labor of any sort, and enjoy a needed rest. He had, at different times, seen about all there was to be seen of the northern part of the Western hemisphere, and he planned for a journey in foreign countries. He set sail on May 17, 1877, from Philadelphia on the steamer Indiana, accompanied by his wife, his son Frederick and a private secretary, his first objective point being England. His departure was the occasion for a memorable demonstration. Distinguished men from both civil and military life assembled to do him honor. A fleet of naval and commercial vessels and river craft, gaily decorated with the choicest banners, convoyed his steamer; crowds lined the shore, making the air resound with their repeated cheers; bells on all sides pealed lustily in his honor; whistles from mills and factories in every direction added their cheerings to the general din, and flags without number saluted as he floated down the stream toward the ocean. On the 28th of May he received the first of the grand series of ovations in foreign lands, which for two years and four months constituted a triumphal tour never experienced by even a Roman or Oriental monarch. On his arrival at Liverpool the river Mersey was covered with vessels displaying the flags of all nations, and vieing with each other in their demonstrations of welcome. He was entertained by Queen Victoria and the Prince of Wales, and accorded the "freedom" of the chief cities, which meant the granting of citizenship. Upon leaving England he visited the continent, and his welcome by every class of people, from royalty to peasants, was of the most heartfelt kind. He received the most elaborate of hero worship. The U.S. man-of-war Vandalia had been placed at his service, and on board that vessel he made a cruise of the Mediterranean, visiting all the adjacent countries. Thence on Jan. 23, 1879, he sailed for India, arriving in Bombay, Feb. 12th; from there visiting such points of interest as suited his pleasure. The greetings he received were the greetings given to a loved emperor making a triumphal tour through his own realms. He visited Burmah, the Malacca peninsula, Siam, Cochin China, Hong Kong. He went into the interior of the mighty empire of China. At Pekin, he was officially asked by the reigning prince to act as "sole arbitrator" in the settlement of a dispute between his country and Japan, concerning the Loo Choo islands. Grant's plans prevented his spending time to enter upon the duties pertaining to an arbitrator, but after an examination of the questions involved, he gave his advice on the subject, and the matter was subsequently settled without war between the nations involved. On June 21st he reached Nagasaki, Japan, where he became the guest of the Mikado. The entertainments given in his honor exceeded anything ever before known in the history of the empire. He sailed from Yokohama for home Sept. 3, 1879, and touched the American shores at San Francisco, Sept. 20th. He had not been on the Pacific coast since he had served there as a second lieutenant, twenty-seven years before. The reception that was given him on his arrival was royal in the extreme; the demonstration in the harbor of San Francisco on his arrival forming a pageant never before witnessed on the Pacific shore. Banquets and receptions met him everywhere, until he sought the retirement of his private home. In 1880 he visited Cuba and Mexico, and another series of ovations persistently followed him. On his return to the United States he went with his family to his old home, Galena, Ill. The popular feeling in his favor was such that in 1880 a movement was begun for his renomination to the presidency of the United States. Overtures were made to draw him into an active canvass for the purpose of accomplishing the result. The convention gathered in Chicago, in June 1880, and when his name as the candidate was presented, there was a wild excitement. For thirty-six ballots the iron-clad vote for Grant was 306, with slight variations ranging between 302 and 313. There was a strange opposition in certain directions, for, while he had many warm friends, there was a traditional sentiment against a "third presidential term." The contest was very hot, and in honor of the loyalty of the "306" pledged friends of Grant, an iron medal was cast and secured by each of the "loyal 306" as a souvenir of the effort to secure Grant for a third term. After a long and exciting contest, a compromise was effected by the nomination of Gen. James A. Garfield, who was subsequently elected. On Christmas eve of 1883, while in front of his residence at Long Branch, N.J., Gen. Grant slipped upon an icy

sidewalk, and received such injuries, especially in the region of the hip, that he was never after able to walk without the aid of a crutch. His military and public life having ended, and finding his income insufficient for the proper maintenance of his family, he invested his entire capital of saved moneys in a banking house, where one of his sons was interested. He took no part in the management of the business, but trusted the firm implicitly. In May, 1884, through a series of unblushing frauds, the firm became bankrupt, and the man who had wielded the destinies of a nation found himself completely swindled by the skillful manipulation of a single unscrupulous partner. In order to save the firm with which his name was connected from absolute ruin, Gen. Grant, at the suggestion of Ferdinand Ward, the wrecker of this concern, went to William H. Vanderbilt, and sought temporary financial relief for the firm. Vanderbilt granted it as a personal favor to Gen. Grant, and drew his check for $100,000. The check was used. In a few days the firm collapsed. Vanderbilt had not required any security, but Grant, true to the instinctive integrity of his nature, immediately went to his friend and deposited with him all the swords, gifts, medals and valuables of every kind that he had at different times received, as a partial security for the loan. The entire collection of swords, gold-headed canes, medals, rare coins, and specially prepared documents presented by different cities, governments and nations, were afterward returned by Mr. Vanderbilt to Mrs. Grant, and eventually the entire collection was deposited in the National Museum at Washington. Among the portraits painted of Gen. Grant, that by Healy for the Union league club in 1865, and one executed in Paris in 1877, one by Le Clear for the White House in Washington, a second by the same artist for the Calumet Club of

Chicago, and one by Ulke for the war department, are regarded as among the best. A marble bust in the war department by Hiram Powers, is ranked among the finest of sculptured work. In 1884, at the age of sixty-two, Gen. Grant was attacked by a disease which proved to be cancer at the root of the tongue, and which ultimately caused his death. On March 4, 1885, congress unanimously passed a bill creating him a general on the retired list, thus restoring him to his former rank with full pay. On June 16th of that year the progress of his disease became so alarming that the suffering warrior was removed to Mt. McGregor, near Saratoga, where the cottage of Joseph W. Drexel had been placed at his disposal. Two days after his arrival he wrote upon a card: "It is just a week to-day since I have spoken. My suffering is continuous." An anxious month then ensued, during which the united heart of the nation was stirred to its inmost depths with sympathy and sorrow. On July 21st an alarming relapse set in, and from that time the entire grief-stricken family were gathered about his bedside, until Thursday morning, July 25, 1885, when death released him from his pains. Almost the only contribution to literature that Gen. Grant ever indulged in, previous to the fading days of his life, was an article, entitled "An Undeserved Stigma" published in the "North American Review" for December, 1882, which he wrote in reference to the case of Gen. Fitz-John Porter. Soon after this the "Century" magazine asked him for a series of articles on his campaigns. He prepared four. In 1884, after receiving handsome offers from several publishers, he began the preparation in two octavo volumes of "Personal Recollections," in which he told the story of his life down to the close of the war. He signed the contract for the publication of this work Feb. 27, 1885, and finished the

proof-reading four days before his death. Eight years later Mrs. Grant had already received nearly $500,000 from the sales of this work. As a man Grant had simple habits, marked force of character, and great pertinacity. In war he was remorseless; in peace magnanimous. In manner he was modest and unassuming, and possessed a character of singular purity. He wrote in his "Personal Recollections" that he had never uttered a profane word, and never told or willingly listened to an impure story. Among the numerous institutions which stand as monuments to his memory is the U.S. Grant university, Chattanooga, Tenn., to the erection of which he made the first contribution. The university was founded for the benefit of the poor whites of the mountain districts of Tennessee, and Gen. Grant, on making his contribution, said: "I want to help the class of people for whom this school is being established, for I believe a Christian education among the masses of the mountainous Central South is now a necessity." His remains were taken to New York, escorted by a detachment of U.S. troops, and a body of veterans of the war. The public funeral occurred Aug. 8, 1885, and was by far the most impressive spectacle of the kind ever known in this country. The morning dawned that day upon weather of well-nigh perfect loveliness, and not a hitch of mishap marred the execution of the truly admirable programme. New York, a city that has witnessed so many splendid pageants in its history, and has ever been among the first to render popular tribute to the nation's heroes, was filled with countless throngs of strangers, pouring in from every corner of the land, without distinction of color or section, to add to the mighty host of sincere mourners. The streets were draped in black, stores and residences alike being covered with the emblems of grief; flags drooped at half-mast, and even the surging crowds on the sidewalks, pressed against each other in a compact mass, spoke only in murmurs, and wore an attitude of hushed expectancy. It was shortly after ten o'clock when the procession finally started from the venerable City hall, the place where the beloved and honored remains had been lying in state for two days, viewed by 250,000 people, while a guard of honor, chosen from the national troops, the state militia, the comrades of the Grand army of the republic, and the police of the city, had watched the bier with jealous care continuously. The line of march was up Broadway to Fourteenth street, Fifth avenue and Boulevard to Riverside park. The procession was divided into three main sections—the military escort, the veteran mourners, and the civic division. At the head rode the dignified figure of Maj.-Gen. Winfield Scott Hancock, U.S.A., commanding military department of the Atlantic. Behind him in columns of eights were the mounted aides, the cream of the national guard and U.S. army and navy officers—a splendid company of fifty-six in all; then came a detachment of 500 regular troops, and after them a naval brigade of 875 marines, led by Com. H. B. Robeson, on duty at the navy yard, with three aides. The state troops appeared next, commanded by Maj.-Gen. Alexander Shaler and twelve aides. New York was represented in the first, second, third and fourth brigades; Massachusetts, Connecticut, New Jersey, and Virginia sent full contingents, and the veteran guards swelled this division to over 12,000. The funeral car was now in sight, drawn by twenty-four horses draped in mourning, led by as many colored grooms. The catafalque was preceded by the six carriages of the clergy and physicians, and the eight carriages occupied by the pallbearers, twelve men, whose names would have added lustre to any funeral rite, and are worthy of

record here: Gen. William T. Sherman, U.S.A.; Lieut.-Gen. Philip H. Sheridan, U.S.A.; Adm. David D. Porter, U.S.N.; Rear-Adm. John L. Worden, U.S.N.; Gen. Joseph E. Johnston of Virginia; Gen. Simon B. Buckner of Kentucky; A. J. Drexel of Pennsylvania; George S. Boutwell of Massachusetts; George W. Childs of Pennsylvania; John A. Logan of Illinois; George Jones and Oliver Hoyt of New York. Two of this number traveled many miles to pay a fitting tribute at the obsequies of him whom they had known in war as a brave soldier and honorable foe, and in after life as a statesman of iron principles and noble ambition. Following the funeral car were the 350 carriages of the mourners, among whom, besides the immediate family and relatives, were Grant's old staff and cabinet, President Cleveland, Vice- President Hendricks, members of the cabinet, Ex-Presidents Hayes and Arthur, members of the U.S. senate and house of representatives, members of the U.S. supreme court, governor of New York and staff, foreign ministers, diplomatic and consular officers who had served under Grant, the governors of sixteen states, the mayors of ten cities, the committee of one hundred, and Gen. Schofield, Adm. Jouett, and Com. Chandler, with their respective staffs. The veterans and G.A.R. posts mustered over 18,000 men, and were commanded by Maj.-Gen. Daniel E. Sickles and a large staff. The civic division, under the command of Maj.-Gen. M. T. McMahon and aides, which contained large deputations from such organizations as the Society of the Cincinnati, New York historical society, Chamber of commerce, Union league club, ex-Confederate veterans' association, New York stock exchange, Produce exchange, Cotton exchange, and Maritime association, ended this vast array of marshaled hosts, which reached the total number of 42,500. It was close upon five o'clock when the funeral car arrived at the temporary tomb in Riverside park, where another great throng had been waiting for hours to view the ceremony of interment from the best possible vantage ground. The minute guns from the men-of-war in the placid river below belched forth their salutes, and the government band played a solemn dirge as the coffin was lifted from the car and placed at the door of the vault. Surrounding the bier, in addition to the small family group, were President Cleveland and cabinet, Ex-Presidents Hayes and Arthur, Gens. Sherman, Sheridan and Hancock, also the Confederate generals Johnston and Buckner, with faces expressive of deep emotion, William M. Evarts, John Sherman, and others equally well known to fame. The Grand army ritual was impressively performed by Grant's old post (George G. Meade post No. 1 of Philadelphia). It commenced with the words "God of battles! Father of all! Amidst this mournful assemblage we seek Thee, with whom there is no death!" Succeeding the utterance of the word "Amen" a wreath of evergreen was laid on the casket, together with a spray of white flowers. A bugler of the regular army played a call; the reverential crowd lifted their hats in unison, and Bishop Harris pronounced the benediction in measured tones. "Taps" were then sounded by the trumpeter. As the sweet, plaintive notes rolled out they actually seemed to falter a moment- the trumpeter could scarcely control his feelings. Sherman's gray head drooped at the familiar sound and he wept as a child; Sheridan brushed his hand quickly across his face; tears came to Johnston's eyes, while Buckner's stern countenance trembled with evident emotion. As the casket was slowly borne within the dark recesses of the tomb, the two Southerners turned instinctively to the grief-stricken relatives and extended their hands in silent sympathy. The iron gates were closed, and immediately the momentous fact was announced to the sorrowing city and country for miles around by thundering salutes from the artillery. A company of eight regulars then mounted guard opposite the entrance, and the immense assemblage gradually dispersed from the scene. The temporary vault was a small square-walled shell of red and black brick, with stone trimmings, and a high semi-cylindrical roof of brick, coated with asphalt. Each of the barred gates discloses the letter "G" in the centre of a wreath. In almost every detail it is an exact copy of the tomb of Henry Meigs, near Callao, Peru. The magnificent monument, of which the cornerstone was laid by ex-President Harrison Apr. 27, 1892, is one of the most superb mausoleums in the world; an appropriate tribute from the people of the United States to the memory of the savior of the Union. The Grant biographies include: "Military History of Ulysses S. Grant, from April, 1861, to April, 1865," by Adam Badeau (3 vols., New York, 1867–68); "Life and Public Services of Gen. U.S. Grant," by James Grant Wilson (1868; revised and enlarged edition, 1886), and "Around the World with General Grant," by John Russell Young (1880).

GREENE, GEORGE SEARS, soldier and civil engineer, was born at Apponaug in the town of Warwick, R.I., May 6, 1801, a descendant in the seventh generation from John Greene, who came in 1635 from Salisbury, England, and settled in Warwick, R.I., in 1642. He was graduated at the United States Military Academy at West Point, N.Y., in June 1823. In the last year of his academic course he was acting assistant professor of mathematics. He was appointed second lieutenant of artillery on being graduated, and detailed for duty at the military academy for four years as assistant

professor in the department of mathematics and of engineering, when he joined his regiment, the 3d artillery, and served in garrisons in Virginia, Rhode Island, Massachusetts and Maine, and on ordnance duty until 1836, when he resigned from the army and entered upon the practice of civil engineering. He was engaged in the location and construction of railroads in the states of Maine, Massachusetts, Rhode Island, New York and Maryland until 1856, when he entered the service of the Croton aqueduct department of the city of New York, designed and built the reservoir in Central Park, enlarged High Bridge and built a new aqueduct over it. After the civil war broke out he re-entered the army, January 1862, as colonel of the 60th regiment of New York volunteers, stationed in the department of Washington. He was appointed a brigadier-general of volunteers, April 28, 1862, joined the army in northern Virginia, and was engaged in the battle of Cedar Mountain, Aug. 9, 1862,

being in command of his brigade. At the battle of Antietam (September, 1862) he commanded the 2d division of the 12th army corps of the army of the Potomac, and repulsed the enemy with signal loss to them; his horse was shot under him in this engagement. He was engaged in the battle of Chancellorsville in command of his brigade. At the battle of Gettysburg on the night of July 2, 1863, with his brigade reduced to less than 1,500 men, he held the entrenchments on Culps Hill, on the right wing of the army of the Potomac against repeated attacks by a division of Confederate troops from six until ten o'clock at night, thereby averting the serious consequences of having a strong division of the enemy in the rear of the main body of the army on Cemetery Ridge. In September, 1863, Gen. Greene in command of his brigade was sent with the 11th and 12th army corps from the army of the Potomac, then on the Rappahannock in Virginia, by rail, via Washington, Wheeling, Cincinnati and Louisville, to Nashville, Tenn., to reinforce the army at Chattanooga. On Oct. 28, in an attack at night by the enemy at Wauhatchie, at the foot of Lookout Mountain, near Chattanooga, he commanded his brigade, and was severely wounded by a shot through his upper jaw, which disabled him from active service in the field until January 1865, when he went to Newbern, N.C., and joined a provisional division under Generals Schofield and Cox, taking part in the battle of Kingston, N.C., where his horse was shot under him. He then commanded a provisional brigade and joined Sherman's Army at Goldsboro', N.C., and also commanded a brigade in Baird's division of Slocum's army corps on the march from Goldsboro' to Washington. He received the commission of major-general by brevet on March 13, 1865, and was on duty in Washington until April 30, 1866, when he retired from the service. The legislature of his native state, Rhode Island, presented him with a vote of thanks for his services during the war. On retiring from the army he returned to the service of the Croton aqueduct department of the city of New York, and planned the stone dam at Boyd's Corner, which was nearly completed under his administration of the department. He became chief engineer and commissioner of the Croton aqueduct department in 1867, and held the office until the department was merged in the department of public works. In 1871 he was appointed chief engineer of public works in Washington, D.C. and made the plans for the entire sewerage of that city. He was consulting engineer of the Central Park commission in making the plans of streets for the annexed districts of the city of New York. From 1875 to 1877 he was president of the American Society of Civil Engineers, of which he was one of the original projectors. He was made an honorary member of the society in 1888, and was employed as consulting engineer in various public works. He was president of the New York Genealogical and Biographical Society for several years. *He died in Morristown, New Jersey, on Jan. 28, 1899, in his 98th year, having lived longer than any other Civil War general.*

GREENE, SAMUEL DANA, naval officer, was born at Cumberland, Md., Feb. 11, 1840, the second son of George Sears Greene. He was graduated from the United States Naval Academy in 1859, and served as midshipman on the Hartford, of the China squadron. In 1861 he volunteered for service on the ironclad Monitor, then building in New York city, which afterward left New York, March 6, 1862, for Hampton Roads, Va. Reaching that place March 9, 1862, she at once proceeded to attack the Merrimac, and Lieut. Worden, her commander,

directed the movements of the vessel from the pilot-house, while Lieut. Greene had charge of the guns in the turret, personally firing every shot until near the close of the action. In the delay incident to a change of command from Lieut. Worden to Lieut. Greene, the former having been wounded, the vessels drifted apart. Lieut. Greene forthwith turned the Monitor again toward the Merrimac, but that vessel was already in retreat toward Norfolk. After firing a few shots after her, Lieut. Greene returned to the vessels which had been saved by the arrival of his own craft. He was afterward engaged in the attack on Fort Darling and in other naval actions on the James River. After the loss of the Monitor, which foundered off Cape Hatteras, Dec. 29, 1862, he served as executive officer of the Florida on blockade duty, 1863, of the Iroquois in search of the Alabama, 1864–65, and on various other vessels from 1865 until 1869. He was promoted to be lieutenant-commander in 1866, and to commander in 1872, and commanded the Juniata in 1875, the Monongahela in 1876–77, and the Despatch in 1882–84. He was assistant professor of mathematics 1866–68, at the United States Naval Academy, of astronomy 1871–75, and was assistant to the superintendent of the institution 1878–82. He received a vote of thanks from the legislature of Rhode Island for his services in the action between the Monitor and the Merrimac. He died at Portsmouth, N.H., U.S. navy-yard, Dec. 11, 1884.

GREGG, DAVID McMURTRIE, soldier, was born in Huntingdon, Pa., April 10, 1833, being descended from David Gregg, of Scotland, a captain in Cromwell's army. His great-grandfather came from Londonderry, Ireland, to Pennsylvania in 1712, and died at Carlisle in 1789. His grandfather, Andrew Gregg, was a member of congress and U.S. senator from 1791 to 1813. At the age of eighteen, David, after a good preliminary education, obtained at the Milwood academy and the University of Lewisburg, entered the U.S. military academy, where he was graduated in 1855. He was brevetted second lieutenant of dragoons and sent to the far West, where he spent about five years, and participated in a number of engagements with the Indians along the Pacific coast from California to Washington, and March 21, 1861, was promoted to first lieutenant. At the outbreak of the civil war he came East, and served in the defense of Washington. *He was captain in the 3d U.S. Cavalry May 14–Aug. 3, 1861, and then a captain in the 6th U.S. Cavalry until named colonel of the 8th Pennsylvania Cavalry, Jan. 24, 1862.* He participated with the regiment in all the engagements of the peninsular campaign from March to August, 1862. In the Maryland campaign, with the army of the Potomac, from September 1862, to March 1863, he engaged

in several important skirmishes on the march to Falmouth. On Nov. 29, 1862, he was made brigadier-general of U.S. volunteers in the army of the Potomac. In the Pennsylvania campaign he was engaged at Brandy Station, June 9, 1863; took a leading part in the cavalry charges at Gettysburg, in the operations in central Virginia, and the actions at Rapidan Station, Auburn, and New Hope Church. In the Richmond campaign he was in charge of the 2d cavalry division of the army of the Potomac from Aug. 1, 1864 to Feb. 5, 1865. He was made brevet major-general of U.S. volunteers Aug. 1, 1864, for "highly meritorious and distinguished conduct throughout the campaign, particularly in the reconnoissance on the Charles City road." While in command of the cavalry he took part in many actions, skirmishes, and battles. He resigned from the army Feb. 3, 1865, and engaged in farming. He served as consul at Prague, Austria, under President Grant, and then returned to Reading. Gen. Gregg was of a retiring and modest disposition. Among old soldiers he was a favorite, and frequently attended reunions, camp-fires, and other social gatherings. As an extemporaneous public speaker he stood among the foremost. In personal appearance he was dignified and stately, six feet in height and of slender build. Upon the death of Hancock, Gen. Gregg succeeded to the command of Pennsylvania commandery, military order of the Loyal legion. He was also a member of the G.A.R. Post 76, of Reading. He was a pall-bearer at the funerals of Gens. Hancock and Hartranft, and accompanied the Count of Paris over the battle-field of Gettysburg on the occasion of his last visit to this country. In 1891 he was the nominee of the republican party for the office of auditor-general of Pennsylvania, and was elected by a handsome majority. *He died Aug. 7, 1916.*

GREGG, JOHN IRVIN, soldier, was born at Bellefonte, Pa., July 19, 1826. He volunteered for the Mexican war as a private in December, 1846; became first lieutenant of the 11th regular infantry in February, 1847, and on Sept. 3d of the same year was appointed captain. He was discharged after serving through the war, in 1848, and then engaged in the iron business in Centre county, Pa. At the outbreak of the civil war he became captain of reserves, and in 1861 was made captain of the 6th cavalry. He was made colonel of the 16th Pennsylvania cavalry in October, 1862, and commanded a cavalry brigade in the army of the Potomac from April, 1863, until April, 1865. His command was engaged in numerous battles, including Deep bottom, where he was severely wounded. He was brevetted major-general of volunteers, and brigadier-general for gallant and meritorious services at the close of the war. During the reconstruction of the South he was inspector-general of freedmen in Louisiana, and under the establishment of July 28, 1868, became colonel of the 8th cavalry. With his regiment he was stationed on the Pacific coast until he was retired for disability incurred in line duty, April 2, 1878. Gen. Gregg died of heart disease in Washington, D.C., Jan. 6, 1892, and was buried in Arlington Cemetery.

GREGG, MAXCY, soldier, was born in Columbia, S.C., in 1814, son of James and Cornelia (Maxcy) Gregg. His father (1787–1852), was a graduate of the University of South Carolina, where he subsequently taught. He was admitted to the bar in April, 1813, and became a prominent attorney of Columbia. In 1830 he was elected to the state senate, and became colonel of the 23d militia regiment. His son, Maxcy, was also educated at the College of South Carolina, where he was graduated in 1836. He then studied law, and was admitted to the bar in 1839. He was appointed major of the 12th infantry March 24, 1847, and was sent to Mexico; but arrived there too late to share in any of the important battles of the war. He was a delegate from Richland district to the state convention of South Carolina of 1852; was a member also of the state convention of 1860–61, which, on Dec. 20, 1860, passed the ordinance of secession, and was a member of the special committee that framed the ordinance. He was appointed colonel of a regiment, and was stationed on Morris island during the bombardment and capture of Fort Sumter, April

12th and 13th. He left Charleston on April 22d for Virginia, and his was the first volunteer regiment to enter that state. Previous to the battle of Manassas Gregg's regiment was stationed at Centreville and near Fairfax Court House, and in the affair at Vienna Station he

commanded the Confederate infantry. His regiment was also engaged in the battle of Manassas, forming a part of Bonham's brigade. In August his regiment was reorganized, and four months later Col. Gregg was made a brigadier-general, and sent to South Carolina to take charge of the regiments there that had been assigned to his brigade. He soon returned to Virginia, and his brigade, consisting of Gregg's 1st, the 12th, 13th and 14th South Carolina regiments and Orr's 1st regiment of South Carolina Rifles, was assigned to A. P. Hill's light division, Jackson's corps. The brigade was present at Seven Pines, but was not engaged; was engaged at Mechanicsville, *Gaines Mill (sometimes called first Cold Harbor),* Frazer's farm, Malvern hill, Cedar mountain, Warrenton springs and second Manassas, where Gen. Gregg immortalized himself and his brigade by what some considered the bravest stands recorded in modern history. From early morning until late in the afternoon of Aug. 29, 1862, his brigade withstood six determined assaults of the Federal forces, who sought to overwhelm Jackson's corps before Longstreet could arrive and take his position. Gen. Hill sent a messenger to ask Gen. Gregg if he could hold his position. "Tell Gen. Hill that my ammunition is exhausted, but that I will hold my position with the bayonet." Then taking his position before his troops, he marched up and down exclaiming: "Let us die here! let us die here." At this juncture the brigades of Pender and Fields of their division appeared on their right and left, and saved the day. The brigade was again engaged at Ox Hill, Harper's Ferry, Sharpsburg, where Gen. Gregg was slightly wounded; Shepardstown, Snicker's gap, and Fredericksburg, where he was mortally wounded. *He died Dec. 15, 1862, two days after the battle.*

B. H. Grierson

GRIERSON, BENJAMIN HENRY, soldier, was born at Pittsburg, Pa., July 8, 1826. When quite young he settled in Trumbull, Ohio, and afterward removed to Jacksonville, Ill., where he engaged in the produce business. At the outbreak of the civil war, he was appointed aide-de-camp to Gen. Prentiss, and in *October, 1861* was promoted major of the 6th Illinois cavalry. *In April 1862, he was commissioned colonel,* and in December of that year placed in command of a cavalry brigade. He took part in most of the cavalry skirmishes and raids in Northern Mississippi and Western Tennessee. In April, 1863, Gen. Grierson made a particularly fortunate cavalry raid from La Grange to Baton Rouge, which furthered Gen. Grant's movements in the vicinity of Vicksburg. *He was brigadier-general* of volunteers June 3, 1863; major-general, May 27, 1865, and colonel of the 10th U.S. cavalry July 28, 1866. In recognition of his raid into Arkansas he was promoted *to brevet* brigadier and major-general of the U.S. army on March 2, 1867. During 1868–73 he commanded the district of the

Indian territory, and took a prominent part in engagements against the Comanches, Kiowas, Cheyennes, and various other Indian tribes; he was also engaged in scouting and exploring expeditions and in ejecting intruders from the Indian territory. Gen. Grierson was employed in exploring Western Texas and New Mexico, and took part in different actions against hostile Indians during 1875–81. On Nov. 3, 1886, he was appointed commander of the district of New Mexico with headquarters at Sante Fé, and in 1890 he was appointed brigadier-general to succeed Gen. Nelson A. Miles. *He died Sept. 1, 1911.*

GRIFFIN, CHARLES, soldier, was born in Licking county, O., *Dec. 18, 1825.* He was graduated from West Point in 1847, assigned to the 2d artillery, and ordered to Mexico. He was in command of a company under Gen. Patterson during the campaign from Vera Cruz to Pueblo. He became first lieutenant in 1849, and served in New Mexico against the Navajo Indians until 1854. After seeing further frontier service, he was appointed instructor of artillery

at West Point, and acted in this capacity from 1859–61. He commanded the "West Point battery" at Bull Run, and was made brigadier-general of volunteers, June 9, 1862, and was present in the peninsula campaign, distinguishing himself at the battle of Gaines's Mills. In command of the artillery at Malvern Hill he supported his brigade, repulsing Gen. Magruder and driving back the enemy, which was a signal factor in the success of the day. At the second battle of Bull Run Gen. Pope charged Gen. Griffin with declining to take part in the action, while he "spent the day in making ill-natured strictures upon the commanding general." He was arrested on this charge, but soon released. After being promoted to the command of a division, he was present at Antietam and Fredericksburg and in Hooker's campaign. He was brevetted major-general of volunteers Aug. 1, 1864, and received the brevet of colonel in the regular army Aug. 18th. *He had been ill and did not participate in the battle of Gettysburg, though he arrived on the field July 3.* He received the arms and colors of the army of Northern Virginia, as commander of the 5th corps, by order of Gen. Grant, and was brevetted brigadier and major-general in the regular army May 13, 1865. He was appointed to command the district of Maine Aug. 10, 1865, his headquarters being at Portland, *and had been promoted to the full rank of major-general of volunteers to rank from April 2, 1865.* He was made colonel of the 35th infantry July 28, 1866. He commanded the department of Texas in 1867, with headquarters at Galveston. During the yellow fever epidemic at Galveston he temporarily commanded the fifth military district after the removal of General Sheridan, and was directed to make his headquarters at New Orleans. His reply was, that "to desert Galveston at such a time was like deserting one's post in the time of battle."

He remained at his post, and fell a victim to the scourge and died Sept. 15, 1867.

GRIFFIN, SIMON GOODELL, soldier and legislator, was born at Nelson, Cheshire co., N.H., August 9, 1824, son of Nathan and Sally (Wright) Griffin. Both his grandfathers, Samuel Griffin and Nehemiah Wright, were revolutionary soldiers and both were in Reed's regiment and fought from behind the rail fence at Bunker hill. His first American ancestor was Humphrey Griffin, who died at Rowley, Mass., 1661. Simon Griffin attended only the district schools of Nelson, but began a successful career as a teacher at the age of eighteen. While teaching he studied law; next represented his native town for two years in the legislature, and was admitted to the bar at Concord, in 1860. The civil war breaking out, he volunteered as a private; was chosen to the command of the company, and was mustered into the U.S. service as captain of company B, 2d New Hampshire volunteers. He commanded his company at the first battle of Bull run, and was promoted to lieutenant-colonel, and soon afterward to colonel of the 6th New Hampshire volunteers. He commanded his regiment at the battles of Camden, N.C.—in Burnside's expedition—second Bull run, Chantilly, South mountain, Antietam, and Fredericksburg, handling it with skill and sound judgment. In 1863 he commanded a brigade under Burnside, in Kentucky, and under Grant and Sherman at Vicksburg and Jackson, Miss.; the 2d division of the 9th corps in its march to East Tennessee; and the following winter was in command of Camp Nelson, Ky., with about 9,000 men, to protect that important depot of supplies from threatened raids. In the spring of 1864 the 9th corps reorganized at Annapolis, Md., and Col. Griffin was assigned to the command of the 2d brigade, 2d division. The corps joined the army of the Potomac, and was engaged in the battle of the Wilderness, May 6th. At Spottsylvania,

for his prompt and vigorous support of Hancock, in his famous charge, and holding the enemy in check in his countercharge, he was promoted to brigadier-general of volunteers, made on the field of battle, upon the recommendations of Gens. Grant and Burnside. He commanded his brigade at the battles of North Anna river, Tolopotomy creek, Bethesda church, and Cold harbor. Arriving in front of Petersburg at daybreak on the 17th of June, with his own and Curtin's brigade, he forced the enemy's lines at the Shands house, capturing about 1,000 prisoners, four pieces of artillery, 1,500 stands of arms and one stand of colors. He led his brigade gallantly at the time of the mine explosion at Petersburg, and at Weldon railroad, Poplar Spring church and Hatcher's run. On the 2d of April, 1865, he led the assaulting column of the 2d division, 9th corps, in connection with Gen. Hartranft, of Pennslyvania, with his division, that broke through the enemy's main line, at the Jerusalem plank road and won Petersburg and Richmond. For gallantry in that act he was brevetted a major-general of volunteers. Gen. Potter having been severely wounded, Gen. Griffin succeeded to the command of the 2d division, 9th army corps, which he led at the surrender of Lee, at the grand review in Washington, and until it was mustered out of service. At the close of the war he resided at Keene, N.H., and represented that town in the legislature in 1866, 1867, 1868, serving the last two years as speaker of the house. Dartmouth College conferred upon him the honorary degree of M.A. In 1871, and again in 1873, he was nominated for congress by the Republicans, but the opposition party carried the state. In 1887 and 1888 he was commander of the Massachusetts Commandery of the Military Order of the Loyal Legion of the United States. In 1850 he was married to Ursula J., daughter

of Jason Harris, of Nelson, who died in 1852. In January, 1863, he was married to Margaret R. Lamson, of Keene, N.H., by whom he had two sons. *He died Jan. 14, 1902.*

GRIFFING, JOSEPHINE SOPHIE WHITE, philanthropist, was born in December, 1816, at Hebron, Conn. She was descended, on her father's side, from Peregrine White, who was the first child born of Pilgrim parents in New England, and on her mother's, she was the lineal descendant of Peter Waldo, the founder of the sect called the Waldenses. *She was married in 1835 and moved to Litchfield, Ohio, in 1842.* Soon after her marriage, in 1838, she moved to Ohio, where she made her house a refuge for fugitive slaves. In 1849 she began speaking in public at the anti-slavery conventions which for years were interrupted by all sorts of riotous proceedings. She possessed great ability and persuasiveness as a public speaker, and did much to enlighten and change public sentiment. Her history is not only interwoven with that of abolition but with that of woman suffrage; and later she became an active member of the Woman's Loyal League and the Sanitary Commission, *an outgrowth of the Women's Central Relief Association, which was founded in 1863.* In connection with the last she lectured through West, and organized societies for the relief of the soldiers and freedmen. While engaged in this work her mind was roused to the condition of the thousands of slaves who, in 1863, were pouring into Washington, and to the need of an organized system of protection, help, and education. She went to Washington and submitted her plans for their relief and employment to Pres. Lincoln and Sec. Stanton, who approved them and gave her their assistance. Through her efforts, in December, 1863, a bill for a bureau of emancipation was presented to the house of representatives, but it was not passed until March, 1865. While this was pending, by her energetic solicitations for money and supplies and the use of her own property, she greatly relieved the suffering of thousands hidden away in alleys and stables, attics and cellars, many of them old and infirm and unable to work. She opened at once industrial schools for the women, who were clothed with the garments when finished, and three ration houses where 1,000 could be fed daily. She caused old barracks to be made into comfortable shelter for them and distributed army blankets and wood, given her by the personal order of Sec. Stanton. Large supplies of food and clothing she also obtained from the northern aid societies. The bill having been passed, and the freedmen's bureau established, her plans were adopted, and the freedmen and women sent, at government expense, to homes at the North, and employment offices opened in New York City and Providence, R.I. Private generosity assisted in this work, and congress appropriated $166,000 for the purchase of supplies of which more than half were distributed by Mrs. Griffing at her own house. In about two years she personally arranged and superintended the departure of over 7,000 freedmen and women from Washington. It would be impossible to state the whole number she assisted, but at one time there were in Washington 30,000 of these homeless people. To Horace Greeley, who alone of the prominent men of the day refused her recognition and encouragement, she gave a summary of her work as follows: "A freedmen's bureau; sanitary commission; church sewing societies; orphan asylums; old people's home; hospital and almshouse for the sick and blind; minister-at-large to visit the sick, console the dying and bury the dead." She was president of the Universal Franchise Association, and secretary of the National Woman Suffrage Association. After the bureau was abolished she continued to work for the freedmen, at request of such men as Sumner, Stanton, Wade, Wilson and others, and only relinquished it when failing strength compelled her. She died in Washington, Feb. 18, 1872. Of her Mr. Garrison said that she belonged to the honorable women "whose self-abgenation and self-sacrifice in the cause of suffering humanity having been absolute, and who have nobly vindicated every claim made by their sex to full equality with men in all that serves to dignify human nature."

GRIMES, BYRAN, soldier, was born in Pitt county, N.C., Nov. 2, 1828, the son of Byran Grimes, a farmer, and grandson of William Grimes, a patriot of the revolution. Byran was brought up on the farm, and entered the University of North Carolina, from which he was graduated in 1848. He then engaged in farming, and was distinguished for his success and enterprise. He was a member of the convention of Raleigh which passed the ordinance of secession in 1861. He immediately entered the Confederate service, and was appointed by Gov. Ellis major of the 4th regiment of the North Carolina state troops. He served gallantly throughout the whole war. He was with Lee at Sharpsburg and Gettysburg, and was severely wounded at South Mountain. He was promoted through the several grades of service, and attained the position of senior major-general of Stonewall Jackson's corps. His division made the last charge at Appomattox immediately before the final surrender to Gen. Grant. After the war he returned to his farm in Pitt county, and was the constant advocate of all improvements that were issued in by the new order of things consequent upon the change in the labor system of the state. Gen. Grimes was twice married—first, to Bettie Davis, and, upon her decease, to Charlotte Bryan, daughter of the late John H. Bryan. On Aug. 14, 1880, while returning from Washington, N.C., to his home, in a buggy, he was fired upon by some miscreant in ambush, and killed. The alleged cause of the assassination was the impending testimony of Gen. Grimes in a forthcoming trial, which would incriminate certain persons who, it is supposed, took this means to close his lips forever.

GRIMES, JAMES WILSON, third governor of Iowa (1854–58), was born at Deering, Hillsboro co., N.H., Oct. 20, 1816, son of John and Elizabeth (Wilson) Grimes. His ancestors were Scotch-Irish emigrants from the north of Ireland, who settled at Londonderry, N.H., in 1719. His father was a thrifty farmer of sterling integrity and worth. The son received his classical education at Hampton Academy and Dartmouth College. He studied law under James Walker, at Peterboro, N.H., and in May, 1836, began practice at Burlington, Ia., which was then a part of the Black Hawk purchase in Wisconsin territory. He was highly successful as a lawyer, and from 1841 to 1853 practiced in partnership with Henry W. Starr. His first public service was as secretary of the Indian commission at Rock island, Sept. 27, 1836, where the Sacs and Foxes relinquished to the United States their lands along the Missouri river. During 1837–38 he was assistant-librarian in the Wisconsin library, and after the formation of Iowa territory represented Des Moines county in its legislature in 1838 and 1843, serving in the general assembly of the state in 1852. In August, 1854, he was elected by both Whig and Free-Soil Democratic parties as governor of Iowa. Though reared among Whig principles, his whole career was marked by freedom from party bias. During his

administration he opposed the Missouri compromise and did much to foster Free-Soil sentiment throughout Iowa. In 1856 the capital of the state was changed from Iowa City to Des Moines. He served as a commissioner for founding the Insane Hospital at Mt. Pleasant, giving careful attention to the trust; and in July, 1856, he convened a special session of the general assembly to act on land grants received from congress for the construction of railroads. In August of the same year he addressed a remonstrance to Pres. Pierce against the treatment of Iowa settlers in Kansas. He relinquished his office as governor in January, 1858, and in the same year was elected to the U.S. senate for a term of six years. He served by re-election from March 4, 1859, until Dec. 6, 1869, when he resigned on account of ill-health. He was one of the founders of the Republican party, which he represented in the senate. Though seldom making a set speech, he was always a ready and vigorous debater. He was a prominent worker on the pensions, naval affairs, District of Columbia and other committees; and on July 4, 1861, he obtained an order from the secretary of war setting free the escaped slaves confined in the Washington jail, thus inaugurating the first official act of emancipation. He urged the building of iron-clads, and on March 13, 1862, spoke on the achievements of the western naval flotilla, becoming a recognized authority in all matters pertaining to the navy. Among the works due largely to his advocacy were the return of the Naval Academy from Newport to Annapolis, the establishment of a national armory at Rock island and of a navy yard at League island. Politically he was remarkable for independence of character, and, though a Republican, opposed a high protective tariff and Pres. Lincoln's enlargement of the regular army. During the impeachment trial of Pres. Johnson, he considered himself in the light of a judge rather than a representative; and though his physical condition required severe fortitude to do so, he entered the senate and cast his vote for acquittal. Later he said: "Neither the honors nor the wealth of the world could have induced me to act otherwise than I did; and I have never for a moment regretted that I voted as I did. I shall always thank God that He gave me courage to stand firm in the midst of the clamor, and by my vote not only to save the Republican party, but prevent such a precedent being established as would in the end have converted ours into a sort of South American republic, in which there would be a revolution whenever there happened to be an adverse majority in congress to the president for the time being." Though then greatly censured by his party, the New York "Times" said years afterward: "No braver or more faithful man ever sat in the senate than Mr. Grimes, who, almost alone, saved his party from an incalculable blunder . . ." He founded a free library in Burlington, a professorship in

Iowa College (Grinnell), and scholarships both at that college and Dartmouth. The degree of LL.D. was conferred upon him by both Dartmouth and Iowa colleges in 1865. He was married at Burlington, Ia., Nov. 9, 1846, to Elizabeth Sarah Nealley. After a two years' residence in Europe, with temporary intervals of improved health, he died suddenly at Burlington, Ia., Feb. 7, 1872.

GRIMKÉ, ANGELINA EMILY, reformer, and wife of Theodore Dwight Weld, to whom she was married May 14, 1838, was born in Charleston, S.C., February 20, 1805, the daughter of Judge John Faucheraud Grimké of South Carolina. They were wealthy slaveholders and Episcopalians, but Angelina and her sister Sarah became Quakers in 1826, and on the death of their parents they emancipated the slaves they had inherited. Her "Appeal to the Women of the South" was published in England in 1836, with a preface by George Thompson. After reading it, Mr. Wright, the secretary of the American Anti-

Slavery Society, invited her and her sister to come to New York to lecture in private houses. This they did, and afterward visited New England, receiving much attention, making favorable impressions wherever they lectured, and causing considerable excitement. Angelina is said to have been very handsome, and to have had a magnetic charm of manner. Of her address at Hanover, Rev. Samuel J. May said that he had "never heard from any other lips, male or female, such eloquence as that of her closing appeal." After her marriage to Mr. Weld she aided him in educational and reformatory work. She also wrote "Letters to Catherine E. Beecher," on the slavery question, which was published in Boston in 1837. *She died Oct. 26, 1879.*

GRIMKÉ, THOMAS SMITH, reformer, was born in Charleston, S.C., Sept. 26, 1786, the son of John Faucheraud Grimké, and was graduated from Yale College in 1807. He desired to enter the ministry, but yielded to his father's wishes that he should become a lawyer. He became a member of the bar association of South Carolina, and in 1827 advocated the codification of the laws of that state. He was state senator from 1828 to 1830, and in 1828 made a speech in which he supported the general government on the tariff question; in 1834 he argued the South-Carolina test-oath question. He was one of the first to take up the temperance cause, was a distinguished member of the American peace society, and lectured and wrote in their behalf, besides contributing large sums to help on their work. He thought that even defensive warfare was wrong, and said that if he were in control of Charleston when attacked by the enemy, he would lead the Sunday-school children to welcome the invaders. He opposed the classics and mathematics in education, advocating more

extensive religious training. He was one of the early advocates of reform in spelling, making the changes advocated by Noah Webster and many others introduced by the spelling-reform association. In 1834 before the Western literary institute at Cincinnati, he delivered an address on "American Education." His published work is "Addresses on Science, Education, and Literature" (New Haven, 1831). As a man Mr Grimké was much beloved, even by those whose ideas were totally opposed to his. He died near Columbus, O., Oct. 11, 1834.

GROVER, CUVIER, soldier, was born in Bethel, Me., July 24, 1829. He went to West Point, where he was graduated in 1850; was assigned to the 1st artillery, and served on the frontier till 1853; and from Apr. 14, 1853 till July 17, 1854, on the Northern Pacific railroad exploration, after which he served at various western stations. He was promoted first

lieutenant March 3, 1855; captain Sept. 17, 1858; brigadier-general of volunteers Apr. 14, 1862, and transferred to the army of the Potomac; brevetted lieutenant-colonel May 5th following, for services at the battle of Williamsburg, Va., and colonel May 31st for gallantry at Fair Oaks. At the second battle of Bull Run his brigade advanced boldly in face of a destructive artillery and infantry fire, and distinguished itself by a bayonet charge that drove away the Confederate forces holding the railroad embankment. He forced a passage between two Confederate brigades; but, reserves coming to their aid, he was obliged to fall back to his first position, after a bitter and prolonged hand-to-hand fight, in which the losses were very severe on both sides. Gen. Grover was then transferred to the department of the Gulf, where he took command of a division of the 19th corps, and was in command of the right wing of the forces besieging Port Hudson, La., in May, 1863. He was promoted major Aug. 31, 1863, and, returning to the east, commanded a division in the Shenandoah campaign from August to December, 1864. On the 19th of October, 1864, he was wounded at the battle of Cedar Creek, and was the same day brevetted major-general of volunteers for gallantry at Winchester and Fisher's Hill. He was brevetted brigadier-general, U.S. army, March 13, 1865, and on the same date major-general, U.S. army. At the close of the war he was mustered out of the volunteer service and returned to frontier duty; was promoted lieutenant-colonel 38th infantry July 28, 1866; transferred to Jefferson barracks, Mo., Nov. 7th; assigned to the 3d cavalry in 1870, and promoted colonel of the 1st cavalry, holding that rank until his death in Atlantic City, N.J., June 6, 1885.

H

HALLECK, HENRY WAGER, soldier, was born at Westernville, Oneida county, N.Y., Jan. 16, 1815. After a common-school education received at Hudson academy, and a partial course at Union college, he entered the United States military academy July 1, 1835, graduating four years later third in a class of thirty-one. July 1, 1839, he was appointed second lieutenant in the engineer corps of the army, and from his marked ability and skill as an instructor, while still a cadet, was retained as assistant professor of engineering at the academy until June 28, 1840. During the next year he acted as assistant to the board of engineers at Washington, D.C., and was thence transferred to assist in the construction of the fortifications in New York harbor. Here he remained several years, with the exception of

time spent in 1845 on a tour of inspection of public works in Europe, receiving while absent a promotion to first lieutenant. At the outbreak of the war with Mexico, he was sent to California as engineer of military operations for the Pacific coast, and after a seven-months' voyage in the transport Lexington, reached Monterey, Cal., which he partially fortified as a port of refuge for the Pacific fleet, and a base for incursions into California by land. In his military capacity he accompanied several expeditions; in that of Col. Burton into Lower California, he acted as chief of staff to that officer, and took part in the skirmishes of Palos Prietos and Urias, Nov. 19–20, 1847; with a few volunteers made a forced march to San Antonio, March 16, 1848, surprising a large Mexican garrison and nearly capturing the governor, and was engaged at Todos Santos, March 30th. He was also aide-de-camp to Com. Shubrick in naval operations on the coast, among which was the capture of Mazatlan (of which for a time he was lieutenant-governor), and for "gallant and meritorious services," received the commission of captain by brevet, to date from May 1, 1847. As secretary under the military governments of Gens. Mason and Riley, he displayed "great energy, high administrative qualities, excellent judgment and admirable adaptability to his varied and onerous duties," and as a member of the convention, called to meet at Monterey, Sept. 1, 1849, to frame a constitution for the state of California, he was substantially the author of that instrument. He might easily have been elected one of the new U.S. senators also, but, preferring his military profession, remained as aide-de-camp on the staff of Gen. Riley. Dec. 21, 1852, he was appointed inspector and engineer of lighthouses; from Apr. 11, 1853, was a member of the board of engineers for fortifications of the Pacific coast, receiving the promotion of captain of engineers July 1, 1853, and retained all these positions until Aug. 1, 1854, when he resigned from the army to become the head of the most prominent law firm in San Francisco, with large interests and much valuable property in the state, with whose

Dec. 21, 1861, he issued an order fixing the penalty of death on all persons who should attempt the destruction of railroads and telegraphs, and requiring that the same should be repaired by, and at the expense of, the towns and counties where such destruction was done.

development and prosperity his name was identified. From 1850 to 1861 he was director-general of the New Almaden quicksilver mine, and in 1855 was made president of the Pacific and Atlantic railroad, from San Francisco to San José, Cal. In 1860–61 he was major-general of the militia of California, and at the outbreak of the civil war tendered his services to the government, and was appointed major-general of regulars at the urgent recommendation of Gen. Scott, his commission dating Aug. 19, 1861. Nov. 18th he took command of the department of Missouri (embracing that state, Iowa, Minnesota, Wisconsin, Illinois, Arkansas, and the western portion of Kentucky), with headquarters at St. Louis, where his vigorous rule soon established order; the elaborate fortifications, undertaken at immense expense, and without regard to the laws of engineering, were suspended; the army reorganized and in preparation for the plan of campaign intended by him, thrown back to Rolla, while treason, sharply defined, was summarily dealt with.

Four days later a qualified martial law was declared in his department, to be enforced in and about all the railroads in the state, though it was expressly stated that no interference was intended with the jurisdiction of any court loyal to the government of the United States, and which would aid the military authorities in enforcing the order and punishing criminals. The oath of allegiance was required even of the faculty of the State university, and sympathizers with secession brought to subjection, or sent beyond the lines. In less than six weeks the lower portion of the state was cleared of Confederates, and their general (Price) driven back into Arkansas. For the campaign of 1862 (a simultaneous advance of all the Union forces having been ordered by President Lincoln for Feb. 22d), he planned, in December, 1861, three successive lines of attack upon the Confederates from the line of the Mississippi: the first, to drive them from the protection of the neutrality of Kentucky; the second, advance upon Chattanooga, from Memphis as a base;

and the third, from Vicksburg, through Montgomery, to Atlanta, co-operating always with the fleet on the Mississippi river. The efforts of Grant, to whom he had assigned the district of Cairo, including also Paducah, Tenn., were accordingly directed against the center of the enemy at Forts Henry and Donelson, as weaker than either of the flanks protected by the fortifications at Columbus and Bowling Green, and in a little over three months after his accession to the command in the West, both places had been turned and abandoned, and Nashville was in the possession of the Federal troops, while Curtis, dispatched against the Confederates in Missouri, fought and won the battle of Pea Ridge, driving the enemy to White rive~ a. 'and No. 10 was taken by Pope, with the combined action of the fleet. The first line of the Confederates being thus annihilated, the second was next to be undertaken, and in pursuance of the tactics recently successful, Grant was ordered to ascend the Tennessee, then in full water, and make a lodgment about

Florence, or Tuscumbia, Ala., or even Corinth, Miss. (the latter the left center of the enemy), but that general, failing to receive word or communication of any kind, ascended the Cumberland instead, and was relieved by Gen. A. J. Smith. The arrival of Buell secured the victory at Shiloh, after which Halleck himself took the field, having, March 11, 1862, succeeded to the command of the department of the Mississippi, into which those of Kansas and Ohio had been merged, and which now stretched from the Alleghany to the Rocky Mountains. That the march upon Corinth consumed six weeks has been invidiously commented upon, but it is to be remembered that it was accomplished with troops demoralized at Pittsburg Landing, whose reinforcement and rehabilitation from a considerable distance consumed two weeks, and that the route lay, moreover, through extreme difficulties of country, a hostile people, and amid the discouragement of drenching rains. So carefully was guard maintained,

however, that no attack was ventured by the enemy, notwithstanding the proclamation of Beauregard to "the soldiers of Shiloh and Elkhorn," May 2d; and one month after the march had been begun (May 27th) the siege of Corinth was initiated, with its fifteen miles of heavy entrenchments and impregnable natural defences, notwithstanding vigorous efforts to prevent the advance of the Federal troops. On the morning of the 30th, the town was evacuated, Pope dispatched in pursuit of the enemy, Buell in the direction of Chattanooga, and Sherman to Memphis (taken before his arrival by the fleet). In the midst of the fortification of Corinth against a return of the enemy from the South, and the repairing of the railroad communication with Columbus, Halleck was visited by two assistant secretaries of war and one U.S. senator, to urge his acceptance of the office of general-in-chief, which had been tendered him, but which he declined, continuing his preparations against the third and last remaining line of the enemy, until events in the Peninsular campaign forced his acceptance of the honor on July 23d. From Washington, where, from this time his annual reports as commander-in-chief notified the country that the army had a military head, he ordered the recall of the Federal forces from Harrison's Landing, not obeyed for eleven days, and Oct. 28th he wrote the letter which constitutes "the only official explanation of the final removal of McClellan from command, Nov. 7th." After Gen. Grant became lieutenant-general of the army, he remained at Washington as chief-of-staff from March 12, 1864, to Apr. 19, 1865, and from Apr. 22d to July 1st of the same year he was in command of the military division of the James, with headquarters at Richmond, from which place he issued the orders, under the direction of his superiors in office, "to pay no regard to any truce or orders

of Gen. Sherman respecting hostilities," and "to push onward, regardless of orders from any one except Gen. Grant, and cut off Johnston's retreat," which gave offence to Gen. Sherman, and for a time caused a coolness between the two friends. Aug. 30, 1865, he took command of the division of the Pacific, from which he was relieved by Gen. George H. Thomas, and March 16, 1869, was transferred to that of the South, with headquarters at Louisville, Ky. As an author, Gen. Halleck enjoys a reputation distinct from that gained by him in arms. In 1840–41, he prepared a work on "Bitumen: Its Varieties, Properties, and Uses," embracing all the then known applications of asphalt to military structures. His "Report on Coast Defence," published by congress, led to the delivery by him of twelve lectures before Lowell institute, Boston, in 1845, on the "Science of War," published, with an introductory chapter on the justifiableness of war, in 1846, as the "Elements of Military Art and Science." A second enlarged edition, in 1861, contained notes on the Mexican and Crimean wars, and, during the war, was considered as standard authority on military matters. In 1859 appeared "A Collection of Mining Laws of Spain and Mexico;" in 1860 a translation of "De Fooz on the Law of Mines, with Introductory Remarks," and in 1861, his masterpiece, "International Law; or, Rules Regulating the Intercourse of States in Peace and War," which, with its abridgment of 1866, for schools and colleges, takes rank among the highest authorities. In 1864 the translation of "La Vie Politique et Militaire de Napoléon" (Baron Jomini), undertaken in 1846, on the voyage to California, was published in four octavo volumes, with an atlas. In 1848 he declined the professorship of engineering in the Lawrence scientific school of Harvard university, and in 1862 received the degree of

LL.D. from Union college, which in 1843 had made him an A.M. Gen. Halleck died at Louisville, Ky., Jan. 9, 1872.

HAMILTON, CHARLES SMITH, soldier, was born in Erie county, N.Y., Nov. 16, 1822, son of Zayne Alasman and Sylvia Jane (Putnam) Hamilton. The original representative of his line in America was William, son of the famous Scotch physician, Galliton Hamilton, and a descendant of James, Duke of Hamilton, at one time heir to the throne of Scotland. He was married to Lucy Berry of England, and settled at North Kingston, R.I., in 1668. From them the descent is traced through their son Samuel; his son Benjamin; and his son Hosea, father of Zayne A. Hamilton, a surgeon by profession. His wife was a niece of Gen. Israel Putnam, of revolutionary fame, and daughter of Joseph Putnam, also a soldier in the same conflict. Charles S. Hamilton entered the United States Military Academy, West Point, in 1839, and on graduation was appointed brevet second lieutenant in the 2d U.S. infantry. After two years of service at Buffalo, he was, in 1845, promoted to full rank in the 5th U.S. infantry and ordered first to Copper Harbor, Mich., then to the Rio Grande. Joining Gen. Taylor's army of occupation, he participated in the siege and storming of Monterey, being, with George H. Thomas, the first to scale the outworks. He was then ordered to join Scott's army, and with it fought all the way from Vera Cruz to Molino del Rey, where he was dangerously wounded and promoted first lieutenant. During the remainder of the war he held the command of the company, and was brevetted captain for gallant and meritorious conduct in battle, and appointed regimental quartermaster of his regiment. He served until 1853 at Pascagoula, Miss., Rochester, N.Y., and Fort Towson, I.T., and then, resigning his commission, engaged

in the linseed oil business. Upon the outbreak of the civil war, he enlisted as a volunteer, and was made colonel of the 3d Wisconsin regiment. In May, 1861, he was promoted brigadier general, and after serving under Gen. Banks through the Shenandoah campaign, he led the advance division down the Potomac to Fortress Monroe and thence to Yorktown. In May, 1862, he was transferred to the army of Western Virginia, and placed in command of a division in Rosecrans' army. During the succeeding summer he served in various engagements in northern Mississippi and Tennessee, and on Sept. 19, 1862, with his single division of less than 5,000 men met and defeated a Confederate force of 18,000 at Iuka. Gen. Rosecrans was not present on the field, and the credit of the victory was awarded to Gen. Hamilton. *An exaggeration. Hamilton's division did bear the brunt of the fighting at Iuka, but most of the fighting on the Confederate side was also done by a single division of similar strength. And Rosecrans was present in overall command of his two divisions.* Again on *Oct. 3d and 4th* he rendered memorable service to the Federal cause by his admirable handling of his division, which changed the battle of Corinth from disastrous defeat to a glorious victory. Several of Gen. Rosecrans' movements had failed and been badly executed, and Hamilton's movements were precisely timed for effectual help. *This account also exaggerates Hamilton's role at the expense of Rosecrans.* Gen. Grant always ascribed the success of the repulse at Corinth to Gen. Hamilton. He was then transferred to the command of the left wing of Grant's army—Sherman having the right and McPherson the centre—and, *on Sept. 19, 1862,* was promoted major-general of volunteers. He resigned from the service *in April, 1863,* and, returning to his home in Wisconsin, resumed active business. For twenty years from 1869, he was president of the Milwaukee Oil Works, and was prominent in civil and political life as well. He was president of the board of regents of Wisconsin State University (1869–76), and U.S. marshal through both of Grant's administrations. Gen. Hamilton was married, in 1848, to Sophia J., daughter of Charles Shepard of Dansville, N.Y. They have six sons, all living. He died in Milwaukee, Wis., *April 17, 1891.*

HAMLIN, HANNIBAL, vice-president, was born at Paris Hill, Oxford Co., Me., Aug. 27, 1809, the son of Cyrus and Anna Hamlin who was a daughter of Deacon Elijah Livermore, one of the original owners of the township that now bears his name. His paternal ancestors were of English origin and among the early settlers of Massachusetts. His grandfather, Elijah Hamlin, was a resident of Pembroke, Mass., and commanded a company of minutemen in which five of his sons were enrolled in the revolutionary war. Young Hamlin's boyhood was passed upon a farm and in attendance at the district schools in its vicinity. His parents were not in affluent circumstances, and the lad was early trained to habits of industry and economy. He was prepared for college at the Hebron Academy, but his father dying suddenly when Hannibal was about eighteen years old, the lad was obliged to relinquish his expectations of a collegiate education and assume the management of the farm. Two years later, in connection with Horatio King, he purchased the "Jeffersonian," a weekly political paper published at Paris. Desiring to acquaint himself with every detail of the business, he applied himself to learning the printing art, and soon became an expert compositor. At the end of six months he sold his interest in the paper to his

partner and resumed the study of law, which had been interrupted by his father's untimely death. In January, 1833, Mr. Hamlin was admitted to the bar at Paris, and the following May began the practice of his profession in Hampden, Me. He at once took a foremost place as a lawyer, and acquired an enviable reputation as a public speaker. In December, 1833, Mr. Hamlin was married to Sarah J., daughter of Judge Stephen Emery, one of the most prominent lawyers in Maine. By a singular coincident Judge Emery was the opposing counsel in the first law case that Mr. Hamlin won. He early connected himself with the democratic party, and in 1835 was elected to represent his town in the state legislature, and re-elected for five successive terms, being speaker of the house in 1837, '39, '40, and in the latter year was nominated for congress by his party. Mr. Hamlin introduced during this campaign the custom of joint debates between the candidates, which was the first time the practice had been adopted in Maine. After a vigorous campaign he was defeated, in common with most of the democratic candidates in the exciting year of the campaign of "Tippecanoe and Tyler too," the election having been postponed one year on account of a new apportionment required. After the census of 1840 Mr. Hamlin was again a candidate for congress and was elected, and re-elected in 1845. Early in his political life he identified himself with the anti-slavery movement, and when Texas was annexed to the United States, he emphatically announced to his constituents that further attempts to extend slavery would meet with his most strenuous opposition. The prominent part he took in connection with the famous Wilmot proviso, and his pronounced anti-slavery views, made him many enemies in his own party. The Wilmot proviso was an amendment to a bill, then pending, granting $2,000,000 for the purpose of negotiating a peace with Mexico. It declared that it be an "express and fundamental condition to the acquisition of any territory from Mexico, that neither slavery nor involuntary servitude shall exist therein." Mr. Wilmot being detained at the White House by President Polk on the day the amendment was presented (intentionally as was subsequently thought), after waiting vainly for him to appear, Mr. Hamlin gained the floor at the last moment, and presented the amendment and secured its passage by a vote of 115 to 106, and took an active part in the exciting contest that followed. *Although Hamlin strongly supported the Wilmot Proviso, David Wilmot of Pennsylvania personally introduced this measure in the House.* Though not then an avowed abolitionist, he was uncompromising in his anti-slavery views. Speaking of this amendment in his "Twenty Years in Congress," Mr. Blaine says: "It occupied the attention of congress for a longer time than the Missouri compromise; it produced a wider and deeper excitement in the country, and it threatened a more serious danger to the peace and integrity of the Union. The consecration of the United States to freedom became from that a rallying cry for every shade of anti-slavery sentiment." In 1848 Mr. Hamlin was elected to the U.S. senate to fill the unexpired term of Senator Fairfield. In 1851 he was re-elected for a full term, resigning in 1857 to become governor of Maine, having been elected to that position by the recently organized republican party. He resigned the executive chair on Feb. 20, 1857, and was re-elected to the U.S. senate by the legislature for a full term from March 4, 1857. In January, 1861, he again resigned his seat in the senate, having been elected vice-president of the United States on the ticket with Abraham Lincoln, and in this position from March 4, 1861, to March 3, 1865, presided over the U.S. senate. Mr. Hamlin was in the senate when Mr. Lincoln was in the house, but they never met until after the election in November, 1860. Mr Hamlin then called on Mr. Lincoln in Chicago, and each recalled having heard the other speak in congress. They were on the most cordial terms during the whole of Mr. Lincoln's first term, and Mr. Hamlin left behind him the record of having been one of the few vice-presidents who always maintained most friendly relations with the chief executive, and Mr. Lincoln did not refrain from expressing his disappointment that the convention of 1864 did not renominate Mr. Hamlin for vice-president. *There is no record that Lincoln expressed disappointment at this outcome.* Mr. Hamlin was collector of the port of Boston. 1865–66, and from 1861–65 acted as regent of the Smithsonian Institution, being reappointed in 1870, and for the subsequent twelve years continued regent, and also at one time became dean of the board. From 1869–81 Mr. Hamlin remained in the senate, and resigned in the latter year to accept an appointment as minister to Madrid. He remained in Spain but a short time, when he resigned and retired from public life. His career is a part of the history of the nation; he was in office continuously for nearly fifty years, and probably since the death of Abraham Lincoln no man was more generally mourned. Mr. Hamlin, in a speech made in 1888, gave the following version of the history of Lincoln's part in the emancipation proclamation: "The emancipation proclamation was the crowning glory of his life. That proclamation made 6,000,000 freemen. It was the act of Abraham Lincoln, not the act of his cabinet. He was slow to move, much slower than it seemed to us he should have been, much slower than I wanted him to be. But he was right. I urged him over and over again to act; but the time had not come in his judgment. One day I called at the White House, and when I was about to leave, he said to me: 'Hamlin, when do you start for home?' 'To-day.' 'No, sir.' 'Yes, sir.' 'No, sir.' 'Well, Mr. President, if you have any commands for me, of course I will stay.' 'I have a command for you; I want you to go to the Soldiers' Home with me to-night—I have something to show you.' We went to the Soldiers' Home that night, and after tea he said: 'Hamlin, you have often urged me to issue a proclamation of emancipation. I am about to do it. I have it here and you will be the first person to see it.' Then he asked me to make suggestions and corrections as he went along—a most delicate thing to do, for every man loves his own child best. I suggested the change of a single word, saying: 'Now, Mr. President, isn't that your idea?' and he said yes, and changed it at once. I made three suggestions, and he adopted two of them. Now, what I desire to show you is this—the proclamation of emancipation was the proclamation of Abraham Lincoln." Thus, not only during Mr. Lincoln's life did Mr. Hamlin show his esteem for him, but throughout his own life was ever jealous that the memory of his friend should be held in esteem, and that justice, which had been somewhat tardy, would award him his place in history. The span of his political life covered a period fraught with great events, and scarred with many records that have not stood the test of time, but the historian will not detect a blemish in recounting the career of Hannibal Hamlin. His death occurred at Bangor, Me., July 4, 1891.

HAMMOND, WILLIAM ALEXANDER, surgeon-general, U.S. army (1862–64), was born in Annapolis, Md., Aug. 28, 1828, son of John W. and Sarah (Pinkney) Hammond and a descendant of John Hammond who emigrated from the Isle of Wight to Annapolis, Md., with his wife Mary Howard in 1685. His mother was a niece of William Pinkney, the statesman. In 1835 his father, a physician, moved to Harrisburg, Pa., where the son received his early education. He was graduated M.D. at the University of the City of New York (later New York university) in 1848 and served his internship in the Pennsylvania hospital, Philadelphia, Pa., beginning the practice of medicine at Saco, Maine, in 1849. Later in the same year he entered the U.S. army as an assistant surgeon, with the rank of first lieutenant, subsequently being promoted to captain. A decade of active service followed at army posts in the Southwest and in Florida, Kansas and Michigan, with a tour of duty at the U.S. military academy and a trip abroad to study military medical services, including hospital methods and administration in Europe. During this period Hammond made researches in physiology and physiological chemistry and had published numerous monographs on these subjects, some of which were reprinted in England and translated into French and German. One of these, on "The Nutritive Value and Physiological Effects of Albumen, Starch and Gum when Singly and Exclusively Used as Foods" (1857), was awarded the American Medical Association prize. While in the field he also made large collections of fauna, which were presented to the Smithsonian Institution and the Philadelphia Academy of Natural Sciences. On Oct. 31, 1860, Hammond resigned from the army to accept the chair of anatomy and physiology at the University of Maryland,

but on the outbreak of the Civil war he returned to the army as assistant surgeon. After organizing hospitals at Hagerstown, Frederick and Baltimore, he was made medical inspector of camps and hospitals on the staff of Gen. Rosecrans, in West Virginia. His work in that position attracted so much attention that on Apr. 28, 1862, at the urgent request of the sanitary commission, President Lincoln

appointed him surgeon-general of the army with the rank of brigadier-general. Under his guidance the medical department was thoroughly reorganized and revolutionary improvements made in provisions for the care of sick and wounded soldiers. Not only were the requirements for admission to the medical corps made more stringent but 233 general hospitals and a large number of post and garrison hospitals were constructed, efficient methods of hospital administration were inaugurated, the most advanced hygiene, heating and ventilating facilities were installed, crowding was strictly prohibited, the food of the patients was prepared with the best possible care and, in the words of the sanitary commission, the sick and the wounded "received a skillful and humane treatment, unexampled in military history." As a result of these measures the mortality rate in the hospitals of the Federal army during the Civil war was lower than that of any other army in modern times. Hammond also carefully nurtured plans for the formation of an army ambulance service and for the compilation of the "Medical and Surgical History of the War of the Rebellion," proposed the establishment of an army medical school and laboratory and founded in 1862 the army medical museum in which specimens, collected from the army hospitals and illustrating the character of wounds inflicted by the weapons and missiles of war, were exhibited for the benefit of the medical fraternity. That was the first and at the time of Hammond's death was still the only military medical museum in the world though its scope was later extended to include specimens illustrating every known disease. As a result of strained relations between Hammond and secretary of war Edwin M. Stanton, the former was tried by a court-martial on trivial charges and was dismissed from the service, Aug. 18, 1864. Fifteen years later (1879) after a re-examination of this proceeding, under the authority of a special act of congress, he was completely exonerated and was restored to his rank in the army as brigadier-general and surgeon-general on the retired list. After leaving the military service in 1864 he began the practice of medicine in New York city, specializing in the treatment of mental and nervous diseases. He soon joined the faculty of the college of physicians and surgeons and delivered there in 1866–67 the first course of lectures ever given on diseases of the mind and the nervous system. In 1867 he accepted a chair on this specially created for him at the Bellevue hospital medical college and remained there until 1874 when he resigned to accept a similar professorship in the medical school of the University of the City of New York. In 1882 Hammond and some of his colleagues left that institution and founded the New York Post-Graduate medical school in which he became professor of diseases of the mind and nervous system. For a number of years he was connected in the same capacity with the University of Vermont. Returning to Washington, D.C., in 1888 he founded there in 1889 the Hammond sanitarium for mental patients, which he conducted until his death. Hammond made many original investigations and was the first to discover and describe a number of diseases, among them being the nervous condition later universally known as athetosis, which was so named by him. In his later years he was greatly interested in the therapeutic employment of animal extracts and did much to instruct the medical profession in their use. A facile writer, he also made many contributions to medical literature. He was the author of a "Treatise on Hygiene with Special Reference to the Military Service" and "Physiological Memoirs" (1863); "Lectures on Venereal Diseases" and "Military, Medical and Surgical Essays" (1864); "On Wakefulness: With an Introductory Chapter on the Physiology of Sleep" (1865); "Insanity in its Medico-Legal Relations" (1866); "On Sleep and Its Derangements" (1869); "The Physics and Physiology of Spiritualism" (1870); "Treatise on the Diseases of the Nervous System," which was announced as the "first textbook on nervous diseases in the English language" and was translated into French, Italian and Spanish (1871; 9th ed. 1890); "Insanity in its Relations to Crime" (1873); "Clinical Lectures on Diseases of the Nervous System" (1874); "Spiritualism and Allied Causes and Conditions of Nervous Derangement" (1876); "General Hyperennia, the Result of Mental Strain or Emotional Disturbances" (1878) and "A Treatise on Insanity in Its Medical Relations" and "On Sexual Impotence in the Male" (1883). Hammond also wrote a number of novels, including "Robert Severne" (1867); "Dr. Grattam" and "Lal" (1884); "Mr. Oldmixon" and "A Strong Minded Woman" (1885); "On the Susquehanna" (1887) and "The Son of Perdition," a strong novel which had for its subject the character and conduct of Judas Iscariot (1898). He also translated Meyer's "Electricity" (1869) and contributed to various professional and literary magazines and to the transactions of professional societies. His literary work also included the editing of a number of magazines. He was co-editor of the "Maryland and Virginia Medical Journal" in 1860–61 and in 1867 founded the "Quarterly Journal of Psychological Medicine and Medical Jurisprudence," of which he was the editor until 1872. He collaborated in founding and editing the "New York Medical Journal" (1867–69), "Physiological and Medico-Legal Journal of New York" (1874–76) and "Neurological Contributions" (1879–81).

Hammond was affiliated with many scientific societies at home and in Europe and was one of the dominant personalities of his generation in American medicine. Professionally one of the pioneer neurologists of the United States, he was a man of vision, courage, rare executive ability, wide intellectual interests and of enormous industry. He was married twice: (1) in July 1849 to Helen, daughter of Michael Nisbet, of Philadelphia, Pa., and they had five children: Clara, wife of the Marquis Manfredi Lanza di Mercato Bianco (of Italy), Graeme Munro, Summerville Pinkney, William Alexander and Helen Nisbet Hammond; she died in 1885; (2) in 1886, to Ester Dyer, daughter of John F. Chapin, of Providence, R. I. Hammond's death occurred in Washington, D.C., Jan. 5, 1900.

HAMPTON, WADE, soldier and forty-eighth governor of South Carolina (1876–78), was born in Charleston, S.C., Mar. 28, 1818, son of Col. Wade and Ann (Fitzsimons) Hampton,

and grandson of Gen. Wade Hampton, of revolutionary fame. His mother's ancestry can be traced back for five hundred years to one of the first primates of Ireland, while his father was of English descent. The son was graduated at South Carolina University in 1836, and

afterward studied law for a time, but without the intention of practicing his profession. His early manhood was largely devoted to his plantation interests. Later he was elected a member of the South Carolina legislature, but on account of his unpopular political opinions, did not serve long in that capacity. His speech against reopening the slave trade was characterized by the New York "Tribune" as a "masterpiece of logic, directed by the noblest sentiments of the Christian and the patriot." When the civil war broke out he enlisted as a private, but subsequently raised the "Hampton Legion," which he commanded with distinguished gallantry to the close of the war. At Bull Run, 600 of his men held Warrenton road *against Brigadier-General Keyes' brigade;* while for his services at the battle of Seven Pines, where his legion suffered severely and he himself was wounded, he was raised to the rank of brigadier-general of cavalry. In September, 1862, he was engaged in the battle of Antietam, and in the following month took part in the raid into Pennsylvania. He fought with splendid bravery at the battle of Gettysburg, receiving three wounds, and was appointed major-general, dating from August, 1863. In June, 1864, by giving Sheridan's forces a severe check at Trevellian Station, he probably saved Lynchburg. *Hampton had succeeded General J. E. B. Stuart as commander of the Army of Northern Virginia's cavalry corps after Stuart was mortally wounded in the battle of Yellow Tavern, May 11, 1864.* In twenty-three days he captured over 3,000 prisoners and much material of war, with a loss of 700 men. He was assigned to Lee's cavalry in August, with the rank of lieutenant-general, and in September attacked the rear of the Federal army, securing 400 prisoners, besides 2,486 beeves. *He was not promoted to lieutenant-general until Feb. 15,*

1865. It was about this time that his son lost his life in battle. Being transferred to South Carolina, he commanded the cavalry forming the rear guard of the Confederate army, and attempted to arrest Gen. Sherman's advance northward. After the destruction of Columbia by fire, each of the generals accused the other of willfully burning the city, and a spirited correspondence ensued, establishing the fact that it was not ordered by either Sherman or Hampton, but was caused by the large accumulation of cotton and other inflammable substances, which it was deemed advisable to destroy before the city was evacuated. At the close of hostilities, Gen. Hampton retired to his estate and engaged in cotton planting. During the reconstruction period, he favored a conciliatory policy, and in 1866 referred to the negro as follows: "As a slave he was faithful to us; as a free man let us treat him as a friend. Deal with him frankly, justly, kindly, and my word for it, he will reciprocate your kindness, clinging to his old home, as his own country and his former master." His views were not then favorably received by Southerners. The ballot had been placed in the hands of the recently liberated negroes, whom slavery had not fitted to exercise this privilege, and who, in South Carolina, outnumbered the whites by nearly 400,000. For a time the negroes were in a majority in the legislature. Affairs continued in a more or less demoralized condition until the election of Gen. Hampton as governor in 1876. His election was disputed by his opponent, Daniel H. Chamberlain, and two governments were organized, but Mr. Chamberlain finally withdrew his claim. The period during which Gov. Hampton directed the fortunes of the state was one of the most critical in her history; and it required great tact and wisdom to steer between the dangers of negro domination and carpet-bag rule. In 1878, he was re-elected governor, but being sent in that year to the United States senate, his term was filled by Lieut.-Gov. W. D. Simpson. He was a member of the senate till 1890, and while in that body his course was that of a conservative Democrat, advocating a sound currency and resisting all inflation. He served on the committees on epidemic diseases, fisheries, and military affairs, and as chairman of the committee on coast defenses. In 1893, he was appointed U.S. commissioner of Pacific railroads by Pres. Cleveland, and was retained in this office by Pres. McKinley, until the fall of 1897, when he was succeeded by Gen. James Longstreet. A historian says of him: "Gen. Hampton's services to the state as general, governor, senator, and more recently as her most distinguished private citizen, are comparable only to those of John Rutledge or Charles C. Pinckney in the days following the revolution." He was married first, to Margaret, youngest daughter of Gen. Francis Preston; and second, to a daughter of Gov. McDuffie, of South Carolina. He died in Columbia, S.C., Apr. 11, 1902.

HANCOCK, WINFIELD SCOTT, soldier, was born at Montgomery Square, Pa., Feb. 14, 1824. He came of English ancestry; his father, however, Benjamin Franklin Hancock, having been born in the city of Philadelphia Oct. 19, 1800. Winfield Scott Hancock and Hilary B. Hancock were twins. The family were Baptists, and Gen. Hancock's father was a deacon of that church, besides being superintendent of the Sunday-school for more than thirty years. Gen. Hancock's mother came from English and Welsh ancestry. The political principles of the family, after the presidency of John Adams, were anti-federal or democratic, so that the subject of this sketch may be said to have been a natural democrat. At the time of the birth of

the twin brothers, Gen. Winfield Scott was the most admired of American soldiers, and Mr. Hancock, who was naturally patriotic, named one of his sons after him. The two boys were sent in early boyhood to Norristown academy. Here Winfield first began to display his military tastes by continually marching and

countermarching with his playmates, among whom he organized a military company, of which he was chosen captain. In his fifteenth year the boy received a marked expression of public esteem, in being appointed to read in public at Norristown the declaration of independence. In 1840. at the age of sixteen, young Hancock entered the West Point military academy. His class graduated twenty-five, among whom were Gens. U. S. Grant, George B. McClellan, William B. Franklin, William F. Smith, Joseph J. Reynolds, Rosecrans, Lyon, and others of the Federal army; and Longstreet, Pickett, E. K. Smith, and "Stonewall" Jackson of the Confederate army. Hancock was graduated on June 30, 1844, and was brevetted second lieutenant of the 6th infantry July 1st. He was afterward sent to join his company in the Indian country, near the Red river, on the border of Texas, and in this rough but exhilarating duty he remained until 1846, when he was commissioned second lieutenant in a company stationed on the frontier of Mexico, where he remained until the outbreak of the Mexican war. But it was not until Gen. Scott, passing through New Orleans on his way to Mexico, heard from some friend of Hancock's that he was still detained in his former post, that he joined the army of invasion under peremptory orders from that general. who had previously met him, and taken a fancy to him, partly on account of his name, and partly because of his already excellent record. Hancock's first active service was at the National bridge, on the way from Vera Cruz to Puebla, where he was in command of a storming party, and captured the bridge and a strong barricade. Hancock was brevetted first lieutenant "for gallant and meritorious conduct in the battles of Contreras and Churubusco in the war with Mexico." Between 1848 and 1855 he served as regimental quartermaster and adjutant on the upper Missouri. In 1849 he was ordered to Fort Snelling, Minn., but was then granted five months' leave of absence, and returned to his home in Pennsylvania. On Jan. 24, 1850, Lieut. Hancock was married to Almira Russell, daughter of Samuel Russell, a merchant of St. Louis. Of this marriage there were born two children, Russell and Ada Elizabeth, both now dead. In 1855 Lieut. Hancock was appointed quartermaster with the rank of captain, and ordered to Florida, where the Seminole war was going on, and where, under Gen. Harney, he performed difficult and arduous service. Next occurred the disorders

in Kansas, and Capt. Hancock was ordered to Fort Leavenworth, and after the Kansas troubles were over he accompanied Gen. Harney's expedition to Utah. Following the Utah outbreak, Capt. Hancock was ordered to join his regiment, the 6th infantry, at Fort Bridger, and made the trip with sixteen soldiers, a distance of 709 miles, in twenty-seven days with a train of wagons. He was next ordered to Benicia, Cal., and the entire journey which he made from Fort Leavenworth to that station, 2,100 miles, was performed by Capt. Hancock on horseback. Later he returned to the East on leave, and rejoined his family, but, after a short sojourn, was again ordered to the Pacific coast, and stationed at Los Angeles, Cal. Here he was when the civil war broke out, and his position at this time became critical, as he had a depot of military stores under his control, with supplies and munitions of war, and there was a good deal of pro-slavery feeling at the station. He succeeded in holding it within the Union until the arrival of reinforcements. He was then ordered to the East, reaching New York Sept. 4, 1861, when he reported at Washington for service. He was at once commissioned brigadier-general, and placed in charge of a brigade, including the 5th Wisconsin, the 6th Maine, the 49th Pennsylvania, and the 4th New York. Gen. Hancock's energies were at first devoted to aiding Gen. McClellan in the organization of what was gradually becoming the army of the Potomac. In the spring of 1862 the division of which his brigade was a part was assigned to the 4th army corps, and had its first serious conflict with the enemy at Lee's Mills on Apr. 16th. He saw sharp fighting at Williamsburg and Frazier's Farm and in the Maryland campaign. At the battles of South Mountain and Antietam he commanded the 1st division of the 2d army corps, which fought brilliantly during the second day of the battle of Antietam. He was assigned as commander of the 1st division, 2d army corps, on the field of Antietam. This corps contained many of the best regiments in the service. Two days after the battle Gen. Hancock's corps marched to Harper's Ferry, where the corps continued encamped until the movement to Warrenton and Fredericksburg in October and November. In the battle of Fredericksburg he commanded the 1st division, 2d army corps, in the magnificent attempt to storm Marye's Heights, Dec. 13, 1862, when he led his men through such a fire as has rarely been encountered in warfare. He left nearly half his division on the field. The following spring Hancock's division fought at Chancellorsville, and on June 25th, he was ordered by the president to assume command of the 2d army corps. In the consultation prior to the battle of Gettysburg, Gen. Hancock located the situation which was afterward the scene of that celebrated conflict. In the fight of July 3d he commanded the left centre, the main point assailed by the Confederates, and was shot from his horse, being dangerously wounded, but remained on the field until he saw that the enemy's attack had been repulsed by his corps. For his services in this campaign Gen. Hancock received, on Apr. 21, 1866, a resolution of thanks passed by congress. His wound kept him from active duty until March, 1864, during which period he was engaged in recruiting the 2d army corps up to its former strength. He resumed command in the spring campaign of that year, and fought in the battles of the Wilderness and Spottsylvania, also at the second battle of Cold Harbor, and in the assault on the lines in front of Petersburg. On Aug. 12, 1864, he was appointed brigadier-general in the regular army "for gallant and distinguished services in the battles of the Wilderness, Spottsylvania, and Cold Harbor, and in the operations of the army in Virginia under Lieut.-Gen. Grant." At Ream's station on the Weldon railroad on Aug. 25th Gen. Hancock's corps met with a serious disaster, being attacked by a powerful force of the enemy, and many of his men slain and captured. In the movement against the South side railroad in October of that year Gen. Hancock took a leading part. On Nov. 26, 1864, he was called to Washington to organize a veteran corps of 50,000 men, and continued in the discharge of that duty until Feb. 26, 1865,

when he was assigned to the command of the military division, and ordered to Winchester, Va. After the assassination of President Lincoln, Gen. Hancock's headquarters were transferred to Washington, and he was placed in command of the defence of the capital. On July 26, 1866, he was appointed major-general of the regular army, and on the tenth of the following month assigned to command of the department of the Missouri. Here he fought the Indians until relieved by Gen. Sheridan, when he was placed in command of the fifth military district, comprising Texas and Louisiana. In 1868 he was given command of the division of the Atlantic, with headquarters in New York city. The following year he was sent to the department of Dakota, but in 1872 was again assigned to the division of the Atlantic, in which command he remained until the time of his death. In 1868 and in 1872 Gen. Hancock was a candidate for the presidential nomination, and in 1880 was nominated by the democratic convention at Cincinnati. The election in November, however, gave the opposing candidate, James A. Garfield, both a popular plurality, and a majority in the electoral college; the vote being: Garfield, republican, 4,454,416; Hancock, democrat, 4,444,952; James B. Weaver, greenback, 308,578; Neal Dow, prohibition, 10,305. After the conclusion of this election Gen. Hancock continued to devote himself to his military duty. On the occasion of the funeral of Gen. Grant the arrangements were carried out under his supervision, and this was the last time that he appeared in public. Gen. Hancock's death was felt as a national calamity. More than any other officer on either side, perhaps, he was the embodiment of chivalry and devotion to the highest duties of the soldier. Gen. Grant, best qualified to judge, said of him: "Hancock stands the most conspicuous figure of all the general officers who did not exercise a general command. He commanded a corps longer than any other one, and his name was never mentioned as having committed in battle a blunder for which he was responsible. He was a man of very conspicuous personal appearance, tall, well-formed, and, at the time of which I now write, young and fresh-looking; he presented an appearance that would attract the attention of an army as he passed. His genial disposition made him friends, and his presence with his command in the thickest of the fight won him the confidence of troops who served under him." During the presidential canvass of 1880 Gen. Sherman said of him to a reporter: "If you will sit down, and write the best thing that can be put in language about Gen. Hancock as an officer and a gentleman I will sign it without hesitation." McClellan gave him the name of "The Superb." Among all who knew him he was the Bayard of the northern army, *sans peur et sans reproche*. He died at Governor's island, New York harbor, Feb. 9, 1886.

HARDEE, WILLIAM J., soldier, was born in Savannah, Ga., *Oct. 12, 1815*. He was admitted to the United States military academy, from which he was graduated in the class with Gen. Beauregard in 1838, entering the army as second lieutenant of dragoons. He was promoted to first lieutenant of the dragoons Dec. 3, 1839, after a year's service in Florida. During the whole course of his studies he showed so much aptitude and so much proficiency in all the details of war, and paid so much attention to the observance of military discipline that he soon won the admiration of all with whom he came in contact, and his advancement was rapid and steady. In 1838 he was sent by the U.S. secretary of war to the military school of St. Maur, in France, and during his stay there, was attached to the

cavalry of the French army. After his return to America he served as captain of dragoons on the frontier, and in 1846 was one of the officers who went with Gen. Taylor across the Rio Grande. In 1844 he was promoted to the rank of captain. His company, which was the first to attack the Mexican troops at Curricitos, was defeated by the superior numbers of the enemy, and Capt. Hardee was taken prisoner; he was, however, exchanged, so that he was able to be present at the siege of Monterey. On March 25, 1847, he was made brevet major for meritorious and gallant services. In 1855 he was brevetted major of the 2d regular cavalry, and in 1856 appointed to the command of the cadets at West Point academy, with the rank of lieutenant-colonel. While at West Point he gave courses of instruction in artillery, cavalry, and infantry tactics. In 1860 he was brevetted a lieutenant-colonel of cavalry and in January, 1861, resigned his commission in the U.S. army to enter the Confederate service, and was appointed brigadier-general, soon attaining the rank of major-general. Shortly after the Mexican war Gen. Hardee was instructed by the war department to prepare a system of

tactics for use in the infantry; the result of which was "Hardee's Tactics; or The U.S. Rifle and Light Infantry Tactics." His work was drawn chiefly from French sources, and made his name famous, afterward becoming the standard for use by the militia in the regular army. At the battle of Shiloh, in 1862, Gen. Hardee was placed in command of the 3d corps, and at the battle of Perryville, Oct. 8th of that year, he commanded the left wing of Gen. Bragg's army, and also held a position at the battle of Murfreesboro; and at Chattanooga, in November, 1863, he had charge of Gen. Bragg's right wing. Gen. Hardee was also for a time stationed in Kentucky, where he defeated a small body of United States troops at Munfordsville. He was subsequently assigned to commands in South Carolina and Georgia, evacuating Savannah Dec. 20, 1864, and Charleston Feb. 18, 1865. He was made lieutenant-general for meritorious and gallant services at Perryville and other engagements, and took part in the battle of Bentonsville, N.C., March, 1865, surrendering to Gen. W. T. Sherman, with Joseph E. Johnston's army, at Durham, N.C., Apr. 26, 1865. After the war Gen. Hardee lived quietly on his plantation in Alabama. He died at Wytheville, Va., Nov. 6, 1873.

HARNEY, WILLIAM SELBY, soldier, was born at Haysboro', Davidson county, Tenn., Aug. 27, 1800, son of Thomas Harney, who served as an officer in the war of the revolution from the state of Delaware. The war over, he emigrated with his family to Tennessee in 1791, and subsequently settled in Louisiana. William Selby's elder brother, John Milton Harney, a physician, poet, journalist, and Dominican monk, was born March 9, 1789, and died at the monastery at Bardstown, Ky., Jan. 15, 1825. William Selby was appointed second lieutenant

in the 19th U.S. infantry from Louisiana Feb. 13, 1818, promoted to be first lieutenant Jan. 7, 1819, to a captaincy May 14, 1825, as major and paymaster May 1, 1833, lieutenant-colonel, 2d dragoons, Aug. 15, 1836, colonel Jan. 30, 1848, and brigadier-general *June 14, 1858*. As Maj. Harney he took part in the Black Hawk war, also in the Florida war; as lieutenant-colonel, distinguishing himself at Fort Milton and at Carloosahatchie July 23, 1839, and was in command of several expeditions into the Everglades, gaining by his superior officership the brevet of colonel in December, 1840, "for gallant and meritorious conduct." He was with the army in the war with Mexico, and was mentioned for bravery at Medellin, March 25, 1847, and for his part in the battle of Cerro

Gordo was brevetted brigadier-general. After the close of the Mexican war he was on frontier duty, and on Sept. 3, 1855, met and defeated the Sioux Indians at Sand Hills, on the Platte river. Upon receiving his commission as brigadier-general in June, 1858, he was assigned to the command of the department of Oregon. One of his acts was to take military possession of the island of San Juan, claimed by the British government as a part of British Columbia. This led to a dispute with Great Britain, and the recall of Gen. Harney. He was subsequently appointed to the command of the department of the West, with headquarters at St. Louis. In April, 1861, while Gen. Harney was *en route* for Washington to meet the incoming administration and receive orders incident to the reorganization of the army, he was arrested by the Confederates at Harper's Ferry, Va., and carried to Richmond. Gens. Lee and Johnston both strongly urged him to join the fortunes of the South, at the same time deprecating the necessity that forced them to take up arms against the government. Gen. Harney was released, and allowed to report at Washington. On his return to St. Louis he warned the people of Missouri against secession, and the disasters that would surely follow the act. With a view of saving the state from taking such a step, he agreed with Gen. Sterling Price, commanding the state militia, to make no military movement on the part of the U.S. government so long as peace was

maintained by the state authorities. This agreement was made May 21, 1861. On May 29th he was relieved of his command by Gen. Nathaniel Lyon, and was placed on the retired list Aug. 1, 1863. At the close of the war he was brevetted major-general "for long and faithful services." He died in St. Louis, May 9, 1889. L. U. Reavis published his life and military services (St. Louis, 1887).

HARPER, FLETCHER, was born Jan. 31, 1806. He was the youngest of the four brothers, and after having served his apprenticeship with the firm, and become a partner in 1825, he soon, like the other brothers, fell into his natural place in the house and became one of its sustaining pillars. In the arrangement which grew up naturally, James Harper superintended the mechanical operations of the establishment; John made most of the purchases and became the financial manager of the firm; Wesley read the final proofs of the most important works, while conducting the correspondence of the house; and Fletcher, after being for a time foreman of the composing room, grew into the charge of the publishing departments. It was to his suggestion that the publication of the "Weekly" and the "Bazar" was due; while the idea of the "Magazine" originated with James Harper. Fletcher Harper was not a writer himself, but he was always shrewd and acute in his suggestions to the editors. Like his brothers he was a lifelong and consistent member of the Methodist denomination. In private life he was genial and hospitable. Harper & Brothers have grown to be the largest publishing house in the United States, and probably in the world. Before 1825 the firm gave employment to fifty hands and kept ten large hand-presses constantly in use; removing in that year to Cliff Street, the demands of their business required the addition of one

building after another, and at as early a period as was practicable steam-power was introduced into their establishment, and every new discovery and invention which could be of use to them was applied to their business. The firm began stereotyping their works in 1830. From that time forward they became known for their collections of standard publications, and the firm was rapidly achieving the highest success when, on Dec. 10, 1853, it met with a terrible blow in the destruction of its buildings by fire. A plumber, who was engaged in mending some pipes on the premises, threw a bit of lighted paper in a trough which he thought contained water. It was actually filled with camphine, used for cleaning ink-rollers. It burst into flame, which almost instantly swept through the rooms, and in a few hours the nine buildings, wherein were conducted the operations of the house, were totally destroyed, the loss being nearly a million dollars. The brothers met immediately after this catastrophe at the residence of Mr. John Harper, to make arrangements for rebuilding. Soon after, the present structure was planned, extending

Private Office

between Cliff Street and Franklin Square; a fire-proof building, or rather two buildings united by bridges. The Franklin Square building is five stories high above the street, and contains the business offices, warerooms, editorial rooms, and the art and engraving departments. The Cliff Street building is six stories high, and therein are conducted the various processes of bookmaking, which are complete from the type-setting and electrotyping to the stitching, binding and lettering. Fronting Franklin Square, and occupying the first floor above the street, are the book store and counting-rooms, in the latter of which, facing the windows, are to be daily seen the members of the third generation of the Harper & Brothers, engaged in the conduct of the business of the firm. The basement story of the Cliff Street building is devoted to the engine-rooms and press-rooms of the "Weekly," "Bazar," "Young People," and "Franklin Square Library". The second story contains the presses devoted to the "Magazine" and book work. Sheets are dried and pressed by steam on the next floor; and on

the others are the folding, collating, stitching, binding, and electrotyping rooms. The ground area of the building is about three-fourths of an acre. It is thoroughly fire-proof, well-lighted and ventilated. The whole number of employees in the establishment is about 1,000. While, as book publishers, Harper & Brothers have conducted a vast business of the greatest importance to the literature and education of the country, it is in their periodicals that they have made, perhaps, their most extraordinary success. "Harper's Magazine," established in 1850, gave a new impetus to periodical literature, which has since become such a field for authorship and artistic effort. Its influence upon art, taste and general culture can hardly be overestimated. A second periodical, in all respects representative of the taste and liberality of the Harpers, and one which has, moreover, wielded great influence, social and political, is "Harper's Weekly, a Journal of Civilization," whose first number was issued Jan. 3, 1857. This paper, which was suggested and originated by Mr. Fletcher Harper, has been remarkable for the high character of its literary and art work, and not less for the remarkable force and vitality of its editorials. Its services during the civil war were of the greatest value to the country, while hardly less so, in relation to the city of New York, in the vigor and earnestness with which it handled the corruptions of the Tweed "ring." "Harper's Bazar," more particularly devoted to the interest and taste of women; and "Harper's Young People," which supplies appropriate illustrated literature for children, complete the list of periodicals published by Harper & Brothers. Among the editors connected with the Harpers have been Henry J. Raymond, who was editor of the "Magazine" during the first three years of its existence; George Ripley and Dr. Alfred H. Guernsey, who succeeded him in that position; and Henry M. Alden, who has been the editor since 1869. Mr. George William Curtis has had the charge of the "Editor's Easy Chair" of the "Magazine" for many years, besides having the editorial supervision of the "Weekly." The first editor of the "Editor's Drawer" in the "Magazine" was Lewis Gaylord Clark, who was succeeded by S. Irenaeus Prime, who was followed by W.A. Seaver and Charles Dudley Warner. The catalogue of the publications of Harper & Brothers is in itself a considerable volume of 200 pages. Prominent in this is Harper's "Library of Select Novels," which was for many years so popular with the readers of fiction, and which included 615 numbers. This series was replaced by Harper's "Franklin Square Library," which ran through 700 numbers; while the "Handy Series," "Half-Hour Series," "Library of American Fiction" and others, have been convenient forms for their respective classes of books. The index to "Harper's Magazine", from the beginning down to 1888, is a large octavo volume, and is a comprehensive key to a perfect library of literary wealth. Fletcher was the last one of all the brothers, passing away after a long illness, on May 29, 1877.

HARRIS, ISHAM GREEN, governor of Tennessee, was born near Tullahoma, Tenn., Feb. 10, 1818, the son of a poor farmer. He became clerk in a country store at the age of fourteen, attended a country school, and at the age of nineteen settled in Tippah county, Miss.,

where he engaged in business on his own account and became a successful merchant. He studied law at night, and was admitted to the bar in 1841. He was elected to the Tennessee legislature *in 1847*, and was a representative

in congress from 1849 to 1853; refused a re-nomination in the latter year, and removed to Memphis, where he settled as a lawyer. In 1856 he was a presidential elector; was elected governor of Tennessee in 1857; was re-elected in 1859, and a second time in 1861. His sympathies were with the South during the war, and he was finally forced to leave the state on account of the success of the Federal arms. He subsequently entered the Southern army as a volunteer, served as aide to Gen. A.S. Johnston, and was with him at Shiloh. At the close of the war he was penniless, but not wishing to be captured, he traveled abroad for a few years, and in 1867 returned to Memphis and practiced his profession. In 1877 he was elected to the U.S. senate, was re-elected in 1882, and again in 1888. He was a member of the select committee on the levees of the

Mississippi; of the committee on claims, and chairman of the committee on the District of Columbia. He was an opponent of all class legislation. He was a man of strong intellect and great power in debate, and very few men had more influence in the politics of his native state. *He died July 8, 1897.*

HARTRANFT, JOHN FREDERICK, governor of Pennsylvania (1872–78), was born in New Hanover township, Montgomery Co., Pa., Dec. 16, 1830, of German ancestry, a descendant of the religious denomination of Schwenkfelders, who settled in eastern Pennsylvania at the time of William Penn, and by his special invitation. Young Hartranft obtained his preparatory education at Marshall College, in Pennsylvania, and was graduated from Union College, N.Y., in 1853, where he showed great proficiency in the higher mathematics. As a civil engineer he engaged in running the line of the Mauch Chunk and Wilkesbarre Railroad, and then for several years was deputy sheriff of his native county. While he held that office he studied law with James Boyd, of Norristown, Pa., and was admitted to the bar in 1859. At the opening of the civil war he was colonel of a militia organization, which became the 4th Pennsylvania Regiment in the three months' service. Its term having expired one day before the battle of Bull Run, Col. Hartranft was immediately assigned to the staff of Gen. William B. Franklin, and in that engagement distinguished himself by rallying two regiments which had been thrown into confusion. He then raised and was commissioned colonel of the 51st Pennsylvania regiment and accompanied Gen. Burnside on the expedition to North Carolina in 1862. At Roanoke Island his regiment led the advance through what was supposed by the enemy to be an impassable swamp and captured nearly the entire

Confederate force in front of them. At Newbern, N.C., he led the charge on the works defending the town, which soon fell. In July, 1862, his regiment was assigned to the 9th army corps in Virginia, and was afterward identified with all of its achievements. Col. Hartranft showed remarkable skill and strategy in handling his troops at Second Bull Run, Chantilly, South Mountain, and at Antietam he led the famous charge which captured the stone bridge, resulting in one of the most brilliant achievements of the war. After winning fame for his bravery at Fredericksburg, he and his command were transferred to the army of the West in 1863, and were engaged in the battle of Campbell's Station and the successful defence of Knoxville. He commanded a brigade at Vicksburg, and on the march upon Jackson, Miss., directed its movement while lying sick in an ambulance. While in command of the second division of the 9th corps his talent and military skill were conspicuously shown on the retreat from Loudon to Knoxville, previous to the siege of that city by Gen. Longstreet. The next year he commanded a brigade which did valiant service under Grant in the Wilderness campaign. By his characteristic bravery and presence of mind at an eventful moment in the conflict at Weldon Railroad, he saved his entire corps from discomfiture. In December, 1864, he was assigned to the command of a division of 6,000 Pennsylvania troops, and with them recaptured Fort Stedman. Immediately thereafter, he was given the rank of major-general by brevet. *He had earlier been promoted to brigadier-general of volunteers on May 12, 1864.* The last brilliant achievement in Gen. Hartranft's military career was to break the cordon of works in front of Petersburg, causing the surrender of that city Apr. 2, 1865. Soon after the close of the war he declined the offer of a colonelcy in the regular army. In October, 1865, he was elected auditor-general of Pennsylvania, and was re-elected in 1868. He was chosen governor of the state in 1872, and served two terms of three years each. Under the amended constitution, adopted in 1873, the term was extended to four years, and the executive could not be a candidate for re-election. During Gov. Hartranft's administration the state militia was reorganized by him, and placed on a military basis. He commanded it in person during the great "strike" of 1877 in the coal regions of Pennsylvania and at Pittsburg, and without bloodshed soon brought about a peaceful condition of affairs. He devoted much time and attention to municipal reform, and the plan recommended by him in 1876 was adopted in 1885. When his term of office ended, he removed to Philadelphia, was appointed postmaster of that city by President Hayes, and from 1880 to 1885 was collector of the port of Philadelphia. He declined the office of commissioner of pensions, but accepted the position of major-general of the National Guard of Pennsylvania, which organization erected a handsome monument to his memory at Norristown, Pa. Gov.

Hartranft was married in 1854 to Sallie D. Sebring. He died Oct. 17, 1889, leaving one son and two daughters.

HARTSUFF, GEORGE LUCAS, soldier, was born in Tyre, Seneca county, N.Y., May 28, 1830. His parents moved to Michigan during his childhood, and he entered West Point from that state, graduating from the military academy in 1852. He was assigned to a second lieutenancy in the 4th artillery, and served in Texas and afterward in Florida in the Indian campaign; was wounded and sent to West Point as instructor in artillery and infantry tactics in 1856. He was promoted assistant adjutant-general, March 22, 1861, and ordered to Fort Pickens, Fla., where he served until July 16, 1861, then in West Virginia; was commissioned brigadier-general of volunteers Apr. 15, 1862; took charge of Abercrombie's brigade and

commanded it both at Cedar mountain and Antietam. In the latter battle he was severely wounded. He became major-general of volunteers, Nov. 29, 1862; was appointed to assist in revising the rules and articles of war, and prepare a code for the government of the armies in the field; was ordered to Kentucky and assigned to the command of the 23d corps, Apr. 27, 1863; promoted lieutenant-colonel and assistant adjutant-general, U.S. army, June 1, 1864; brevetted brigadier-general and major-general, U.S. army, March 13, 1865, and commanded the works in the siege of Petersburg, March and April, 1865. Having been mustered out of the volunteer service at the close of the war he was adjutant-general of the 5th military division, U.S. army (Louisiana and Texas), in 1867–68, and of the Missouri division in 1869–71, when, by reason of disability from wounds received in battle, he was retired from active service, June 29, 1871. He died in New York city, May 16, 1874.

HATCH, EDWARD, soldier, was born at Bangor, Me., Dec. 22, 1832. He was graduated at the Norwich (Vt.) Military Academy in 1852, and soon afterward removed to Iowa. In April, 1861, he was one of the first to volunteer for the defense of Washington, D.C., and upon his arrival at that place he was stationed on duty at the White House. He was ordered soon afterward to take charge of the camp of instruction at Davenport, Ia. On Aug. 12, 1861, he was commissioned captain in the 2d Iowa cavalry, which he had assisted in raising; he was made major on Sept. 5th, lieutenant-colonel, Sept. 11th, and colonel June 13, 1862. He was engaged at the captures of New Madrid and Island No. 10, and in the battles of Iuka and Corinth; and he was in command of the cavalry raid through central Mississippi, which was devised in order to withdraw the attention of the Confederates from the movements of the Federal army about Vicksburg. He participated in the actions at Thompson's station and Hatchie, and in the subsequent operations of

Gen. Grant's Mississippi campaign, being in command of a cavalry brigade. He was then assigned to the command of a cavalry division in the army of the Tennessee, and took part in the actions of Salisbury, Colliersville, La Grange, Palo Alto, Birmingham, Jackson, and Wyatt, where he was severely wounded, December, 1863. On Apr. 27, 1864, he was commissioned brigadier-general of volunteers, and commanded a cavalry division in Gen. Andrew J. Smith's campaign, being engaged in the actions at Florence, Lawrenceburg, Campbellville, and Spring hill. He led his division at the battle of Franklin, Tenn., Nov. 30, 1864, and for his gallant conduct was brevetted brigadier-general. He also distinguished himself in the battle of Nashville, Dec. 15–16, 1864, and in the pursuit of Gen. Hood's army; receiving the brevets of major-general of volunteers, and major-general, United States army. He was mustered out of the volunteer service, Jan. 15, 1866, and on July 28th of that year he was commissioned colonel of the 9th cavalry, which command he held for twenty-three years. Upon the death of Gen. Gordon Granger in 1876, Gen. Hatch was assigned to the command of the military department of Arizona, which included New Mexico. In 1880 he was appointed a member of the Ute investigating commission, of which he was president, and after making a treaty with that tribe, he went to New Mexico, and took the field against Victorio, the Apache chief, whom he defeated. He died at Fort Robinson, Neb., Apr. 11, 1889.

HATCH, JOHN PORTER, soldier, was born at Oswego, N.Y., Jan. 9, 1822, son of Moses Porter and Hannah (Reed) Hatch, grandson of Timothy and Abigail (Porter) Hatch and a descendant of Thomas Hatch, who came from England in 1633. He was graduated at the

United States Military Academy and was appointed brevet second lieutenant of 3d infantry July 1, 1845. During the Mexican war he participated in numerous engagements from Palo Alto to the final surrender of the City of Mexico, and he was breveted first lieutenant and later captain for gallant and meritorious conduct at the battles of Contreras, Churubusco and Chapultepec. He was employed from the close of the Mexican to the opening of the civil war in garrison and frontier duty and in numerous expeditions against the hostile Indians. He was promoted to a captaincy in 1860, and in 1861 was appointed brigadier-general of volunteers and commanded a cavalry brigade under Gen. King. He distinguished himself by several daring reconnoissances in the vicinity of Gordonsville, the Rapidan and the Rappahannock. He commanded the cavalry of the 5th corps in the Shenandoah valley and northern Virginia. In July, 1862, he was transferred to the infantry division, and Gen. King being disabled by sickness he commanded his division. He was wounded at the second battle of Bull run, participated in that at Chantilly, and was again severely wounded at the battle of South mountain, where he commanded a division, Sept. 14, 1862. He commanded various divisions in the South, and was appointed major of the 4th cavalry Oct. 27, 1863. He had command of the forces operating on John's island, S.C., July 1–10, 1864, and of the coast division department of the South Nov. 29, 1864, to Feb. 26, 1865, also at the attack on Honey Hill, S.C., Nov. 30th and that at Tullafumy river Dec. 3, 1864. He then co-operated with Gen. Sherman in his advance up the coast and participated in various skirmishes. He was breveted from major to major-general for his gallantry during the war, notably at Manassas and South mountain, and for his services throughout the war was breveted brigadier-general, United States army. In 1881 he was promoted colonel of the 2d cavalry, and was retired by the operation of the law in 1886. He was married Jan. 14, 1851, to Adelaide Goldsmith, daughter of Christian J. Burchle of Oswego, N.Y., and had two children, Mark B. and Harriet Hatch. He died in New York city, Apr. 12, 1901.

HAUPT, HERMAN, civil engineer, was born in Philadelphia, Pa., March 26, 1817, son of Jacob and Anna Margaretta (Wiall) Haupt. He was educated in Philadelphia and afterward at West Point, where he was graduated in 1835, and was commissioned second lieutenant in the U.S. army. He resigned this position in the fall of 1835 to accept that of assistant engineer on the corps of H. R. Campbell in Philadelphia. Being appointed the following year principal assistant engineer in the service of the state of Pennsylvania, he located the Gettysburg railroad across South mountain. In 1840 Mr.

Haupt became principal assistant of the York and Wrightsville railroad; at the same time began to investigate the strength of timbers and the magnitude and distribution of strains in bridges and other trusses, which resulted in a publication: "The General Theory of Bridge Construction" (1852). This book was generally adopted as a text-book in engineering and technical schools, and has since been of invaluable use in the great bridge structures of modern times. After being connected with the Pennsylvania College as a professor of mathematics and civil engineering in 1842–47, he was appointed principal assistant engineer on the Pennsylvania railroad in 1847, and assistant to John Edgar Thompson in 1847–49. In 1849 he was instructed to inspect the principal railroads of New York and New England, with a view to comparing their systems of book-keeping and management, and prepared a plan for the business organization of the Pennsylvania road. This was adopted without change, and Mr. Haupt was made superintendent of transportation Sept. 1, 1849, and general superintendent in the following year. In 1853 he was unanimously elected chief engineer, and completed the Allegheny tunnel and the Mountain division of the Pennsylvania railroad. Withdrawing, in 1856, from the Pennsylvania railroad, he began the construction of the Hoosac tunnel in Massachusetts. In 1862 he became chief of construction and operation of the military railroads of the United States. The corps which he organized became a model of efficiency; accompanied Gen. Sherman in his famous march to the sea, and, under the supervision of E. C. Smeed, constructed a railroad bridge across the Chattahoochee in Georgia, 780 feet long and ninety feet high, in four and one-half days, taking the timber from the stump; a feat never before or since witnessed and one of untold value to the army. A military bridge, built on the line of Fredericksburg railroad, in 1862, by details of unskilled, common soldiers, was spoken of thus by Pres. Lincoln at a meeting of the war committee: "Gentlemen, I have witnessed the most remarkable structure that human eyes ever rested upon. That man, Haupt, has built a bridge across Potomac creek in nine days with common soldiers, and, upon my soul, gentlemen, there is nothing in it but bean poles and corn stalks." On taking charge of the bureau, Mr. Haupt was appointed colonel and aide-de-camp to Gen. McDowell, and was subsequently promoted to brigadier-general for meritorious services. In 1862 a work, "Haupt on Military Bridges," was published by D. Van Nostrand & Co. After the war he was chief engineer on the Shenandoah Valley railroad, 1875; general manager of the Richmond and Danville system, 1879, and chief engineer on the Seaboard Pipe line. In 1881 he became general manager of the Northern Pacific railroad. He was appointed president of the Dakota and Great Southern railroad in 1884, and in 1892 became occupied in the development of compressed air motors and in different kinds of engineering work. Mr. Haupt was married, in 1838, to Anna Cecilia, daughter of Rev. Benjamin Kellie, and they had eleven children. One of his sons, Lewis Muhlenberg Haupt, born in 1844, was a civil engineer of wide reputation, and has been professor of civil engineering in the University of Pennsylvania since 1872, and was one of the three U.S. commissioners on the Nicaragua canal. He was author of "Engineering Specifications and Contracts"; "Working Drawings and How to Make Them"; "The Topographer: His Methods and Instruments"; "Essays on Road-Making," etc. *He died Dec. 14, 1905.*

HAWKINS, RUSH CHRISTOPHER, soldier and officer of the Legion of Honor of France, was born at Pomfret, Vt., Sept. 14, 1831. Both his paternal and maternal ancestors were distinguished for bravery in the war of the revolution, and doubtless from them he inherited his soldierly instincts. He attended the district school of his native village, and then was for a short time at the military school, Norwich, Vt. In 1847 he enlisted in the second dragoons, and was sent to Carlisle barracks, and afterward joined his regiment in Mexico, where he remained during the last nine months of our occupation. At the commencement of the civil war, he raised the 9th New York volunteers, known as the Hawkins zouaves, of which he was colonel; and he also had the honor of being the first individual to offer his services to the governor of New York. He rendered important service in the capture of Hatteras inlet, Roanoke Island and Winton, and took an active part in the Virginia campaign of 1862, and subsequent movements of the army of the Potomac, in which he commanded a brigade and then a division. He retired from the army brevet brigadier-general, and a similar commission in the National guard of New York was conferred upon him by the governor of that state. In recognition of his services, fifty prominent citizens of New York presented him with an elegant sword of honor. He shared, with Generals Kearny and Wadsworth, claim to the credit of having discovered McClellan's inability to command the army. He has been actively engaged in nearly every important reform movement undertaken in New York city since the close of the war, and has also spent much of his time in Europe, traveling and studying art at the great art centres, and has written extensively on art topics. In 1872 he was a member of the New York legislature, and in 1889 of the United States commission of fine arts at the Universal exposition held at Paris, where his particular department achieved a notable success. He is a man of peculiar endowment as regards culture, and an authority on art bibliography, more particularly in the history of wood engraving and early printing. Among the more important of his published works are: "A Statement" (1872), exposing the corrupt character of the New York legislature of that year; "Horrors in Architecture, and So-called Works of Art in Bronze in the City of New York" (1884); "First Books and Printers of the Fifteenth Century," and a number of others of varied character and great worth. *He died Oct. 25, 1920.*

Rush C. Hawkins

HAYES, RUTHERFORD BIRCHARD, nineteenth president of the United States, was born at Delaware, O., Oct. 4, 1822. His ancestry this side of the Atlantic ocean began with George Hayes, Scotchman, who came to the colony of Connecticut in 1680 and settled at Windsor. His son Daniel, when twenty-two years old, was taken prisoner by Indians in Queen Anne's war and spent five years in captivity in Canada. By the year 1690 he had located in Salmon Brook, Conn., where he became a prosperous farmer and a pillar in the church, and was often employed in public affairs. The third son of Daniel was Ezekiel, who became a blacksmith of merit and an extensive maker of scythes, who built for himself a large brick house at Branford, Conn.

Ezekiel's second son, Rutherford, settled at Brattleboro, Vt., and there was born to him and his wife a son Rutherford, father of the subject of this sketch. He prospered as a merchant at Dummerston, Vt., but in September, 1817, with his household goods stored in two large wagons, he removed himself and family to the native place of the future president of the republic, but died in the July preceding his birth. Rutherford B. Hayes had for a mother Miss Sophia, daughter of Roger and Drusilla Birchard, of Suffield, Conn. The founders of the whole family came from England to America in 1635. When the father died his mother trained him in reading and spelling. It is recorded, too, that he was a pupil at the village district school of a thin, wiry little Yankee, Mr. Daniel Granger, who left upon his pupils a very deep impression of the rod as an agent in education. An uncle, Sardis Birchard, who had removed to Ohio with the Hayes family and was successful in business, supplied the eager demands of the boy and his favorite sister for books. On a visit to eastern relations made in 1834 by Mrs. Hayes with her son and daughter it was decided that the son should have a college education, and should begin to prepare for it immediately. In the summer of 1836 he was sent to an academy at Norwalk, O., but soon afterward became a pupil of Mr. Isaac Cobb, of Middletown, Conn. He was finally graduated from Kenyon College, Gambier, O., in 1842 after the full four years' course of study. Here he had excelled in logic, mental and moral philosophy and as a debater in the college societies, and was the valedictorian of his class. Immediately after graduation he entered an office at Columbus, O., as a law student. In August, 1843, he went to the law school of Harvard University, proposing to pursue other branches of education as well as the studies of the legal course. His life at Cambridge, Mass., ended in January 1845, and he was admitted to the Ohio bar in May of that year. He had forced himself to severe mental discipline, and four rules which he laid down for himself at Harvard are worth quoting: "First, read no newspapers. Second, rise at seven and retire at ten. Third, study law six hours, German two, and chemistry two. Fourth, in reading Blackstone, record any difficulties." Young Hayes soon opened a law office at Lower Sandusky, O., forming a partnership in 1846 with R. P. Buckland; but rushing into practice with feverish energy his health failed, and he was inclined to join the U.S. army and take service in the Mexican war; but a physician forbade this, and he went for recuperation first to New England, and then to Canada and, when winter approached, to a plantation in Texas. When he returned (1849) with health restored he found his future wife, Lucy W. Webb, whom he married Dec. 30, 1852. As a temporary resident of Delaware in December, 1849, he had commenced the practice of his profession at Cincinnati, O., forming a partnership early in 1850 with Mr. J. W. Huron. This was succeeded in 1854 by another with Mr. H. W. Corwin and Mr. W. K.

When his term of office ended in April, 1861, a political reaction had set in; the municipal election occurring prior to the bombardment of Fort Sumter, the entire city republican ticket was defeated, Mr. Hayes, who ran for re-election among the rest. Apr. 13th, at a mass-meeting called to appeal to the patriotism of the people in response to President Lincoln's proclamation calling for 75,000 troops, he was chairman of the committee appointed to draw

Rogers. In 1856 he was nominated for judge of the court of common pleas, but declined the honor. Up to this time he had acted with the whig party. When the republican party was formed he took an active interest in its first campaign, proving himself a capital political speaker. In 1858 he was chosen city solicitor of Cincinnati by a majority of over 2,500 votes.

up resolutions expressive of the intense feeling which had now been aroused. Forthwith the members of the literary club to which he belonged organized a military company of which he was chosen captain, and President Lincoln sent him a commission as colonel of volunteers, which he declined, saying that he was not ready for so much responsibility for the services and lives of other men. At the same time he entered upon a methodical course of drill and study, for June 1, 1861, he accepted a commission from the governor as major of the 23d regiment of state volunteers, a body of 900 men recruited in forty-two counties of the commonwealth. Its colonel was W. S. Rosecrans. In July, 1861, it was ordered to duty in western Virginia under Gen. Geo. B. McClellan. Sept. 19th, Maj. Hayes was made judge advocate of the department of Ohio, but on the 24th of October was back with his regiment as its lieutenant-colonel, and took an active and commendable part in all its engagements until his retirement from the army. In the famous Cedar Creek fight (that of "Sheridan's Ride" from Winchester), Oct. 19th, while attempting to rally the soldiers in the contest at the dawn of day, he had a horse killed under him, but escaped capture, and was ready to take his part in the second battle and the brilliant victory with which the day ended. Here he was slightly wounded in the head by a spent ball. That night Gen. Sheridan said to him: "You will be a brigadier-general from this time." His commission arrived a few days afterward, and on March 13, 1865, he received the rank of brevet major-general "for gallant and distinguished services during the campaign of 1864 in West Virginia, and particularly at the battles of Fisher's Hill and Cedar Creek, Va." His war record ended with the memorable campaign in the Shenandoah Valley. In the second volume of his "Personal Memoirs" Gen. U. S. Grant wrote: "On more than one occasion in these engagements Gen. R. B. Hayes, who succeeded me as president of the United States, bore a very honorable part. His conduct on the field was marked by conspicuous gallantry as well as by the display of qualities of a higher order than mere personal daring. Having entered the army as a major of

volunteers at the beginning of the war, Gen. Hayes attained by his meritorious services the rank of brevet major-general before its close." Aug. 6, 1864, a republican convention at Cincinnati had nominated him for congress. He was then on the field, and to a friend, who suggested that he leave it and make the political canvass, he replied: "Your suggestion about getting a furlough to take the stump ws certainly made without reflection. An officer fit for duty who at this crisis would abandon his post to electioneer for a seat in congress ought to be scalped." When the election came on, however, he was chosen to the U.S. house of representatives by more than 2,400 majority. His resignation from the army was formally accepted to take effect June 8, 1865. In congress he was appointed chairman of the library committee, and succeeded in greatly amending the copyright law, as well as in trebling the area, contents, and usefulness of the congressional library, the additions including the invaluable historical and scientific collection of the Force library and those of the Smithsonian Institution. His votes in matters affecting the reconstruction of the South were given with his party, his first vote being for a resolution affirming the sacredness of the public debt, and denouncing every form of repudiation. In August, 1866, the republican convention of his congressional district gave him the high honor of a nomination by acclamation, and he was re-elected by a majority of 2,556. The fortieth congress was that of the reconstruction measures, including negro suffrage, and Gen. Hayes gave hearty support to the policy of his party associates, sustaining the movement for the impeachment of President Johnson. His own reputation was already established, not as a talking member, but as a vigorous worker and a man of good judgment. June 8, 1867, the democratic party of the state of Ohio placed in nomination for governor an able and respected leader, A. G. Thurman. On the 19th of the month, at the republican state convention, by a handsome majority and on the first ballot, Gen. Hayes was named as his competitor, a proceeding taken without any expression whatever of ambition upon his part. He resigned his seat in congress to go home and fight the battle upon the issues of the hour, including "manhood suffrage." He was elected, as was the rest of his state ticket, but a proposed manhood suffrage amendment to the constitution of the state was buried under an adverse majority of 50,000, a democratic legislature was chosen, and Mr. Thurman was returned by it to the U.S. senate. Gen. Hayes was inaugurated Jan. 13, 1868. During his term as governor he steadily increased his personal popularity among intelligent men of all parties, and in 1869 was nominated by acclamation and elected, receiving at the polls a majority of 7,506 votes over his democratic competitor, George H. Pendleton. His first message to the Ohio legislature in his second term advocated measures embodying the entire doctrine of civil service reform, as it is now understood. In January, 1872, he was proffered the Ohio U.S. senatorship, but rejected it that it might go to John Sherman. During that year the political current in the state set against the republicans, and he was defeated in his contest for a seat in congress by William Allen, democrat. Shortly after, he declined the position of U.S. treasurer at Cincinnati, which was tendered to him by President Grant, and retired to private life at Fremont, O., in accordance with his own plans and wishes of his uncle, Sardis Birchard, who proposed to make him his heir. Here he designed to create a model home, and over 1,000 trees were set out in his spacious grounds as a partial means to that end. His uncle dying in 1874 he came into possession of the estate. But these purposes of retirement were broken in upon by his political friends, who, *in June 1875*, nominated him a third time for governor of Ohio, to which position he was chosen by a majority of 5,500 after a canvass

which had drawn to him the attention of the whole country. And now Gov. Hayes began to be talked about as a possible presidential candidate. When the convention came together in Cincinnati (June, 1876), he was so nominated on the seventh ballot. His democratic opponent in the ensuing canvass was Samuel J. Tilden, of New York, and the result of the election became the subject of violent contention, the leaders of each of the great parties charging fraud upon the other. Gov. Hayes's position in this strife is shown by a letter of his, dated Nov. 17, 1876, addressed to John Sherman at New Orleans, La. He said: "You feel, I am sure, as I do, about this whole business. A fair election would have given us about forty electoral votes at the South, at least that many. But we are not to allow our friends to defeat one outrage by another. There must be nothing curved on our part. Let Mr. Tilden have the place by violence, intimidation, and fraud, rather than undertake to prevent it by means that will not bear the severest scrutiny." The facts turned out to be when the forty-fourth congress met, that the canvassing boards of several southern states declared the republican electors chosen, and Gen. Hayes had a majority of one in the electoral college. And these returns were sent to Washington by the state governors. But others were sent as well which certified the choice of the democratic electors, and in this emergency an electoral commission, the only one in American history so far, consisting of five U.S. senators, five U.S. representatives, and five judges of the U.S. supreme court, was appointed by congress, which was to decide upon all contested cases, the decision of this commission to be final unless set aside by concurrent vote of the two houses of congress. This commission refused, by votes of 8 to 7 in each case, to go behind the returns made by the governors of the states. The republican

candidate was, March 2, 1877, declared to have been elected president of the United States, and on March 5th was duly inaugurated. As to an important issue before the country, the pacification of the southern states, the inaugural address which President Hayes made at this time, assured both white and colored people in that section that he should put forth his "best efforts in behalf of a civil policy which will forever wipe out in any political affairs the color and the distinction between the North and the South, to the end that we may have not merely a united North or united South, but a United Country." He had given evidence of this already by taking into his cabinet as postmaster-general David M. Key, of Tennessee, and withdrawing the U.S. troops from the state house in South Carolina, and from that in Louisiana. In the matter of civil service reform, then a new political topic, Gen. Hayes as president advocated the same views which had been noted as characterizing his gubernatorial administration in Ohio. And he now proceeded to give them practical effect according to the possibilities of the case, refusing to allow senators and representatives to control nominations in their states and districts. They might advise, and their advice estimated at its proper value, but they were not to be allowed to dictate. In the summer of 1877, on the call of the governors of West Virginia, Maryland, and Pennsylvania, he sent detachments of U.S. troops to the places where they were needed to quell extensive railroad riots; when September of that year came, with Mrs. Hayes and a large party of public personages he made a tour of the southern states, being everywhere received with kindness and in many places with enthusiasm, usually by all political parties. In the second session of the forty-fifth congress, while steadily pressing his measures for civil service reform, and that, too against the will of the professional politicians of all party connections, his exertions to keep inviolate the good faith of the nation in its financial policy are especially to be noted. Vetoing an act to authorize the coinage of the silver dollar (412½ grains), and to restore its legal tender character (February, 1878), he said: "I cannot approve a bill which in my judgment authorizes the violation of sacred obligations." But the bill was passed over his veto in both houses by majorities exceeding two-thirds. On Jan. 1, 1879, specie payments were resumed by the government without trouble, to the patent advantage of the country at large. In the thirty-sixth congress the democrats were in a majority in house and senate alike, and pursued their previous policy of withholding supplies, or passed appropriation bills with clauses in them which could constrain the executive to abandon his policy already entered on, of restoring civil order and securing free elections at the South. The whole matter, so far as it involved the adoption of legislation by means of special clauses or "riders" attached to appropriation bills was received by the president in connection with his veto of an army appropriation bill which had been passed with such objectionable attachments Apr. 9, 1879, and although the same policy was attempted by his opponents in the passage of other appropriation bills, he vetoed each as they came before him for his signature, and the house was obliged by the pressure of popular opinion to pass such amended and proper bills as the president required. March 2, 1880, he sent to congress a special message accompanied by copies of correspondence between the government of the United States and foreign powers in regard to the inter-oceanic canal project then under general discussion. It was a plain application of the Monroe doctrine to this question, declaring that "the policy of this country is a canal under American control. The United States cannot consent to surrender this control to any European power or to any combination of European powers." Congress now made one more attempt to attach a modification of election laws to an appropriation act, but the deficiency bill, to which it was affixed, received a veto May 4, 1880, and congress once more receded, removed the objectionable matter and passed the bill in such a form that the president could conscientiously sign it. The national republican convention met at Chicago, Ill., June 5, 1880, and the president had absolutely refused to have his name mentioned in connection with a re-nomination. This was in strict conformity with the declaration in his letter of acceptance of the republican candidacy in 1876. His last presidential message went to congress Dec. 6, 1880, and in it he set forth his views on civil service reform and its required legislation, the protection of Indian rights, the advanced but imperfect state of social order and civil rights of the South, the treatment of the exit of polygamy in Utah, popular education, silver coinage, etc. etc. He also recommended the creation of the grade of captain-general of the army with proper pay as a suitable acknowledgement for the services rendered to his country by Gen. Grant. President Hayes's last important official acts were a proclamation convening the U.S. senate in special session, March 4, 1881, to receive communications from his successor, and the veto of the act "to facilitate the refunding of the public debt." In closing the history of the work done at Washington during the four years of his official term, mention is to be made of the deep impression made by President Hayes and his wife upon its society, habits, customs. Alcoholic stimulants were for the first time banished from the highest public life, and at the same time a hospitality was exercised at the executive mansion, of which it has been said that it surpassed any known by a veteran American statesman during his forty years' experience. When the ex-president returned to his home sat Fremont, O., in 1881, it was largely to resume the management and development of his property, the beautifying of "Spugel Grove" (the residential name), the education and settlement of children. Three fields of public activity to which his energies were turned when he became a private citizen were the presentation of the personal associations of the old army while seeking to promote the welfare of its surviving members, the promotion of prison reform, and the advancement of popular education. He was president of the John F. Slater Educational Fund, president of the National Prison Reform Association, and of other charitable and educational institutions. Kenyon College, Harvard, Yale, and Johns Hopkins Universities all gave him LL.D. More than one Life has been written and well written, but that to which the author of this sketch was especially indebted is the Life by W. O. Stoddard (N.Y., 1889). He died Jan. 17, 1893.

HAYS, ALEXANDER, soldier, was born in Franklin, Venango county, Va., July 8, 1819. He was selected by the representative of his congressional district for a cadetship at the U.S. military academy, West Point, and admitted to that institution in 1840. He was graduated in 1844 in the class with Gens. Hancock and Pleasonton. His commission as second lieutenant in the U.S. army assigned him to the 8th infantry. The Mexican war gave the young soldier an opportunity for active service, and he won special distinction on the field near Atlixco. At the

close of the war he resigned his commission and settled in his native county, where he engaged in the manufacture of iron from 1848 to 1850. He then entered the employ of a railroad company as assistant civil engineer, where he remained four years, when he removed to Pittsburg and established himself as a civil engineer. At the beginning of the civil war in 1861, Lieut. Hays proffered his services to the government and was made colonel of the 63d Pennsylvania regiment of volunteers. The rank of captain in the U.S. army was conferred upon him, and he was assigned to the 16th regular infantry, his commission to date from May 14, 1861. His active service was with the 63d Pennsylvania, and he was at its head throughout the peninsular campaign, attached to the 1st brigade of Kearny's division, Heintzelman's corps. At the close of the seven days' contest before Richmond he had won, by his bravery on the field, the brevet of lieutenant-colonel in the regular service, and that of brigadier-general of volunteers after the Maryland campaign of 1862. He engaged in the battle of Chancellorsville, where he was wounded while leading his brigade. At the battle of Gettysburg, Gen. Hays commanded the 3d division of the 2d corps, and after Gen. Hancock was wounded Gen. Hays was temporarily in command of the corps until it could be assumed by Gen. Gibbon of the 2d division. Here he gained the brevet of colonel in the regular army. Upon the reorganization of the army of the Potomac, Gen. Hays commanded the 2d brigade of

Birney's 3d division of the 2d corps, and under Gen. Grant took part in the march upon Richmond. During the first day's fighting in the battle of the Wilderness, while Gen. Hays was cheering on his men to a desperate struggle against largely opposing numbers at the junction of the plank and brick roads, he received a mortal wound. The date of his death was May 5, 1864.

HAZEN, WILLIAM BABCOCK, soldier and signal officer, was born at West Hartford, Vt., Sept. 27, 1830. He was graduated from the West Point military academy in 1855, after which he spent five years with the 8th infantry on the western frontier, where he was twice badly wounded. At the breaking out of the civil war he was appointed temporary instructor at West Point, but he soon went to the front as colonel of the 41st Ohio volunteers, serving during the remainder of the war. In 1864 he was promoted a major-general "for long and continued services of the highest character, and for special gallantry and service at Ford McAllister." For fifteen years from 1865— with the exception of two six-month sojourns in Europe in 1870–71, and 1876–77—he did duty with the regular army on the frontier. In December 1880, he was promoted a brigadier-general and assigned as chief signal officer of the U.S. army. He took up his headquarters at Washington, and remained there until his death. His two visits to Europe referred to above were made in the interests of the U.S. government for the special purpose of studying European war methods; the first during the Franco-Prussian war, the second as a military attaché of the U.S. legation at Vienna during the Turco-Russian war. The results were afterward published in book form. Gen. Hazen is also the author of "Our Barren Lands" (1875), and of "A Narrative of Military Service," relating to

the civil war (1885). As chief signal officer he did much to improve the scientific character of the U.S. signal service. He employed expert physicists, meteorologists and electricians to conduct careful investigations, "emphasizing especially," to quote his own words, "the necessity of the study of instruments and methods of observing and investigation of the laws of changes going on in the atmosphere." Gen. Hazen heartily encouraged state weather bureaus and all institutions and societies of the science of meteorology. "One of his first acts," writes Prof. Abbe, "was the request for co-operation on the part of the National academy of sciences. He improved the opportunity to help Prof. Langley in the determination of the absorbing power of the atmosphere; he accepted Prof. King's offer to carry observers on his balloon voyages; he heartily furthered Lieut. Greely's efforts to maintain an international polar station, and joined with the coast survey in establishing a similar station under Lieut. Ray at the northern point of Alaska; he co-operated with the bureau of navigation in securing weather reports from

the ocean; he powerfully assisted the Meteorological society in its labors for the reformation of our complicated system of local times, the result of which was the adoption by the country of the present simple system of standard meridians one hour apart." He endeavored to elevate the personnel of the signal corps by securing the services of college graduates, and by establishing regular courses of instruction. He also devised many means for increasing the practical usefulness of the service to commerce and agriculture, co-operating with the telegraph and railroad companies and local boards of trade in displaying daily telegraph bulletins, railroad train-signals and flood-warnings. He died at Washington Jan. 16, 1887.

HEINTZELMAN, SAMUEL PETER, soldier, was born at Manheim, Lancaster co., Pa., Sept. 30, 1805. Through the influence of James Buchanan, he was appointed to the West Point Military Academy, where he was graduated in 1826. For seven years he was on garrison duty at various military posts in the West, and during 1832–34, he was engaged in surveying the Tennessee river. He saw considerable service in the Indian wars in Florida, and served in the quartermaster's department. He was commissioned captain, Nov. 4, 1838. He organized troops for the Mexican war at Louisville, Ky., was actively engaged in the battles of Paso las Ovejas and Huamantla, and the action of Atixco. He was commissioned major, Oct. 19, 1847, "for gallant and meritorious conduct." *This was a brevet appointment.* After the war, he was stationed at Fort Hamilton, New York harbor. In 1850–51, he led an expedition against the Yuma Indians, California, which terminated hostilities there, and established Fort Yuma, at the junction of the Gila and Colorado rivers. At the outbreak of the civil war, he assisted Gen. Scott in the defense of Washington, and was in command of the invasion of Virginia under Gen. Mansfield, having been commissioned brigadier-general of volunteers, May 17, 1861. He led his division in the first battle of Bull Run, when he was wounded in the arm. Upon the organization of the army of the Potomac, Heintzelman was assigned to the command of the 3d corps, and was in the siege of Yorktown and the battles of Williamsburg, Seven Pines, and Fair Oaks. He was brevetted major-general for his gallantry at Williamsburg. After the battle of Manassas he was assigned to the command of the northern department, with headquarters at Columbus, O., and in the uprising of 1864, he aided in organizing, arming, and sending off 40,000 Ohio militia in two weeks' time. He was relieved, Oct. 1st, and during the remainder of the war was waiting orders, or on court-martial duty. He was mustered out of the volunteer service, Aug. 24, 1865; resumed the command of his regiment at Hart's island, New York harbor, and after various routine duties he was retired with the rank of colonel, Feb. 22, 1869, which became major-general by special act of congress. He died May 1, 1880.

HELM, BEN HARDIN, soldier, was born *in Bardstown, Ky., on June 2, 1831,* the son of John Larue Helm, the governor of Kentucky in 1850–52, and re-elected in 1867. The father was descended from the pioneer settlers of Kentucky, who had become distinguished in

Indian warfare. He was educated to the law, and after admission to the bar was appointed county attorney. He served in the legislature in 1826–37; was state senator in 1844–48, and again in 1865–67, when he resigned. During seven years of the seventeen he served in the legislature he was presiding officer. In 1848 he was elected lieutenant-governor; became governor in 1850, retaining the office until 1852, and in 1854 was elected president of the Louisville and Nashville railroad. His constituency again chose him governor in 1866, and he was inaugurated at his residence in Elizabethtown Sept. 3, 1867. His death occurred five days afterward. Ben H. was graduated from West Point military academy

in 1851, assigned to the dragoon service, and went to the cavalry school at Carlisle, Pa., and afterward to frontier duty at Fort Lincoln, Tex. He resigned from military life Oct. 9, 1852, studied law, was admitted to the bar, practiced in Elizabethtown 1854–58, and in Louisville in 1858–61. He was a member of the legislature in 1855–56, and state's-attorney in 1856–58. At the breaking out of the civil war he joined the Confederate army, and was elected colonel of the 1st Kentucky cavalry, served with honor at Shiloh, and for bravery on the field was made brigadier-general March 14, 1862; took part in the battles of Peroyville and Stone river, when he was assigned to the command of a Kentucky brigade in Breckinridge's division, army of Tennessee, and ordered to Vicksburg. Thence he went in command of a brigade to Chickamauga, where he lost his life in battle, Sept. 20, 1863. *Helm was married to Emily Todd, one of Mary Todd Lincoln's sisters.*

HERRON, FRANCIS JAY, soldier, was born in Pittsburg, Pa., Feb. 17, 1837. He was graduated at the Western University of Pennsylvania in 1854, and removed in 1856 to Dubuque, Ia., where for some years he was a successful merchant, and also studied law. While a resident of Dubuque, he became captain of the "Governor's Grays," a military company, and on Jan. 15, 1861, tendered their services (the first proffer of troops to the government) to Secretary of War Holt, but the offer was declined on the ground that the "government had no need of troops at the time." In April, 1861, he was made captain in the 1st Iowa volunteers, and served under Gen. Lyon in the brilliant Missouri campaign, in which Lyon was killed. In September, 1861, he was made lieutenant-colonel of the 9th Iowa regiment, and commanded it during the subsequent operations in Arkansas, Missouri, and the Indian Territory.

At the battle of Pea ridge he was wounded and taken prisoner, but soon exchanged. He was promoted to brigadier-general of volunteers, July 16, 1862, and as commander of the army of the frontier, in November, 1862, marching 114 miles in three days, he fought the battle of Prairie grove, Dec. 7th, which destroyed Confederate rule north of the Arkansas river. The Confederates under Gens. Hindman, Marmaduke, Parsons, and Frost lost 1,317 in killed and wounded, and the Federal loss was 167 killed, 798 wounded, and 183 missing. For this he was made major-general of volunteers. During the siege of Vicksburg he commanded the left wing of Grant's army, and was one of the three officers selected to lead a division into the city after its surrender on July 4, 1863. Later he led the expedition that captured Yazoo City and the Confederate boats and supplies gathered there. He next commanded the 13th army corps on the Texas frontier and, acting under private instructions, gave material aid to Pres. Juarez, of Mexico, then at war with Maximilian, for which he received the thanks of Secretary Seward, and an offer from Juarez of a high command in the Mexican army. In March, 1865, he took command of the northern division of Louisiana, and in June, 1865, he received the surrender of Gens. Buckner and Smith, commanding the Confederate forces west of the Mississippi. *General Sterling Price escaped to Mexico and was not part of this surrender.* In July, 1865, he was appointed Indian commissioner. He resigned as commissioner and major-general *in June 7, 1865.* He commenced the practice of law in New Orleans, and aided in the work of reconstruction. During 1867–69, he was U.S. marshal for the district of Louisiana, and in 1872–73 secretary of state of Louisiana. In *1877* he removed to New York city, where he was president of a large manufacturing company. He was one of the most gallant and capable of the volunteer officers who served in the Union army during the civil war. Gen. Herron died in New York, Jan. 8, 1902.

HETH, HENRY, soldier, was born in Virginia in 1825, of old French war descent. His grandfather, William Heth (1735–1808) was an officer in Gen. Montgomery's regiment during the French war, and carried wounds received at Quebec. In the war of the revolution he joined the Continental army, and was in 1777 commissioned lieutenant-colonel of the 3d Virginia regiment, remaining in command until the end of the war. After the war he was duly remembered by Gen. Washington, by an appointment to a lucrative position. Henry Heth was graduated from West Point military academy in 1847, assigned to the 6th infantry, and rapidly advanced by successive grades until he had reached a captaincy in 1855. On the breaking out of the civil war he resigned from the Federal army, and cast his fortunes with the Confederacy, accepted a commission as major of a corps of infantry, March 16, 1861, and as colonel of the 45th Virginia infantry, June 17, 1861. He was made brigadier-general of *the Provisional Army of the Confederate States (P.A.C.S.),* Jan. 6, 1862, and was assigned to A. P. Hill's division, army of Northern Virginia *in February 1863; Heth had spent the previous eighteen months in West Virginia and Kentucky.* On May 24, 1863, he was commissioned major-general in the Confederate service. At Gettysburg in July, 1863, he led a division composed of Pettigrew's, Archer's, Davis's, Cook's, and Brockenborough's brigades, 3d corps, army of Northern Virginia, and performed brave service. After the close of the war he was engaged in business in South Carolina. *He died Sept. 27, 1889.*

HILL, AMBROSE POWELL, soldier, was born in Culpeper county, Va., Nov. 9, 1825, the son of Maj. Thomas Hill, a politician and merchant. He was graduated from West Point in 1847, and entered the United States army as second lieutenant of the 1st artillery. He afterward served in the Mexican and Florida wars, and attained the rank of captain. At the outbreak of the civil war he was connected with the United States coast survey, but at the secession of Virginia at once offered his services to his native state, and was appointed colonel of the 13th Virginia regiment, and ordered to Harper's Ferry. He was with Johnston at Manassas, and, after the battle, was brevetted brigadier-general *Feb. 26, 1862.* He occupied a conspicuous position at Williamsburg, and was soon afterward made a major-general *May 26, 1862.* He opened the seven days' fight around Richmond by driving the forces of McClellan from Meadow bridge, and took part in the second campaign against Pope and the second battle of Bull Run, and received the surrender of the Federal troops at Harper's Ferry Sept. 17, 1862, and, by making

a forced march, arrived at Sharpsburg in time to render Lee valuable service. His division formed the right of Jackson's corps at Fredericksburg, and the centre at Chancellorsville, and participated in the flank movement which crushed Hooker. Gen. Hill was severely wounded in this engagement. May 20, 1863, he was brevetted lieutenant-general, and *commissioned to the full rank of lieutenant-general May 24.* He was placed in command of a corps, which he led at Gettysburg, and participated in all the operations around Petersburg until he met his death. Contrary to the wishes of Gen. Lee, he attempted to reach Heth's division, and was shot from his horse by stragglers from the U.S. army. His body was recovered, taken to Coalfield and buried in the family burial-ground, and later his remains were removed to Hollywood cemetery, Richmond, Va., and recently (1891) have been interred in their final resting-place at the intersection of Laburnum avenue and the Hermitage road, Richmond, Va. A handsome monument is erected there to his memory by the A. P. Hill monument association. His wife was a Miss Morgan, sister of the Confederate general, John Morgan. He died near Petersburg, Va., Apr. 2, 1865.

HILL, BENJAMIN HARVEY, lawyer and statesman, was born in Jasper county, Ga., Sept. 14, 1823, son of John and Sarah (Parham) Hill, the latter a native of South Carolina, of Irish descent. Early in the nineteenth century John Hill removed to Jasper county, Ga., and thence to Troup county, where he continued the occupation of farming, aided by his sons. In 1840 Benjamin entered *the University of Georgia, located in Athens, Ga.*, and in 1844 was graduated there with first honors, receiving later the degrees of A.M. and LL.D. from that institution. He at once began the study of law;

was admitted to the bar in 1845, and opened an office at La Grange. While ever faithful to professional work, he gave considerable time to public questions, and in 1851 was elected by the Whigs to the lower house of the legislature. He was re-elected in 1852 and 1858, and served in the state senate in 1859–60. *Hill served a single term in the lower house 1851–52 and a single term in the state senate 1859–60. He had run for Congress in 1855 and for governor in 1857, losing both races.* In 1856 he was an elector for the state at large on the American, or Know-nothing ticket, and supported Millard Fillmore in speeches of great eloquence and power. His name was on the Bell and Everett electoral ticket of 1860, and he was sent as a Unionist to the state convention of 1861, where he opposed the passage of the secession ordinance, but finally voted in favor of that measure. He was elected to the provisional congress of 1861, and soon after to the senate of the Confederate States, where he remained until the war closed, heartily supporting the policy of Pres. Davis, who said of him, as distinguished from some others in the councils of the Confederacy, "I could place my hand upon his shoulder and feel that its foundation was as firm as marble." At the close of the war Sen. Hill was arrested at his home and was imprisoned for a few months at Fort Lafayette in New York harbor. He resumed the practice of his profession immediately after his liberation, and was not only successful, but was a potent factor in saving the property of his fellow citizens from the efforts of unauthorized agents of the government. He did not again enter politics until 1867, when he reorganized the Democratic party in Georgia for the purpose of resisting these measures. In a pamphlet from his pen entitled "Notes on the Situation," which had a widespread influence, occurs this striking passage: "Who saves his country saves himself, saves all things; and all things saved do bless him. Who lets his country die, dies himself ignobly, and all things dying curse him." Mr. Hill supported Horace Greeley for the presidency in 1872. In 1875 his political disabilities having been removed, he was elected to the national house of representatives to fill a vacancy, and on Jan. 11, 1876, had a memorable debate with James G. Blaine on the question of amnesty, in the course of which he defended Pres. Davis against Mr. Blaine's

charges of direct responsibility for the deaths of Union prisoners at Andersonville, and in the course of which he said, speaking for the South: "We are in the house of our fathers. Our brothers are our companions, and we are at home to stay, thank God!" Another notable speech was that delivered on June 11th, on the use of troops at elections. He was re-elected without opposition in 1876, but before taking his seat was elected to the senate, and served for four years, up to the time of his death. Among the speeches made in congress was one denouncing William Mahone's coalition with the Republican party. He was recognized as the leader of the senate, and was chiefly potential in his efforts to bring about a complete reconciliation between the North and South. His speeches and writings were models of beauty and force, replete with splendid imagery and cogent reasoning, blending the elegant graces of a Virgil with the exact logic of a Plato. He loved the Union and the constitution with an idolatrous devotion, and gave the best energies of his life to their preservation. He only consented to the secession of the southern states as he would to the death of his father—from necessity—and in opposing the madness of secession he exclaimed: "I would not give the American union for African slavery, and if slavery dares strike the Union, slavery will perish." In the reconstruction period, when the bravest hearts quailed and almost despaired, Sen. Hill rose to the grandest heights of statesmanship, when spoilsmen threatened constitutional liberty and the very life of the American government, his voice rang out clear and strong in such sentences as "The Constitution inviolate, the Union its surest defense"; "My country, my whole country, and nothing but my country!" Sen. Hill was married at Athens, Ga., Nov. 27, 1845, to Caroline E., daughter of——and Sarah (Moore) Holt. She bore him two daughters and two sons. The eldest daughter, Mary, became the wife of J. Edgar Thompson of Atlanta, in 1867; the younger the wife of Dr. Robert B. Ridley of La Grange, Ga., in 1875. Benjamin Harvey Hill, Jr., was associated with his father in the practice of law. In 1877 he was appointed a solicitor-general; in 1882 was re-elected; in 1885 refused a third election, and was appointed by Pres. Cleveland U.S. attorney for the northern district of Georgia. He was married, in 1874, to Mary Carter, of the distinguished Virginia family of that name. She died without

issue, and in 1893 he was married to Janie M. Hill, of Wilkes county, Ga. Charles Dougherty Hill, the second son, was married, in 1870, to Caroline Hughes. He has been for many years solicitor-general of the Atlanta circuit. Sen. Hill died Aug. 16, 1882, at Atlanta, which had been his home for many years. A statue of heroic size, carved from Italian marble, stands in the grounds of the state capitol, "Erected by his fellow-citizens in commemoration of the indomitable courage, unrivalled eloquence and devoted patriotism characterizing the illustrious dead."

HILL, DANIEL HARVEY, soldier, was born at Hill's iron works, York district, S.C., July 12, 1821. On both his father's and his mother's side he was descended from American soldiers, and his earliest aspirations were for a soldier's life. In furtherance of this desire he, at sixteen, secured an appointment to West Point, and was, in 1842, graduated from that institution in a class that afterward furnished twelve generals to the Federal army and eight to the Confederate. Upon graduation he was assigned to the 4th artillery, and served in various garrisons until the opening of the Mexican war. He took part in every important battle of this war, and was one of the few officers in the whole army who were twice brevetted, having been made brevet captain for "gallant and meritorious conduct" in the battles of Contreras and Churubusco, and brevet major for being a volunteer in the desperate storming party at Chapultepec. In the assaults on the works of Chatultepec, he and Lieut. Stewart had a foot-race, to see which could first force his way into a stoutly defended Mexican fort. At the close of the war the state of South Carolina presented him with a gold sword as a token of its appreciation of his services. Shortly after the treaty of peace was ratified, Maj. Hill resigned his commission, and accepted the professorship of mathematics in what later became Washington and Lee university, but was then known as Washington college. After five years of work there, he was elected to the same chair in Davidson college, N.C., where he did much to build up a high standard of scholarship. In 1859 he was called to the presidency of the North Carolina military institute at Charlotte, an institution from which were culled many of the noblest young officers that fell in the Confederacy. In 1861 Gov. Ellis invited Maj. Hill to Raleigh, to organize the first camp of instruction in the state. Shortly afterward, as colonel of the 1st North Carolina regiment, he fought, at Big Bethel, the first important battle of the war. Promoted to be a brigadier-general, he took part in the Yorktown defences, and then, as a major-general, he commanded a division in the great battles around Richmond. At Seven Pines his division drove Casey from his entrenchments and, aided only by Jenkins's brigade, repulsed, after a desperate battle, the whole of Keyes's corps. He took part in the Maryland campaign, and during Lee's retreat into Virginia he fought, single-handed, the battle of South Mountain, or Boonesboro, one that has often been called the Thermopylae of the war, for, with 5,000 men Gen. Hill held these mountain passes against McClellan's 80,000, from sunrise until three o'clock, and by this bold stand enabled Jackson to reunite with Lee, and this junction saved the Confederate army from being crushed. *The battle of South Mountain occurred on September 14, 1862, as a prelude to the battle of Antietam three days later, not "during Lee's retreat." Union forces in this battle were about 28,000, not 80,000, and while Hill originally had about 5,000 men he was reinforced to a strength of nearly 15,000 before the battle was over.* Gen. Hill was hotly engaged at Sharpsburg, and at Fredericksburg. During Gen. Lee's invasion of Pennsylvania, he entrusted Gen. Hill with the command of the defences around Petersburg and Richmond. In the fall of 1863 he was promoted to be a lieutenant-general, and sent to command a corps in the western army, and his command made a brilliant record in the bloody battle of Chickamauga. For some years after the war Gen. Hill conducted a monthly magazine, "The Land we Love," at Charlotte, N.C. In 1877 he was invited to assume the presidency of the University of Arkansas, and labored successfully there until 1884. After a year's rest in Macon, Ga., he accepted the presidency of the Military and agricultural college at Milledgeville, and remained there until within a few weeks of his death. Gen. Hill was a constant contributor to periodical literature, and is the author of three books: "A Consideration of the Sermon on the Mount" (1858); "The Crucifixion of Christ" (1860), and "The Elements of Algebra." Gen. Hill died at Charlotte, N.C., Sept. 24, 1889.

HOKE, ROBERT FREDERICK, army officer and industrialist, was born in Lincolnton, N.C., May 27, 1837, son of Michael and Frances (Burton) Hoke, grandson of John and Barbara (Quickel) Hoke, great-grandson of John and Maria Sabina (Swope) Hoke, and great-great-grandson of Michael Hoke, who came to America from Alsace or Lorraine (later part of France) in 1709 and settled in New York city, later removing to York County, Pa. His father was a lawyer. After receiving his preliminary education at the Male Academy, Lincolnton, Robert F. Hoke was graduated at the Kentucky Military Institute in 1854. After leaving the military school he remained in Lincolnton to help his widowed mother in the management of various family business

interests. These included cotton, paper, iron, and linseed and cottonseed oil mills. The cottonseed oil mill, one of the earliest established in this country, was built in 1819, and the cotton mill was founded by one of his great-grandfathers and the iron works by another. Later he also studied law in Washington, D.C. In 1861 he enlisted as 2d lieutenant in Co. K, 1st North Carolina Volunteers, and participated in the first battle at Bethel, N.C. He was promoted rapidly, becoming a major of the regiment in 1861. He later was made a lieutenant colonel of the 33d North Carolina Infantry and colonel of the 21st North Carolina Regiment. In the latter capacity in December, 1862, he commanded a brigade that was posted in the second line at the Battle of Fredericksburg. Following a Federal assault on the front line which resulted in the capture of a brigade and the death of a general, Hoke, without hesitation and without waiting for orders, brought his troops forward, restored the line, released the captured Confederate brigade, and captured the Federal forces. For this distinguished action in January, 1863, he was commissioned brigadier general and assigned to command of

a brigade comprising the 6th, 21st, 54th and 57th North Carolina regiments, which brigade served in the Army of Northern Virginia in the division of Jubal A. Early. Hoke himself was wounded at the Battle of Chancellorsville and thus did not take part in the fighting at Gettysburg. Late in 1863 he was sent to the piedmont region of the Carolinas to deal with the problems of desertion and outlawry and later was assigned to tidewater North Carolina. In April, 1864, with the aid of the ram "Albemarle," he captured from Federal troops the town of Plymouth, N.C., taking many prisoners and much equipment. For the success of this important maneuver, he was promoted to major general on the battlefield by Jefferson Davis and given command of a full division known as Hoke's Division, composed of several brigades of the Army of Northern Virginia. Hoke served with distinction at the Battle of Cold Harbor, where his division withstood the brunt of the Federal forces' onslaught. Later, returning to North Carolina, he took part in engagements at Wilmington and Bentonville, and in 1865 he was in command of a division in the army of Joseph E. Johnston. He surrendered with Johnston at Durham Station on Apr. 26, 1865. Following his discharge from the Confederate Army Hoke was engaged in various business activities until the close of his life. Among his principal interests were gold and iron mining in Lincoln County, N.C., his association with the Cranberry (N.C.) Iron Mines, and his building of a narrow gauge railroad called the East Tennessee & Northwestern from Johnson City, Tenn., to Cranberry. In addition he owned his own feldspar and kaolin mines at Brown Mountain, N.C. He built and became president in 1890 of the Georgia, Carolina & Northern Railroad Co. (later part of the Seaboard Air Line Co.), and continued in that capacity for eight years. He was also president at one time of the North Carolina Home Insurance Co. Zebulon B. Vance, former governor of the state, appointed Hoke a director of the North Carolina Railroad Co., in which post he continued until his death. Hoke County in North Carolina was named in his honor, and during the Second World War a Liberty Ship was christened with his name. His religious affiliation was with the Episcopal church. Politically he was a Democrat. He was married in New York city, Jan. 7, 1869, to Lydia Ann, daughter of William Van Wyck of that city, an attorney, and had six children: Robert Frederick; Van Wyck; Michael; Lydia, who married Alexander Webb; Frances Burton, who married William Durward Pollock; and Anderson. His death occurred in Lincoln, N.C., July 3, 1912.

HOLLINS, GEORGE NICHOLS, naval officer, was born in Baltimore, Md., Sept. 20, 1799. At the age of fifteen he entered the navy as a midshipman, and served on the sloop-of-war Erie, being on board that vessel at the time of her attempt to break the British blockade in the Chesapeake bay. Later he was assigned to the President, under Com. Decatur. Having grounded while going to sea, the President was surrounded by three British frigates, being compelled, after an obstinate resistance, to surrender. Twenty-five of her crew were killed, sixty were wounded and the remainder taken prisoners. Hollins was held at Bermuda until the establishment of peace. In 1815 he again served under Decatur in the Algerian war, where for his bravery exhibited in the capture of a frigate he received from the commodore a magnificent Turkish sabre. He afterward served on the Guerriere, the Columbus, the Franklin, the Washington, then took command of an East Indian merchantman; *was promoted lieutenant in 1828 and commander in 1841.*

While he was serving off the coast of Nicaragua in *1854* the American residents of Greytown being harassed by the local authorities, appealed to Hollins for protection. He acted promptly in demanding reparation and proper treatment for the Americans, and his demands not being complied with, he as promptly shelled the town. Nicaragua being then under the protection of the British government, an international complication arose. The English residents resented what they deemed an interference, and claimed that their property and lives had been imperilled by the "encroachments" of the United States. Thus serious difficulties between Great Britain and the United States were for a time apprehended. In 1861 Com. Hollins resigned his commission with a view to joining the Confederate navy, but his resignation was refused and an order issued for his arrest. He skilfully eluded the authorities, however, and, making his way to the South, was commissioned commodore, in charge of the Confederate battering ram Manassas. On the night of Oct. 12, 1861, while the Federal fleet was lying at anchor inside the southwest pass of the Mississippi, Hollins drove his ram against the sides of the Richmond, striking her below the water line with such force as to knock a hole in her timbers and tear her from her fastenings. Thereupon an effective broadside was poured into the ram, but Hollins signaled for support, and five ships came down the river, threatening the complete destruction of the fleet. In this effort to break the Federal blockade of the Crescent City great reliance was placed upon the Manassas. This vessel had the appearance of a floating roof, with two smoke-stacks projecting from its ridge pole; and though carrying a single heavy gun, being iron-clad, was very effective as a ram. She was sunk in April, 1862, during a fight with the Federal fleet. For his services to the

Confederate navy Hollins was appointed flag captain of the New Orleans station, but was superseded by Com. Wm. C. Whipple prior to Farragut's attack in 1862. After the war he retired to civil pursuits, and became a crier in the city court of Baltimore. He was a man of rare abilities, and experienced strange vicissitudes during his career. He died in Baltimore, Md., Jan. 18, 1878.

HOLMES, OLIVER WENDELL, jurist, was born in Boston, Mass., Mar. 8, 1841, son of Oliver Wendell Holmes, the eminent physician, essayist, novelist and poet, and Amelia Lee (Jackson) Holmes. His grandfather, Abiel Holmes, was pastor of the First Congregational Church at Cambridge, Mass., for forty years and an historian of note. His mother was a daughter of Charles Jackson, a member of the Supreme Judicial Court of Massachusetts, on which her son was to sit for twenty years. Young Holmes grew to manhood in an exhilarating intellectual environment peopled by such celebrities in the domain of letters and philosophy as, besides his father, Ralph Waldo Emerson, John Greenleaf Whittier, Henry Wadsworth Longfellow, Wendell Phillips, Theodore Parker, Henry David Thoreau, James Russell Lowell, Nathaniel Hawthorne, Edward Everett and others of a distinguished company representing the "golden age of American literature." From his early association with such men as these, he derived much of the culture and love of learning that distinguished in a superlative degree his own career. After obtaining his preparatory education at T. R. Sullivan's Latin school in Cambridge, Holmes went to Harvard where he was graduated with an A.B. degree in 1861. On the outbreak of the Civil war, in April 1861, he joined the 4th battalion of infantry in Boston and in July was commissioned a first lieutenant in the 20th

regiment, Mass. volunteer infantry, known as the "Harvard regiment," which stood fifth on the roll of northern regiments that suffered the heaviest losses during the war. In his first battle, at Ball's Bluff, Va., on the Potomac, Oct. 21, 1861, a Confederate bullet pierced his breast, barely missing his heart. After a long convalescence in Boston, he rejoined his regiment in the spring of 1862 and was promoted to the captaincy of company G, which he commanded at the Battle of Seven Pines and through the Seven Days' campaign on the Virginia peninsula. At Antietam, Md., *Sept. 17, 1862,* he was again dangerously wounded, a ball passing through his neck. His father hastened from Boston to care for him and his efforts to locate his wounded son furnished the inspiration for his essay, "My Hunt After the Captain." After another prolonged recovery at home, Holmes returned to his regiment in November 1862 and a month later participated with it in the battle of Fredericksburg, Va., where the Federal army suffered a crushing defeat. On May 3, 1863, when the 20th Mass., with other Federal army units, crossed the Rappahannock at Fredericksburg en route to Chancellorsville, where both sides were massing troops for another historic battle, it was met by Confederate artillery fire from Marye's hill and Holmes received a third serious wound, a shrapnel fragment mangling one heel so badly that for a time it was feared he would lose the leg. He was again invalided home where he made a safe recovery but was unable to return to his command until Jan. 29, 1864. He was then appointed aide-de-camp on the staff of Maj. Gen. Horatio G. Wright and was brevetted lieutenant colonel. On the expiration of his term of enlistment in July 1864, he was mustered out of the service, returned to Boston and in the fall of that year entered Harvard law school. Two years later he was graduated with an LL.B. degree. He then went to London where he formed lifelong friendships with Frederick Pollock and Frederic Maitland, who were destined to do for English law what Holmes later did for American law. After a walking tour of England and a sojourn in Switzerland mountain climbing with Sir Leslie Stephen, he returned to Boston and spent several months reading law in the office of Robert M. Morse. He was admitted to the bar in 1867 and for fifteen years practiced law in Boston, first in partnership with his brother, Edward Jackson Holmes, then with the firm of Chandler, Shattuck & Thayer, and from 1873 until 1882 as a member of the firm of Shattuck, Holmes & Munroe. During this period he held various teaching appointments at Harvard, being an instructor in constitutional law in 1870, instructor in the Constitution of the United States in 1870–71, university lecturer in 1871–72 and lecturer on jurisprudence in the law school in 1872–73. From 1876 to 1882 he served on the university's board of overseers. For three years (1870–73) he was also an editor of the "American Law Review," then the leading legal periodical in this country. To this publication he contributed numerous learned articles, reviews and editorials which commanded wide attention and revealed thus early the exceptional qualities of his mind and his remarkable insight into the law. During this same period he edited the 12th edition of James Kent's "Commentaries on American Law" (4 volumes, 1873), which he annotated with English and French decisions that brought the "Commentaries" down to date from the death of its author twenty-five years before. This work, which made Holmes famous on both sides of the Atlantic, has since remained the standard edition of Chancellor Kent's noted text. During his editorship of the "American Law Review," Holmes had written several

articles on the common law and in the winter of 1880–81 he delivered at the Lowell institute in Boston, a series of lectures on the same subject. These articles and lectures he later elaborated into a book, "The Common Law," which established his reputation as a legal scholar of the first magnitude (1881). "The Common Law," which was translated into the principal languages of continental Europe, was the fruit of an amazing amount of research into the origins of law. It was in reality a work on comparative law, utilizing the Roman and other systems to illustrate the beginning and growth of English law, and has been called the first "worth while work in pure legal history as distinguished from anthropology." The London "Spectator" pronounced it "the most original work on legal speculation which has appeared in English since the publication of Sir Henry Maine's 'Ancient Law,' whose materials it supplements and whose generalizations it exemplifies in many respects." The renown that resulted from its publication led to a professorship at Harvard law school in 1882 and, in December of the same year, to an appointment as an associate justice of the Supreme Judicial Court of Massachusetts, on which he took his seat, Jan. 3, 1883. On Aug. 2, 1889, he became chief justice of the court, serving for more than three years. To the already high standing of that tribunal, Holmes made a distinguished contribution both by the pre-eminent quality of his work and by the influence of his strong and vivid personality on his colleagues. There he gave one of the earliest and best-known of his famous dissents, in Vegelahn v. Gunter (167 Mass. 92), wherein he upheld the right of striking employees to picket their employer's premises, indicating unmistakably his attitude toward the legal aspects of social questions. This opinion asserted that the "policy of allowing free competition justifies the intentional inflicting of temporal damages, including damage of interference with a man's business, by some means, when damage is done not for its own sake, but as an instrumentality in reaching the end of victory in the battle of trade." After twenty years of eminent service as a member of the Massachusetts court, President Theodore Roosevelt appointed Holmes an associate justice of the Supreme Court of the United States in December 1902, to succeed Justice Horace Gray, resigned. He sat with the nation's highest tribunal until Jan. 12, 1932, when, being then in the ninety-first year of his age, he resigned. At the time of his retirement he was the senior of any of his associates by many years and the oldest member in the history of

the court. Even then his remarkable mental faculties showed no signs of impairment but his physical strength had begun to fail. In his nearly fifty years of service on the bench Holmes signally elevated the level of American jurisprudence, leaving upon it the imprint of his scholarship and philosophy. Although an aristocrat by birth and breeding and all his life a firm believer in the régime of private property, he consistently championed in his opinions the constitutional provisions made to safeguard the rights of the individual man and defended the right of legislatures to advance the cause of human rights as against property rights. It was said of him that he stood first among the jurists of the English-speaking world in the development of the sociological or social-scientific method of modern jurisprudence. It was one of the cardinal principles of his juridical faith that the framers of the Constitution intended it to conform with realistic public policy and changing social and economic conditions and that the legislatures of the several states should be permitted to experiment with reforms which they believed would promote the common good without judicial interference unless their enactments violated some express prohibition in the Constitution of the United States or in the state constitutions. Thus, in one of his wisest opinions (dissenting in Truax v. Corrigan, 257 U.S. 404), he deprecated the extension of the Constitution beyond its expressed limitations "to prevent the making of social experiments that an important part of the community desires . . . even though the experiments may seem futile or even obnoxious to me and to those whose judgment I most respect." "If there is one principle of the United States Constitution," he wrote in another opinion, "that more imperatively calls for attachment than any other, it is the principle of free thought. Not free thought for those who agree with us but freedom for the thought that we hate." In this thesis, which Holmes emphasized again and again, he clearly revealed his conviction that the private opinions of judges as to the merits of a law should not be permitted to interfere with their determination of its constitutionality. Thus, he was a strong supporter of the national prohibition act, not because he believed in prohibition as a government policy but because he believed the American people had the right to have prohibition if they wished it and the right to enforce it by every reasonable method. He had little regard for the sanctity of precedents purely as precedents, declaring that "It is revolting to have no better reason for a rule of law than that it was laid down in the time of Henry IV." To an extraordinary degree he possessed the ability to approach every case that came before him with a mind wholly aloof from any consideration except that of reaching what seemed to him the correct result, without regard to its apparent magnitude or the degree of public interest in the decision. The singularly liberal trend of his mind was further illustrated in opinions which he wrote sustaining a state law guaranteeing bank deposits (the banks bearing the cost); affirming the right to compel employers to bear the burden of industrial accidents through liability insurance; holding that corporations could be taxed for owning stock in other corporations, though individuals holding the same stock were exempt, and declaring that railroads could be forced to eliminate grade crossings without receiving compensation. These enactments benefited the humble citizen at the expense of private property and it is a tribute to Holmes's persuasive power that he was able to convince his colleagues that there was nothing in the Constitution to prevent them. "Constitutional rights," he said, "like others, are matters of degree and the great constitutional provisions are not to be pushed to a logical extreme, but must be taken to permit the infliction of some fractional, relatively small losses, without compensation, for at least some of the purposes of wholesome legislation." In his nearly thirty years as a member of the Supreme Court of the United States, Holmes wrote more than 1000 of its decisions. Although he concurred with the majority of the court in about 90 per cent of the cases, he was probably best known for his dissenting opinions. One of the first and most famous of these was filed in the celebrated Northern Securities case (Northern Securities Co. v. United States, 193 U.S. 400). James J. Hill and J. Pierpont Morgan had organized the Northern Securities Co. as a holding company to consolidate the ownership of the Northern Pacific, the Great Northern and the Chicago, Burlington & Quincy railroads. By direction of President Theodore Roosevelt, Attorney General Philander C. Knox instituted proceedings seeking dissolution of the company as a combination in restraint of competition and therefore in violation of the Sherman antitrust law. When the case reached the Supreme Court of the United States on appeal in 1903, the government's contention was sustained by a five-four decision, Holmes writing a dissenting opinion which astonished and deeply irritated the President who had so recently appointed him a member of the court. Seventeen years later, in the railway act of 1920, congress in effect upheld the position Holmes had taken by authorizing the consolidation of the railway lines of the country. Illustrating his passionate devotion to the principle of liberty of thought and speech were his dissenting opinions in Abrams v. United States (250 U.S. 616) and United States v. Schwimmer (279 U.S. 644). In the former action, in which three radicals had been convicted under the espionage act,

Holmes declared that "In this case sentences of twenty years' imprisonment have been imposed for the publication of two leaflets that I believe the defendants had as much right to publish as the government has to publish the Constitution of United States," adding that "the most nominal punishment seems to me to be all that possibly could be inflicted, unless the defendants are to be made to suffer not for what the indictment alleges but for the creed that they avow—a creed that I believe to be the creed of ignorance and immaturity." In the Schwimmer case, the majority decision denied citizenship to Madam Rosika Schwimmer, a Hungarian socialist, because she refused to take the usual oath to bear arms in defense of the United States. After remarking that the defendant, being a woman, "would not be allowed to bear arms even if she wanted to," Holmes closed his dissent with the statement: "Recurring to the opinion that bars this applicant's way, I suggest that the Quakers have done their share to make the country what it is, that many citizens agree with the applicant's belief, and that I had not supposed hitherto that we regretted our inability to expel them because they believe more than some of us do in the teachings of the Sermon on the Mount." In his dissent in Lochner v. New York (198 U.S. 45), in which the majority of the court had held unconstitutional a statute that limited employment in bakeries to ten hours a day, Holmes gave a famous expression of his liberal views on economic problems, stating, in effect, that the court could not apply to child labor, or the minimum wage, to public utilities or the exercise of governmental power, the methods or principles which the nineteenth century deemed final. In numerous cases based on the 14th Amendment, Holmes's powerful dissents were directed against those conservative judges who saw in every legislative attempt to better the conditions of the common man an invalid taking of property "without due process of law" as in the civil rights cases his dissents were aimed at those who saw in every exercise of the constitutional right of free speech a violation of some harsh sedition law and a menace to property rights. His opinions were distinguished not only for their erudition and for his liberal and philosophic interpretations of law or the Constitution, but for their perfect clarity, brilliant witticisms, epigrams and faultless diction. No one was ever left in doubt as to the meaning that his words sought to convey or failed to be impressed by the logic and strength of his reasoning. Always his opinions made fascinating reading. The epigrammatic quality of his style was disclosed in such classic aphorisms as these: "The Fourteenth Amendment . . . did not destroy history for the states and substitute mechanical compartments of law all exactly alike"; "The Fourteenth Amendment does not enact Mr. Herbert Spencer's 'social statics'"; "Legal obligations that exist but cannot be enforced are ghosts that are seen in the law but that are elusive to the grasp"; "The life of the law has not been logic; it has been experience"; "The law . . . cannot be dealt with as if it contained only the axioms and corollaries in a book of mathematics," and "That at any rate is the theory of our Constitution. It is an experiment, as all life is an experiment." One of Holmes's greatest assets, both on and off the bench, was the surprising quickness with which he assimilated and arranged facts and arrived at conclusions. His opinions which he wrote with a pen—he never dictated—in a firm, unwavering hand, ordinarily were prepared much more speedily than those of his colleagues and he was sometimes called upon to write opinions for other justices. On one occasion, he even wrote the majority opinion in a case in which he was actually dissenting. Possessed of that passionate devotion to the law which a great painter feels for art or a scientist for science, Holmes dedicated to its service all the resources of his rich and varied talents. Yet he was a man of many interests. Driven by insatiable intellectual curiosity, not only did he keep abreast of the latest philosophic and economic trends, but he read widely outside those special fields. An omnivorous reader, he enjoyed books of all kinds, ranging from the works of Plato, Thucydides and Horace Walpole down to the latest popular novels. He was fond of the theatre and of etchings and paintings, wrote a number of excellent poems and took little interest in politics. A gallant gentleman of the old New England school, he had many personal friends in all walks of life and was a social favorite in Washington. His conversation was characterized by rare brilliance and charm. In the company of women he had the ease and gaiety of a Parisian or a Viennese and whatever the type of man that life threw in his path he met him with singular ease and understanding and treated him as an equal. With an indomitable spirit and intellectual and moral integrity so obvious and absolute as to be apparent to all the world, he combined ardent patriotism, dauntless courage, thoughtfulness, generosity, unfailing courtesy and an unquenchable spirit of youth. When he read an opinion in court or delivered a public address, his auditors listened to him with profound interest, charmed by the wealth of his culture, fascinated by his rare gift of style, enriched in their own intellectual lives by the examples of his wisdom, his humanity and his forward-looking social philosophy. Among American judges and lawyers he was easily the foremost figure of his time and to many he ranked with the classic figures of Anglo-American legal history. In sweep and strength of intellectual power and wise statesmanship, he was frequently compared to John Marshall, famed chief justice of the United States. Many of the leading legal authorities of the English-speaking world acknowledged the debt they owed to his teaching and illustrious example. John H. Wigmore, long dean of Northwestern university law school, wrote of him: "He enriched our law, our literature and our philosophy . . . His opinions shine with an historical light which, in its lustre of distinction, ought to be even as the Penang diamond, a lure to the avid ambition of the judicial world." The opinion of Holmes held by Justice Benjamin N. Cardozo, his successor on the Supreme Court of the United States bench, who saw in him "the greatest of our age in the domain of jurisprudence and one of the greatest of the ages," was thus epitomized: "To the lips of eager youth comes at times the halting doubt whether law in its study and its profession can fill need for what is highest in the yearnings of the human spirit. Thus challenged I do not argue. I point the challenger to Holmes." The British estimate of him was well expressed by Prof. Harold J. Laski, professor of political science at the University of London, in these words: "Since John Marshall revealed to the American people what their new Constitution might imply, none has so clearly molded its texture as Mr. Justice Holmes. He stands out in its history not merely as one of the two or three most significant figures in the record, but also as one of the supreme expositors of principle in the annals of the Common Law . . . To read his opinions as a whole is to know what Montesquieu would have been like had he presided over a modern court. He too, like that great pathfinder, has made his place in the canonical succession of those who push forward the boundaries of wisdom in legal institutions." Besides his "The Common Law", Holmes published two volumes, "Speeches" (1891, 1913), and "Collected Legal Papers" (1920). He was a corresponding fellow of the British Academy and a member of the Massachusetts Historical Society. He was awarded the honorary LL.D. degree by Yale (1886) and Harvard (1895) universities and Williams college (1912); that of D.C.L. by Oxford university (1909), and that of J.U.D. by the University of Berlin (1910). In 1924 he received the Roosevelt medal from the Roosevelt Memorial Association for "the development of public law." In his will Holmes bequeathed the residue of his very substantial estate to the U.S. government. He was married at Cambridge, Mass., June 16, 1872, to Fanny, daughter of Epes Sargeant Dixwell, principal of Dixwell's Latin School, Cambridge, and died, without issue, in Washington, D.C., Mar. 6, 1935.

HOLMES, THEOPHILUS HUNTER, soldier, was born in Sampson county, N.C., *Nov. 13, 1804,* son of Gabriel Holmes, who was governor of that state (1821–24). He was graduated at the U.S. Military Academy, West Point, in 1829, and was promoted second lieutenant, 7th infantry, July 1, 1829. He served on frontier duty in Louisiana, on Arkansas river and in the Indian Territory, 1830–36; became first lieutenant 7th infantry, March 26, 1835; served on recruiting service and in removing the Cherokees to the West, 1838–39; became captain of 7th infantry, Dec. 9, 1838; served in the Seminole wars in Florida, 1839–42; was on garrison duty in Louisiana and Mississippi, 1842–45; was in the military occupation of Texas, 1845–46; in the war with Mexico, 1846–48, and was brevetted major for gallantry at Monterey, Mexico, Sept. 23, 1846. He served in Florida against the Seminoles in 1849–50; was on garrison duty in Missouri, Kansas,

Indian Territory, Texas and New Mexico, 1850–59; was promoted major 8th infantry, March 3, 1855, and was superintendent of the general recruiting service July 1, 1859, to April 6, 1861. He resigned April 22, 1861, and on June 5, 1861 was appointed by Pres. Davis a brigadier-general in the Confederate army. He was first assigned to duty in North Carolina, where he selected officers for the state troops; was promoted major-general, Oct. 7, 1861, and was in command of the district of Fredericksburg, Va., and of the forces that held the Potomac in the winter of 1861–62; was transferred to the district of North Carolina in 1862. He was promoted lieutenant-general, Oct. 10, 1862, and put in command of the district of Arkansas, and was at one time in command of Daniels', Walker's and Wise's brigades, army of northern Virginia. In August, 1863, he was in command of the paroled prisoners of Mississippi, Arkansas, Missouri, Texas and Louisiana, recently a part of the garrison of Vicksburg. In 1864 his health became poor, and he was assigned in April to command the reserve forces in North Carolina, with headquarters at Raleigh. These he organized and put on a strong footing. After the war was over he cultivated a farm near Fayetteville, N.C. He was married, June 4, 1841, to Laura, daughter of Ichabod Wetmore, of Fayetteville, N.C., niece of Hon. George C. Badger. They had eight children. He died at his home, *June 21, 1880.*

HOOD, JOHN BELL, general, was born at Owenville, Ky., June 1, 1831. He was graduated from the West Point military academy in 1853, served in California from 1853 till 1855, and then became connected with the 2d cavalry under Albert Sidney Johnston. In 1858 he was promoted first lieutenant, and from 1859 till 1860 he was cavalry instructor at the military

academy. He resigned his commission at the outbreak of the civil war, to enter the Confederate army, in which he became colonel, and soon after, brigadier-general of the Texas brigade. He was ordered back to the peninsula, and in the battle of Gaines's Mills, in which he lost half of his men, was shot in the body. His bravery on this occasion was immediately rewarded, and he was brevetted major-general on the field. He served in both campaigns in Maryland, in the second engagement of Bull Run, and in the battles of Boonesborough, Fredericksburg, and Antietam, and at Gettysburg July 1–3, 1863, was so severely wounded that he lost the use of his arm. In September he rejoined his command, and was ordered to Tennessee to reinforce Gen. Bragg, and in the second day's fight at Chickamauga, fought in the most courageous manner, rallying the wavering troops, and charging at the head of the Texas troops, to fall, badly wounded in the leg. He was removed to the hospital, where his leg was amputated, but the undaunted soldier refused to leave the service to accept a civil position that was offered him. After six months he returned to the field, was assigned to a command in Gen. Joseph E. Johnston's army, and took an active part in the fighting that occurred during the retreat from Dalton to Atlanta. On July 17, 1864, Gen. Johnston was removed from the command of the Confederate army, by order of President Davis, and Gen. Hood was put in charge; the army turned over to him consisting of some 50,600 veterans. Gen. Hood lost no time in assuming the aggressive, and arranged for a battle on the 20th, which took place not far from Decatur, and was repeated on the 22d, in a desperate engagement known as the battle of Atlanta,

with heavy losses on both sides. Gen. Hood compelled the evacuation of Decatur in November; and then made a movement into Tennessee, where, on the 30th of that month, he was defeated at Franklin by Gen. John M. Schofield, and as a result of this engagement, and that at Nashville on Dec. 16th, in which he was opposed by Gen. Thomas, Gen. Hood's army was reduced to about 23,000 men. After this battle Gen. Hood, who, though the bravest of fighters, was not considered, by many of the Confederate service, the equal of Gen. Johnston in military ability, requested to be relieved from command, and was succeeded by Gen. Richard Taylor. At the close of the war he removed to New Orleans, where he engaged in the commission business, and became president of the Louisiana branch of the Life association of America. His experiences were recorded by him in "Advance and Retreat: Personal Experiences in the United States and Confederate Armies" (New Orleans, 1880). Gen. Hood lost his wife and eldest child during the yellow fever epidemic of 1879, and died of the same disease on Aug. 30th of that year.

HOOKER, JOSEPH, soldier, was born at Hadley, Mass., Nov. 13, 1814. He received a good preliminary education, *and when eighteen years of age* entered the West Point military academy, from which he was graduated in 1837, *at the age of twenty-two,* in the same class with Gens. Jubal Early and Braxton Bragg. At the beginning of the Mexican war he received a commission on Brig.-Gen. Hamar's staff, being a second lieutenant in the 1st artillery. He was present at the battle of Monterey, and exhibited in that engagement the daring and courage which ever after characterized him. In this engagement he so distinguished himself that he was brevetted captain, and in March, 1847, obtained the full rank of captain with the

post of assistant adjutant-general. He was with Scott at Vera Cruz, *and was brevetted major and lieutenant-colonel* for gallant conduct at the National bridge and Chapultepec. Col. Hooker remained in the army until 1853, but the conditions of a time of peace were objectionable to him, and in that year he

resigned his commission and went to California. He settled in Sonoma county, and for several years worked his own farm. In 1858 he was appointed superintendent of military roads in Oregon, and obtained some other military surveying. For the next three years he was colonel of California militia, and on the outbreak of the civil war was still in a condition of military training to enable him to take full advantage of his past experience and natural aptitude for the art of war. He offered his services to the government, and in May, 1861, was made a brigadier-general in the army of the Potomac. The actual time of issuing Gen. Hooker's commission was in August, but it was dated back to May 17th. Gen. Hooker was present at the battle of Bull Run, but took no part in it. From July to the next February, he was stationed on the north bank of the Potomac, in southern Maryland, with orders to watch the enemy, and to defeat any effort on their part to cross the river for the purpose of moving on Washington from that

direction. He commanded the 2d division in the 3d corps of the army of the Potomac under Gen. Heintzelman. This division afterward formed part of McClellan's army in the peninsular campaign. At the siege of Yorktown, which lasted from Apr. 5th to May 4, 1862, Hooker distinguished himself, and on the day after the evacuation he was appointed a major-general of volunteers. As soon as it was learned that the enemy had evacuated Yorktown, Stoneman was sent forward to harass the Confederate rear with his cavalry, while Hooker with his division was ordered to support him. This movement brought about the battle of Williamsburg, in which Hooker's division held the entire Confederate army in check, though he had to contend with overwhelming numbers. Seeing that the retreating army had halted, and that reinforcements were being sent back, Hooker sent to Heintzelman for assistance. He stubbornly held the road, which was the centre of his operations, while waiting for the requested aid, and three times the hostile columns pushed up to this key to his position, and were driven back, shattered and bleeding. He fought all the forenoon, and soon after midday Longstreet came up with a fresh division in support of the Confederates, and attacked so sharply that though Hooker repulsed him, it was with the loss of four of his guns. At this juncture, Kearny came up with his division, and relieved him. Hooker's loss in this fight was 2,228 men killed and wounded, and it is stated that 30,000 national troops stood by

and looked on, while his division was being cut to pieces. *This is a distortion. Parts of three other Union divisions also fought at Williamsburg. Total Union casualties there were 2,283, of which Hooker's division suffered 1,575.* Hooker distinguished himself on the Peninsula at the battles of Fair Oaks, Frazier's Farm, Glendale, and Malvern Hill, during McClellan's celebrated change of base. On account of the part which he took in these battles, his division became known as "Fighting Joe Hooker's Division," thus giving him the sobriquet by which he was afterward always known. When the army of the Potomac was called from the Peninsula to assist Pope in front of Washington, Heintzelman's corps with Hooker's division was one of the first to reach him at Warren's Junction. Here, on Aug. 27th, he was attacked by Gen. Ewell, whom he repulsed and attacked in turn, driving him along the railroad, and compelling him to leave his dead, many of his wounded, and much of his baggage in the Federal hands. This rapid defeat of Ewell saved the army from a very critical situation. In *May,* Hooker was appointed major-general, and when the army was reorganized in September, preparatory to the Maryland campaign, he was assigned to the command of the 1st army corps. On the 14th of September occurred the battle of South Mountain, when Hooker, as a corps commander, added still more to his laurels. The attack was made by Gen. Reno early in the morning, and was kept up for seven hours under a heavy fire, when

Hooker came up with his corps, and at three o'clock in the afternoon formed his line of battle at the base of the mountain. The passes through South Mountain had been carried, and Hooker attacked the mountain side on the right of the gap, while Gen. Reno attacked on the left; the enemy retreated precipitately before this terrible onslaught. Three days later occurred the battle of Antietam, in which Hooker bore a most important part. Lee's army lay behind the heights which line the western bank of Antietam creek, extending from near its mouth, where it enters the Potomac, for several miles up. McClellan's plan was to send across Hooker's corps above, supported by Mansfield, Sumner, and Franklin, and to have them come down on the Confederate left. When he had turned it, Burnside was to cross on a stone bridge on the Federal left, and force back Lee's right, pushing on to Sharpsburg, and thus getting in the enemy's rear, and preventing him from escaping across the Potomac. Hooker made his first movement on Sept. 16th, and there was some artillery firing that night. Early in the morning the battle of Antietam began. A terrific attack was made by the enemy, and the right wing of the Federal army, under Gen. Sumner, was badly shattered. Gen. Hancock, who commanded a brigade in Smith's division, pushed forward in support of the Federal army, and succeeded in driving back the force which had attacked Sumner with such determination. After this engagement the Federal army was so firmly established on that part of the field, that the enemy did not again assail it with infantry, although it suffered considerably from artillery fire at very short range. In this fight Gen. Hooker was shot in the foot, but remained on the field until the close of the engagement. The battle of Antietam was important, since it arrested Gen. Lee's march of invasion, and compelled him to retreat across the Potomac

into Virginia. Hooker was unable to take the field again until November, when he superseded Gen. Fitz John Porter in the command of the 5th corps; on Burnside's assuming the chief command. Hooker was assigned to the centre grand division of the army of the Potomac, comprising the 3d and 5th corps. When Burnside commenced his movement on Fredericksburg, Hooker brought up the rear of the grand army. He had no faith in the promise of Burnside's anticipated surprise of Lee, and he took no part in the great battle of Fredericksburg, which proved a frightful mistake, in which the loss of the Federal army was over 12,000 killed, wounded, and missing. *A strange error. Hooker's center grand division participated heavily in the battle and suffered more than a quarter of the army's casualties.* Early in January, 1863, the divisions of Franklin and Hooker were put in motion in two parallel columns, with the idea of moving across the

Rappahannock and along its banks six miles above Fredericksburg. A terrible storm of rain came up in the night, and lasted two days, converting the country into a continent of mud, through which the columns struggled on in what is known in army history as the "mud march." Finding that Lee was fully informed of his grand movement, Gen. Burnside recalled the army to its quarters. On Jan. 26th Burnside was relieved of the command, at his own request, and Gen. Joseph Hooker was appointed by the president in his place. The result of this change of commanders was to revive in the army that zeal and confidence, which had certainly been considerably weakened by the recent disaster, and the feeling of doubt generally prevalent concerning the capacity of Gen. Burnside. After his appointment to the command, Gen. Hooker wisely determined not to attempt any large operations on the impassable roads during the winter season, and he spent three months in efforts to bring the army into a condition of efficiency after the demoralization produced by Burnside's ill-starred command. He effected a number of improvements in the organization: such as abolishing the "grand divisions;" perfecting the several departments; consolidating the cavalry under able leaders, and improving its efficiency; and introducing corps badges, for the double purpose of distinguishing to what corps a soldier belonged, and forming *esprit de corps*. Before the spring campaign opened Hooker found himself at the head of 120,000 infantry, and 12,000 well-appointed cavalry. The Confederate army numbered scarcely half that force; two divisions under Longstreet having been detached, which did not rejoin it until after the battle of Chancellorsville. Gen. Hooker now formed the bold plan of marching up the Rappahannock, crossing it and its tributary, the Rapidan, turning Lee's flank near Chancellorsville, and sweeping him *en reverse*. His turning column was put in motion Apr. 27, 1863, including the 2d, 5th, 11th and 12th corps. The movement resulted in the battle of Chancellorsville, which was attended by great loss of men, and resulted disastrously. Hooker was badly defeated, a fact which enabled Lee to concentrate a heavy force against him, and he was compelled to recross the river, narrowly escaping total destruction. It was a terrible disaster, and what made it worse was, that on Apr. 30th Hooker had issued the following boastful address to his army: "It is with heartfelt satisfaction that the general commanding announces to the army, that the operations of the last three days have determined that our enemy must ingloriously fly, or come out from behind their defences, and give us battle on our own ground, where certain destruction awaits them." The result that actually occurred angered the whole country. Hooker had declared that the army of the Potomac had failed to take Richmond on account of the incompetency of its leaders, and he had so conducted himself that there was no sympathy felt for him in his defeat. Lee was so elated with the knowledge that he had defeated the army of the Potomac, with half its numbers, that he formed a bold plan to invade Maryland and Pennsylvania. He moved his army nearly 150 miles around by the Shenandoah valley to the Potomac, and crossed the latter near Hagerstown. The neglect of Hooker to stop this invasion caused the greatest dissatisfaction, and *at Frederick, Md.,* he resigned his command, and Meade was appointed in his place. His failure as commander-in-chief of the army of the Potomac had been complete, but it did not blind the administration to Hooker's great merit as a soldier. He was placed in command of the 11th and 12th corps, and was sent to reinforce Rosecrans at Chattanooga. It was understood that as a division or corps leader Hooker had no superior. Soon after Grant assumed command at Chattanooga, his line being complete from the northern end of Lookout Mountain to the northern end of Missionary Ridge, Hooker made his splendid attack on the former position, which has passed into history as the "battle of the clouds." This was on Nov. 24, 1863. All up the side of the mountain the battle raged furiously, the scene being hidden from Grant and Thomas down below in Chattanooga by the low-hanging clouds, which wrapped the contending armies from sight. Suddenly the fog lifted, and the whole army in Chattanooga were witnesses of this strange fight among the clouds, and saw the enemy driven from his works upon the summit, and that the mountain stronghold was Hooker's. Later Hooker joined in the pursuit of Bragg from Missionary Ridge, and pushed on until the demoralized army of the Confederates took refuge in Dalton. When Gen. Sherman organized his celebrated "march to the sea" by the invasion of Georgia, Hooker remained in command of the 20th corps—which was the consolidation of the 11th and 12th corps—and added to the laurels gained at Lookout Mountain by his splendid fighting at

Resaca, Dallas, and in the attack on Atlanta. After the death of McPherson, who commanded the army of the Tennessee, Hooker expected to succeed him, but was disappointed. Sherman did not altogether like Hooker, and advised the president to appoint Gen. Oliver O. Howard to the vacant post. This was done, and Hooker asked to be relieved July 30th, and was placed upon waiting orders until Sept. 28th. He was remembered, however, and his services respected. He was brevetted a major-general in the regular army under date of March 13, 1865. After the close of the war Hooker was placed in command of the department of the East, with headquarters in New York city. In August, 1866, he was sent to Detroit, and put in command of the department of the Lakes. Sept. 1, 1866, he was mustered out of the volunteer service, and for some time was a member of a board for the retirement of officers. He was stricken with paralysis, however, and being incapacitated for further active service, he was retired at his own request on Oct. 15, 1868, retaining the full rank of major-general. For the remainder of his life Gen. Hooker resided in New York, and at last in Garden city (Long Island), N.Y., where his remains lie buried. Hooker was a valiant and

able soldier and general. As has been already said, in command of a division or corps he had no superior, but precisely as Ney and Murat could not be turned into Napoleons by placing them in chief command of an army, so Hooker was out of place and unsuccessful when given the supreme charge, in the conduct of which so many other experienced officers had failed. He died in Garden city, Oct. 31, 1879.

HOVEY, ALVIN PETERSON, twenty-first governor of Indiana (1889–91), was born at Mount Vernon, Ind., *Sept. 26, 1821,* son of Abiel and Frances (Peterson) Hovey, grandson of Rev. Samuel and Abigail (Cleveland) Hovey, and a descendant of Samuel and Elizabeth (Perkins) Hovey, of Windham, Conn. His parents, who came from Vermont, were early pioneers of Posey county, Ind., and both died while Alvin, their youngest child, was yet a lad. He became a student in the law office of John Pitcher, at Mt. Vernon, reading evenings after his day's work with the trowel. In 1843 he was admitted to the bar, where he soon rose to distinction. In 1849 he was elected a delegate to the Indiana constitutional convention, and in 1850 was made judge of the circuit court of southern Indiana. *Four years later, in 1854,* at the age of thirty-two, he was appointed a supreme court judge of Indiana, thus becoming the youngest member of the supreme court in the history of the state. In 1856 Pres. Pierce appointed him U.S. attorney for the district of Indiana. In the split which occurred in the Democratic party between Pres. Buchanan and Stephen A. Douglas, Mr. Hovey supported Douglas so heartily that it was not long before Pres. Buchanan removed him as district-attorney, naming as his successor Daniel W. Voorhees. When Fort Sumter was fired upon, Judge Hovey at once began the organization of a company of troops, and in a short time the

1st regiment Indiana legion, of which he was commissioned colonel, was ready for the field. Later he became colonel of the 24th Indiana, which joined Frémont's army in Missouri. He was with Gen. Grant in the Vicksburg campaign, and was appointed a brigadier-general for gallant conduct at Shiloh. In the battle of Champion's hill, Miss., May 16, 1863, Hovey's brigade suffered one-third of all the losses of the Federal forces there engaged. Gen. Grant in his memoirs gives special credit to Hovey for his part in this battle. In July, 1864, he was appointed *brevet major-general* and ordered by Gen. Grant to raise 10,000 new troops. Only men not married were invited to enlist; from which it resulted that when the quota was filled it was found that many of the new troops were mere boys. For this reason they were known as "Hovey's babies," but there were no troops more effective in the march to the sea. *Very few of these troops participated in the march to the sea.* In the latter part of 1864 Hovey was appointed by the secretary of war military commander for Indiana, an office made necessary by the growing hostile feeling in the state at that time towards the national government. Gen. Hovey caused the arrest of a number of persons belonging to the so-called Sons of Liberty, a treasonable organization in the state, and five were found guilty and sentenced to be hanged, but their sentence was commuted to life imprisonment by Pres. Lincoln. In 1865 he was appointed minister to Peru at the request of Gen. Grant. He served until 1870, when he returned home and resumed the practice of law at Mt. Vernon. In 1872 his friends wished him to be the Republican candidate for governor, but he would not consent to it, declaring that he did not want to re-enter political life. Fourteen years later, however, in 1886, he accepted a unanimous nomination for congress in the first district of Indiana, and defeated McCullough, Democrat, by 1,357 majority. In congress he championed the cause of Union veterans in the matter of pension legislation. When the Republican state convention met at Indianapolis in June, 1888, he was unanimously nominated for governor, and in the November election that followed he was elected, over C. C. Matson, Democrat, by 2,200 votes. During his term of office an act was passed changing the method of selecting and supplying school books for the schools of the state. By that law the state board of education was made a board of commissioners to determine what text books should be used in the schools, no other books being allowed. Gov. Hovey strongly urged that all text-books be furnished at the expense of the state. Another important measure, which passed during his incumbency, was the adoption of the "Australian" ballot, thus changing the whole system of elections. At the national Grand Army encampment held at St. Louis in 1888, Gov. Hovey was unanimously elected president of the Service Pension Association of the United States, and in December, 1889, he issued an appeal from the association, addressed "to the loyal people of the United States and their representatives in congress" demanding, on behalf of many surviving Union soldiers of the late war, the passage of a service pension law. Gov. Hovey was twice married. His first wife was Mary, daughter of Col. E. R. James, a prominent citizen of southern Indiana, and his second wife was a daughter of Caleb B. Smith, secretary of the interior in Pres. Lincoln's cabinet. He died in Indianapolis, Ind., Nov. 23, 1891.

HOWARD, OLIVER OTIS, soldier, was born at Leeds, Kennebec county, Me., Nov. 8, 1830. He came of a family who were in comfortable circumstances but not wealthy, and during his

boyhood he worked on a farm, attending the district school, and at the age of nine, after the death of his father, lived for two years with his uncle, John Otis, at Hallowell. Here he began to obtain the advantages of a higher education. Having finished preparation at Monmouth and Yarmouth, at the age of sixteen he entered Bowdoin college, from which he was graduated in 1850, with a fair standing. An opportunity was now afforded him by his uncle, Mr. Otis, to enter the United States military academy, and he became a cadet in that institution, graduating in 1854. He stood fourth in his class; by his own request being assigned to the ordnance department with the brevet rank of second lieutenant. His first service was at Watervliet, N.Y., and Kennebec arsenal, Me. He next served in Florida, being chief ordnance officer during Gen. Hardey's campaign against the Indians. The following year he was promoted first lieutenant, and was assigned to duty as acting professor of mathematics at West Point, which position he continued to hold until the breaking out of the civil war. In the meantime he had received the degree of M.A. from Bowdoin college. In 1861 Lieut. Howard volunteered his services to the governor of his native state. He was finally, by a regimental election, made colonel of the 3d regiment, Maine volunteers. The other officers of this regiment were: lieutenant-colonel, I. N. Tucker, of Gardiner; major, H. G. Staples of Augusta; adjutant, Edwin Burt of Augusta; quartermaster, W. H. Haley of Bath; surgeon, Gideon S. Palmer of Gardiner; chaplain, A. J. Church of Augusta; sergeant-major, Charles H. Plaisted of Waterville; quartermaster-sergeant, W. H. Smith of Gardiner; commissary-sergeant, B. W. Graves of Augusta; hospital steward, Getchell of Bath. His commission bore date May 28th, and by June 1st he was on his way to the national capital with a full regiment. Col. Howard commanded the 3d brigade of the 3d division during the battle of Bull Run July 21st. For his conduct during this campaign he was, the 3d of September, created brigadier-general of volunteers. He was assigned by Gen. McClellan to a brigade, which finally became the 1st brigade, 1st division, 2d army corps. He bore a prominent part in the movement toward the Rappahannock in the spring of 1862, and was then transferred to the Peninsula, where he participated in the advance against Richmond. He was twice wounded in the right arm at the battle of Fair Oaks May 31, 1862, while leading his brigade in a charge against the enemy. He lost that arm by amputation. He was invalided but a few days, during which he was at home in Maine. When able, he addressed the public, and exercised his personal influence to promote enlistments in the army. In two months and twenty days after Fair Oaks, Gen. Howard returned to his corps, and was in the Pope campaign in Virginia, participating in the second battle of Bull Run. During the retreat from Centreville to Washington, he commanded the rear guard of the army, which was under fire during that movement. In the Maryland campaign he commanded a brigade until Antietam, where Gen. Sedgwick was wounded, when he took charge of his division, which he also commanded at Fredericksburg. In November, 1862, he was promoted to the rank of major-general of volunteers. In the following spring he succeeded Gen. Sigel as commander of the 11th army corps, which he led during the sanguinary battles at Chancellorsville and Gettysburg. Gen. Howard's corps did good service during the three days' fight at Gettysburg, securing, the first day, the final battle-ground, Cemetery ridge, and was thanked by congress. In October, 1863, Gen. Howard's corps was engaged in the fighting in Lookout valley. He received Gen. Thomas's commendation in further orders the following month, when he fought under Grant in the

battle of Chattanooga, gaining distinction. During Sherman's Atlanta campaign in the spring of 1864, Gen. Howard was in command of the new 4th corps, a consolidation of two others, which formed part of the army of the Cumberland, seeing severest service for 100 days. When Gen. McPherson fell before Atlanta, Gen. Howard succeeded him as commander of the army and department of the Tennessee, and throughout the whole of the grand march through Georgia his corps formed the right of Sherman's army. For his part in this campaign he was appointed brigadier-general in the regular army. He commanded the same wing during the movement through the Carolinas, and assisted in the operations by virtue of which Johnston's army was forced to surrender in 1865. For this portion of the campaign Gen. Howard was brevetted major-general of the regular army. On May 12, 1865, Gen. Howard was assigned to duty in the war department in the bureau of refugees, freedmen, and abandoned lands. One of his first orders was to the effect that lands in the states recently in rebellion, which had been abandoned by their disloyal owners, and were now under cultivation by freedmen, should be retained in the possession of the latter until the crops, then growing, should be secured for their benefit, unless full and just compensation should be made for their labor and its products, and for expenditures. Gen. Howard remained commissioner of the Freedmen's bureau from May, 1865, to July, 1874, when he was assigned to the command of the department of the Columbia. In 1877 he commanded a successful expedition against the Nez Perces Indians, his infantry marching over 1,400 miles, and the following year another, nearly as extended, against the Bannocks and Piutes. In 1881–82 Gen. Howard was superintendent of the United States military academy. From 1882–86 he commanded the department of the Platte at Omaha, Neb. In 1886 he was commissioned major-general and placed in command of the division of the Pacific. After the death of Gen. Sheridan, and the assignment of Maj.-Gen. Schofield to command the U.S. army, Gen. Howard was appointed to the command of the division of the Atlantic, with headquarters at Governor's island in the harbor of New York. The degree of LL.D. was conferred upon him four different times: by Waterville college, Maine, 1865; by Shurtliff college, Illinois, 1865; by Gettysburg theological seminary, Pennsylvania, 1866; and by Bowdoin college, Maine, 1888. The French government made him a Chevalier of the Legion of honor in 1884. He was author of "Donald's School Days;" "Chief Joseph; or, The Nez Perces in Peace and War;" also author and translator of "Life of the Count De Gasparin"—from the French, and of numerous articles and monographs published in magazines and reviews. *He died Oct. 26, 1909.*

HOWE, ALBION PARIS, soldier, was born in Standish, Me., March 13, 1818. He entered the Military Academy at West Point in 1837; was graduated in 1841, and assigned to the 4th artillery. He served on garrison and frontier duty for a time, and then as professor of mathematics at West Point until the Mexican war. While in the Mexican campaign he occupied the staff position of adjutant of 4th artillery from Oct. 1, 1846, to March 2, 1855, and participated in many battles. For gallant and meritorious conduct at Contreras and Cherubusco, he received the brevet of captain, Aug. 20, 1847, a full captaincy being granted March 2, 1855. In the interim between the Mexican and civil wars he was on garrison duty, four years of the time being given as instructor at the Artillery School at Fortress

Monroe. At the opening of the civil war he was appointed Gen. McClellan's chief of artillery in the army of the Potomac during the campaign on the peninsular in 1862, after having served in West Virginia in 1861. In 1862 he commanded a brigade of light artillery in the peninsular campaign; was brevetted major July 1st, for bravery at Malvern Hill, Va; lieutenant-colonel, May 3, 1863, for gallant action at Salem Heights, Va.; colonel, Nov. 7, 1863, for daring and meritorious work in the battle of Rappahannock Station, Va.; and brigadier-general and major-general, March 13, 1865, and further brevetted major-general of volunteers, July 13, 1865, for faithful and meritorious services during the war. Gen. Howe was on duty in Washington as chief of artillery in 1864-6, and was a member of the military commission that tried the conspirators against President Lincoln and his cabinet after the terrible assassination of Apr. 14, 1865. He was mustered out of service Jan. 15, 1866, and retired June 30, 1882, with the rank of colonel of the 4th artillery, his commission dating from Apr. 19, 1882. During the latter part of his active military service he was stationed on the Pacific coast, where he held the rank of major. *He died Jan. 25, 1897.*

HOWE, SAMUEL GRIDLEY, philanthropist and educator, was born in Boston, Mass., Nov. 10, 1801, son of Joseph N. and Patty (Gridley) Howe. His father was a ship-owner and manufacturer, and his mother a relative of Clol. Gridley, who constructed the fortifications before the battle of Bunker Hill. He was graduated at Brown University, Providence, R.I., in 1821, and at the Harvard Medical School in 1824. The Greek revolution was then in full progress, and Howe, sailing for Greece, offered his services to the government as surgeon, becoming later in the war surgeon-in-

chief of the Greek fleet. Many and romantic were his adventures on sea and on land, and great were the hardships and privations which he suffered in common with the native soldiery. In 1827 he returned to America to raise money for the starving people of Greece. About $60,000 and a great quantity of clothing was contributed in New England and New York. Howe hastened back to Greece, and personally superintended the distribution of these supplies, which saved a large part of the population from actual starvation. He also founded a colony of exiles on the isthmus of Corinth, laboring night and day to secure its prosperity, until forced by a severe malarial fever to leave the country in 1830. His many and varied services gained for him the title of "The Lafayette of the Greek Revolution," and were commemorated in Whittier's poem, "The Hero." He next spent some time in Paris, continuing his medical studies. On his return to America in 1831, he became interested, through his friend Dr. John D. Fisher, in the project of starting a school for the blind, and once more crossed the ocean to study such schools in England, France, and Germany. At the request of Lafayette, he carried relief (sent out from America) to the Polish refugees in Prussia, and was imprisoned in consequence without trial in Berlin, for five weeks *au secret*. In 1832 he entered upon the great work of his life, the education and uplifting of the blind. Gathering together a few children from the highways, he taught them in his father's house, giving exhibitions of their progress throughout New England and arousing much interest and enthusiasm. In 1833 the school was transferred with thirty pupils to a large mansion, the gift of Col. Perkins, and was named the Perkins Institution. Dr. Howe at a later period addressed the legislatures of seventeen states, to induce them to provide for the education of the blind, and great success attended the movement everywhere. As the pioneer of this cause in America, he was obliged to create his own working machinery, inventing a new kind of map, much lighter, better and cheaper than any in use, compiling text-books for his scholars, as well as teaching and superintending in person every detail of the establishment. He founded a printing-press for the blind, and printed a large number of books, including the Bible, in raised type. Through his improvements the bulk of the volumes was diminished fifty per cent, and the expense seventy-five per cent. His most famous achievement was the education of Laura Bridgman, the first blind, deaf, and dumb person ever taught the use of language. His reports, containing the story of her instruction, awakened the most intense interest abroad as well as at home, and were translated into the European languages. In April, 1843, he was married to Julia, daughter of Samual Ward, a well-known banker of New York, and with his talented young bridge visited England and the

continent, studying, as was his life-long custom, the benevolent institutions and prisons, and receiving many social attentions. In 1844 he resumed his labors as superintendent of the Institution for the Blind, retaining this position to the end of his life. He was actively interested in prison reform as early as 1845, and was one of the founders of the Society for Aiding Discharged Convicts, continuing to be its president until his death. In 1845 he served on the Boston school committee, and brought about several important reforms. In 1846 he was a member of the state legislature and co-operated with Dorothea L. Dix to improve the condition of lunatics. He induced the legislature to appoint a commission to inquire into the number and condition of idiotic and feeble-minded children in Massachusetts, and his report as chairman produced a profound sensation. Through his efforts, a school for these unfortunates (the first in America) was founded, in 1848, at South Boston, and he retained supervision of it throughout his life. In 1844, in co-operation with his friend, Horace Mann, he attempted to introduce the teaching of articulation to the deaf pupils in the asylum at Hartford, Conn., and it was largely through his efforts and testimony that the articulation method was adopted in Masschusetts in 1867. In 1845, when the Texas question assumed prominence, he was one of the "Conscience Whigs," joining strongly in the opposition to slavery, and becoming chairman of a vigilance committee to prevent the return of fugitive slaves. He was one of the founders, in 1851, of the "Commonwealth," an anti-slavery paper, and edited it for more than a year, assisted by Mrs. Howe. He was an active member of the Kansas committee, formed at the East to assist the free-state men in their contest with the slaveholders, and was a friend and admirer of John Brown. During the civil war he was one of the heads of the sanitary commission, and in 1863 was appointed with Hon. Robert Dale Owen and Mr. James McKay on a commission to inquire into the condition of the freedom of the South. In 1863 a board of state charities (the first in America) was created in Massachusetts, and Dr. Howe, taking his place on it in 1864, served as chairman and wrote the annual reports from 1865 until 1874. His life-long experience in charities, his powers of organization and insight into principles, made these of great value. Says his biographer, F. B. Sanborn: "The system he devised for Massachusetts now prevails to a great extent there, and in a less degree in many other American states, while it has been introduced in European countries in some of its features." During the Cretan rebellion of 1866 he collected a large amount of money and clothing, and went to Greece to distribute it among the Cretan refugees, for whom he also established industrial schools at Athens. In 1870 Dr. Howe, together with Hon. Benj. F. Wade and Hon. Andrew D. White, were sent by Pres. Grant to San Domingo to inquire into the resources of that island and the disposition of its inhabitants with regard to annexation. Their report was favorable to the project. Dr. Howe continued his active labors until shortly before his death, failing health obliged him to retire. He was a vigorous and prolific writer, chiefly on educational and philanthropic themes. His reports rank among the classics of pedagogy, and his "Historical Sketch of the Greek Revolution" (published in 1828) passed through several editions. He received many medals and diplomas from European countries for his work among the blind, and decorations from the Greek government for his services in the Greek revolution. He also received the degree of LL.D. from Brown University. Five children survived him: Julia Romana Anagnos (who

shared his devotion to the blind), Florence Howe Hall, Prof. Henry Morton Howe, Laura E. Richards and Maude Howe Elliott. Dr. Howe died in Boston, Mass., Jan. 9, 1876.

HUGER, BENJAMIN, soldier, was born in Charleston, S.C., *on Nov. 22, 1805*, son of Francis Kinloch Huger, patriot, who aided in liberating Gen. Lafayette from the fortress of Olmutz, and was arrested, imprisoned, and persecuted by the Austrian government, and after eight months released and sent across the frontier. He afterward joined the U.S. army and served through the war of 1812. The mother of Benjamin was a daughter of Gen. Thomas Pinckney. His grandfather was Benjamin Huger, the revolutionary patriot, who was killed while reconnoitering the position of the British army then occupying Charleston, S.C., May 11, 1779, and his great-great-grandfather was Daniel Huger (1651–1711), the refugee who fled from France before the revocation of the edict of Nantes and settled in South Carolina. Benjamin Huger was educated for the army and entering as cadet at the U.S. military academy, West Point, 1821, was graduated, in 1825, with the brevet rank of second lieutenant in the 3d artillery. He served on topographical duty three years, when he visited Europe on leave of absence. On his return he was promoted captain of ordnance, May 30, 1833, and commanded the arsenal at Fortress Monroe for seven years. From 1839 to 1846 he was on the ordnance board of the department and in 1840–41 was a member of a military commission sent to Europe to study the art of war. From 1841 until 1846 he again commanded the Fortress Monroe arsenal. Upon the outbreak of hostilities with Mexico, Capt. Huger was made chief of ordnance of the army under Gen. Scott, and had charge of the siege train at Vera Cruz. For gallantry in this siege he was brevetted major,

March 29, 1847. For Molino del Rey he was brevetted lieutenant-colonel Sept. 8, 1847, and for Chapultepec a colonel Sept. 13, 1847. South Carolina, in 1852, presented her valiant son a sword of honor for meritorious conduct and gallantry in Mexico. On his return from Mexico, Col. Huger again assumed command of the arsenal at Fortress Monroe, remaining in charge until 1851. From 1851 to 1854 he commanded the armory at Harper's Ferry. Capt. Huger was promoted a major, Feb. 15, 1855, and stationed at Pikeville arsenal, Md., from 1854 to 1860, when he was transferred by Secretary Floyd to the arsenal at Charleston, S.C. On March 16, 1861, he was commissioned colonel of artillery in the Confederate states army. On Apr. 22, 1861, he tendered his resignation as an officer in the U.S. army, and on June 17, 1861, was made a brigadier-general in the provisional army of the Confederate states. He commanded the troops from South Carolina at Norfolk, Va., May 23, 1861, and on May 26th was given command of all the troops and defences around Norfolk until occupied by the Federal forces, May 10, 1862. He was promoted a full major-general, provisional army Confederate states, Oct. 7, 1861. In the defence of Richmond against McClellan in 1862, he had a division composed of the brigades of A. R. Wright, Mahone, Blanchard, and Armistead. After the battle of Malvern Hill, July 1, 1862, he was relieved of his command under the charge of failing to cut off McClellan's retreat after the battle had been won by the Confederates. He was transferred to the trans-Mississippi department, and assigned to duty in the ordnance department. Here he continued until the surrender of Lee, when he returned to Virginia and became a farmer. He afterward removed to his native city and died there Dec. 7, 1877.

HUMPHREYS, ANDREW ATKINSON, soldier, was born in Philadelphia, Pa., Nov. 2, 1810, son of Samuel Humphreys, who was appointed chief contractor of the navy in 1815, and held that position until his death. His great-great-grandfather, Daniel Humphreys, was a Welsh Quaker, who settled in Haverford, Pa., and is grandfather, Joshua Humphreys, was widely known as the leading shipbuilder of his day. He was graduated from the U.S. Military Academy in 1831, and began his active life in the 2d artillery, serving in garrison at West Point, South Carolina, Georgia, Florida and Cape Cod. He was an excellent draughtsman, and, having a decided turn for surveying and engineering, was frequently detailed for such work. He took part in the Seminole war, and was engaged in the battles of Oloklikaha and Micanopy, bearing himself bravely, but modestly withal, and gaining experience and breadth of view rather than honor. He was a serious-minded man, whose tendencies were rather towards engineering and science than to the life of a soldier. As there were but few educated civil engineers at that

time in the country, and as the system of internal improvements was just being started, Humphreys, after serving five years, resigned his commission in the army, and was immediately employed by the government as a civil engineer to construct light houses, under Maj. Bache, on the Delaware Bay. The corps of topographical engineers was authorized by congress in 1838, and in July of that year, Humphreys was offered and accepted the rank of first lieutenant. From that time he led a most active, studious and laborious life, serving on the harbor works and defenses of the great lakes, in the bureau of topographical engineers at Washington, again in the bureau of topographical engineers, and then in charge of the coast survey office. He was made captain in 1848, and for the next twelve years had charge of the surveys and examinations of the Mississippi river, being assisted in this work by Henry L. Abbott. The result of their joint

labors brought their names into distinction throughout the world, and it is justly regarded as an enduring monument to their learning and ability. On account of ill health, in 1851, he gave up this work and went to Europe, both to recuperate and to study the means of protecting delta rivers from overflow. On his return, in 1854, he was assigned to the additional duty at Washington of supervising the explorations and surveys for a railroad from the Mississippi to the Pacific. At that time the railroad system was in its infancy, and the construction of a line to the Pacific was deemed to be an event of the indefinite future, if not an impossibility; but Humphreys, scarcely yet recovered from the breakdown which had culminated in a sunstroke, with his accustomed intensity threw himself into this new task, and was able to make a preliminary report before congress adjourned. In 1855 he was made a member of the lighthouse board, on which he served until 1862. The numerous resignations which took place at and before the time of the outbreak of the rebellion brought him to the rank of major. Shortly after, he was promoted to be brigadier-general of volunteers. He was assigned to duty on Gen. McClellan's staff, and accompanied the army of the Potomac to the peninsula, and as chief topographical engineer took part in all the operations and battles of that campaign. On Sept. 12, 1862, Halleck, then general-in-chief, assigned Humphreys to the command of the third division of Fitz-John Porter's fifth corps, composed entirely of new Pennsylvania troops, which he led to the field of Antietam. At the battle of Fredericksburg he led a gallant charge, which won the admiration of all who beheld him, and made him the most conspicuous figure on the field that day. Humphreys' division had a bloody encounter at Chancellorsville, and maintained its high reputation for steadiness and courage. When the army withdrew to the north side of the Rappahannock, the time of most of his men having expired, his division was broken up, and Humphreys was transferred to the command of the second division of the third corps, under Gen. Sickles. He made a creditable defense at the battle of Gettysburg. When Gen. Meade was made commander of the army of the Potomac, he appointed Humphreys his chief of staff, but he declined the honor offered him in order to participate in the impending battle with his division. Four days after the battle he accepted the position, and held it for sixteen months. On Nov. 26, 1864, he was again given command of the second corps, which was engaged under his direction in the siege of Petersburg, and in following up the retreat of Lee. His services in this last campaign brought him to the very front rank of corps commanders, and showed him to be possessed of the highest military talents. From December, 1865, to August, 1866, he was in charge of the Mississippi levees, where he was mustered out of the volunteer service. He was then made brigadier-general and given command of the corps of engineers, the highest scientific appointment in the U.S. army, with charge of the engineer bureau in Washington. This office he held until June 30, 1879, when he was retired at his own request, serving during three years on many commissions, including that to examine into canal routes across the isthmus connecting North and South America, and also on the lighthouse board. Gen. Humphreys was elected a member of the American Philosophical Society in 1857, a member of the American Academy of Arts and Sciences in 1863, and was one of the incorporating members of the National Academy of Sciences in the last named year. He also held honorary memberships in foreign scientific societies, and received the degree of LL.D. from Harvard in 1868. He published "The Virginia Campaigns of 1864 and 1865" (New York, 1882), and "From Gettysburg to the Rapidan" (1882), and a number of reports concerning his engineering work. Gen. Humphreys possessed the gentle and refined manner and habits of a scholar. He was an indefatigable worker and a remarkably courageous soldier. All who have witnessed his conduct in battle concur in the statement that it was simply perfect, as if inspired solely by the sense of duty, and absolutely uninfluenced by danger or the sense of fear. No emergency ever found him unprepared, and no fire unwilling to face it. The only wonder is that an officer of such conspicuous intrepidity should have escaped alive from any battle in which his troops took part. He died in Washington, D.C., Dec. 27, 1883.

HUNT, HENRY JACKSON, soldier, was born in Detroit, Mich. Sept. 14, 1819, son of Samuel W. Hunt, lieutenant in the 3d infantry, and grandson of Thomas Hunt, colonel of the 3d infantry. He accompanied his father on the expedition that established Fort Leavenworth, in 1827, and after attending school in Missouri, entered the U.S. Military Academy, where he was graduated in 1839. During the Canada border disturbances of that year, he served in the 2d artillery on the frontier. He was promoted first lieutenant, June 18, 1846, and subsequently, for gallantry during the Mexican war, was brevetted captain. *On Sept. 28, 1852,* he became captain, and on May 14, 1861, was promoted major. He took an active and important part in many campaigns of the civil war, including the battle of Bull Run, the defense of Washington and the peninsular campaign. In September, 1862, he was made brigadier-general of volunteers, and became chief of artillery of the army of the Potomac,

Henry J. Hunt [signature]

holding the office until the close of the war and participating in all the battles fought by that army during 1862–65. He was brevetted colonel, July 3, 1863, for his services at Gettysburg; major-general of volunteers, July 6, 1864, and brigadier-general in the regular army, March 13, 1865. In 1866 he was president of the permanent artillery board, afterward commanding various forts and being promoted to colonel of the 5th artillery, April 4, 1869. On Sept. 14, 1869, he was retired from active service, receiving the appointment of governor of the soldiers' home. Among Gen. Hunt's publications are: "Instruction on Field Artillery," many papers on artillery projectiles, army organization, and three articles in the "Century Magazine" on the battle of Gettysburg. He died at Washington, D.C., Feb. 11, 1889.

HUNTER, DAVID, soldier, was born in Washington, D.C., July 21, 1802. His father was Andrew Hunter, clergyman, who was appointed a brigade chaplain in 1775, and afterward received the public thanks of Gen. Washington

for rendering valuable aid at the battle of Monmouth. His mother was a daughter of Richard Stockton, one of the designers of the declaration of independence. David Hunter was graduated from the West Point military academy in 1822, and was appointed second lieutenant in the 5th infantry; in 1828 he was promoted first lieutenant, and in 1833 became captain in the 1st dragoons. He had a taste of frontier duty, and twice crossed the plains to the Rocky Mountains. In 1836 he resigned his commission, and engaged in business in Chicago. Afterward he re-entered the military service as paymaster, with the rank of major. He was with Gen. John E. Wool in the Mexican war, and was, later on, stationed successively at New Orleans, Washington, Detroit, St. Louis, and on the frontier. He had the honor of accompanying President-elect Lincoln when he set out from Springfield for the capital, in February, 1861, but at Buffalo he was disabled

D. Hunter [signature]

by a broken collar bone, the result of an accident in the jostling crowd. On May 14th he was appointed colonel of the 6th U.S. cavalry, and three days later was commissioned brigadier-general of volunteers. He commanded the main column of McDowell's army in the Manassas campaign, and was one of the heroes at Bull Run, July 21, 1861, when he was severely wounded. On Aug. 13th of the same year, he was made a major-general of volunteers, served under Gen. Frémont in Missouri, and on Nov. 2nd succeeded him in the command of the western department. Under date of Feb. 19, 1862, Gen. Halleck wrote to him: "To you, more than any other man out of this department, are we indebted for our success at Fort Donelson. In my strait for troops to reinforce Gen. Grant I applied to you. You responded nobly, placing your forces at my disposition. This enabled us to win the victory." In March, 1862, Gen. Hunter was transferred to the department of the South, with headquarters at Port Royal, S.C. On May 9th he issued the famous general order declaring

his department (Georgia, Florida, and South Carolina) under martial law, adding thereto this pregnant clause: "Slavery and martial law, in a free country, are altogether incompatible. The persons in these three states, heretofore held as slaves, are therefore declared forever free." This order, however, was proclaimed without the sanction of President Lincoln, who was somewhat annoyed at this undue assumption of authority on the part of Gen. Hunter, notwithstanding the fact that they were intimate friends. The president therefore declared this order null and void within ten days after its issue, wisely wishing to bide his own time for the settlement of a most momentous question. Later, the general successfully organized the 1st South Carolina volunteers, the first regiment of black troops in the Federal service. Naturally this created a decided sensation. Congress was asked to secure more definite information on the subject, and the secretary of war communicated with the general forthwith, receiving speedily this memorable response: "No regiment of fugitive slaves has

been or is being organized in this department. There is, however, a fine regiment of persons whose late masters are fugitive rebels—men who everywhere fly before the appearance of the national flag, leaving their servants behind them to shift, as best they can, for themselves." In August Jefferson Davis issued an order to the effect that, if Gen. Hunter or any other U.S. officer, known to have been drilling slaves as soldiers, should be captured, he should be denied the privileges of a prisoner of war, but held in close confinement for execution as a felon. In September the general was summoned to Washington, and made president of a court of inquiry to investigate the causes of the surrender at Harper's Ferry. In May, 1864, he took charge of the department of West Virginia. In June he defeated the Confederate forces at Piedmont and Lynchburg. Afterward he served on various courts-martial, being president of the commission that tried the persons who conspired for the assassination of President Lincoln. In March, 1865, he was brevetted major-general, U.S.A., and finally was retired from active service, full of honors, July 31, 1866, making his home thereafter in Washington. Gen. Hunter married a daughter of John Kinzie, who was noted for having been the first permanent citizen of Chicago. The general died Feb. 2, 1886.

HUNTER, ROBERT MERCER TALIAFERRO, statesman, was born in Essex county, Va., April 21, 1809, son of James and Maria (Garnett) Hunter. His father, a representative of a noted Scotch-American family, was a landed proprietor of considerable means and high standing, and for two terms a member of the Virginia legislature; his mother was a daughter of Muscoe Garnett, another wealthy planter of Essex county. His maternal grandmother, Grace Fenton Mercer, belonged to the distinguished family of that name, one of the most prominent members of which was Charles Fenton Mercer (1778–1858), the well-known philanthropist, who was a member of congress from Virginia (1817–40). Two of his uncles, James Mercer Garnett, and robert Selden Garnett, were also representatives in congress from the Essex district, for two and five terms respectively. With so many of his immediate family in public life, the young man's mind turned naturally to the study of current politics. The science of government, history and biography were always his favorite studies, but with active mind, comprehensive intellect and retentive memory, few fields of learning escaped his attention. After receiving a careful home training and the best the schools of the vicinity afforded, he entered the University of Virginia at its first session, in 1825, having for his classmates Prof. Gessner Harrison, Prof. Henry Tutwiler, and others little less distinguished, and was one of its first graduates, in 1829. On leaving college he entered the law school of that eminent jurist and publicist, Judge Henry St. George Tucker, of Winchester, and in 1830 established himself in professional practice in his native county. In 1835, when but twenty-six years of age, he was elected to the house of delegates from Essex, and served during two sessions (1835–37). This period is memorable for the discussion and adoption of the Virginia resolutions on the northern anti-slavery associations and the formal denial of the power of congress to legislate on the subject, and further by the discussions on the Expunging Resolutions. Upon the latter he made probably his first speech in the house, on Feb. 26, 1836. In 1837 he was elected to the national house of representatives, where he served continuous, until 1847, with the exception of one term. During the sessions of 1839–41 he was speaker

of the house, and his rulings are still regarded as of high authority on questions of parliamentary law. He advocated the annexation of Texas, the compromise of the Oregon question, the retrocession of Alexandria to Virginia, and supported the Walker tariff of 1846. In December 1847, he was elected by the general assembly to the U.S. senate, and soon took a leading position in that body, among such distinguished statesmen as Calhoun, Clay, Webster, Cass, and Benton; and at a later period, he, with Davis of Mississippi, and Toombs of Georgia, constituted what was known as the "Southern Triumvirate." Early in his congressional career he adopted in the main the state-rights and low tariff views of Mr. Calhoun, and was among the ablest of the disciples and supporters of that eminent statesman. He voted for the Clayton compromise, and the extension to the Pacific coast of the line *36°30′*, established by the Missouri compromise of 1820. As chairman of the committee on finance in the senate, he made an able and exhaustive report on the coinage of the country; he was the author of the tariff of 1857, which effected a considerable reduction in duties and enlarged the free list; he originated the bonded warehouse system, under which imported goods were allowed to remain in government warehouses until the owners desired to put them upon the market, paying the duties at the time of withdrawal. He was a prominent candidate for the presidency in 1860, having secured the Virginia delegation over ex-Gov. Henry A. Wise, a fact attesting his great popularity in the state, as the delegates were elected by conventions held in each congressional district. On Feb. 22, 1858, he delivered a stirring oration at the unveiling of Crawford's equestrian statue of Washington in the capitol square of Richmond. His address delivered in the same city in the campaign of

1852, in which he traced the growth and history of parties, and demonstrated the soundness of the state-rights view of the Federal compact, is one of the ablest popular disquisitions on that subject; and his address in the African Church in the memorable Know-nothing campaign of 1855, on the dangers to be apprehended from secret political parties, is still referred to as a masterpiece of eloquence, oratory, and overwhelming logic. When Virginia seceded, he resigned his seat in the senate, and was soon afterwards invited by Pres. Davis to accept the office of secretary of state of the Confederacy in his second cabinet. He filled this position until elected, in 1862, to the Confederate States senate, in which he served until the evacuation of Richmond and the dispersion of the Confederate government. He was one of the three Confederate commissioners appointed by Pres. Davis to treat with Pres. Lincoln and Secy. Seward at the Fortress Monroe conference, his associates being Alexander H. Stephens, of Georgia, vice-president of the Confederacy, and John A. Campbell, of

Louisiana, ex-associate judge of the U.S. supreme court. He was among the prominent Virginians summoned by Mr. Lincoln to meet him in Richmond, to confer as to the restoration of Virginia to her relations in the Federal union —a meeting which was to have been held in April, 1865, and was prevented by Lincoln's assassination. *This is garbled. Lincoln did not summon Hunter to meet personally in Richmond; Hunter wanted to meet with Lincoln in Washington, but a telegram containing this request reached the Union War Department on April 14 after Lincoln had departed for Ford's Theatre.* Mr. Hunter was soon after arrested, and confined for several months in Fort Pulaski, with James A. Seddon, the last Confederate secretary of war, and other distinguished men. Having been released, through the efforts and intercession of friends in both the North and South, he returned to his home, and devoted himself to study and to agricultural pursuits. Thereafter he seldom participated in public affairs; his speech in New York city in the presidential campaign of 1872, and an occasional appearance in his own state, are the only instances now recalled. In 1874 he was elected by the legislature treasurer of Virginia, and discharged the duties of the office until January, 1880, when he was defeated for re-election, in consequence of the triumph of what was then called the Readjuster party. In 1885 Pres. Cleveland appointed him collector of the port of Tappahannock, a position which he held to the time of his death. There have been few men in this country whose public career extended over a longer period, or who filled so many exalted positions with such conspicuous ability. In private life, he was as distinguished for his simplicity of manner, amiability and purity of character, and the philosophical equanimity with which he bore the reverses of fortune, as he was in public for

his fervent patriotism, eminent ability and fidelity to duty. No citizen of any age has left a more stainless record, and he illustrated by his life the grand maxim of Robert E. Lee, that "Human fortitude should be equal to human calamity." Mr. Hunter was married, in 1836, to Mary Evelina Dandridge, of Jefferson county, Va., a lineal descendant of Gov. Alexander Spottiswoode, a relative of Martha Washington (neé Dandrige) and a niece of Judge Henry St. G. Tucker. He died at his home in Essex county, Va., July 18, 1887.

HURLBUT, STEPHEN AUGUSTUS, soldier, was born at Charleston, S.C., Nov. 29, 1815. He practiced law in his native city from 1837, and served for a time against the Seminoles in Florida, as adjutant of a South Carolina regiment. Settling at Belvidere, Ill., in 1845, he was a member of the state constitutional convention in 1847, a presidential elector on the Taylor ticket in 1848, and in the legislature 1859 and 1861. May 17, 1861, he was commissioned brigadier-general of volunteers. In 1862 he had command of Fort

Donelson, and bore a prominent part in the battles of Pittsburg Landing and Shiloh; for services at the latter was made major-general Sept. 17th, and after Corinth, led the pursuit of the enemy. He held command at Memphis in September, 1863, was at the head of the 16th army corps when Gen. Sherman took Meridian, Miss., in February 1864, and succeeded Gen. Nathaniel P. Banks in command of the department of the Gulf during the last year of the war, after which he was honorably mustered out of the service. He was again in the Illinois legislature in 1867, a republican elector-at-large in 1868, minister to the United States of Colombia 1869–72, a member of congress 1873–77, and minister to Peru in 1881. He died at Lima, March 27, 1882.

I

INGALLS, RUFUS, soldier, was born at Denmark, Me., Aug. 23, 1820, son of Cyrus and Sarah (Barker) Ingalls. He was graduated at the United States Military Academy, July 1, 1843, being assigned to the rifles. He served on frontier duty at Fort Jesup, La., and Fort Leavenworth, Kan., 1843–46, and was made second lieutenant in the 1st dragoons, Mar. 17, 1845. In the Mexican war he took part in the engagements at Embudo, Jan. 29, and Pueblo de Taos, Feb. 4, 1847, and was promoted first lieutenant, Feb. 16, 1847. On Jan. 12, 1848, he was appointed assistant quartermaster, with the rank of captain, and was ordered to California, where he served at Monterey, Los Angeles, and Fort Tuma, till 1853. He accompanied Col. Steptoe on his expedition across the continent, 1854–55; he was on duty at Washington, D.C., 1855–56; and on the commission to examine the war debt of Oregon and Washington Territory, 1856–60. On the outbreak of the civil war he served in the defense of Fort Pickens, Fla., until July, 1861, when he was assigned to duty with the army of the Potomac, and on Sept. 28th of that year, he was appointed aide-de-camp to Gen. McClellan. On Jan. 12, 1862, he was promoted major in the quartermaster's department, and on July 10th was made chief quartermaster of the army of the Potomac, performing the duties of that office with great ability and dispatch till the close of the war. He was commissioned brigadier-general of volunteers, May 23, 1863, and received the brevets of lieutenant-colonel, colonel, and brigadier-general, United States army, July 6, 1864, for meritorious and distinguished services. He was present at the battles of South Mountain, Antietam, Fredericksburg, Chancellorsville, Gettysburg, Wilderness, Spottsylvania and Cold Harbor; at the siege of Petersburg, and at the surrender of Gen. Lee. He was brevetted major-general of volunteers, and of the United States army, March 13, 1865, for faithful and meritorious

services during the war, and he was promoted in the regular service, assistant quartermaster-general with the rank of colonel, July 29, 1866. He was mustered out of the volunteer service, Sept. 1, 1866. He was chief quartermaster of the division of the Atlantic, 1867–75; of the Pacific, 1876–78, and of the division of the Missouri, 1878–81, and on Feb. 23, 1882, he was made quartermaster-general of the army, with the rank of brigadier-general, being retired, July 1, 1883, at his own request. After residing in Oregon eight years, he removed to New York city, and died there, Jan. 15, 1893.

IVERSON, ALFRED, senator, was born in Burke county, Ga., Dec. 3, 1798. He was

educated at Princeton, from which college he was graduated in the class of 1820. On his return to Georgia, he studied law and commenced the practice in Columbus. He was elected to the lower house of the legislature of Georgia three times and to the upper house once, when he was appointed by the legislature judge of the supreme court for the Columbus circuit. In 1844 he was elected one of the presidential electors at large for Georgia, voting for James K. Polk, and in 1846 was sent to represent his district in the thirtieth congress. He was afterward chosen by the legislature to represent Georgia in the senate of the United States, serving in the thirty-fourth, thirty-fifth and thirty-sixth congresses, withdrawing with his colleague, Robert Toombs, on the secession of their state in 1861. In the senate he was for several sessions chairman of the committee on claims, and a member of the committees on military affairs and the Pacific railroad. He was an advocate of state rights and one of the leaders in the secession movement. He died at Macon, Ga., March 4, 1873.

J

JACKSON, CLAIBORNE FOX, soldier and governor *of Missouri*, was born in Fleming county, Ky., *Apr. 4, 1806.* He removed to Missouri in 1832, and at once raising a company of volunteers, served as its captain against Black Hawk, taking part in the battle of Bad Axe, Aug. 1–2, 1832, when the chief was overwhelmed, and forced to surrender on the 27th of the same month. Capt. Jackson was then elected to the state legislature, and for one term was speaker of the house. He reorganized the banking system of the state, and was for several years its bank commissioner. He was elected governor in 1860, and being a strong southern sympathizer, he endeavored to carry the state out of the Union, and opposed the movements of the general government, which he characterized as "invasion of the state." He established a secession rendezvous called "Camp Jackson," which Gen. Nathaniel Lyon broke up when Gov. Jackson issued a call for 50,000 militia to defend the state against invasion. On the approach of Gen. Lyon with 1,500 men Jackson retreated from the capital, and in July, 1861, *the state convention which had been called into session to consider secession but rejected it and became, in effect, the Unionist governing body of the State, deposed him from the governorship.* He at once entered the Confederate army, with the rank of brigadier-general. He did some service at Boonville, and at Carthage; but his health failing, he was obliged to resign, and take up his home at Little Rock, Ark., where he died Dec. 6, 1862.

JACKSON, THOMAS JONATHAN ("Stonewall" Jackson), soldier, was born at Clarksburgh, W. Va., Jan. 21, 1824. His first ancestor in this country was John Jackson, of Scotch and Irish descent, who sailed from England in 1748 for America, and during the voyage fell in love with Elizabeth Cummins, daughter of a public-house owner in London, who, after disagreement with her stepfather, who was also her uncle, had hurled a silver tankard at his head, and then fled from home. On the vessel she formed the friendship of a family of colonists bound for Maryland, and agreed to serve them for a certain term of years after reaching land, thereby securing her immediate future. Two years after this she was married to Jackson, in Calvert county, Md. The couple forthwith made their way to West Virginia, and Elizabeth Jackson then had ample opportunity to display her intrepid spirit. She never quailed, it is said, at the Indian war-whoop, and her voice inspired the men around her to heroic resistance of the savages. She lived to be 105 years old, dying in 1828. In the war of the revolution John Jackson and his son bore honorable part as soldiers. The second son was Edward, grandfather of "Stonewall," and Jonathan, father of the latter, was a lawyer, who married Julia Beeleith, daughter of Mr. Neale, a merchant at Parksbury, W. Va. He died in middle life, and left his family without property, Thomas Jonathan then being three years of age. When six years old he was separated from his mother, and sent to live at the house of an uncle. Summoned within a twelvemonth to the dying bedside of that mother, it is said that her prayers, counsels, and triumphant death made an impression upon his mind that was never effaced. "His boyhood," says his latest biographer, "showed that the child is the father of the man." The same energy, determination, perseverence, that marked him in after years were visible then. At school he was studious and persevering; on the farm and in the mills, which belonged to his uncle, he was a valuable assistant. As soon as he was old enough he rode his uncle's racers; but although he made for him a good deal of money, it is stated that he never had the least propensity to the vices which belong to sporting characters, and had a reputation for uprightness, industry, and truth. He possessed talent for mathematics in an eminent degree. When he was but eighteen years old, by the influence of his uncle he was made sheriff of the county. Then, hearing of a vacancy in the appointment for the cadetship at the U.S. military academy at West Point, N.Y., in the gift of the member of congress from his district, he besought his friends to aid him in securing it; and to one who asked him if he did not fear that his education was insufficient to enable him to enter and

sustain himself at West Point, he replied: "I know that I shall have the application necessary to succeed; I hope that I have the capacity; at least, I am determined to try, and I want you to help me." Being encouraged to hope that his application would be successful, he resolved to make it so, if possible, and accordingly went to Washington, where the secretary of war was so pleased with his manliness and resolution that he gave him the appointment, and said to him: "Sir, you have a good name. Go to West Point, and the first man who insults you, knock him down, and have it charged to my account." In June, 1842, he went to West Point, and was admitted to the academy. Deficient as he was

in preparation, he was obliged to employ every expedient to keep up with his class. A classmate said of this period: "We were studying algebra, and maybe analytical geometry, that winter, and Jackson was very low in his class standing. All lights were put out at 'taps,' and just before the signal he would pile up his grate with anthracite coal, and lying prone before it on the floor, would work away at his lessons by the glare of the fire, which scorched his very brain, until a late hour of the night. He rose steadily year by year, until we used to say, if we had to stay here another year 'old Jack' would be at the head of the class." He himself said that he studied very hard for what he got at West Point. He was graduated in 1846, seventeenth in a class of seventy. Among his classmates were Gens. G. B. McClellan, Foster, Reno, Stoneman, Couch, Gibbon *(1847 graduate)*, A. P. Hill *(1847 graduate),* Pickett, Maury, D. R. Jones, W. D. Smith, and Wilcox. While at the academy he compiled for his own use a set of rules and maxims relating to morals, manners, dress, choice of friends, and the aim of life. Perhaps the most characteristic of these was, "You may be whatever you resolve to be." Of the others, let these quotations suffice: "Through life let your principal object be the discharge of duty." "Disregard public opinion when it interferes with your duty." "Sacrifice your life rather than your word," etc. Upon his graduation he was ordered at once to New Orleans, La., and sailed thence for Mexico to join the American army, under Gen. Winfield Scott. He was in most of the battles of the Mexican war for the ensuing two years. After the operations which ended in the capture of Vera Cruz, March, 1847, he became second lieutenant in Capt. J. B. Magruder's battery of light field artillery. In the engagement of Churubusco he took the place of the first lieutenant, and for his gallantry was promoted to the brevet rank of captain. In the battle of Chapultepec his conduct was such that Capt. Magruder wrote: "If devotion and industry, talent, and gallantry are the highest qualities of a soldier, then he is entitled to the distinction which their possession confers." For this he received the brevet of major. Years after, when his pupils at Lexington, Va., were asking him

for particulars of the Chapultepec fight, he modestly described it, when one of them exclaimed in astonishment, "Major, why didn't you run when your commander was disabled?" With a quiet smile he answered: "I was not ordered to do so. If I had been ordered to run, I would have done so; but I was directed to hold my position, and I had no right to abandon it." In after years he confessed that the part he played in stepping out and assuring the men that there was no danger, when the cannon ball passed through his legs, was the only willful falsehood he ever told in his life. After the capture of Mexico city, he had a few months of leisure in that capital, and was charmed with what he saw of its social life. Here, too, he began the religious life which was so marked in all his future career. Col. Francis Taylor, the commandant of his regiment, the 1st U.S. artillery, who was an earnest Christian, was the first of all ever to speak to Jackson upon personal religion. Characteristically, Jackson determined to study the Bible for himself. In his quest for truth, moreover, as he had no preference for sects, he sought out the Roman Catholic archbishop of Mexico, with whom he had several interviews, although he was not convinced by him as to the correctness of the Roman Catholic faith. In the summer of 1848, the U.S. troops returned from Mexico, and for *two years* Maj. Jackson was stationed at Fort Hamilton, L.I. Here he attended to his religious duties, but afterward acknowledged that he went through them with no feeling stronger than that of having performed a duty. Sunday, Apr. 29, 1849, however, he was baptized at St. John's Protestant Episcopal church, at the Fort, by Rev. Mr. Schofield. He did not apply for the rite of confirmation. In 1851 he was ordered to Ford Meade, near Tampa Bay, Fla., and remained there but six months. Then, having been elected (March 27, 1851) professor of natural and experimental philosophy and artillery tactics in the Lexington (Va.) military institute, he at once resigned from the U.S. army to accept the position. Here he spent the next ten years of his life. In the early part of his stay at Lexington, he identified himself with the Presbyterian church in that place, making his public profession of religion Nov. 22, 1851, and soon after was chosen a deacon in the church. The subject of becoming a preacher, moreover, seriously engaged his attention. Forthwith he began Christian labor among the negroes, getting up a large Sabbath-school class among them, the Sabbath-school which grew out of it being now in existence. Influenced by a sermon from his pastor, he called on him to know if he (Jackson) was to be deterred from making public prayer because of modesty or false shame, saying that he had not been used to public speaking, was naturally diffident, and feared that he would not edify those who were present, but added, "You are my pastor, and the spiritual guide of the church, and if you think it my duty, I shall make the effort." But when he was called on, his embarrassment was such that the service was almost as painful to the audience as to himself. Jackson was not asked to pray again, and after several weeks he renewed his visit to the pastor's to know if this was because of the latter's unwillingness to inflict distress upon him. Being answered in the affirmative, his reply was: "Yes; but my comfort or discomfort is not the question; if it is my duty to lead in prayer, then I must persevere in it until I learn to do it right, and I wish you to discard all consideration for my feelings." The man's crystalline truthfulness may be added as another moral trait. It is said that if in conversation he unintentionally made a misstatement about a matter of no moment whatever, he would lose no time in hastening to correct it, even if he

had to go upon the mission in a pouring rain; and upon being remonstrated with for this extreme action would say, "I went simply because I have discovered that it was a misstatement, and I could not sleep comfortably to-night, unless I corrected it." He was an abstainer from the use of intoxicating drinks on principle, and said during the civil war, "No, I thank you, I never use it (the social glass); I am more afraid of it than of Federal bullets." Testimony as to the profound nature of his religious character, and the extent of his habitual submission to the will of God may be found in the "Life and Letters," published by his wife in 1892, from which much of this sketch is derived, and is of extraordinary interest. He was twice married: first to Elinor, daughter of Rev. George Jenkins, president of Washington college, Va., who died about fourteen months after the union; then (July 16, 1857) to Mary Anna, daughter of Rev. Dr. R. H. Morrison, president of Davidson college, N.C., who, with one daughter, survives him. In the summer and fall of 1856, he made a five months' tour in Europe. Of his ten years' experience at Lexington as military instructor the concurrence of testimony is, that it was not especially successful, one writer going so far as to say that he was a laughing stock to the institute students. Near the close of that year, and as the civil war cloud began to darken, Mrs. Jackson's "Life" declares that her husband was, in his feelings, "strongly for the Union, but at the same was a firm state's rights man. In politics he had always been a democrat, but never a very strong partisan." "He never," she adds, "was a secessionist, and maintained that it was better for the South to fight for her rights in the Union than out of it." She adds: "I am very confident that he would never have fought for the sole object of perpetuating slavery." When Virginia seceded from the Union, the superintendent of the Lexington institute was notified by Governor Letcher that he should need the services of the more advanced classes of the cadets as drill-masters, and they must be prepared to go to Richmond at a moment's notice, under the command of Maj. Jackson. Sunday morning, Apr. 21, 1861, Jackson received the summons, and at once departed from Lexington with his small command, and did not return to his home. He had no furlough, and was never absent from his troops in all his subsequent military service. At Richmond he was made colonel of the Virginia forces, and ordered to take command at Harper's Ferry. When Virginia adopted the constitution of the Confederate states, he advised his wife by letter, to manage all home interests so that she could return to her father's roof in North Carolina. Up to this date, she declares that he had hoped that the gathering storm might pass over without bloodshed. At Harper's Ferry he promptly took possession of Maryland Heights, but as to his plans in general and in detail, displayed the reticence and secrecy which marked his subsequent campaigns. It was his maxim that, in war, mystery was the key to success, and to one of a committee of the Maryland legislature who visited his camp at this time, and asked him: "Colonel, how many troops have you?" he answered only, "I should be glad if Lincoln thought I had 15,000." When the Confederate authorities located at Richmond, Gen. Joseph E. Johnston was sent to Harper's Ferry, and superseded Jackson in command. The Virginia troops were organized into a brigade, and Col. Jackson was made its commander. This body afterward became the "Stonewall" brigade. July 3, 1861, Gen. R. E. Lee, commander of the Confederate army, forwarded to him his commission as brigadier-general in the Confederate army. Gen. Johnston having evacuated Harper's Ferry, after removing from it its valuable machinery and war materials, fell back to Winchester, Va., and in the month of July pressed on to Manassas Junction to the relief of Gen. Beauregard, who in the first battle of Bull Run (July 21st) was sorely pressed by the Federal forces. *Jackson's brigade had arrived at Manassas Junction, July 20, and reached the key position on the battlefield about noon on July 21.* The troops of South Carolina, commanded by Gen. Bernard E. Bee, had been overwhelmed, and he rode up to Jackson in despair, exclaiming,

"They are beating us back." "Then," said Jackson, "we will give them the bayonet." Bee rode off to rejoin his command, and cried out to them to look at Jackson, saying, "There he stands like a stone wall. Rally behind the Virginians!" Bee then led his troops in another charge, but fell dead while making it. This was the genesis of the sobriquet which did not leave Jackson thereafter, by which he is known in history, and which pertained thenceforth to his brigade. His distinguished career was now fairly begun. For his conduct at Bull Run he was commissioned major-general (September, 1861) and placed in command of the Confederate forces in the lower Shenandoah valley. Some apparently profitless and wearisome marches and movements in that quarter during the next five months brought no material military results, but, severely testing the mettle of his troops, somewhat impaired his popularity with them. In March, 1862, he found himself at Winchester, Va., with but 3,400 men and eighteen guns, while Gen. N. P. Banks was approaching him from the Potomac with a largely superior force. Jackson's instructions were to detain as large a hostile body as possible in the valley without risking the destruction of his own troops. He fell back as far as Strasburg, but turned, on the 23d of the month, and fought the battle of Kernstown the same day, after a forced march of from fourteen to twenty-five miles. In this action he was worsted, and forced

to retire up the valley to Swift Run Gap, in the Blue Ridge, on the south fork of the Shenandoah river, which he struck about the 9th of April. Meanwhile an adversary, Gen. Milroy, was marching across the mountains from the west to unite with Banks. But reinforcements for Jackson were approaching under Gen. Ewell, and another Confederate force, under Gen. Edward Johnson, was at Buffalo Gap, just west of Staunton. Giving orders to Ewell to hold Banks in check, while he, forming a junction with Johnson, should take the offensive against Milroy, Jackson encountered and defeated that officer in a severe action at McDowell, May 8, 1862, and forced him to retreat with a heavy loss in supplies. Then, retracing his steps, he effected a junction with Ewell, and throwing himself into the Luray valley by a forced march, day and night, he stole upon the flank and rear of Banks's army at Winchester, and captured detached bodies of Federal troops, artillery, and wagon trains. This brought the immediate concentration of strong Federal columns from different quarters in the Shenandoah valley upon Jackson's rear for his destruction. They threatened him. Jackson detached Ewell to meet Frémont, approaching from the *northwest,* and with his own division, encumbered with 2,300 prisoners and over 9,000 stand of captured arms, promptly threaded the Luray valley to White House, and passing around another Federal general (Shields), took position near Ewell at Fort Republic, equally distant between Shields and *Frémont.* On the 8th and 9th of June the Confederate generals worsted their opponents in sharply contested engagements. The effect of Jackson's operations was to neutralize an aggregate of nearly 70,000 Federals, with a highly adverse influence upon the Federal Gen. McClellan's campaign against Richmond, added to the gravest apprehension excited at

Washington and throughout the whole Union, for the safety of the national capital. *Banks retreated across the Potomac into Maryland two weeks earlier, after his defeat at Winchester, May 25.* It has been said that in this "campaign of the valley, Jackson displayed true military instinct, and the highest military art. By vigilance, sagacity, celerity, and secrecy of movement, and faultless tactical skill on the field of battle, he achieved the greatest possible results with the smallest possible means. His reputation was now fixed in the estimation of friend and foe, and while the Confederacy was filled with the renown of his achievements, the Federal forces were in constant apprehension of his prowess." At once, when these results had been secured, Jackson was summoned to Richmond to concert with Lee for the deliverance of the Confederate capital, then almost invested by McClellan. Appointed forthwith to command a corps, he suddenly reversed himself to the Federal forces at New Chancellorsville, Va., and in a series of desperately fought battles, routed the besieging army, and drove McClellan to shelter at Harrison's Landing, on the James river. *Jackson's performance during these battles was sub-par.* When Richmond was thus relieved, without pause Jackson confronted Pope, who was threatening the Confederate capital from the north, and in the battle of Cedar Run (Aug. 9, 1862) inflicted signal defeat upon the general, compelling him to retrace his steps across the Rappahannock. Then Pope was reinforced by the army of the Potomac and by fresh troops from the northern states, but on the field of Manassas (Aug. 30, 1862), in the second Bull Run battle, he suffered as severe an overthrow as had fallen to McDowell's lot at the first battle in July of the previous year. On the 25th of the month, Jackson, under orders, had passed around

Pope's flank with 2,500 men, seized his depot at Manassas, and broken up his communications. In the action of Aug. 30th, his was also the conspicuous figure. Then came the invasion of Maryland by the Confederates, in which Jackson was detached by Lee for special operations at Harper's Ferry, Va., and soon reported to his superior that this fortified position had fallen into his hands with 11,000 men, an equal number of small arms, seventy-three pieces of artillery, 200 wagons, and large stores of camp and garrison equipage. The withdrawal of Jackson's force for this service, however, weakened Lee's army so seriously that the Confederate leader was brought to bay at Antietam, Md., before Jackson could rejoin him, and was compelled to accept battle under every disadvantage. The timely arrival after of Jackson's division not only averted an otherwise inevitable disaster for the Confederates, but secured Lee from the destruction that awaited him if defeated with his rear resting upon the Potomac river. In Gen. Burnside's attack on Lee at Fredericksburg, Va., *Dec. 13, 1862,* Jackson, who had been promoted to the rank of lieutenant-general, held the Confederate right. When, in April, 1863, the Federal Gen. Hooker made a feint of passing the Rappahannock river below Fredericksburg, the movement was confronted by Jackson, and at his own suggestion he was entrusted with his last flank operation, a swift march around, and descent upon, the Federal right and rear. On the 2d of May, in the afternoon, he fell upon the 11th Federal corps and completely routed it, but was checked in his advance by Federal batteries hastily brought into line. Between eight and nine o'clock Jackson rode beyond his own lines with a small party to reconnoitre. On his return he and his suite were mistaken by some of his own troops for Federal cavalry, and were fired upon by

Lane's brigade. Jackson fell with three wounds, one ball shattering his left arm two inches below the shoulder. Another passed through the same arm below the elbow. A third entered the palm of his right hand. These volleys drew an immediate answer from the Federal force. A sharp conflict began between the Federals and Confederates, in which the Federal soldiers charged over the very body of the Confederate leader. That was recovered, however, in a counter-charge, and carried from the field under a terrible fire, by which one of the litter-bearers was slain. By the fall of the litter Jackson was grievously contused. "Meanwhile," says one biographer, "his charge to the surgeons in attendance was, 'Do not tell the troops that I am wounded.'" The doubly wounded arm having been amputated, he was left serene, cheerful and hopeful, talking freely of the battles, the bravery and the deserts of his subordinates, and of his old "Stonewall" brigade. Pneumonia supervened, and, in his weakened condition, he died May 10, 1863. His remains were taken to Richmond, Va., and after a public funeral in that city, to Lexington, where they were buried. A bronze statue, paid for by English subscriptions, was unveiled at Richmond, Va., in 1875. It is probably a fair judgment which says of this extraordinary man that, "the more his operations in the spring, summer, and fall of 1862 are studied, the more striking must the merits of this almost uniformly successful soldier appear, with all his intense perception of the value as well as right method of the active defensive of which he may indeed be regarded as the very incarnation." His life was written by R. L. Dabney (N.Y., 1863); by John Esten Cooke (1866), and by Mary Anna Jackson, his wife (N.Y., 1892).

JACKSON, WILLIAM HICKS, soldier and capitalist, was born at Paris, Tenn., Oct. 1,

1835, son of Dr. Alexander and Mary W. (Hurt) Jackson. His parents early removed from Halifax county, Va., to Paris, and thence to Jackson, Tenn. They belonged to the best stock of Virginia, and bequeathed to their sons, Howell Edmunds and William Hicks, the high qualities which made them both eminent men. Descended from such ancestors and trained by such parents, William Hicks Jackson displayed in early life the strong impulses, and acquired the complete self-control, which have so distinguished his manhood. His preparatory education was received in the best schools of Jackson, and at West Tennessee College, where he evinced strong intellectual powers. He gained reputation among his schoolmates as the stout defender of the weak against the strong. In 1852 he was appointed a cadet to West Point. Although hard study and severe regulations were irksome to his fiery spirit, he was guided by his firm resolve to gratify the wishes of his father, and was graduated in 1856 with credit to himself. In his career at West Point he

displayed the same traits that marked his boyhood, and was recognized as a leader among his comrades. After the usual furlough and some months spent at the barracks at Carlisle, Pa., he was sent, in 1857, to Fort Union, New Mexico, where, as an officer in the regiment of mounted rifles, he took an active part in the principal Indian fights in that territory with such men as Kit Carson, La Rue, and others as his guides. The adventurous character of this service was well suited to the bold and ardent temperament of the young soldier. He was frequently complimented in orders from headquarters of both department and army for his gallantry and good judgment. Although not an advocate of secession, his intense loyalty to his native state induced him, when the first shot was fired in the civil war, to resign his commission in the U.S. regular army, and to offer his services to the Confederate States. After an adventurous journey in running the blockade at Galveston, he finally arrived in Tennessee, was appointed a captain of artillery by Gov. Harris, and summoned before the state military board at Nashville, which retained him two weeks in consultation on the subject of the equipment of cavalry and artillery. He then reported to Gen. Pillow at Memphis, and served on his staff in the campaigns of Missouri and Kentucky. He was assigned to the duty of organizing a light battery at Columbus, Ky., with which he reported to Gen. Pillow. On Nov. 7, 1861, followed the battle of Belmont, in which he performed the exploit of conducting three regiments of infantry to the rear of Grant's army, routing it and securing a Confederate triumph. For this service he was promoted to the rank of colonel. In this battle his horse was shot under him, and he received a minie-ball in the right side, which, inflicting a wound at the time supposed to be fatal, has never been extracted. He was placed by Gen. Albert Sidney

Johnston in command of all the cavalry in western Tennessee, and was engaged in many severe minor battles there and in northern Mississippi. He led the brilliant dash on Holly Springs, Miss., Dec. 20, 1862, that resulted in the capture of 1,800 infantry, many cavalry, millions of dollars' worth of stores, and Gen. Grant's private papers. The loss of this secondary base of supplies compelled Gen. Grant to abandon his campaign by land against Vicksburg, caused him to return to Memphis and organize his river campaign. This brilliant service gained him promotion to the rank of brigadier-general, and the unique distinction of being mentioned in Gen. Grant's "Memoirs" as the only man who came near capturing him. Gen. Jackson was next assigned to the command of the second division of cavalry under Gen. Van Dorn in Tennessee, the first division being commanded by Gen. Forrest, and soon after participated in the battle of Thompson's Station, which resulted in the capture of Col. Coburn's Federal brigade of 1,600 infantry. *In the summer of 1863,* at the request of Gen. Joseph E. Johnston, Gen. Jackson joined him at Canton, Miss., and commanded the cavalry of his army in the

movement for the relief of Vicksburg. Later, at Johnston's request, he was transferred with him to the army of Tennessee, and during the Georgia campaign commanded the cavalry on the left wing. Among the gallant exploits during this period were the defeat of Kilpatrick at Lovejoy Station, and in connection with Gen. Wheeler, the capture at Newnan, Ga., of 1,500 Federal cavalry. Gen. Jackson was selected by Gen. Hood to join him in the invasion of Tennessee. His division led the advance in pursuing Gen. Schofield's retreating forces, held them at bay for an entire night at Spring Hill, participated in the battle of Franklin, Nov. 30, 1864, and led the Confederate advance to a point only a few miles from the fortified city of Nashville. At Murfreesboro, Jackson defeated the Federals and drove them back to their intrenchments, and after the battle of Nashville, his division covered the retreat of Hood's army. He was now placed in command of Forrest's cavalry troop, and the Texas brigade, and was recommended for promotion by Gens. Dick Taylor, N. B. Forrest, Joseph E. Johnston, and previously by Polk and Hardee; but having incurred the displeasure of Pres. Davis on account of arresting a friend of the

president's brother, Joseph, he failed to receive the promotion. Gen. Jackson next served in the Alabama campaign, defeating Gens. Croxton and McCook, and arrived at Marion Junction, where he learned of Forrest's defeat at Selma. Then came the final surrender at Gainesville, Ala., May 9, 1865. Gen. Jackson performed his last military service as Confederate commissioner in association with Gen. Dennis, Federal commissioner, for the parole of the troops at Gainesville and other points. Returning to his home at Jackson, Tenn., the retired soldier entered upon his peaceful career as a cotton planter. On Dec. 15, 1868, he was married to Selene, daughter of Gen. W. G. Harding, a highly accomplished and lovely woman. She died Dec. 13, 1892, leaving three children: Eunice, wife of Albert D. Marks, a son of ex-Gov. Marks, and a prominent attorney of Nashville; Selene Harding, wife of William R. Elliston; and William Harding Jackson, who succeeds his father in the management of "Belle Meade," and gives promise of emulating his father's usefulness. At the request of Gen. Harding, Gen. Jackson became his assistant in the management of the vast stock farm, "Belle Meade," comprising 5,500 acres, where he found opportunity not only to indulge the tastes so firmly implanted in him as a boy on his father's plantation, but also to devote his mind to the development of scientific agriculture. He was the projector and moving spirit of the agricultural journal known as the "Rural Sun," which was long the most popular agricultural publication in the South. He was president of the company with Col. J. B. Killebrew as chief editor. In his own language, "Agricultural journals, like almanacs, should be calculated for the latitudes they are designed to serve. . . . My observation has taught me that many young men of the South, in their efforts to apply the teachings of the northern journals

to the conditions of the South, have led them into disastrous errors." Refusing the highest political offices which his fellow-citizens desired to thrust upon him, preferring rather to be the power behind the throne than the shadow upon it, he has proved his public spirit and shown the highest attributes of citizenship by devoting his energies to contributing to the material development of the country, and has accepted positions tending to promote the public welfare. He has been president of the state association of farmers; was organizer and for many years president of the national agricultural congress, and state bureau of agriculture of Tennessee. In the latter capacity he was influential in creating the office of state commissioner of agriculture, and in promoting the publication of that notable work, "The Resources of Tennessee," of which the secretary of the board, Col. J. B. Killebrew, was editor. This work has been published in many different languages and scattered abroad, and, according to leading authorities, was the most eminent agency in first attracting immigration to Tennessee. As president and fiscal agent of the state bureau of agriculture, no money could be spent without his signature. So well was this duty discharged, that the whole work of the department was completed, including the publication of the "Resources of Tennessee" (1874), at a total cost of $13,500, leaving $6,500 out of an appropriation of $20,000 to be returned to the state treasury. In recognition of this distinguished service and economical expenditure, he was complimented by a vote of thanks by the general assembly of Tennessee. In addition to his work as an agriculturist, Gen. Jackson has been an active promoter of various public enterprises: as president of the Safe Deposit Trust Co., of Nashville, of the Nashville Gas Light Co., and of the Nashville street railway, which he took over when in the hands of a receiver in a disordered condition, and reorganized and rehabilitated, financially and materially. In no instance has his genius been more conspicuously displayed than in the perfection of the great "Belle Meade," celebrated in poetry and song, which experts from England pronounce to be the best managed and most complete stock farm in the world. It is the home of Iroquois, the most famous race-horse, and now one of the most valuable stallions in the world, who won on the English turf an unequaled triumph. Here are also Luke Blackburn (imp.), Great Tom, Tremont, Loyalist (imp.), Clarendon, and other "kings of the turf," as well as extensive herds of thoroughbred Jersey cattle, Shetland ponies, and the finest deer park in America. "Belle Meade" is a typical southern home, the frequent scene of true southern hospitality, and here Gen. Jackson has entertained Pres. and Mrs. Cleveland, cabinet officers, statesmen, authors, poets, and many foreigners, including members of the nobility from different countries. In many other ways, also, he contributed to the material prosperity, and stimulated the progress, of his native state. He erected at Nashville the finest office and apartment building in Tennessee, a model of architecture. He was a moving spirit in promoting the great Tennessee centennial exposition of 1896–97, and declining the presidency served as chairman of its executive committee. After the close of the war he was the advocate of sectional conciliation, and exerted his powerful influence at all times and at all places, but especially in the Confederate Veteran Association, in which he held high rank. By promoting such public enterprises and exerting an influence so salutary and potent, Gen. Jackson furnished an illustrious example of the private citizen of public spirit who, declining political office, "does more than armies for the commonweal."

The well-known author and scientist, Col. J. B. Killebrew, who knew him over a quarter of a century, has well said: "Gen. Jackson is a strong man, mentally, physically and morally. He never does anything by halves. He never rests as long as there is an improvement to be made. Whatever he puts his hands on, prospers. He has an intuitive knowledge of men, and therefore his agents are always the best for accomplishing the purposes for which he selects them. In the organization and conduct of the many large enterprises with which his name is associated, he has acquired the habits of thought peculiar to all successful men. He goes directly to the point, and he has all the precision of a martinet, with the power of a conqueror. Broad, but accurate; diligent, but deliberate; patient, but prompt; kind, but firm; fearing no weight of responsibility, yet not careless of it, he always meets and overcomes difficulties." *He died March 30, 1903.*

JEFFERS, WILLIAM NICHOLSON, naval officer and gun inventor, ws born in Gloucester county, N.J., Oct. 6, 1824. He was appointed

a midshipman in the navy Sept. 24, 1840, and until 1843 was attached to the frigate United States, of the Pacific squadron. In 1844–45 he served on the Congress, of the Brazil squadron, and in 1846 studied at the naval school in Philadelphia. He was promoted to be passed midshipman in July of the year last named, and, during the Mexican war, as an officer of the Vixen, participated in the attacks on Alvarado, San Juan and Vera Cruz, and the capture of Tuspan and Tampico. He was promoted to be master in June, 1854, commissioned as lieutenant in January, 1855, and in 1856 commanded the Water Witch on the river La Plata. While commander of the Water Witch he rescued the Spanish steamer Cartagena, and for this service was presented with a sword by the queen of Spain. In 1857 he was on special duty at Washington, and then, until 1860, was attached to the home squadron. At the opening of the civil war he was assigned to ordnance duty at Norfolk, but was shortly made commander of the Philadelphia, and during the closing months of 1861, and the winter and spring of 1862, commanded the Underwriter, engaging brilliantly in the capture of Roanoke Island and Elizabeth City, and in frequent actions in the waters of Albemarle sound. He was advanced to the rank of lieutenant-commander in July, 1862, and commanded the ironclad Monitor in the actions at Sewell's Point and Fort Darling. Thereafter, and until the close of the war, he was on ordnance duty in Philadelphia and Washington. He was commissioned as commander in March, 1865, and after two years' service at the Washington naval observatory, was promoted to be captain in July, 1870. In April, 1873, Capt. Jeffers was made chief of the bureau of ordnance of the navy department, and served in that position with splendid and lasting results until his death. In 1875 he perfected a system of bronze and steel boat howitzers, and in 1876 effected improvements which doubled the power of the Dahlgren guns, and designed a complete system of breech-loading guns. He was the author of: "Short Methods in Navigation" (1849); "Theory and Practice of Naval Gunnery" (1850); "Inspection and Proof of Cannon" (1864); "Marine Surveying" (1871); "Ordnance Instructions for U.S. Navy" (1866 and 1880), and a large number of pamphlets on naval and scientific topics. He was promoted to the rank of commodore in February, 1878, and died in Washington, D.C., July 23, 1883.

JENKINS, MICAH, soldier, was born at Edisto Island, S.C., *Dec. 1, 1835*, son of John and Elizabeth (Clark) Jenkins. His earliest American ancestor was Joseph Jenkins, who came from Wales. His son, Joseph, was married to Martha Hand, and the descent runs through their son Joseph, who was married to Phoebe Chafin; their son, Richard, who was married to Martha Rippon, and their son, Joseph, who was married to Elizabeth Evans, and was the father of John. He was an officer in the revolutionary war, and for many years was a member of the state legislature. Micah Jenkins was graduated at the South Carolina Military Academy in 1854, and in connection with a classmate, Col. A. Coward, established a military school at Yorkville, S.C., in 1855. He was elected colonel of the 5th South Carolina volunteers at the beginning of the civil war, and reorganized it at the end of its year's enlistment as Jenkins' Palmetto sharpshooters. He commanded a brigade in the seven days' battles around Richmond, Va., and after Gaines' Mill and Fraser's farm, brought out his sharpshooters, originally numbering more than 1,000, with but 125 men, his personal aid having been killed at his side, and his own hat pierced by five, and his clothing by twelve, bullets. His sabre when partly drawn, was struck by a minie ball which cut through the edge of the blade and scabbard (killing his horse) and immediately after the lower half of sabre and scabbard were shot away. The remnant, in its partly drawn condition, is now in the possession of his family, a prized and curious relic. He was promoted brigadier-general and was at the second battle of Manassas (Bull Run) where he was severely wounded and had two of his colonels and his adjutant killed. In the spring of 1863 he led a corps of observation on the Blackwater, near Richmond and Petersburg. In September following he went to Georgia with Longstreet but reached there too late for the battle of Chickamauga. He then commanded Hood's division and accompanied Longstreet to Tennessee. He removed thence in the spring to Virginia, where he met his death at the hands of Mahone's brigade (the same which killed "Stonewall" Jackson) by mistake, *about noon on the second day of Grant's advance through the "Wilderness," May 6, 1864. Not true; Jackson was accidentally shot by soldiers in General James H. Lane's brigade.* In his "Battle of Seven Pines," Maj.-Gen. Gustavus W. Smith says, at page 63: "It is believed that the annals of war show few, if any, instances of more persistent, skillful and effective battlefield fighting, than was done by the two South Carolina regiments under Col. Jenkins on the afternoon of May 31st." In 1856 he was married to Caroline, daughter of Gen. D. F. Jamison, president of the South Carolina secession convention. He was a resident of Orangeburg county, and author of "Life of Bertrand du Guesclin." Mr. and Mrs. Jenkins had four sons.

JOHNSON, ANDREW, the seventeenth president of the United States, was born in

Raleigh, N.C., Dec. 29, 1808. His parents were poor but respectable, and when he was only five years of age he had the misfortune to lose his father while the latter was attempting to save another from drowning. When the boy was ten years of age, his mother was obliged to apprentice him to a tailor, on account of her extreme necessity. He learned to read while he was learning his trade, but it is a fact that he offers the exception of an American boy who never went to school a single day of his life. He completed his apprenticeship in 1824, and then went to Laurens Court House, South Carolina, where he worked as a journeyman tailor until May 1826, when he removed to Greenville, Tenn. At this time Mr. Johnson had the good fortune to obtain for a wife Eliza McCardle, a woman whose capacity and whose devotion to him exercised a marked influence on his future life. Under her tuition, he progressed rapidly in the attainment of useful knowledge, and soon among his townspeople he began to be recognized, through his self-reliance and persistent energy, as a born leader. He identified himself with the laboring classes, a fact which they recognized by giving him their votes when he was a candidate for alderman in 1828, insuring his election to that position, which he held until 1830, when he was elected mayor. In 1834 he interested himself in the adoption of a new constitution for the state of Tennessee, guaranteeing important rights to the people, and this action resulted in fairly starting him in public life. In politics he was a democrat of the Jackson school, and as such he was elected in 1835 and again in 1839 to the legislature of the state. In 1840 he was one of the presidential electors on the Van Buren ticket and stumped the state for his candidate, proving himself very effective as a speaker. In 1841 he was elected to the state senate, where he became a useful and active member as he had previously been in the house. His services and abilities were by this time fully appreciated, and in 1843 he was elected to congress from his district. There he remained, constantly re-elected until 1853, when he was chosen governor of Tennessee, being re-elected to that position two years later. In 1857 Mr. Johnson was elected to the United States senate, where he remained until 1862, when he was appointed the military governor of Tennessee. Andrew Johnson was recognized by this time as "a representative of the people." He never permitted any sneers at his calling, nor any attempted disparagement of the laboring classes to pass unrebuked. Once, when Jefferson Davis superciliously asked him, "What do you mean by the laboring classes?" Johnson replied, "Those who earn their bread by the sweat of their face and not by fatiguing their ingenuity." While in congress, having been born and reared in a slave state he accepted slavery where it existed, but was no advocate of its extension. He denounced the John Brown raid in December, 1859, but he readily acquiesced in the election of 1860 of Abraham Lincoln to the

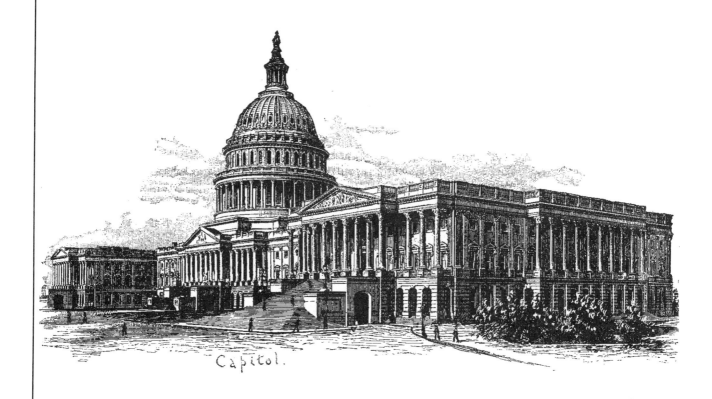

Capitol.

presidency. He bitterly opposed and denied the right of any state to withdraw from the Union. For himself he was one of the strongest of Union men and on July 26, 1861, introduced a resolution into the senate, which was passed, to the effect that the war had been forced upon the country by the disunionists of the southern states, that it was not prosecuted on the part of the Union in any spirit of oppression, but to defend and maintain the supremacy of the constitution and laws, and to preserve the Union with all its dignity and equality and the rights of the southern states unimpaired, and that as soon as those objects were accomplished the war ought to cease. Johnson's course in congress had brought down upon him the wrath of leading secessionists, and he was burned in effigy at Memphis, threatened with lynching on his return to Tennessee, a price being set upon his head and personal violence threatened if he remained within the state. His home was assaulted, his slaves confiscated, his sick wife and her child driven into the street and his house turned into a hospital barracks by the Confederates. This was in 1861. In the early part of 1862 Gen. Grant entered Tennessee and the secessionists left it. President Lincoln appointed Mr. Johnson military governor of the state, with the rank of brigadier-general of volunteers. His course as military governor was fearless, but cool and judicious. He did

Birthplace of Johnson.

much to hold Tennessee within the Union, as he alleged that it had never been out of that condition. *On June 8, 1864,* Andrew Johnson was unanimously nominated by the national republican convention at Baltimore as the candidate for the vice-presidency, and soon after a mass-meeting was held at Nashville to ratify the nomination and to congratulate Mr. Johnson. In speaking to this meeting, Mr. Johnson said: "Slavery is dead, and you must pardon me if I do not mourn over its dead body. You can bury it out of sight. Now, as regards emancipation, I want to say to the blacks that liberty means liberty to work and enjoy the fruits of your labor. Idleness is not freedom." On March 4, 1865, Vice-President Johnson was duly qualified and assumed his position. On the 15th of April Abraham Lincoln fell by the hands of an assassin, and Mr. Johnson took the oath of office as president of the United States in his private apartments at the Kirkwood House, in the presence of Mr. Lincoln's cabinet officers and others. After subscribing to the oath, President Johnson spoke as follows: "Gentlemen: I must be permitted to say that I have been almost overwhelmed by the announcement of the sad event that has so recently occurred. I feel incompetent to perform duties so important and responsible as those which have been so unexpectedly thrown upon me. As to an indication of any policy which may be pursued by me in the administration of the government, I have to say that that must be left for development as the administration progresses. The message or declaration must be made by the acts as they transpire. The only assurance I can give of the future, is by reference to the past. . . . I must be permitted to say, if I understand the feelings of my own heart, I have long labored to ameliorate and elevate the condition of the American people. Toil and an honest advocacy of the great principles of the government have been my lot. The duties have been mine-the consequences are God's. This has been the foundation of my political creed. I feel that in the end the government will triumph and that these great principles will be permanently established." It was during the administration of President Johnson that the territories of the United States assumed their final form. Dakota was taken from the northern part of Nebraska, Arizona from the western part of New Mexico; Idaho was organized as an independent territory, and afterward the territory of Montana was cut off from Idaho, and the territory of Wyoming from portions of Idaho, Dakota and Utah. On March 1, 1867, the territory of Nebraska was admitted into the Union as a state, and on the 30th of that month, the United States received from Russia, for the sum of $7,200,000, the cession of the territory of Alaska. Soon after his accession to the presidency a serious disagreement took place between Mr. Johnson and congress, the principal question at issue relating to the reorganization of the southern states and the relation which those states sustained to the Union during the civil war. President Johnson maintained that the seceded states had never been out of the Union and that their ordinances of secession were null and void. On the other hand, congress maintained that, while the acts of secession were unconstitutional, yet, by those acts, seceded states had actually been out of the Union and that they could not be restored to their former status without legislation. President Johnson cut this gordian knot by issuing proclamations establishing provisional governments over the seceded states. Congress answered this by passing the civil rights bill admitting the freedmen of the South to all the rights of citizenship, over his veto. In August, 1866, President Johnson,

accompanied by his cabinet in part, and by Gen. Grant, Adm. Farragut and other prominent persons, made the tour of the northern states, which afterward became known as "Swinging Round the Circle." During this tour the president spoke freely in denunciation of congress and in favor of his own policy, the result being that the journey was the cause of intense excitement and partisanship. At the second session of congress in 1867, the policy of the president was severely condemned, and the affairs of the administration grew more critical. Congress passed several acts over the president's veto, and eventually the work of the reconstruction was continued under the congressional plan. In the months of June and July, 1868, Arkansas, Alabama, Florida, Georgia, North and South Carolina, and Louisiana, were admitted into the Union, but in every case such readmission was effected over the veto of the president. On Feb. 21st President Johnson dismissed Edwin M. Stanton, the secretary of war, from office. Congress held that this act was a usurpation of power and a violation of the tenure-of-office law. Therefore, in accordance with the constitutional provision to that end, on March 3, 1868, articles of impeachment were agreed to by the house of representatives against the president and remanded to the senate for trial. The trial, which was presided over by Chief Justice Chase, was conducted, on the part of the house of representatives, by Benjamin F. Butler. It commenced March 23rd, and continued until May 26th, resulting in the president's acquittal. Upon leaving the presidential chair, Mr. Johnson retired to his old home at Greenville, Tenn., where he lived a somewhat secluded life until 1875, when the legislature of Tennessee chose him United States senator, and President Grant having called a special session of the senate, Mr. Johnson took his seat in that body,

March, 5, 1875. Later, while on a visit to his daughter, Mr. Johnson was stricken with paralysis. He lingered some days in an unconscious state and died on the last day of July, 1875.

JOHNSON, BRADLEY TYLER, lawyer and soldier, was born in Frederick City, Md., Sept. 29, 1829. He was graduated from Princeton in 1849, receiving the prize in mathematics; studied law at Harvard; was admitted to the bar *in Maryland* in 1851, and was elected district attorney of Frederick county in November. He was democratic candidate for state comptroller in 1857, chairman of the democratic state central committee in 1859–60, and a delegate to the National democratic convention at Charleston and Baltimore in 1860, from which he withdrew with a majority of the Maryland delegation, and united in the nomination of Breckinridge and Lane. When the war broke out he formed a company at his own expense, which was mustered into the service of the Confederacy, Mr. Johnson himself acting as

captain. His promotion thenceforth was rapid. On June 16th he was made major, July 21st lieutenant-colonel, and March 18, 1862, colonel. He took part in all the battles of Jackson's valley campaign, and in the seven days' battles around Richmond. Owing to hard service, the regiment became rapidly depleted in numbers, and in August 1862, the remnant was mustered out, and Col. Johnson was then assigned to Jackson's division. On June 28, 1864, he was commissioned brigadier-general of cavalry. After his services in the defeat of Dahlgren, he was mentioned in a general order, and Gen. Wade Hampton presented him with a sabre. In December, 1864, Gen. Johnson was assigned to post duty at Salisbury, N.C. When the prisoners under his charge were near starvation, he showed the depth of his humanity by stopping a train bound for the army of northern Virginia, and appropriating the provisions with which it was loaded, for the benefit of the prisoners. He also wished to carry these same prisoners to Goldsboro, and release them on parole. After the war Gen. Johnson settled in Richmond, Va., and resumed the practice of law. In 1872 he was delegate again to the National democratic convention at Baltimore; in 1875 he was elected to the Virginia senate, serving on the committees on finance and federal relations. In 1879 he removed to Baltimore, and in 1883 published an "Examination into the Foundation of Maryland, and the Maryland Act Concerning Religion." In 1884 he was president of the electoral college of Maryland. *He died Oct. 5, 1903.*

JOHNSON, EDWARD, soldier, was born in Chesterfield county, Va., Apr. 16, 1816. He was graduated at the United States Military Academy, in 1838, and was assigned to the 6th infantry as a second lieutenant. He participated

in the war against the Seminole Indians, 1838–41, and was promoted first lieutenant, Oct. 9, 1839. He was on frontier duty, 1842–46, and in the Mexican war was engaged at Vera Cruz, Cerro Gordo, Amazoque, Churubusco, Chapultepec, Molino del Rey, and in the assault and capture of the City of Mexico. He received the brevet of captain, Sept. 8, 1847, for his gallantry at Molino del Rey, and that of major, Sept. 13, 1847, for conduct at Chapultepec; he was also presented with swords of honor by his native state and county for his gallant services during the war. He was on sick leave, 1848–50, and on Apr. 15, 1851, he was promoted captain. He served on frontier duty in Kansas and Dakota, 1851–55, and was engaged in quelling the disturbances in Kansas, 1856–58. He took part in the Utah expedition and in the march to the Pacific coast in 1858. At the beginning of the civil war he was in garrison at Fort Columbus, N.Y., and resigned, June 10, 1861, to enter the Confederate army. He was appointed colonel of the 12th Georgia regiment, July, 1861, and he was commissioned brigadier-general, Dec. 13, 1861, being assigned to the command of a brigade in Gen. Loring's division, with which he served in western Virginia. He was promoted major-general, Feb. 28, 1863, and at the battle of Gettysburg he was in command of the old division of "Stonewall" Jackson. He also participated in the battles of the Wilderness and in the battle of Spottsylvania, where he was captured with his entire division. After his exchange he was placed in command of a division in Gen. Stephen D. Lee's corps of Gen. Hood's army, and at the battle of Nashville, Tenn., Dec. 16, 1864, was again taken prisoner. *He was captured at the battle of Franklin on Dec. 16, not at the battle of Nashville.* After the surrender of the Confederate forces, he returned to his home in Virginia, near Chesterfield Court House, and engaged in agricultural pursuits. He died in Richmond, Va., *March 2, 1873.*

JOHNSON, RICHARD W., soldier, was born near Smithland, Livingston co., Ky., *Feb. 27, 1827,* son of James and Louisa (Harmon) Johnson and a descendant of James Johnson, who came from England in 1648, having procured a grant of land either from the Crown or from Lord Baltimore, for the purpose of planting. The family has contributed much to the civic, scientific and national life of America and includes such noted names as Vice-pres. Johnson, Reverdy Johnson, William Cost Johnson of Maryland, Richard W. Johnson, late senator from Arkansas; W. H. and R. M. Johnson of Mississippi, and Dr. John M. Johnson of Atlanta, Ga. Richard W. Johnson, the subject of this sketch, was graduated at the United States Military Academy in 1849 and assigned to the 6th infantry. He was promoted second lieutenant, 1st infantry, June 10, 1850; first lieutenant, 2d cavalry, Mar. 3, 1855, and captain Dec. 1, 1856. In 1849–61 he served on frontier and scouting duty, mainly in the

Southwest, and was engaged in guarding the upper Potomac and took part in the action at Falling Water, Va., July 2, 1861. He was appointed lieutenant-colonel of the 1st Kentucky cavalry and volunteers (Federal army), Aug. 28, 1861, and on *Oct. 11* of the same year was commissioned brigadier-general of volunteers. In the Mississippi campaign (Oct., 1861, to June, 1862) he commanded a brigade. *He was ill during the battle of Shiloh and missed the fighting but participated in the siege of Corinth.* He commanded a division of the army of the Ohio in the Tennessee campaign and distinguished himself at the battles of Stone River, Liberty Cap, Chickamauga and Missionary Ridge, receiving the brevets of lieutenant-colonel and colonel for his gallant services. He was in command of a division of the 14th corps of the army of the Cumberland in the Georgia campaign and took an active part in all the engagements up to and including the

battle of New Hope Church, May 28, 1864, where he was severely wounded. At the battle of Nashville, Dec. 15–16, 1864, he commanded a division of cavalry and displayed great ability and gallantry, for which he was breveted major-general of volunteers and brigadier-general United States army. He was then assigned to the staff of Gen. George H. Thomas and served as provost-marshal-general and acting judge-advocate of the military division of the Tennessee (1865–66), doing much to ameliorate conditions between the warring factions. On March 13, 1865, he received the brevet of major-general, United States army, for gallant and meritorious services in the field during the war, and on Jan. 15, 1866, he was mustered out of the volunteer service. He served as acting-judge-advocate of the department of the Tennessee from August, 1866, until March 15, 1867, and of the department of the Cumberland until Oct. 12 of the latter year, when he retired from active service with the brevet rank of major-general. He was professor of military science at the University of Missouri in 1868–69, and at the University of Minnesota in 1869–70. General Johnson was the author of "A Soldier's Reminiscences in Peace and War," "Life of General George H. Thomas," "Pistol Practice," "History of Fort Snelling," and various magazine articles. He was married first, at Mendota, Minn., Oct. 30, 1850, to Rachel E., daughter of Gen. James Steele, by whom he had three sons: Alfred Bainbridge, Richard W. and Henry Sibley; second, at Catasauqua, Pa., Feb. 14, 1894, to Julia Macfarlane, daughter of James Clinton Carson, by whom he had one son, John Macfarlane. General Johnson died in St. Paul, Minn., Apr. 21, 1897.

JOHNSTON, ALBERT SIDNEY, soldier, was born at Washington, Mason co., Ky., Feb.

2, 1803, son of John and Abigail (Harris) Johnston, and grandson of Archibald and Sarah (—) Johnston. His grandfather, his first known paternal ancestor, was living at Salisbury, Conn., when he was commissioned captain of the 1st Dutchess county (N.Y.) regiment for service in the Revolutionary war. His father practiced medicine at Salisbury until 1788 when he moved to Washington, Ky. Josiah Stoddard Johnston, judge and U.S. senator from Louisiana, was his half-brother. Albert S. Johnston studied under private tutors, at a school in western Virginia and at Transylvania university and was graduated in 1826 at the U.S. military academy, where he won mathematical honors and as a first-classman was corps adjutant. At West Point he formed a friendship with Jefferson Davis which lasted until his death. After graduation he was assigned as second lieutenant to the 2d infantry. In 1832 he served throughout the Black Hawk war as chief of staff to Gen. Henry Atkinson. Owing to the serious illness of his wife, he resigned from the army in 1834 and took up farming, in which he was only moderately successful. In 1836 he enlisted as a private in the Army of the Texas Republic and promptly was appointed by Gen. Thomas J. Rusk as adjutant-general of the army on the Coleta. His success in organizing these ill-disciplined troops secured for him in January 1837 the appointment as senior brigadier-general of the army. A disappointed aspirant to this office, Gen. Felix Houston, then in command of the army, challenged Johnston to a duel and seriously wounded him. He resigned in May 1837. In the following year he was appointed secretary of war by President Mirabeau B. Lamar. In this office he carried out those plans for the security of the border against the annual Mexican invasion which, as commander of the army in the field, he had repeatedly but unsuccessfully urged upon the government. He resigned in 1840 and again engaged in farming until the outbreak of the Mexican war, when he organized and became colonel of the 1st Texas rifles. On the disbandment of this force he became inspector-general of Butler's division at Monterey. Subsequently he resumed farming until Dec. 2, 1849, when he was commissioned as paymaster in the U.S. army. In 1855 he was appointed colonel of the 2d cavalry, a new regiment, and assigned to the command of the department of Texas, where he remained until 1857. During 1858–60 he served in Utah as brevet brigadier-general, quelling a threatened Mormon uprising without resort to force. In December 1860 he was transferred to the command of the department of the Pacific. When Texas seceded from the Union he resigned his commission, Apr. 10, 1861, but continued in command until his successor Gen. Edwin V. Sumner arrived on April 25. Reaching Richmond, Va., early in September 1861, he was at once assigned to the command of the department of the West. The situation confronting him was one of extreme difficulty. Although the forces under his command were wholly inadequate for a campaign of aggression, he was not dismayed. On October 28 he occupied, with a small army, Bowling Green, Ky., as the center of a line of defense extending from Columbus, Ky., on the west to the Cumberland mountains on the east. This point, strongly entrenched, formed a good basis for military operations and could be held against greatly superior forces. Meanwhile the Federal army had increased by continual reinforcements from 50,000 to nearly 100,000 men. On his side Johnston, with an army never numbering more than 22,000, sent urgent but vain appeals to the governors of Alabama and Georgia, to Gen. Braxton Bragg at Pensacola and to the Confederate government. In spite of the fact that his troops were imperfectly armed he held his position through the whole of the autumn and the early winter of 1861, keeping the Federals by frequent and rapid expeditions through the country in constant expectation of attack where they might chance to be weakest. January 1862 saw the breaking of the military line which his strategic skill had for so many months kept intact in the face of superior forces. Gen. George B. Crittenden, with a small army, was on the upper waters of the Cumberland; Gen. George H. Thomas was marching on the Confederate position there. On January 19 Crittenden resolved to anticipate Thomas by attacking him at Fishing creek. This attack, though spirited, resulted in a Confederate defeat, which during the night turned into a retreat involving the abandonment of artillery and trains. This battle, as it turned Johnston's right flank, involved the loss of east Kentucky. He saw that all the forces of the Confederacy were now needed for the defense of Tennessee. New defensive works were established within the boundaries of that state. Ft. Henry on the Tennessee river and Ft. Donelson on the Cumberland were constructed and strongly fortified. On February 6 Ft. Henry, after a brief resistance, surrendered to a combined military and naval attack under Gen. Ulysses S. Grant and Com. Andrew H. Foote, the bulk of the Confederates, however, retreating before the surrender to Ft. Donelson twelve miles off. Johnston, foreseeing a speedy advance on the latter position, threw into the forest a large force—between 16,000 and 17,000 men— under Gens. Gideon J. Pillow, Simon B. Buckner and John B. Floyd. If held, he hoped to cover his new line at Nashville, to which point he had already begun to fall back. Ft. Donelson, however, assailed by land and water, surrendered on February 16 after a brilliant but ineffectual defense. These losses, opening

to the Federals the Tennessee and Cumberland rivers, rendered inevitable the evacuation of Nashville. The fall of Ft. Donelson created an excitement as extraordinary as it was bitter. The people, acting under the influence of a senseless panic, clamored for Johnston's removal. President Davis was appealed to, and the matter, brought before the Confederate congress, gave rise to acrid debate. The reply of President Davis was: "If Sidney Johnston is not a general, I have none." In the midst of the popular clamor Johnston calmly withdrew his army to Murfreesboro. Here, joined by Crittenden's command and by fugitives from Ft. Donelson, he found his forces increased to 17,000 men. Having decided that the defense of the Mississippi valley was of paramount importance, he crossed the Tennessee and joined Gen. P. G. T. Beauregard (whom he had previously placed in command of West Tennessee and advised of his plan) at Corinth, Miss. He brought with him his munitions and stores and all his depots and machine shops. Here he was speedily reinforced with Bragg's well-disciplined army from Florida and with new levies from Louisiana. These accessions brought his army up to 50,000 men, of whom only 40,000 of all arms could be relied on for battle. His original purpose had been to fight the Federals in detail—Grant first, Gen. Don Carlos Buell after him. This purpose was frustrated, however, by the necessity of organizing and properly equipping the recruits, a work of great difficulty. Grant, swift after the new Confederate center, had already landed as early as March 16 at Pittsburg Landing on the Tennessee, as an advantageous base against Corinth, and had occupied a strong natural position at Shiloh Church. Buell, ready to join Grant at the first summons, still occupied Nashville. Late on Wednesday night (April 2) Johnston heard that Buell was in motion. This precipitated the forward movement. Early the next day the Confederates were on the march, prepared to strike Grant on Saturday morning before Buell could appear. Heavy rains and swollen creeks, however, so impeded the advance that it did not reach the front until Saturday afternoon, instead of, as it had been hoped, on Friday. In view of this unexpected delay and the probability of Buell's speedy junction with Grant, Beauregard, the second in command, strongly urged the necessity for an immediate return to Corinth. Johnston, however, decided against this view. He completed his dispositions during the night for a general advance on the next day (Sunday, April 6). Before daylight the Confederates opened the fight, advancing in three lines of battle under Gens. William J. Hardee, Braxton Bragg, Leonidas Polk and John C. Breckenridge. Johnston's plan was simple. It was to attack constantly by the right and push the Federals from the landing into the angle made by Snake creek and the Tennessee river. Johnston was not for one moment doubtful of the success of his strategy. To those around him during the early hours of Sunday, while the battle was raging, he said confidently: "Tonight we will water our horses in the Tennessee river." By noon the Federal left was almost annihilated. The emergency was a crisis. Fully recognizing this, Gen. William T. Sherman, with Gen. John A. McClernand, fought stubbornly to hold the road crossing Snake creek so that *Gen. Lew Wallace*, away at Crump's Landing with 7,000 men, could come up. It was here, in one supreme effort to drive Sherman back, that Johnston, while leading a successful charge, was mortally wounded. *This attack was made against Union troops commanded by Generals Benjamin Prentiss and Stephen Hurlbut, not Sherman.* His death in the moment of achieving a great triumph was

a severe blow to the Confederate cause. He was married twice: (1) in Louisville, Ky., Jan. 20, 1829, to Henrietta, daughter of Maj. William Preston, U.S. army, and granddaughter of Col. William Preston of Augusta county, Va., who was killed in the Revolutionary war; she died in 1835; (2) near Shelbyville, Ky., Oct. 3, 1843, to Eliza Margaret, daughter of John Caswell Griffin, a planter, of Fincastle, Va., and granddaughter of George Hancock of Fotheringay, a colonel in the Revolutionary war and a member of congress from Virginia. By the first marriage he had three children: William Preston, aide-de-camp to President Jefferson Davis and president of Tulane university; Henrietta Preston, and Maria Pope Johnston (died in infancy); by the second marriage, he had six children: Albert Sidney; Hancock McClung; Mary Hancock (died in infancy); Margaret Strother, who married William Bond Prichard; Griffin, and Eliza Alberta, who married George Jules Denis. His death occurred at Shiloh, Tenn., Apr. 6, 1862.

JOHNSTON, JOSEPH EGGLESTON, soldier, was born near Farmville, Va., Feb. 3, 1807. He entered the U.S. military academy at West Point, graduating in 1829. From the date of his commission as second lieutenant in the 4th artillery, after graduation, to 1834, he served in garrison at various places, and participated in the Black Hawk campaign in 1832. In 1834–35 was on topographical duty, and on July 31, 1836, was promoted to first lieutenant. He acted as aide-de-camp to Gen. Scott in the Seminole war, continuing in that position until May 31, 1837, when he resigned. He was appointed, July 7, 1838, first lieutenant in the corps of topographical engineers, and brevetted captain for gallantry in the Seminole campaign. Capt. Johnston was kept busy discharging important duties with his corps from 1838 to

1841, when he was placed in charge of the topographical bureau at Washington. He left that position to serve as acting adjutant-general

J E Johnston

in the Florida war of 1842–43. In 1843–44 he surveyed the boundary between the United States and the British provinces, and was engaged for the two succeeding years in the coast survey. On Sept. 21, 1846, he was promoted to a captaincy in the corps. The war with Mexico found Capt. Johnston with Gen. Scott at the siege of Vera Cruz. He shared in the battles of Cerro Gordo, Contreras, Churubusco, Molino del Rey, Chapultepec, and the final victorious assault on the City of Mexico. On Apr. 12, 1847, he received his brevet as major, lieutenant-colonel, and colonel, "for gallant and meritorious conduct on reconnoitering duty at Cerro Gordo," where he was severely wounded. He was again wounded September 13th, while leading a detachment of the storming party at Chapultepec, being the first to plant a regimental color on the walls of that stronghold. Aug. 28, 1848, he was mustered

out as lieutenant-colonel of volunteers. Johnston was, however, devoted to his profession, and though passing from the army as a volunteer, he speedily secured his reinstatement, by act of congress, into his old rank as captain of topographical engineers, to date from the original commission, Sept. 21, 1846. Returning to his scientific work, he acted as chief of topographical engineers of the department of Texas. In 1853–55 he was supervising western river improvements, and in 1858 served in the Utah expedition as acting inspector-general. He was commissioned, June 28, 1860, quartermaster-general of the U.S. army, resigning this position Apr. 22, 1861, the Virginia convention having already resolved to submit the secession ordinance to the people. This ended a service of thirty-one years, with but a single break, and that a brief one, as an officer in the army of the United States. Johnston was at once commissioned major-general of volunteers in the army of Virginia. In conjunction with Gen. Robert E. Lee, he was at first engaged in organizing the Virginia volunteers. From this duty he was called to Montgomery, the capital of the Confederacy, to receive his commission as one of the four brigadier-generals provided for by act of congress. He was assigned to the command of Harper's Ferry, covering the valley of the Shenandoah. Johnston did not long remain at this point, as it was wholly unsuitable for a base of operations. Gen. Patterson was already bearing down on the Ferry from the north of the Potomac, and Johnston promptly transferred his army to Winchester. While there, he kept a wary eye upon those military movements which were to culminate in midsummer in the first great battle of the war. On July 18, 1861, Maj. McDowell, with an army of 28,000 men, attacked Beauregard at Manassas. *This was a preliminary reconnaisance in force by*

McDowell, who did not yet have 28,000 troops on hand. The main attack took place July 21. Johnston, leaving Patterson still in the valley watched by Stuart's cavalry, speeded to Beauregard's assistance. He came in time. At 2.30 p.m., July 21st, the Southern outlook was grave. The 5,000 fresh troops thrown into the battle at that hour by Johnston fell upon the Union flank and rear and turned the tide. After Bull Run, Johnston, as ranking officer, remained in command of the combined armies. In the spring of 1862, when McClellan was ready to move, Johnston was prepared to meet him. On May 31, 1862, he attacked the Union army at Seven Pines (Fair Oaks), where he was severely wounded. On March 24, 1863, Johnston, who had been for some time incapacitated by his wound, was assigned to the command of the southwest. Under him were Bragg, Pemberton, and Kirby Smith. He first stationed himself at Chattanooga, believing that field of most importance to the Confederacy. Later, however, when Grant was about to attack Vicksburg in the rear, Johnston was directed to take supreme command of the forces in Mississippi. He had ordered Pemberton "to evacuate Vicksburg and the dependencies, and march to the northeast." Pemberton disregarded this order, and six weeks later Vicksburg fell. After Vicksburg, the war veered to the central west. In December, 1863, Johnston was at Dalton, Ga., in command of *the Army of Tennessee. Confederate armies were generally named for states, Union armies for rivers.* Sherman, fronting him, was in command of the armies of the Cumberland, under Thomas; of the Tennessee, under McPherson, and of the Ohio, under Schofield. The combined Union force numbered 100,000 men; Johnston's barely 68,000. Spring opened with a general Federal advance toward Atlanta. To meet this formidable movement, Johnston,

on withdrawing from Dalton May 12th, resolved on a defensive campaign. He entrenched every foot he fell back; he would not fight unless attacked; he invited battle only when he knew the conditions to be favorable; and even his retreats called for extreme caution on the part of the advancing army. This policy, which enabled Johnston, while preserving his army from any serious mishap during a campaign of seventy-four days, to enter Atlanta with Sherman still out of it, did not meet the approval of the Confederate government. On July 17, 1864, he was relieved from the command, which was turned over to Gen. John B. Hood. By the spring of 1865 Sherman was on his return march from the sea. His purpose was to march to Goldsboro, making junction with Schofield, who was then at Wilmington, while Grant, by extending his left west of Petersburg, would keep Lee from turning against him. Hardee, who had evacuated Charleston, and who was now opposing the Union advance, was making poor headway. Under these circumstances Johnston was assigned to the command of the troops in North Carolina, under the supervision and control of Gen. Lee, with orders from the latter "to concentrate all available forces and drive back Sherman." On Feb. 23d, relieving Beauregard, at Charlotte, he assumed command at that point with a force amounting to about 30,000 men. This new campaign was to be fought on lines far different from those which had marked the Atlanta campaign. Johnston began at once to harass Sherman's front, retarding, although never entirely checking, its advance, by constant attacks by his cavalry under Hampton, Butler, and Wheeler. For some time it was doubtful whether Sherman's objective point was Goldsboro or Raleigh. On March 19th–21st, having obtained definite information that Sherman, with his two wings a day's march apart, was heading for Goldsboro, Johnston struck the Federal left at Bentonville. The action which followed, while well-planned and gallantly fought, was unsuccessful, owing to a failure to concentrate in time the Confederate troops. This was the last attempt to stem the Union progress. On March 23d Sherman and Schofield had united their forces—numbering together upward of 70,000 men—at Goldsboro, remaining there inactive for two weeks. Before this period had elapsed, the Confederacy was in its death-throes. Petersburg had been evacuated, and Richmond captured. On April 9th Gen. Lee surrendered at Appomattox court-house. On the 18th, Johnston and Sherman united on a basis of agreement, which was so generous in its stipulations in favor of the armies and of the people of the South, that it was rejected by the government of the United States, Andrew Johnson then being president. On the 26th—Sherman having, under orders from Washington, announced the termination of the armistice—another agreement was signed by the two commanders, based on that already entered into between Grant and Lee. A reference only can be made here to the unfortunate differences which, rising between Mr. Davis and Gen. Johnston at the opening of the war, grew sharper during its progress, and did much to obscure the latter's undoubtedly brilliant services. Johnston, holding well-pronounced views on the general conduct of the war, found himself in frequent conflict with those of the Confederate government. During the famous march of Sherman toward Atlanta, his strategy was so conspicuously at variance with the plans at Richmond that it led to his being relieved of his command in the face of the enemy, while yet at the head of an army unbroken in spirit and with undiminished confidence in itself. On the restoration of peace, Gen. Johnston did not long remain idle. He met the changed conditions of life with resolution, and, although well advanced in years at the close of the war, he was constantly in the discharge of important duties, both civil and political. In 1877 he served in congress as the representative of the Richmond district of Virginia. *Johnston's single term in Congress was 1879–81.* Subsequently he was appointed by President Cleveland as commissioner of

railroads in the United States. One peculiarity to be noted in Gen. Johnston's military career is the number of times he was wounded in battle. During the civil war, it was a matter of laughing betting among his troops that, in every fight, he would attract a bullet. The fact remains that Johnston bore these marks of valor, received in every campaign, from the Seminole war to that in which he gained his greatest renown. He was the author of a "Narrative of Military Operations Directed during the Late War between the States" (N.Y., 1874). Gen. Johnston died at Washington, D.C., March 21, 1891. He had been suffering for three weeks from an affection of the heart, aggravated by a cold contracted at the funeral of Gen. Wm. T. Sherman, on which occasion he was one of the honorary pall-bearers. Gen. Sherman's death had broken a friendship between these two great chieftains, who, adversaries in war, had learned in peace the lesson of mutual respect. It may be said that the funeral torch of the one had been lighted at the pyre of the other.

JOHNSTON, WILLIAM PRESTON, president of Tulane University *(1884–1899)*, was born in Louisville, Ky., Jan. 5, 1831, eldest son of Albert Sidney Johnston, the Confederate general, and of Henrietta, daughter of Maj. William Preston and his wife, Caroline (Hancock) Preston. When he was four years of age his mother died, and his father departing to undertake military service in Texas, he was left to the care of his maternal relatives in Louisville. He attended schools in that city for a number of years, and afterwards studied successively at Womack's Academy, in Shelbyville; Centre College, in Danville; the Western Military Institute, at Georgetown, Ky., and Yale College. He displayed a quiet and studious disposition while at school, and at

Yale excelled in the study of literature, winning a Townsend prize for English composition and the Clark prize at graduation for an essay on "Political Abstractionists." After graduation he studied law at the University of Louisville; was admitted to the bar in 1853, and entered immediately upon the practice of his profession at Louisville. He took an active part in the stirring political actions of the time, and sympathized strongly with the course pursued by the South. When the trouble culminated in hostilities, he spent the summer of 1861

recruiting and equipping several companies of soldiers for the Confederate army, and in the fall was commissioned major in the 2d Kentucky regiment. Soon afterward he was transferred to the 1st Kentucky regiment, with which he served in the army of northern Virginia during the early operations at Fairfax Court House and the Acotink as lieutenant-colonel. When the regiment was disbanded he was appointed aide-de-camp to Pres. Davis, with the rank of colonel. In this position he continued throughout the war, participating in the battles of Seven Pines, Cold Harbor, Sheridan's Raid, Petersburg and other engagements, and serving always as inspector-general and confidential staff officer to carry communications between Davis and his generals. In the end he was captured, with Pres. Davis, in Georgia, and kept in solitary confinement for three months at Fort Delaware, after which he was released, went to Canada and there lived in exile for a year. He then returned to Louisville and continued his law practice until 1867. In that year, having been appointed professor of history and English literature in Washington College by Gen. Lee, he retired from the bar to devote himself thenceforward to educational and literary labors. In 1877 he became noted as a writer through a work published under the title "Life of Albert Sidney Johnston, Embracing his Services in the Armies of the United States, the Republic of Texas, and the Confederate States." Col. Johnston remained at Lexington until 1880, and then accepted the presidency of the Louisiana State University at Baton Rouge, which, being found in a languishing condition, was thoroughly reorganized. In 1883 he was authorized by the administrators of the Tulane educational fund to organize and take charge of the institution it was intended to found, and in the following year the University of Louisiana was merged into Tulane University, situated at New Orleans, with Col. Johnston as its president. This institution, the most important university of the southwest, embraces law and medical departments, a woman's college, a college of arts and sciences and one of technology, and a post-graduate department for teachers. In addition to the biographical work mentioned, Dr. Johnston has published "The Prototype of Hamlet" and three volumes of verse, "My Garden Walk," "Pictures of the Patriarchs and Other Poems," and "Seekers After God;" also a genealogical volume, entitled "The Johnstons of Salisbury." He has also written extensively for periodical publications, and many of his public addresses and lectures have been printed by the press. The honorary degree of LL.D. was conferred upon him by Washington and Lee University in 1877. He was a regent of the Smithsonian Institution. He was married, July 7, 1853, to Rosa Elizabeth, daughter of Judge John N. Duncan, of New Orleans, and granddaughter of Abner L. Duncan, who served as aide-de-camp of Andrew Jackson at the battle of New Orleans, and at one time was the acknowledged leader of the New Orleans bar. She died in October, 1885, leaving five daughters. Their only son died Jan. 9, 1885, aged twenty-four years. Col. Johnston was married again, in April, 1888, to Margaret Henshaw, daughter of Judge Daniel D. Avery, of Baton Rouge, La., and a descendant of James Avery, one of the early Massachusetts settlers. He died at Lexington, Va., July 16, 1899.

JONES, CATESBY AP ROGER, naval officer, was born in Virginia about 1830, son of Thomas ap Catesby Jones, naval officer, and nephew of Gen. Roger Jones, a soldier of the war of 1812. He was graduated from the U.S. naval academy. When the civil war broke out he resigned and entered the Confederate or Virginia state navy, June 10, 1861. At this critical period the new U.S. frigate Merrimac, one of the three largest steam frigates in the navy, built in 1855, was in commission at the U.S. navy yard at Portsmouth, Va., and under sailing orders. The commandant of the yard, Com. McCauley, delayed departure until Apr. 17, 1861, the date of the passage of the ordinance of secession of Virginia. Then the fires of the Merrimac were ordered to be drawn,

and the guns spiked. During the next two days the commandant was utterly helpless, and to prevent the United States property falling in the hands of the Virginians, he ordered the ships scuttled and sunk or burned, together with the docks, shiphouses, and magazines. This was done on Apr. 20, 1861, the Cumberland alone escaping destruction. In a few days the Virginia government, looking to the formation of a navy to support their secession movement, sought to raise and reconstruct these ships. Lieut. Jones was here prominent, being intrusted with the armament of the Merrimac, and by his skill that vessel, after being raised, was fashioned into a formidable steam ram known as the Virginia. She was a huge floating battery with a long projecting ram, and heavily implated throughout. She was propelled by two engines, and had large furnaces for heating shot, besides an apparatus for throwing hot water. She carried eight eighty-pound rifled guns, besides two guns capable of throwing a 120-pound shell in a 100-pound solid shot. Flag-officer Franklin Buchanan was in command as captain, with Lieut. Minor as second officer, and Jones as executive officer was third in command. The Merrimac (Virginia) thus equipped, officered and manned, represented at that time the most powerful fighting ship in the world. The Federal government felt very uneasy at the tidings received through its trustworthy spies, of the destruction threatened for the northern coasts.

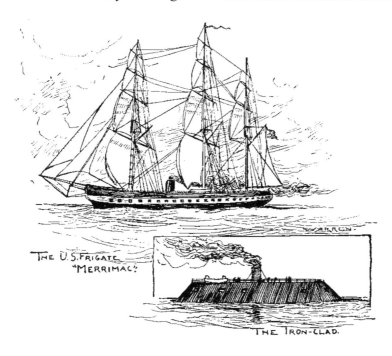

THE U.S. FRIGATE "MERRIMAC."

THE IRON-CLAD.

Up to the last moment previous to her departure, skilled mechanics had been kept at work to effect as nearly as possible her complete equipment before being sent into action. During the memorable conflict commencing on March 8, 1862, which changed the destinies of the world, Lieut. Buchanan and his flag-lieutenant, Minor, were both severely wounded. The command of the Merrimac then devolved upon Lieut. Jones. During his command he had occasion to visit the gun deck. Seeing a division of men standing at ease, he inquired of the officer in command why he was not firing, and the reply was: "After firing for two hours I find I can do the enemy about as much damage by snapping my fingers at him every two minutes and a half." As Lieut. Jones found he could make no impression on the Monitor with his shot, he worked for an hour to run her down, but the Monitor was too agile, owing to her lighter construction, and skillfully avoided all the lunges of her heavier antagonist. The conflict between the Monitor and Merrimac having practically ended in a drawn battle, both vessels retired. Lieut. Jones was superseded in the command of the Merrimac by Com. Tatnall, although his coolness and judgment were generally conceded in naval circles, and it was afterward universally admitted that with all possible skill and judgment any commander would eventually have been worsted in an encounter with such a diminutive but dangerous adversary as the Monitor. Lieut. Jones was promoted to the rank of commander Apr. 27, 1863. *He died June 20, 1877.*

JORDAN, THOMAS, soldier and journalist, was born in Luray Valley, Va., Sept. 30, 1819. He entered the U.S. military academy in 1836, having for a roommate Gen. W. T. Sherman, and was graduated with high honors in 1840. He entered the service as second lieutenant in the 1st infantry. He took part in the Seminole war, and later was stationed on the frontier. His services during the war with Mexico secured his promotion to first lieutenant on June 18, 1846, and to captain and quartermaster on March 3, 1847. From 1848 till 1860 he was stationed on the Pacific coast, where he had charge of the largest depot of stores in the service. When the civil war opened he elected to follow the fortunes of his native state, tendered his resignation on May 21, 1861, and entered the Confederate army as lieutenant-colonel. He was at once appointed by Robert E. Lee adjutant-general of the forces at Manassas, and commanded them until the arrival of Gen. P. G. T. Beauregard. He was made chief-of-staff to Gen. Beauregard in February, 1862, accompanied him to West Tennessee, and for his services at the battle of Shiloh on Apr. 6, 1862, was promoted to be brigadier-general. He was for a short time on the staff of Gen. Braxton Bragg, but soon resumed his former place on the staff of Gen. Beauregard, serving with that general until the close of the war, at Charleston, S.C., in Virginia and the West, and in North Carolina, where Beauregard and Johnston finally surrendered to Gen. W. T. Sherman on Apr. 18, 1865. In 1866 Gen. Jordan became the editor of the Memphis (Tenn.) "Appeal," and while thus employed wrote and published, with J. B. Pryor, "The Campaigns of Lieut.-Gen. Forrest" (N.Y., 1868). In 1869 he was appointed chief of the general staff of the Cuban insurgent army, which he organized and drilled. At the head of 300 men he effected a landing at Mayari, Cuba, and forced his way into the interior. He was soon after made commander of the insurgents, and in January, 1870, with 642 men met and defeated a largely superior force of Spanish regulars at Guaimaro, but seeing that the odds were too great to be overcome he resigned his

commission, returned to the United States, settled in New York city, and became the editor of the "Financial and Mining Record," a weekly paper. A review of the Confederate war policy, which he contributed to "Harper's Magazine" in 1865, attracted wide attention. *He died Nov. 27, 1895.*

JULIAN, GEORGE WASHINGTON, congressman, was born near Centreville, Wayne county, Ind., May 5, 1817. His parents were pioneer settlers of the state, and his early education was acquired in the common schools. He afterward taught school, studied law, and was admitted to the bar in 1840. He entered politics and in 1845 was chosen a representative to the state legislature by the whig party. He became warmly interested in the slavery question, and in 1848 severed his party relations and gave zealous support to Van Buren and Adams. In 1849 he was elected a representative to congress by the free-soilers and democrats of the fourth Indiana district. In 1852 he was a candidate for the vice-presidency on the free-soil ticket. He took a leading part in the formation of the republican party, was re-elected to congress in 1860, and became one of the most active members during the ensuing ten years. He served on the joint committee of the conduct of war and on that which prepared the articles of impeachment against Andrew Johnson. Both in congress and out he strenuously opposed the monopoly and plunder of the public domain. He pleaded for the vigorous prosecution of the war and the policy of striking at slavery as its cause. In 1868 he proposed a constitutional amendment forbidding the denial of the ballot to any citizen on account of race, color, or sex. In 1872 he joined the liberal republicans and supported Horace Greeley for president. In May, 1885, he was appointed surveyor-general of New Mexico. His latter years were devoted mainly to literary work. A volume of his speeches was published in 1872, and in 1884 appeared his "Political Recollections." *He died July 7, 1899.*

K

KAUTZ, ALBERT, naval officer, was born at Georgetown, O., Jan. 29, 1839, brother of August V. Kautz. Appointed acting midshipman under the old law, Sept. 28, 1854, he entered the U.S. Naval Academy, Annapolis, Md., and was graduated in 1858. From that date until July, 1860, he served in the home squadron, as it was then called, on the frigates Colorado, Roanoke and Savannah and the sloop-of-war Saratoga. He was promoted passed midshipman, Jan. 19, 1861; master, Feb. 23, 1861, and lieutenant, April 21, 1861, thus making the three steps in as many months, a most unusual instance of rapid advancement. In May, 1861, he served on the U.S. steamer Flag, of the North Atlantic blockading squadron, and in the following month was placed in command of the prize brig Hannah Balch, off Charleston, S.C., with orders to proceed to Philadelphia. Misfortune now overtook him, as the brig was captured, June 15, 1861, within sight of Cape Hatteras, by the privateer Winslow, Capt. Thomas Crosson. Taken into port in North Carolina, he was placed on parole for two months; then, his parole being withdrawn, he was confined in Henrico county jail, Richmond, Va., by order of Pres. Davis, in retaliation for the imprisonment of captured Confederate privateers in the Tombs prison, New York city. Here he remained until October, 1861, when he was released on parole, and permitted to go to Washington for the purpose of effecting his own exchange. In Richmond he had an interview with the Confederate secretaries Benjamin and Mallory, and in Washington, with Pres. Lincoln and Secs. Seward and Welles, and with Capt. John L. Worden and Lieut. George L. Selden. He was exchanged for three Confederate lieutenants Nov. 14, 1861, who were sent south under a flag of truce. The same exchange included 350 Confederate prisoners, captured at Hatteras inlet in August, 1861, for whom were returned 350 Federal soldiers captured at the battle of Bull Run in July, 1861. This was the first exchange of prisoners authorized by Pres. Lincoln and his cabinet in the civil war. In January, 1862, Kautz was ordered to the flagship Hartford and served on Farragut's staff while commanding the first division of great guns in the engagements with Forts Jackson and St. Philip, the Chalmette batteries, and in the capture of New Orleans in April, 1862. He had command of the howitzers, under Capt. Henry Bell, in New Orleans, and here figured in another historic event, hauling down the lone star flag from the city hall, which Mayor Monroe had refused to strike, and afterwards hoisting the stars and stripes on the custom house. Kautz continued on the Hartford during the engagements with the batteries at Vicksburg in June and July, 1862, but in August he was seized with malarial fever and sent North on sick leave. In 1863 he served in the Juinata, of the West India squadron; and in 1864–65 was first lieutenant of the sloop of war Cyane in the Pacific. He was promoted lieutenant-commander May 29, 1865; served on the Winooski, of the home squadron, and the flagship Pensacola, of the Pacific squadron (January 1866–August 1868); was on the receiving ship New Hampshire, Norfolk (December, 1868–May 1869); on duty at the Boston navy yard (May 1869–August 1871), and was lighthouse inspector at Key West, Fla. (April 1872–October 1873). Being promoted commander, Sept. 3, 1872, he was assigned to the Monocacy, of the Asiatic squadron, there continuing during the next two years (1873–75). He was lighthouse inspector in Cincinnati, O. (January 1876–July 1880); in command of the Michigan on the lakes (August, 1880–August 1883); on duty in the bureau of equipment, navy department (March–July 1884); equipment officer at the Boston navy yard (July 1884–October 1887), and on leave traveling in Europe (November 1887–December 1888). After his promotion as captain, June 2, 1885, he served at the Portsmouth (N.H.) navy yard; was president of the naval examining and retiring board; commandant of the Newport (R.I.) naval station and on other shore duty, and on the receiving ship Wabash in Boston. He was promoted commodore, April 6, 1897, and ordered to the command of the station in Newport, R.I. There he continued until placed in command of the Pacific station, in October, 1898, with the Philadelphia as his flagship. Upon the retirement of Rear-Adm. Bunce, Oct. 24, 1898, he was advanced to rank as his successor. In March, 1899, the condition of affairs at Samoa, which had been serious for some months, reached a climax. The German consul at Apia had been at odds with the British and American consuls and the chief justice, in supporting the claims of Hataafa against those of Malietoa-Tanus, the newly-elected native king. The Philadelphia was accordingly ordered to Apia to protect American rights under the Berlin treaty. On his arrival Adm. Kautz found a state of anarchy which culminated in the murder of an American guard at the consulate and a British seaman by native adherents of Mataafa, encouraged, as was alleged, by an incendiary proclamation issued by the German consul. A conference between the American and British consuls, Adm. Kautz and the commander of a British warship in port resulted in the bombardment of the native positions at Apia under control of Mataafa, and the concentration of the followers of his opponent in the struggle for the kingship. The U.S. government sustained Adm. Kautz in the position he had assumed, and the British government concurred in endorsing her own commanders, but while no official utterance from the German emperor defined his position in the matter, the press throughout the empire bitterly denounced the bombardment as brutal and unnecessary. The affair was further complicated by allegations that shells and weapons of German make had been used by the Samoan insurgents. Upon his return to the United States, Adm. Kautz was retired, having reached the age limit. He died, at Florence, Italy, Feb. 5, 1907.

KAUTZ, AUGUST VALENTINE, soldier, was born at Ispringen, Baden, Germany, Jan. 5, 1828, son of George and Dorothea Kautz. His parents emigrated to America in the year of his birth, settling near Ripley, Brown Co., O., where they engaged in farming, and where the son was educated. At the outbreak of the Mexican war he enlisted as a private in the 1st Ohio volunteers. He served until its close, and

returning home in 1848 he entered the U.S. military academy, West Point, and was graduated in 1852. He was then assigned to the 4th infantry as 2d lieutenant, and during the next few years served in Washington and Oregon territory, gaining distinction as an Indian fighter. He was wounded during the Rogue river hostilities of 1853–55, and again on Puget Sound in 1856. He traveled in Europe in 1859–60, and on his return was appointed captain in the 6th U.S. cavalry (May 14, 1861). With this regiment he served through the peninsular campaign of 1862, was commissioned colonel of the 2d Ohio cavalry, Sept. 2, 1862, and from December of that year till April, 1863, he had command of Camp Chase, Ohio. He was then assigned to the command of a brigade of cavalry, with which he took part in the capture of Monticello, Ky., by Gen. Samuel P. Carter, May 1, 1863, and was engaged in the pursuit and capture of the Confederate raider, John Morgan, whom he prevented from crossing the Ohio near Parkersburg, July 19. He served with the army of the Ohio as chief of cavalry of the 23d corps, and being transferred to the east, was made brigadier-general of volunteers and given command of the cavalry division of the army of the James (May 7, 1864). On June 9, 1864, he attacked Petersburg with his small cavalry force, for which action he was brevetted lieutenant-colonel, and took part in the four days' battles, June 12–16, 1864, in which his efforts were seconded by the colored troops under Gen. Hinks. He took part in Wilson's raid in June, encountered Wade Hampton at Sycamore Church, in September, and as commander of the 1st division, 25th army corps, he participated in the movement leading to the surrender of the Confederates at Appomattox and led his division of colored troops into Richmond, April 3, 1865. He was

brevetted colonel in the regular service for gallantry in the action on the Darbytown road, Va., Oct. 7, 1864, and brigadier-general and major-general for field-services during the war, March 13, 1865. The same year he served on the military commission to try the conspirators in the assassination of Pres. Lincoln. On July 28, 1866, he was appointed lieutenant-colonel of the 34th infantry and in 1869 was transferred to the 15th infantry, commanding the regiment during the expedition against the Mescalero Apaches, whom he succeeded in establishing in their reservation (1870–71). He was promoted colonel of the 8th infantry, June 8, 1874; commanded the department of Arizona from 1875–77; was stationed at Angel Island, Cal., from 1878–86, and then at Niobrara, Neb., till 1890. On April 20, 1891, he was appointed brigadier-general, and on Jan. 5, 1892, was placed on the retired list of the army. Gen. Kautz published several small works and military treatises, among them: "The Company Clerk" (1863); "Customs of Service for Non-Commissioned Officers and Soldiers" (1864); "Customs of Service for Officers" (1886); and "Operations South of the James River" (in "Battles and Leaders of the Civil War"). He died at Seattle, Wash., Sept. 4, 1895.

KEARNY, PHILIP, soldier, was born at No. 3 Broadway, New York city, the site of the present Field building, June 2, 1815. The site of his birth is historical ground, and under the British it was the Post-office. The property belonged to the Watts family, to which also were allied the De Peysters, John Watts de Peyster being "Phil" Kearny's cousin and playmate. Kearny went to school at the corner of Cedar street and Broadway, a place which was kept by a man of the name of Ufford. He afterward attended the famous Round Hill school at Northampton, Mass., which was run on the principle of Eton college by Dr. Joseph G. Cogswell and George Bancroft, and finally entered Columbia college, where he was graduated to begin the study of law. His military

taste, however, from the beginning was too strong for any civil profession to take hold upon him, and March 8, 1836, he obtained an appointment as second lieutenant in the United States dragoons, of which his uncle, Stephen Watts Kearny, was commander. By this time "Phil" Kearny had fallen into possession of his share of the family property, valued at a million dollars. But this did not prevent his going to the frontier and serving with the 1st dragoons, which was the first regiment of cavalry organized after the war of 1812, and in which Jefferson Davis was a lieutenant and adjutant. Kearny was a born cavalry officer. He was a magnificent rider, dashing and adventurous, with the courage of a lion. In 1837, he was stationed at Fort Dearborn, where is now the great city of Chicago, but which was then only a small settlement around the fort and

the house of an Indian agent. Here he remained for two years, when he was appointed by the secretary of war to visit France and study cavalry tactics at the royal cavalry school at Saumur. Once in France, however, he became desirous of more active life and joined the staff of the duke of Orleans, eldest son of Louis Philippe, in the campaign under Marshal Vallée, who was serving in Africa. He afterward became attached to the Chasseurs d'Afrique, and made the campaign against the Arab chief, Abd-el-Kader. In 1840 Lieut. Kearny returned to the United States, when he was appointed aide-de-camp to Gen. Alexander Macomb, commander-in-chief of the army, and on his death filled the same position in relation to Gen. Scott, who succeeded to the command. In 1846 Kearny resigned his commission, but was immediately reinstated on the breaking out of the war with Mexico. He recruited and organized a splendid troop of cavalry, largely defraying the expenses from his private purse. His gallant charge at Churubusco was one of the most remarkable incidents of the war, resulting unfortunately for Kearny, whose left arm was shattered by a shot and had to be amputated. He was the first man to make his way, sword in hand, to the gate of San Antonio of Mexico and was brevetted major for gallantry. In 1851 Maj. Kearny went to California and soon after resigned from the army. He then traveled around the world, and on his return settled in New Jersey, near Newark. In 1859 he went to France, rejoined his old comrades of the Chasseurs d'Afrique, was given command of the cavalry of the guard under Napoleon III in the Italian war, and was present on the field of Solferino where his splendid service gained for him the cross of the Legion of honor. After the close of the war, he lived in Paris for a while and then, returning to this country on the outbreak of the war of the rebellion, entered the service as commander of the 1st New Jersey brigade in Gen. Franklin's division of the army of the Potomac. He served through the engagements in the peninsula and then with the army of Virginia from the Rapidan to Warren. In May, 1862, Kearny was given command of the 3d, afterwards the 1st division, of the 3d corps, his commission as major-general bearing date July 7, 1862. But this commission he never received because he was killed before its issue. At the battle of Williamsburg Kearny's division came nobly to the support of Hooker, retaking ground which had been lost, and saving the day. At Seven Pines he had a horse shot under him, a favorite animal, the loss of which he deeply deplored. It was at this battle that Gen. O. O. Howard lost his right arm, and it is said that Kearny, whose left arm was gone, on seeing Howard being assisted from the field, called out to him, "General, we will have to buy gloves together." Notwithstanding his one arm, Kearny continued to be a splendid horseman, mounting and dismounting with ease. He never passed up and down the line without being heartily cheered by his men. At the second battle of Bull Run, Kearny had the right of the line and forced "Stonewall" Jackson's corps back on the reserve under Longstreet. A few days later, at the battle of Chantilly, after the repulse of the Confederates, he had placed his division, and while reconnoitering rode so far in advance that he penetrated the Confederate line. This was in the evening, and a Confederate soldier who was present relates the incident as follows: "Kearny rode right into our men. Stopping his horse suddenly, he called out, saying, 'Whose troops are these?' Some one replied, 'Hays's Mississippi brigade.' Kearny turned quickly, put spurs to his horse and attempted to escape. Our men fired, and the Federal officer threw himself forward as if to protect himself from the flying bullets, but one struck him at the base of the spine, ranging upward, inflicting a mortal wound." His remains were sent by Gen. Lee under a flag of truce to Gen. Hooker and, being embalmed, were transported to New York and buried in the Watts vault, Trinity churchyard. The date of his death was Sept. 1, 1862.

KEITT, LAURENCE MASSILLON, soldier, was born in Orangeburg district, S.C., Oct. 4,

1824. He was educated at the College of South Carolina, from which institution he was graduated in 1843. He then studied law, and was admitted to practice in 1845. Taking an active part in politics, he was elected to the state legislature in 1848, and to represent his district in the U.S. congress in 1852. He was re-elected continuously until he withdrew, with the other representatives from South Carolina, on the passage of the ordinance of secession by that state in 1860. He was a delegate to the convention that framed the ordinance, and a member of the provisional congress that met in Montgomery, Ala., in 1861. He was a conspicuous member of the committees that framed the provisional as well as the permanent constitution of the Confederate government. In 1862 he entered the army as colonel of the 20th South Carolina volunteers, and, with his regiment, engaged in the principal battles of the army of Northern Virginia, and was mortally wounded at the battle of Cold Harbor, Va., June 3, 1864. *Keitt's regiment did not join the Army of Northern Virginia until the end of May 1864, and Keitt was killed in his first battle with that army. Keitt was shot June 1, and died June 2.*

KELL, JOHN McINTOSH, executive officer of the Confederate cruiser Alabama, was born near Darien, Ga., Jan. 26, 1823. His father, John Kell, a lawyer of Liberty county, Ga., was of Irish descent, his grandfather John settling before the revolution at Old Sunbury. His mother, Margery Baillie, of McIntosh county, Ga., was of Scotch blood, the great-granddaughter of John Mohr McIntosh—chief of clan McIntosh—who emigrated from Scotland to Georgia with Gen. Oglethorpe, and settled at Darien, Ga., then called New Inverness. The subject of this sketch was educated at the Naval Academy at Annapolis, Md., and entered the navy in 1841 as midshipman. He served in 1846 in the Mexican war, and was present at the hoisting of the U.S. flag at Monterey, Cal., when formal possession was taken of that country in the name of the United States. He was an officer in Com. Perry's expedition to Japan in 1853. In 1854, as master of the U.S. frigate Mississippi, he circumnavigated the globe. He was in the Brazilian squadron when an expedition was fitted out against Paraguay to redress indignities to the U.S. consul by Dictator Lopez, and, volunteering his services, he joined the war sloop Preble. He was ordered to duty at the Pensacola navy-yard, and *in 1855* was commissioned lieutenant. Upon the secession of his state he resigned, and tendering his services to the Confederacy was given command of a steamer for coast defence by Gov. Brown. In May, 1861, Adm. Semmes, his warm friend, who had championed him in an early naval trial, applied for him for the steamer Sumter as its executive officer. The Sumter was of 500 tons, with seventy-five men and five guns, was the first vessel that sailed the Confederate flag, captured seventeen ships, and after six months' service became unseaworthy, and these officers took command of the steamer Alabama, of 1,000 tons, with 130 men and eight guns. The Alabama had a dramatic and eventful career. In her twenty-two months' service she captured sixty vessels, pretty nearly clearing the ocean of merchant ships, sinking the Hatteras off Galveston in a thirteen minutes' fight, and rescuing the drowning crew. Her gallant and ill-fated battle with the Kearsarge, under Capt. Winslow, is historic. The orders were not to fight, but to destroy merchant ships. Worn out, she was about to go into the docks at Cherbourg, France, but eager to try a bout, the fight was agreed upon and took place off the shore before thousands. It began at 10 a.m. and lasted one and one-quarter hours. The Kearsarge, in better trim, her machinery protected by chain armor, with heavier guns and better powder, sunk the Alabama, after an heroic struggle; thirty Confederates were drowned and killed, and the 100 drowning men were mostly rescued by the English yacht Deerhound and French pilot-boats. For his brave conduct, Lieut. Kell was made captain. He commanded afterward the ironclad Richmond, in the James river, but at

the surrender was ill at home. Since the war he has lived quietly in his pleasant home at Sunnyside, on the Macon and Atlanta Railroad until 1887, when he was made adjutant-general of Georgia by Gov. Gordon. He married, in 1856, Blanche Munroe, of Macon. Col. Kell was one of the ablest naval officers of the civil war, and connected with its most dramatic events, with honor to its cause and distinction to himself. The executive officer of the two most active cruisers of the South, he was engaged in the most romantic sea experiences of the war, and had a career of danger and excitement. He was a skilful sea-captain, and a bold and successful naval fighter. His career was a continuous naval romance, and a dramatic portion of the naval history of the late war. He was an able and attentive adjutant-general of Georgia, and conducted the state and military affairs in an admirable manner. *He died Oct. 5, 1900.*

KEMPER, JAMES LAWSON, thirty-fourth governor of Virginia (1874–78), was born in Madison county, Va., June 11, 1823, son of William Kemper, a planter, and a descendant of John Kemper, who arrived in Virginia in 1714 as a member of one of the twelve families from Oldenburg seated by Gov. Alexander Spotswood upon his lands at Germania in Virginia. His mother's grandfather was John Jasper Stadler, a colonel of engineers on the staff of Washington. His mother's brother, John Stadler Allison, was a distinguished officer in the war of 1812. Young Kemper studied in the schools of his native county, and was graduated from Washington college with the degree of A.M. He then studied law under George W. Summers of Charleston, Kanawha county. In 1847 he was commissioned by President Polk a captain in the volunteer service of the United States. Afterward he served ten years in the

James L. Kemper

legislature of Virginia, of which body he was two years speaker, and was for a number of years chairman of the committee on military affairs. He served also as president on the Board of visitors of the Virginia Military Institute (VMI). On May 2, 1861, the Virginia secession convention appointed him colonel of the 7th Virginia regiment. He was commissioned brigadier-general in May, 1862, and during the war was engaged in many battles being desperately wounded while leading his brigade in the charge at Gettysburg. From the effects of this wound he sufficiently recovered to be entrusted with the command of the local forces in and around Richmond, *and on Sept. 19, 1864,* he was commissioned major-general. He held command at Richmond until the evacuation, and after the close of the war retired to Madison county, where he resumed the practice of law. He took an active part against the republican party, and in 1873 was elected governor of Virginia, the duties of which office he discharged with that stern conviction of right which had marked his career throughout.

During his gubernatorial term he was waited upon by a committee from the legislative caucus of the democratic party who assured him of his unanimous election as U.S. senator if he would but signify his willingness to accept the honor. This, however, Gov. Kemper declined to do, declaring that the state had already bestowed upon him the highest position in its power—that of governor. On July 4, 1853, he married Miss C. Conway Cave, and after the close of his term as governor, his health having become much impaired, he engaged in farming in Orange county, Va. *He died April 7, 1895.*

KENLY, JOHN REESE, soldier, was born in Baltimore, Md., *Jan. 11, 1818.* He attended private schools in that city, studied law, and was admitted to the bar in 1845. At the outbreak of the war with Mexico he raised a company of volunteers and became their captain. He took part in the battle of Monterey, and when Col. William H. Watson fell, during that engagement, he quickly rallied and re-formed the battalion. On the expiration of his term of enlistment, he returned to Baltimore, where he was tendered the commission of major. He immediately resumed active service until the

close of the war, and then received the thanks of the state for gallantry in the field. Afterward he continued his law practice until the outbreak of the civil war, when he was appointed to the colonelcy of the 1st Maryland regiment, June 11, 1861. He was *at Front Royal* in May, 1862, and aided in saving the force under Gen. Banks from capture. Col. Kenly was severely wounded at the time, and taken prisoner, but was exchanged on Aug. 15th, and a week later became brigadier-general, with the command of all the Baltimore troops outside the forts. After the battle of Antietam he joined McClellan, and was present at Hagerstown and Harper's Ferry. He participated in the recapture of Maryland Heights in 1863, and thereafter, until peace was declared, he commanded various brigades in the 1st and 8th army corps. He was brevetted major-general of volunteers March 13, 1865, and after being mustered out of service, again received the thanks of his native state, and was honored with the presentation of a sword from the corporation of Baltimore. Since then he practiced his profession with success, and wrote "Memoirs of a Maryland Volunteer in the Mexican War" (Philadelphia, 1873). *He died Dec. 20, 1891.*

KERSHAW, JOSEPH BREVARD, soldier, was born at Camden, S.C., Jan. 5, 1822. He received an academic education; studied law, and was admitted to the bar in 1843, beginning the practice of his profession at Camden, S.C. In 1851 he was elected to the state senate, and by re-elections continued a member of that body till 1857. He was chosen a delegate to the secession convention at Charleston, S.C., in 1860, and in April, 1861, he entered the Confederate army as colonel of the 2d South Carolina Volunteers, which he had recruited. He took part in the first battle of Bull Run, July 21, 1861, and was commissioned brigadier-

general, Feb. 13, 1862, being assigned to the command of a brigade in Gen. McLaw's division of Gen. Longstreet's corps, army of northern Virginia. He took a prominent part in the operations in Virginia and Maryland in 1862, and was engaged at the battles of Fair Oaks, Savage Station, Malvern Hill, second Bull Run, South Mountain, and Antietam. He also served with distinction at the battle of Fredericksburg, Dec. 13, 1862, where his brigade was employed in holding the sunken road under Marye's Heights. He participated in the battles of Chancellorsville and Gettysburg, and he was then transferred with his brigade to the west, where he distinguished himself at the battle of Chickamauga, and in the siege of Knoxville, Tenn. After the abandonment of the campaign against Knoxville, he was again ordered to the army of northern Virginia, and on May 18, 1864, was promoted major-general, and assigned to the command of a division composed of the 2d Texas brigade, and the brigade of the late Gen. Mouton. He took part in the battles of the Wilderness, Spottsylvania, Cold Harbor, and all the subsequent battles of the army of northern Virginia, being present at the closing scenes at Appomatox C.H. After his release from Fort Warren, Boston harbor, where he was a prisoner for several months, he returned to Camden, S.C.; resumed the practice of law, and became actively engaged in the politics of his state. In 1865, he was again elected to the state senate, and was judge of the 5th circuit court of South Carolina, from 1877–93, when he was appointed postmaster of Camden. Gen. Kershaw died at Camden, S.C., Apr. 13, 1894.

KEYES, ERASMUS DARWIN, soldier, was born in Brimfield, Mass., May 29, 1810. His father was a surgeon and physician of prominence, and was very well-to-do. In 1824

young Keyes, having passed through the common schools, attended a select school kept by a graduate from the West Point military academy, and there developed the ambition to become a soldier, although his father had destined him for a business life. After passing some time in Maine, where he also studied, an application was made for a warrant admitting him as a cadet to West Point, which was at first unsuccessful, but which afterward, when aided by the special application on his own part, resulted in obtaining for him the desired position. He passed through the Military academy, graduating in 1832, tenth in a class of forty-five. He was assigned to the 3d artillery, and during 1832 and 1833 was on duty in Charleston. This was the period of the nullification troubles between the national government and the state of South Carolina, in which President Jackson and John C. Calhoun were brought into conflict. Keyes served in Charleston all through these troubles. in 1837 and 1841, when he was promoted captain, he served as aide to Gen. Winfield Scott on Indian duty. He was in garrison from that time until

1854. He then went to West Point, where he served as instructor in artillery and cavalry for four years, after which he was again ordered to the frontier, and served against the Indians. He continued engaged in this duty until 1860. A part of this time he was in command of a battery of artillery and had some serious fighting with the Indians in the Northwest. Oct. 12, 1858, he was promoted major. Jan. 1, 1860, he was appointed military secretary to Gen. Scott, and he continued to hold this position until 1861. May 14th of the latter year he became colonel of the 11th infantry, and three days later was made brigadier-general of volunteers. A few months after this he was in New York, assisting in recruiting troops and sending them to the front, and from July 3d was at Washington, and in the battle of Bull Run and the peninsula campaign. From the beginning of 1862 he commanded an army corps of the army of the Potomac, and on May 5th of that year was promoted major-general of volunteers. On the 31st of the same month he was brevetted brigadier-general of the regular army on account of his splendid behavior in the battle of Fair Oaks. Up to that time the career of Gen. Keyes had been eminently successful. He had been fortunate in having Secretary Stanton as his warm friend, and was generally highly respected and commended for his able military services. But in the latter part of 1863 Gen. John A. Dix accused him of having caused the failure of his expedition against Richmond in the summer of that year. Keyes took the position at Fortress Monroe in the spring of 1863, which had been previously held by Gen. Dix, the latter being ordered to New York. Friends of Gen. Keyes always believed that this arrangement had much to do with the charges made against the latter. Some time later in the year, on the return of Gen. Dix to his previous command, he published general orders complimenting a number of officers for their action in several engagements during his absence, but leaving the name of Gen. Keyes out of the list. This course on the part of Dix was viewed by a number of well-known army officers as the result of prejudice. Soon after, Keyes was withdrawn from his command and placed on a board for the retirement of officers. He made many applications to the secretary of war, asking for an opportunity to defend himself against the charges which had been made against him, but was forbidden to visit Washington. He accordingly served on the board already mentioned, and on May 6, 1864, he resigned, and soon after moved to California. From 1867 to 1869 he was president of the Mexican gold mining company, and from 1868 to 1872 vice-president of the California vine culture society. He made, between 1864 and 1884, seven journeys to Europe, where he resided, altogether more than ten years. Gen. Keyes had eleven children, all of whom he educated thoroughly, and his sons, of whom he had five, became rapidly successful in life. Gen. Keyes published, in 1884, a most interesting and important work, entitled "Fifty Years' Observation of Men and Events." This work is delightfully written in the colloquial style, and gives a great many anecdotes of public men, as well as conversations with them; especially Gen. Keyes had a great deal to say about Gen. Winfield Scott, and presents, perhaps, as accurate a word picture of Scott as has ever been written by anybody, not even excepting the general's own autobiography. The account of the appearance of the city of Washington, as seen by Gen. Keyes in 1838, when it took two days to reach there from New York, is most interesting. Later he gives reminiscences of his association with the American officers who were distinguished in the Florida and other wars, and who afterward became noted in the civil war. Among these are W. T. Sherman, George H. Thomas, Cullum, Reno, McClellan, Pickett, "Stonewall" Jackson, Lee, and Grant. Gen. Keyes was in San Francisco in 1849, and gives a very graphic

description of the state of society at that time in California, and the excitement produced by the discovery of gold. He presents interesting accounts, also, of the North American Indians, as he saw them from Florida to Puget's Sound, witnessing their war dances and other ceremonies. In 1855 he was in the extreme Northwest, watching the Puget Sound Indians, among whom there was a considerable outbreak, followed by the massacre of a number of white families on the frontier. Three years later he was in Washington territory, fighting the Indians, and while at Vancouver made the acquaintance of Maj.-Gen. Harney, noted as an Indian fighter, and also a Capt. Pleasonton, afterward a well-known cavalry general. Gen. Keyes resided in California for a very long time, and was as familiar with affairs in the early history of that state and with the pioneers, with most of whom he was personally acquainted, as perhaps any one else in the country. It is an interesting historical fact that, when Gen. Scott was made lieutenant-general, being allowed a military secretary with the rank of lieutenant-colonel, he first offered the

position to Col. Robert E. Lee, by whom it was declined, the rank being lower than his own, whereupon he offered it to Gen. Keyes, who assumed the duties on Jan. 1, 1860, and continued to hold the position until Apr. 2, 1861. In 1862 Gen. Keyes had charge of the Insane asylum at Williamsburg, Va., which was within his lines, and interested himself greatly in the inmates of the asylum. Gen. Keyes makes a very interesting relation, in his work, of the excitement in Washington just prior to and at the outbreak of the civil war. Like his old chief, Gen. Scott, he looked upon the question of secession as something too absurd to be argued, or even considered, while at the same time, he saw the importance and necessity of defining more explicitly the constitution of the United States as to the limits of federal and state jurisdiction. Much of this portion of his work is in the form of a diary, and is especially interesting on account of the anecdotes and personal information contained in it. He wrote also quite freely with regard to the condition at Charleston prior to the bombardment of Fort Sumter and after that occurrence, and commented freely on the attitude of South Carolina in these early days of the struggle. Altogether, one can obtain, probably, a better idea of the character and personality of Gen. Keyes himself by reading his interesting book than could be gathered through any biographical sketch. *He died Oct. 14, 1895.*

KILPATRICK, HUGH JUDSON, soldier, was born near Deckertown, N.J., Jan. 14, 1836. He was graduated from West Point in 1861, appointed a captain of volunteers on May 9th, became first lieutenant of artillery in the regular army on May 14th and was severely wounded at Big Bethel in June. *In September* he was made lieutenant-colonel of a New York cavalry regiment, which he had assisted in organizing.

J. Kilpatrick

In January, 1862, he started for Kansas, intending to accompany Gen. James H. Lane's expedition to Texas as chief of artillery. Finding this was to be abandoned, he rejoined his regiment in Virginia, and was present at Thoroughfare Gap and the second battle of Bull Run. He was promoted brigadier-general of volunteers on June 13, 1863. He received brevets for bravery in the battles of Aldie and Gettysburg, obtaining finally that of lieutenant-colonel, U.S.A. He took an active part in the operations in central Virginia from August till November, 1863, and in the fights at James City, Brandy Station, and Gainesville. In May, 1864, he commanded a cavalry division in the army of the Cumberland when they invaded Georgia. At the battle of Resaca on May 13th he was so severely wounded that he was obliged to retire from service for two months. His zeal and energy, however, were in no wise diminished when he returned to the field, and between the 18th and the 22d of August he especially distinguished himself by making the circuit of Atlanta, tearing up three miles of railroad near Jonesborough, and returning with numerous prisoners, a gun and several flags, captured in an encounter with a division of infantry and a brigade of cavalry. He was now brevetted colonel for gallant conduct at Resaca, and on March 13, 1865, he received the brevet of brigadier-general for the capture of Fayetteville, N.C., and that of major-general for services during the Carolina campaign. He was promoted major-general of volunteers, June 18, 1865; resigned his volunteer commission on Jan. 1, 1866, and in the following year left the regular army. Gen. Kilpatrick was undoubtedly one of the most popular officers

in the Federal forces, and thoroughly worthy of his splendid reputation as a daring and brilliant cavalry leader. *This is an exaggeration. Kilpatrick's reputation was mixed; his vanity and boastfulness probably made him more enemies than friends among his peers.* He was minister to Chili, 1865–68. He endorsed Horace Greeley in 1872, returned to his former party in 1876, and in 1880 was an unsuccessful candidate for congress from New Jersey. In 1881 he was reappointed to the post of Chili by President Garfield. He died at Valparaiso Dec. 4, 1881.

KIMBALL, NATHAN, soldier, was born in Fredericksburg, Ind., Nov. 22, 1822, son of Nathaniel Kimball, and grandson of Nathan Kimball of Massachusetts. He served as captain in the war with Mexico. He was commissioned captain in the Indiana volunteers by Gov. Merton at the outbreak of the civil war, and later was made colonel of the 14th Indiana infantry. He fought at Cheat Mountain, and Greenbrier in 1861; was put in command of a brigade at Winchester, and commissioned brigadier-general Apr. 15, 1862, for the victory gained over "Stonewall" Jackson at Kearnstown, March 23d. At Antietam his brigade, the 1st of the 3rd division of the 2d corps, lost nearly 600 men, but stubbornly held its ground. At the battle of Fredericksburg he was severely wounded. On his recovery he was sent to Vicksburg, Miss., in command of the 3d division 16th corps, up Yazoo river, where, on June 4, 1863, he had an engagement near Satartia, driving the enemy beyond Black river, after which he remained in position at Haines Bluff until after the surrender of Vicksburg to Grant. In August, 1863, he was ordered with his division to Arkansas, where he remained until May 3, 1864, then ordered to join the army of the Cumberland, which he did on May 22, 1864, in command of 1st brigade, 2d division, 4th army corps. He engaged in the battles of the Dallas and New Hope Church, Georgia, and of Kenesaw Mountain, June 27, 1864; after Peach Tree Creek, July 20th, he was for gallantry in that engagement promoted by Gen. Thomas to the command of the 1st division, 4th army corps, and took part in all engagements around Atlanta and battles of Jonesboro' and Lovejoy station, resulting in the capture of Atlanta. After the capture of Atlanta he was taken from field service to Indiana to aid in the suppression of the "Knights of the Golden Circle." His services in this duty resulted in the stamping-out of the organization in Indiana. He commanded the 1st division, 4th corps, army of the Cumberland at Franklin, Nov. 30th, and at Nashville Dec. 15 and 16, 1864. He was brevetted major-general Feb. 1, 1865, and was mustered out of the service the following Aug. 24, 1865. In 1870–71 he was elected treasurer of Indiana, serving two terms,

Nathan Kimball

and was also a member of the legislature. In 1866 he took part in the organization of the G.A.R. of Indiana, and Nov. 22d was its state commander. In 1873 he was appointed surveyor general of Utah Territory by Pres. Grant. He removed from Indianapolis to Salt Lake City, where he took an active part in the organization of the G.A.R. there, and became commander of the Utah department in 1888. *He died in 1898.*

KING, RUFUS, soldier and journalist, was born in New York city, Jan. 26, 1814, son of Charles King of Columbia college and grandson of Rufus King, the American statesman. He was graduated from the U.S. military academy at West Point, in 1833, was immediately appointed lieutenant of engineers. He resigned from the army Sept. 30, 1836, to accept the position of assistant engineer on the Erie railroad. From 1839 to 1843 Mr. King served as adjutant-general of the state of New York, and during a part of the time was connected with the editorial staff of the "Albany Evening Journal." He resigned that position to become editor of the "Albany Advertiser," which position he filled for six years. He then removed to Wisconsin to take charge of the publication of the "Milwaukee Sentinel." He was a member of the convention that framed the constitution of Wisconsin, and served as regent of the state university. In 1849 he was a member of the board of visitors to the U.S. military academy, and was appointed U.S. minister to Rome in 1861, serving in that capacity for five months, when he resigned to take part in the civil war. He remained in the army until 1863, commanding a division at Yorktown, Manassas, Fredericksburg, Groveton, and Fairfax. During the latter part of 1863 he resigned his commission, and was reappointed minister to Rome, where he remained until 1867. From 1867 to 1869 he served as deputy controller of the state of New York. His health failed some time before his death, and in consequence he retired entirely from public life. He died in New York city, Oct. 13, 1876.

L

LANDER, FREDERICK WEST, soldier and civil engineer, was born in Salem, Mass., *Dec. 17, 1821*. His father, Edward Lander, and his grandfather were shipowners engaged in foreign trade. His mother, Eliza West, was the daughter of Nathaniel West, who in early life was for a short time a midshipman on a British man-of-war. Leaving that position Mr. West came home, and taking the command of the Black Prince, a private armed vessel, so distinguished himself during the war of revolution that the Black Prince is mentioned in Cooper's "Naval History" as one of the most prominent of the American privateers. In 1798 he sent from Salem the first vessel from the United States to make a voyage around the world. His great-grandfather, Elias Hasket Derby, sent the first vessel from the United States to the East Indies and thus opened the famous trade that so enriched his native town. *Frederick West Lander* was noted among his playmates for his courage, love of manly sports, adventurous spirit and great physical strength. He received his early education at Franklin and Dummer academies, and afterwards studied civil engineering with Maj. Barton at South Andover. When he had completed his studies, he was employed as a surveyor on the Eastern and other railroads, rising to the position of chief engineer. Meanwhile his interest had been awakened in the scheme of a Pacific railroad, then being agitated by William Whitney, and in 1853 he was appointed chief engineer of the Northern Pacific survey, accompanying Isaac I. Stevens, then lieutenant of engineers, on a tour across the northern plains. At the close of this survey he submitted a report upon the possibilities of the construction of a railroad through that new and unexplored region. In the spring of 1854 he equipped (with the aid of his brother, Edward Lander, then the chief justice of the supreme court of the territory of Washington) a party to examine and report upon a projected road from Puget Sound, by the Columbia and Snake rivers, to the Mississippi, planned to connect with a road to California. His report of this reconnaissance was so thorough that the house of representatives had 10,000 copies of it printed. For the following four years Mr. Lander acted as chief engineer and superintendent of the overland wagon road, and incidentally he was involved in occasional encounters with the Indians, whom he succeeded in defeating and eventually pacifying. He also made improvements in the overland route, greatly aiding emigration, and at the same time managed the sums entrusted to him by congress for this purpose with such economy that he was able to return to the treasury a large unexpended balance. That this was without detriment to the public service is shown by the praise accorded to his labors in the reports of the then secretary

of the interior. At the same time he was studying the problem of a Pacific road, and in 1858, following a resolution requesting information by the house of representatives, he made a full and exhaustive report "as to the practicability and method of construction of railroads," advocating a main line to Salt Lake, with branches to San Francisco and Puget Sound. In 1859 he made a speech at San Francisco, strengthening the feeling he had already created in favor of a Pacific road. While in San Francisco, in the fall of 1860, he was married to Jean Margaret Davenport, a lady of high personal character and of marked literary taste, who was distinguished as an actress, both in England and the United States. By this marriage there were no children. At the commencement of the civil war he volunteered his services in aid of the Federal cause, and was employed on a mission to Gov. Houston of Texas, with authority to order, if he thought best, the troops then in Texas to support the governor. After serving on other important missions he volunteered as aid to Gen. McClellan. In the campaign in Western Virginia he distinguished himself at Philippi and at Rich Mountain, where he guided the column through a pathless forest in the midst of the action, and afterwards displayed extraordinary courage in battle, having his horse shot under him. On May 17, 1861, his gallantry was rewarded with the commission of brigadier-general, and a command was assigned him on the upper Potomac. While reconnoitering at Edward's Ferry, he was severely wounded in the leg, and, his aid being needed to open the Baltimore and Ohio railroad, he did not wait for the wound to heal properly, but on Dec. 27, 1861, assumed command of the Eastern division of the army of the Potomac with that object in view. In the following month he held the town of Hancock with 4,000 men against *Gen. "Stonewall" Jackson with a force estimated at 9,000* men, but was compelled under orders to evacuate Romney and to withdraw to Patterson Creek to

protect the railroad. In February, being largely reinforced, he reoccupied Romney and attacked and defeated the enemy at Bloomery Gap. For this reason he received a letter of thanks from the secretary of war. Feeling that his health was almost exhausted, he reported that he had succeeded in the work entrusted to him and requested to be relieved; but when this was not done, he determined to continue his efforts, and was undertaking an attack upon Jackson, at Winchester, when he was seized with congestion of the brain and died very suddenly, on March 2, 1862. Mr. Lander distinguished himself during his short life as an intrepid soldier, an adventurous and successful explorer, a talented civil engineer and a terse and vigorous writer. His military achievements were of the greatest benefit to the cause he espoused, his explorations opened up the great plains, and his writings and orations were the means of originating a scheme of railroads of incalculable service to the country.

LANE, JAMES HENRY, soldier and educator, was born at Mathews Court House, Va., July 28, 1833, son of Walter Gardner and Mary Ann Henry (Barkwell) Lane; grandson of William and Lucy (Berry) Lane, and great-grandson of Ezekiel and —— Lane. His grandfather was a soldier in the Revolutionary War and his father was a colonel of Virginia militia, a merchant and a member of the Virginia legislature. He was graduated with highest honors at the Virginia military institute in 1854 and subsequently attended the University of Virginia. For a short time he was employed as an engineer on the hydrographic survey of the York river. But the inspiration he had received at the two famous Virginia colleges soon led him back to the academic field. He became successively assistant professor of mathematics at Virginia military institute, professor of mathematics and commandant at the West Florida seminary at Tallahassee, and professor of natural philosophy and instructor in tactics at the North Carolina military institute at Charlotte. By nature and training a soldier, he volunteered promptly at the outbreak of the Civil war. As he was teaching in North Carolina he joined the 1st N.C. volunteers and was elected major. His rise was rapid. He became lieutenant-colonel of his regiment, Sept. 1, 1861, and colonel of the 28th N.C. regiment on September 21 of the same year. When Gen. Branch was killed in the battle of Sharpsburg he took charge of the brigade, and on Nov. 1, 1862, was appointed brigadier general. He was then the youngest general officer in the Confederate army. He was in all the major battles and many of the smaller ones fought by the Army of Northern Virginia. He took part in the first engagements of the war at New Market Bridge, June 8th, and Big Bethel, Va., June 10th. At Gettysburg he led his brigade (July 3) in Gen. Pickett's famous Confederate charge. He surrendered with Gen. Lee at

The National Cyclopedia of American Biography

James H. Lane,

Appomattox. He was wounded three times and won his title as brigadier general for gallantry in action. He was loved and trusted alike by those who served under him and by his superior officers. At the Virginia military institute he had been a student under "Stonewall" Jackson, who during the war showed a teacher's lingering fondness for his old pupil. In the famous night attack at Chancellorsville, where Gen. Jackson received his death wound, his last order, which was given to Lane, was: "Push right ahead, Lane—right ahead." Few officers in the Confederate service had so fully the confidence and approval of both Gen. Jackson and Gen. Lee. At the close of the war, he found his parents in want and the family business and fortune completely wiped out. He applied himself again to the task of teaching the young men of the South, first in schools at Concord, N.C., Richmond, Va., and Wilmington, N.C., and later in the Agricultural and Mechanical College of Virginia (1872–80), Missouri school of mines (1881–82) and Alabama polytechnic institute, where for the last twenty-five years of his life (1882–1907) he was professor of civil engineering. As a teacher Lane was conscientious in the preparation of his work and thorough in his methods of instruction. His pupils admired and respected him and carried his fame to all parts of this country and to many foreign lands. He received the honorary degree of LL.D. from Trinity college (later Duke university), in 1890 and that of Ph.D. from the University of West Virginia in 1896. Reared in the Episcopal church, he allowed nothing to interfere with the conscientious discharge of his duties in it. He was a typical gentleman of the Old South who, after fighting gallantly in its defense through four years of Civil war, devoted himself with equal zeal when peace came to the task of restoring his country to prosperity, training its young men and handing down to them by precept and example the fine virtues and lofty ideals of the old days, thus contributing his share to the making of the new South a worthy successor of the old. He was married in Richmond, Va., Sept. 13, 1869, to Charlotte Randolph, daughter of Benjamin Lincoln Meade, a planter, of Powhatan county, Va., and they had four children: Lidie Hardaway; Mary Barkwell, wife of George Petrie; Kate Meade, and Lottie Everard Lane, wife of Matthew Scott Sloan. He died at Auburn, Ala., Sept. 21, 1907.

LAWTON, ALEXANDER ROBERT, lawyer, was born in St. Peters' Parish, Beaufort District, S.C., Nov. 4, 1818. At sixteen years of age he entered West Point, from which he was graduated in 1839 as 2nd lieutenant, 1st artillery. Resigning from the army in January, 1841, he studied at the Harvard law school, was admitted to the bar in Columbia, S.C., in December, 1842, and settled in Savannah, Ga., January, 1843. He became president of the Augusta and Savannah railroad company in 1849, colonel of the 1st volunteer regiment of Georgia in 1852, representative to the legislature in 1855, and state senator in 1860. He was a brigadier-general in the Confederate army, in command of the military district of Georgia in 1861, served in Virginia, June, 1862, was wounded at Sharpsburg, Maryland, under Stonewall Jackson, and was quarter-master general of the Confederate states from 1863 to the end of the war. He was again a representative to the legislature in 1874, delegate to and vice-president of the constitutional convention of 1877, and chairman of its judiciary committee, president of the Tilden electoral college of Georgia in 1876, and chairman of the Georgia delegation to the national democratic conventions that nominated Gen. Hancock at Cincinnati and Grover Cleveland at Chicago. Gen. Lawton was nominated U.S. minister to Russia, by President Cleveland in 1885, but by his own request his name was withdrawn. President Cleveland appointed him U.S. minister

to Austro-Hungary in 1887. Gen. Lawton has been pre-eminent as statesman, lawyer, soldier and orator. He drafted and secured the charter of the Atlantic Gulf railroad, which united Georgia and Florida, and was an able protector of American interests in his diplomatic career. He had a large practice, and as chief counsel for the Central railroad system, treated questions of corporate rights and contracts in state and national supreme courts with power. His addresses before the Georgia and American bar associations, in 1882 and 1884, on Gen. R. E. Lee, at Savannah, in 1871, and in 1885 to the general assembly of Georgia on laying the corner-stone of the new capitol, were full of eloquence. *He died July 2, 1896.*

LEE, FITZHUGH, soldier and thirty-ninth governor of Virginia (1886–90), was born in Clermont, Fairfax co., Va., Nov. 19, 1835, son of Com. Sydney Smith Lee, U.S. navy. He is the nephew of Gen. Robert E. Lee, and his grandfather was "Light Horse Harry" Lee, of revolutionary fame. After a thorough education in the schools of his native state, he was appointed to the U.S. Military Academy in 1852, and on his graduation, in 1856, was commissioned second lieutenant of cavalry. He saw his first active service in operations against the Indians, and was severely wounded. In May, 1860, he was appointed instructor of cavalry at West Point. On the outbreak of the civil war he resigned his commission, and entered the Confederate service as adjutant-general of Gen. Ewell's brigade, a position in which he remained four months. He was appointed, *in August, 1861,* lieutenant-colonel of the 1st Virginia cavalry, and being soon after promoted colonel, was with the army of northern Virginia through all its campaigns. *On July 24, 1862,* he was appointed brigadier-general, *and Aug. 3, 1863,* major-general. He was severely wounded in the battle of Winchester, Sept. 19, 1864, where he had three horses shot under him, and was disabled

from duty for some months. In March, 1865, he was appointed to command the cavalry corps of the army of northern Virginia; but in April surrendered to Gen. Meade, and returning to his home in Virginia, remained in retirement for several years. He re-entered public life in 1874, when he made a trip to the North. At the Bunker hill centennial, in the following year, he delivered a patriotic speech, which was one of the earliest efforts of the leading men on either side to lay aside the irritating memories of the "lost cause," and draw together in the old bonds of one national life. It made a profound impression throughout the country. During the winter and spring of 1882–83 he made a trip through the South, in behalf of the Southern Historical Society. Gen. Lee was elected governor of Virginia in 1885, and served until 1890, when a constitutional provision prevented his re-election. In 1896 he was sent by

Pres. Cleveland to Havana to fill the important office of consul-general. During his incumbency of this responsible position the last and most serious rising of the Cubans against their Spanish oppressors was raging throughout the island, and under the arbitrary governor-generalship of Gen. Weyler he had ample opportunity to distinguish himself for his calm and judicial but firm protection of American interests whenever threatened. The recall of Gen. Weyler to Spain, and the accession to power in Cuba of Gen. Blanco; the pretense of autonomy for the Cubans, and the strong revolutionary spirit, now mounting to its height, drew upon all the intellectual and diplomatic resources of the consul-general, and made for him a splendid record of patriotism, judgment and determination. Affairs became so serious in Havana, in January, 1898, that Gen. Lee's life was several times threatened and other American residents were in constant danger. In this contingency he had full power to summon the war vessels then lying at Key West for the protection of the lives and interests of Americans, but he did not avail himself of the authority delegated to him. When afterwards it was decided to send a war vessel to Havana, he cabled to the state department recommending that such action should be delayed, but was informed that it was too late, as the Maine was then at sea *en route* to Havana, and could not

Entrance to Havana

be reached. This act was followed a few weeks later by the arrival of the Spanish cruiser Viscaya in New York harbor, there to learn that the Maine had been destroyed by a submarine explosion on Feb. 15th. From this period the popular excitement in Cuba became practically dangerous to Americans. On March 5th, Spain asked for the recall of Consul-Gen. Lee from Havana, which was promptly refused by the U.S. government, but on April 5th all the American consuls in the islands were recalled, and returned with many American citizens to the United States. Gen. Lee was not long idle, however, being placed in command of an army corps, which he organized and held ready for service. Not being ordered to form a part of any of the armies of invasion sent to the West Indies, he was not engaged in active service; nevertheless his famous 7th corps was to be thrown first into Cuba in the operations around Havana, had the war continued; and he was selected by the president to lead the assault against the city. However, late in the year 1898, he was appointed to command the American artillery forces in the district of Havana, and commanded the department of Cuba, consisting of the provinces of Havana and Pinar del Rio. Gen. Lee is the author of the life of his uncle, Gen. Robert E. Lee, in "Great Commander" series. He was married in, 1875, to Ellen Bernard, daughter of George Fowle, of Alexandria, Va. They had two sons and three daughters. *He died April 28, 1905.*

LEE, GEORGE WASHINGTON CUSTIS, ninth president of Washington and Lee university, was born at Arlington, Va., Sept. 16, 1832, the son of Robert Edward and Mary Randolph (Custis) Lee. He was graduated from West Point in 1854, at the head of his class, was commissioned second lieutenant of engineers, in 1855 was assigned to duty in Florida, where he constructed the fort at the mouth of the St. Mary's river, in 1857 was ordered to San Francisco, Cal., to construct works at Fort Point, was promoted first lieutenant in 1859, and entered the engineer bureau at Washington, D.C. At the beginning of the civil war he resigned his commission and entered the Confederate army; on May 10, 1861 he was appointed major of engineers of the provisional army of Virginia, and on July 1st was appointed captain of engineers. The fortifications around Richmond were the result of his engineering skill, and on Aug. 31, 1861 he was appointed aide-de-camp to Jefferson Davis, with the rank of colonel of cavalry, and during a great part of the war was kept on Mr. Davis's staff, contrary to his own eager desire for active service in the field. On June 25, 1863, he was promoted to be brigadier-general and assigned to a brigade that was organized for the local defence of Richmond. In 1864 he was commissioned major-general and assigned to the command of a division in the army of northern Virginia, and served with great skill and bravery in this position until his capture at Sailor's Creek. *This is misleading. Lee did not command a division as such in the Army of Northern Virginia. His local-defense force of militia was attached to that army after the fall*

of Petersburg and Richmond on April 2, 1865. Gen. Lee was appointed professor of military and civil engineering and applied mechanics in the Virginia Military institute in October, 1865. In February, 1871, he was appointed president of Washington and Lee university, succeeding his father, and in the same year the general assembly of Virginia changed the name of the institution from Washington college to its present one, that of Washington and Lee university. Large additions were made to the endowment fund during President Lee's administration through the generosity of William W. Corcoran of Washington, D.C., Robert H. Bayley of New Orleans, La., Col. Thomas A. Scott, John Robinson and Vincent L. Bradford of Philadelphia, and Lewis Brooks of Rochester, N.Y., and other donations of money founded fellowships and scholarships that were open to competition by students of the college. The institution was in a very prosperous condition, and continued to grow and improve. President Lee worthily followed the lofty example set by his father, and resembled him in his integrity of character, courteous bearing, Christian faith, and the same unswerving devotion to duty. In 1887 Tulane university, New Orleans, La., conferred upon him the degree of LL.D. *He died Feb. 18, 1913.*

LEE, ROBERT EDWARD, soldier, was born at Stratford, Westmoreland county, Va., Jan. 19, 1807. He was descended from among the oldest and best of the cavalier gentry of eastern Virginia. His father was the distinguished cavalry general known throughout the revolutionary war as "Light Horse Harry," who, after the termination of that contest, became governor of the "Old Dominion." "Light Horse Harry" was a cousin once removed of Richard Henry Lee, the revolutionary statesman, who, as early as 1766, was the leader of that section of the Virginia aristocracy, which co-operated with Patrick Henry against the stamp act. It was he

who, at the Continental congress of 1774, is said to have penned the address to the king, and who is known to have prepared the second address to the people of Great Britain, together with the appeal to the people of British America, which had been voted by the second congress. He also, on June 7, 1776—nearly a month before the declaration of independence—introduced into the congress at Philadelphia the resolution averring "that the united colonies are, and of right ought to be, independent states." It is also important to remember—because it points to the inherited conviction which led Robert E. Lee to side with his state against the Union—that Richard Henry Lee, like Patrick Henry, vehemently opposed the adoption of the constitution by Virginia. Afterward, like Henry, he strove to make the best of the new *régime*, and accepted the post of Federal senator to secure the adoption of those earlier constitutional amendments, which, it was hoped, would offer a sufficient guarantee of state rights. Robert E. Lee was reared in the knowledge that if such revolutionary patriots as Richard Henry Lee, Patrick Henry, and George Mason had controlled

the Virginia convention—and they came within a hair's breadth of controlling it—the Union in its present form would never have existed. To one conversant as he was with the details of Virginia history, it seemed indisputable that if a state's right to secede had been denied in 1788, the constitution could not have obtained ten votes in the Virginia convention. The opinion that a state had as much right to leave the Union as it had to withdraw from the confederation which had preceded the Union, continued to prevail in Virginia, until it took shape in the act of secession in the spring of 1861. But while in no Virginian was the belief more firmly rooted than it was in Robert E. Lee, he perceived, what was hidden from too many of his countrymen, that the abstract right to secede was one thing, and the practical wisdom of exercising quite another. He was born in the year in which Thomas Jefferson, another son of the "Old Dominion," made his famous embargo experiment, and, therefore, was thirteen years older than Sherman, fifteen years older than Grant, and seventeen years older than "Stonewall" Jackson. At eighteen he entered the Military academy at West Point, where he obtained, like most of the eminent commanders on both sides in our civil war, a thorough technical education.

How well he profited by his opportunities is attested by the fact that when he was graduated in 1829, he received a commission in the corps of engineers. At the date of the outbreak of the Mexican war he had risen to be a captain, and he served with credit during that contest, in the army under Gen. Scott. In the remarkable campaign which ended with the capture of Mexico, he earned particular distinction, and was brevetted colonel for his gallant conduct at the siege of Chapultepec, where he was wounded. The high estimation held by his superiors of his knowledge of the military art, was demonstrated in 1852, when he was appointed, by the secretary of war, superintendent of the West Point academy. Three years later he returned to active service in Texas as lieutenant-colonel of the 2d regiment of cavalry, one of the finest regiments in the army. In March, 1861, he was not only made colonel of the 1st regiment of cavalry, but it was an open secret that Gen. Scott offered to recommend him for the chief command of the Union forces, if he would remain faithful to the old flag. It was with profound distress that Lee saw himself reduced to the alternative of fighting against his native state, or against the Federal government, in whose service the best part of his life had been spent. It was impossible, however, for a man brought up under the doctrine of state rights not to recognize that Virginia had the higher claim upon his sword, and accordingly, after the Richmond convention had passed an ordinance of secession, Lee resigned his commission in the Federal army, and tendered his services to his native state. He was at once made commander-in-chief of the Virginian forces, and, after his state had joined the Confederacy, he was one of the five generals appointed by the Confederate government. For some reason his remarkable abilities do not seem to have been promptly recognized by the Confederate authorities. During a large part of 1861 he was employed in West Virginia, was repulsed in one engagement at Cheat Mountain, and being unable with the force at his disposal to achieve any decisive success, he was recalled by President Davis. Up to June, 1862, it was not suspected at the North that Gen. Lee was to prove the most redoubtable opponent of the Union. When, however, Gen. Joseph E. Johnston was defeated, and severely wounded at Fair Oaks, he obtained his first great opportunity. He was appointed in Johnston's place to the command of the army of Northern Virginia, for the reason, as President Davis said at the time to an aide-de-camp, Col. W. P. Johnston, that he, unlike other Confederate generals, had persistently recommended a vigorous aggressive policy. Owing to his undemonstrative demeanor, and the absence of any melodramatic element in his character, he did not at the time, receive full credit for audacious purposes. The truth is, that, could Lee have had his way, he would never have suffered the Federal armies to recover from their defeats, nor the interval of nearly a year to elapse between the two invasions of Maryland. The effect of his promotion to the supreme control of the defence of Richmond was immediately perceptible. The same Confederates who had been beaten at Fair Oaks (May 31st, June 1st), struck McClellan's army at Mechanicsville on June 26th, and after a series of desperate battles, lasting seven days, drove McClellan to the James river under the protection of his gunboats. How much the sword of one great general weighs when flung into the scale of war, may be computed from the fact that the Washington government, which only thirty days before had deemed its forces in the field adequate for all exigencies, then issued, in a fever of anxiety, a call for 300,000 men. A large army was immediately concentrated for the defence of Washington, and placed under Gen. Pope, who was to receive also the command of McClellan's troops, which were to be transferred from the James river to the Potomac. Before, however, the junction of the Federal forces could be effected, Lee, whose quickness of discernment was equaled by his celerity of movement, fell on Pope, and crushed him so utterly that the remnants of his army were glad to flee for refuge behind the fortifications of Washington. Lee had now been general of the army of Northern Virginia for ninety days, and, whereas at the outset Richmond seemed upon the verge of capture, now, at the end of that brief period, Richmond was safe, while Washington was in imminent peril. The subsequent invasion of Maryland was checked at Antietam, but it is only fair to remember that, in that battle, the Federal forces largely outnumbered the Confederates, and proved unable to prevent Lee

from retiring unmolested across the Potomac. Two months later, at Fredericksburg, Lee inflicted on the greatly reinforced Federal army, under Burnside, a defeat which nothing but the advent of night hindered from becoming an appalling massacre. As it was, the loss of the Federal troops exceeded 12,000 men. Thus ended the year 1862, luminous with hope for the Confederates in Virginia, where Lee commanded, but dark throughout the West, where no captain had proved competent to fill the place left vacant by Albert Sidney Johnston. The three days' battle of Chancellorsville (May 2, 3, and 4, 1863) was one of the most brilliant victories gained on either side during the civil war, by reason of the disparity of forces on that of the victor. Lee, who had dispatched the corps of Longstreet to the West, had only 60,000 men at his disposal. *Two divisions of Longstreet's corps had not gone to the west but to the region near Suffolk, Virginia, south of the James River.* The army of the Potomac, under Hooker, however, numbered over 100,000. Nevertheless, Lee outmanoeuvered and outfought the greatly preponderate forces of his antagonist, and finally drove them back to their old camping ground on the north of the Rappahannock. This truly astonishing achievement was, however, more than counterbalanced in the mind of Lee, and that of the Southern people, by the loss of "Stonewall" Jackson, who, after the evening of his successful onslaught on the Federal right, was mortally wounded by his own men, who mistook his escort for Federal cavalry. Col. William Preston Johnston has recorded that, on meeting Lee in Richmond soon after Hooker's defeat, and condoling with him on the death of Gen. Jackson, Lee responded, with deep feeling, that it was indeed an irreparable loss. Referring to his marvelous rapidity of movement, he mentioned that he had ordered a division to get under way at three o'clock on that eventful morning, or four hours before Jackson started

with his corps, and yet by nine o'clock the latter was ahead. Whether, had Jackson lived two months longer, to act as the unerring executor of Lee's plans at Gettysburg, that battle would have had a different termination, is one of the problems which will always puzzle the student of military history. What is known is, that on the first two days of the three days' carnage, the Confederates were to all appearances successful, and that, although on the third day their magnificent assault on Cemetery Ridge was repulsed by a cyclone of fire beyond the power of human beings to withstand, they were not pursued by Meade in their retreat, but were suffered to leisurely recross the Potomac. In reviewing this tremendous battle it is to be remembered that, while there has been much dispute about the numbers engaged on both sides, no competent military authority has assigned to Lee more than 68,000 men, or to Meade less than 82,000. *The modern consensus of historians is that the Confederate force at Gettysburg was about 75,000 and the Union force nearly 90,000.* Thus Lee had failed in his second invasion of the North, and on the third day at Gettysburg had lost thousands of gallant veterans who were never to be replaced. So great, nevertheless, was his prestige, that the commander of the army of the Potomac did not venture to attack him, and for ten months there was no serious attempt at a renewed advance upon Richmond. When, however, in March, 1864, Gen. Grant was made commander of all the Federal forces, it was evident that Lee was to have "a foeman worthy of his steel." In the following May the Federal army crossed the Rapidan, and the terrible carnage of the two days' battle of the Wilderness ensued. There is no doubt that both here and at Spottsylvania, as well as at the North Anna and Cold Harbor, Lee defeated Grant in the technical sense of blocking the latter's forward movement and inflicting upon him much severer losses than the

Confederates incurred. The ultimate result of the campaign was favorable to the Union, for Gen. Grant, like Zachary Taylor, never knew when he was beaten; but when checked in front, would, instead of retreating, continue to move forward on the left flank of the enemy, and thus after each defeat he drew nearer to the James river. Moreover, Lee's forces were so vastly outnumbered that they could not afford the depletion experienced through a series of desperate engagements, so that when Grant at last sat down in front of Petersburg, they were forced by sheer numerical weakness to remain in a defensive attitude. That nine months should still have intervened before the capture of Petersburg and Richmond is a fact that bears unmistakable testimony to Lee's power of making the most of a hopeless situation, and of achieving remarkable results with small resources. It is even doubtful whether he might not have postponed the evacuation of Richmond still another year, but for Sherman's triumphant march through Georgia and the Carolinas, which threatened the rear of the Confederate capital. When Lee at last abandoned Richmond, the Confederacy was irretrievably shattered, and the only course left open to him as a patriot was to procure the best terms possible for the wreck of his gallant army. Not many months after the surrender at Appomattox, Lee was elected president of the Washington and Lee university at Lexington, Va., and he continued to discharge the duties of that peaceful office until his death in 1870. Col. William Preston Johnston, who was a professor in the same institution, states that Lee avoided discussing the events of the war, or expressing any opinion concerning the political incidents of the reconstruction period. He considered that his own life, so far as it related to public affairs, had ended in 1865, and that the exposition of the war, and of his own part in it, must be left to history. But, although silent, he was conscious that from the hour when he assumed command of the army of Northern Virginia up to the moment when he laid it down, he could not fairly be said to have lost a single battle. *A strange claim, for not only Gettysburg but also several other battles under Lee's command were Confederate defeats.* And yet, there never was a day in that long period when the forces opposed to him were not numerically superior to his own. The trust which he reposed in the historian has been more than justified by the event. He has been awarded a place with

those great captains—Hannibal, Charles XII. of Sweden, and Napoleon Bonaparte—who, although unsuccessful in the end, have gained more glory than their conquerors. Col. Johnston's recollections of his intercourse with Gen. Lee at Lexington, after the war was over, are full of interesting personal details. There was in the great Confederate commander an extraordinary modesty, and an utter lack of self-consciousness. He would usually insist upon deferring to the opinions of the college faculty, although most of its members were much younger men than he. Col. Johnston states that no matter how long or fatiguing a faculty meeting might be, Gen. Lee always preserved an attitude in which dignity, decorum, and grace were united. He was, it is said, a very well-made man, with a symmetrical body, and without the slightest affectation or effort he sat, stood, or walked, a born gentleman. He was never in a hurry. Another fact which seems to bring the great man home to us, is a certain peculiarity of language and pronunciation. Thus he always said "coronel" for colonel, and pronounced walnut "wonnut". In middle life he was still a handsome man, having a rich brown complexion, aquiline features, and fine dark eyes. He was forty-eight years old when Col. Johnston first saw him in 1855, and the thought flashed through the young man's mind, "It was thus that Washington looked." Gen. Lee died suddenly Oct. 12, 1870. Returning from a meeting of the vestry of his church, he found his family waiting for him at the tea-table, and took his place to ask a blessing on the meal. At that moment the fatal stroke fell, and he sank down speechless, never to rise again. There was something singularly appropriate in the circumstance of his taking off. If there was in the Confederacy a man whose effort to divide the Union was disinterested and conscientious, that man was Robert Edward Lee, and it was fitting that his last conscious act on earth should be an act of prayer.

LEE, SAMUEL PHILLIPS, naval officer, was born in Fairfax county, Va., Feb. 13, 1812. He was appointed midshipman Nov. 22, 1825, and ordered to the sloop-of-war Hornet, of the West India station, Feb. 7, 1827. After six months he was sent to the Mediterranean, and at the expiration of three years of service was ordered to the Norfolk school, Oct. 16, 1830. He was promoted to passed midshipman, June 4, 1831; served in various capacities; was promoted lieutenant, Feb. 9, 1837, and ordered on an exploring expedition; then served in the West Indies and on the Atlantic coast. On his own application he received orders to take part in the Mexican war, and was present at the capture of Tobasco. In 1854 he commanded the brig Dolphin in making deep sea soundings, and was promoted commander Sept. 14, 1855. He was ordered to the East Indies, in command of the Vandalia, in 1860, and learning of the civil war at the Cape of Good Hope he assumed the risk of acting against orders, brought his ship back to the support of the Union, and was assigned to the blockade off Charleston, S.C.

When Adm. Farragut organized his expedition against New Orleans Lee was given the command of the U.S. sloop-of-war Oneida, and assigned to Bailey's division, which led the fleet before forts Jackson and St. Philip. In the action of passing the forts the Oneida was one of the three vessels to first encounter the enemy's fleet, and during the engagements relieved the Varuna by driving off two gunboats which had badly rammed her and stove her in, but Lee succeeded in capturing the rebel commander who had made the attack. Lee passed up the river with Bailey, and participated in the capture of the Chalmette batteries below New Orleans. After the capitulation of New Orleans, Farragut sent Lee forward to demand the surrender of Vicksburg, and he took part in passing the batteries. Having been promoted captain, July 16, 1862, Lee was transferred to the command of the north Atlantic blockading squadron and made acting rear-admiral, taking the place of Goldsborough. For two years he fulfilled the arduous duties of blockading the coasts of Virginia and North Carolina, and co-operating with the armies defending Norfolk, Newbern, and Washington. The rivers and sounds were penetrated, watched and guarded, and securely held; guerillas dispersed; and out of a total of sixty-five blockade-running steamers captured or destroyed by the squadron, fifty-four of them were captured or destroyed by the fleet under Lee's command. Besides blockading, which

was the main duty of the squadron, it was, independently or in co-operation with the army, engaged in ninety-one actions and expeditions during the period of his command. The efficiency of his services attracted the approving comment of foreign military observers, especially when the dangers of the coast and the fewness of wrecks in the fleet were considered. When Gen. Butler began his movement on Bermuda Hundred, Lee co-operated with him, and afterwards with Gen. Grant. Lee was anxious to have the Confederate fleet come down the river and attack him, and although he tried every device to bring an attack about, no such opportunity was given him to distinguish himself. On Oct. 21, 1864, he was detached and ordered to the command of the Mississippi squadron. He moved up the Cumberland to support Gen. Thomas, but the flagship was stopped at Clarksville by low water. Nevertheless army communications were kept open, and the lower Mississippi vigilantly guarded against the intervention of the trans-Mississippi Confederate forces. Lee was promoted to commodore, July 25, 1866, and constituted president of the examining board, with the exercise of various duties aboard and ashore until April 22, 1870, when he was promoted rear-admiral and ordered to special duty at the navy department. At the close of the civil war, Adm. Lee had the satisfaction of receiving the surrender of the last of the Confederate fleet on the western waters. He was retired from active service on Feb. 13, 1873, and he died at his home, Silver Spring, Sligo, Md., near Washington, June 7, 1897.

LEE, STEPHEN D., soldier, was born in Charleston, S.C., Sept. 22, 1833. His family was among the most distinguished in the state.

During the revolutionary war, his great-grandfather, William Lee, was one of the forty principal citizens of Charleston confined on a prison-ship and sent to St. Augustine, Fla., after the city was occupied by the British. His grandfather, Judge Thomas Lee, was U.S. judge for South Carolina during President Monroe's administration, presided during the Nullification difficulties, and was a strong Union man. The grandson, upon his graduation in 1854 from the U.S. military academy at West Point, was assigned to the 4th artillery, U.S. army, where he was first lieutenant and regimental quartermaster until 1861, when he resigned to cast his lot with the South in the civil war. Previous to the reduction of Fort Sumter, he was appointed captain in the South Carolina army, and, on becoming aide-de-camp to Gen. Beauregard, he with Col. Chestnut carried the summons to Maj. Anderson, demanding the surrender of the fort, and later, when Anderson declined, they carried the order to open fire on the fort. After the fall of Fort Sumter, Capt. Lee was made quartermaster, commissary and engineer disbursing officer for the Confederate

army in Charleston, having been appointed captain in the regular army of the Confederate states. At his request, he was relieved from these duties, which were distasteful to him, and went to Virginia in command of the light battery of Hampton's South Carolina legion. He was in several fights with Federal gunboats on the Potomac; was promoted major of artillery November, 1861, lieutenant-colonel and colonel of artillery; was with Gen. Johnston in the Peninsula campaign and in the battles around Richmond. He took part in the battles of Seven pines, Savage's station, and Malvern hill; commanded the 4th Virginia cavalry for six weeks, as all the field officers were wounded; was complimented by Gen. Robert E. Lee for activity and gallantry; and commanded a battalion of artillery in Gen. Lee's army in the campaign against Gen. Pope. His services at the battle of second Manassas or Bull Run were brilliant, and attracted the attention of the entire army. At Antietam he did conspicuous service, for which he was made brigadier-general, Nov. 6, 1863, and ordered by President Davis to Vicksburg, Miss., to take command of the garrison and batteries holding the Mississippi river at that point. Here he was signally successful in many important engagements, notably at the battle of Chickasaw Bayou, and subsequently in the battle of Baker's Creek or Champion Hills, where he was greatly complimented for his gallantry. Gen. Lee commanded a part of the intrenchments in Vicksburg near the railroad cut, and immediately after the fall of that city was exchanged, promoted major-general Aug. 3, 1863, and placed in command of all the cavalry in Mississippi, Alabama, West Tennessee and East Louisiana. When Sherman marched from Vicksburg to Meridian, Miss., with an army of 30,000 men, Gen. Lee hung on his front, rear and flanks with a cavalry force of 2,500 men. The infantry force was not large enough to fight a battle and little opposition could be made by the cavalry force. When Gen. Polk was sent from Mississippi to reinforce the Confederate army at Dalton, Ga., Gen. Lee was promoted lieutenant-general June 23, 1864, and assigned to the command of the department of Mississippi, Alabama, East Louisiana and West Tennessee. After the battle of Harrisburg or Tupelo, Miss., Gen. Lee was ordered to Atlanta, Ga., and assigned to the command of Hood's old corps of infantry, Hood having relieved Gen. Johnston in command of the army of Tennessee. Here he was engaged in the battle of July 28th on the left of Atlanta, was also in the battle of Jonesboro' south of Atlanta, and subsequently accompanied Gen. Hood in his flank movement around Atlanta and north as far as Resaca, and then into Tennessee, via Tuscumbia, Ala. When the battle of Nashville was fought and Hood badly routed, Lee's corps held and repulsed the enemy at Overton Hill, and in the disaster his corps was the only one organized for three days after the rout. He was wounded while with the rear guard late in the afternoon of the day after this battle, but did not relinquish command till his corps was relieved by an organized rear guard, composed of infantry and the cavalry corps of Forrest south of Columbia. As soon as Gen. Lee was sufficiently recovered from his wound, he resumed command of his corps in North Carolina, and in time to surrender with the Confederate army commanded by Gen. Joseph E. Johnston. In February 1865, Gen. Lee married Regina Harrison of Columbus, Miss. He has but one child—Blewett Lee. After the war, Gen. Lee labored constantly and energetically to build up the waste places of the South. By profession he was a planter, and was president of the Mississippi agricultural and mechanical college. He had charge of the college from its opening in 1880 to 1897, his administration having been most successful. The college has known nothing but growth and prosperity since the day it first opened its doors. Gen. Lee never aspired to political office. He was twice called into politics, once as state senator, and afterward as a member of the last constitutional convention which framed the present constitution of Mississippi. *He died May 28, 1908.*

LEE, WILLIAM HENRY FITZHUGH, soldier and congressman, was born at Arlington, Va., May 31, 1837, son of Robert E. Lee and brother of George Washington Custis Lee. He was graduated from Harvard in 1857, and the same year was appointed second lieutenant in the 6th regiment U.S. infantry, and in 1858 he accompanied his regiment to Utah against the Mormons, under command of Col. Albert Sidney Johnston. In 1859 he resigned his commission, and returned to New Kent county, Va., to take charge of his estates, but early in 1861, when the civil war broke out, cast his fortunes with the South, and raised a company of cavalry, with which he joined the army of northern Virginia. He was made captain of this company, and from that time until the close of hostilities was actively engaged in the war. He was frequently promoted, serving in the various

grades from captain to major-general of cavalry. He was wounded at Brandy Station early in 1863, and was captured in Hanover county in July following, and taken to Fortress Monroe. Later in the same year he was transferred to the United States prison at Fort La Fayette, where he was confined until March, 1864. After his exchange, he rejoined his command, and served throughout the campaign of 1864. Surrendering with Gen. Lee at Appomattox, he returned to his plantation, on which he continued to reside until 1874, when he removed to Burke's Station. He represented his district in the state senate for one term, declining a renomination. He has been president of the State agricultural society, and was extensively engaged in agricultural pursuits. He was elected to the fiftieth, and re-elected to the fifty-first and fifty-second congresses as a democrat from the eighth Virginia district. He died at Alexandria, Va., Oct. 15, 1891.

LINCOLN, ABRAHAM, sixteenth president of the United States, was born in Hardin county, Ky., Feb. 12, 1809. The earliest American ancestor of the family was probably Samuel Lincoln, of Norwich, Eng., who settled in Hingham, Mass. about 1638. His son, Mordecai, first settled in Monmouth county, N.J., and afterward in Berks county, Pa., and died in 1735; his sons, Abraham, Mordecai, Josiah and Thomas, were citizens of Rockingham county, Va., and one of them at least, Abraham, migrated to Mercer county, Ky. (then a part of the original state of Virginia), in 1782. Abraham, the grandfather of the president, entered a tract of 400 acres of land on the south side of Licking creek, under a government land-warrant, and built a log cabin, near Fort Beargrass, on the site now occupied by the city of Louisville. In the second year of this settlement, Abraham Lincoln, while at work in his field, was slain by an Indian from an ambush. Thomas the younger of the brothers was seized by the Indian, but was rescued by Mordecai, the elder brother, who

shot and killed the Indian. Of Thomas the present subsequently said: "My father, at the time of the death of his father, was but six years old, and he grew up literally without education." Thomas Lincoln was a tall and stalwart pioneer, and an expert hunter. While a lad, he hired himself to his uncle, Isaac Lincoln, living on Watauga creek, a branch of the Holson river. He married Nancy Hanks, a native of Virginia, in 1806, and settled on Larue creek, in what is now Larue county, Ky. They had three children, Sarah, Abraham and Thomas. Sarah married Aaron Grigsby and died in middle life. Thomas, who was two years younger than Abraham, died in infancy. Abraham Lincoln's early education from books was fitful and scanty; schools were infrequent on the wild frontier. In 1816 the Lincoln family removed to Spencer county, Ind., where they built and lived in a log cabin, where Mrs. Lincoln died Oct. 5, 1818, at the age of thirty-five. In the autumn of the following year Thomas Lincoln married his second wife Mrs. Sally Johnston (née Bush). The stepmother of Abraham Lincoln was a woman of some mental ability and great kindness of heart; her influence over the boy was great and beneficent. Aided by her, the lad secured the reading of the few books to be found in the settlement, and became noted as a hungry reader. As he grew older he took to making impromptu speeches among the neighbors on any topic that chanced to be under discussion. His first glimpse of the world was afforded in the spring of 1828, when, in company with a son of one of the traders of Gentryville, Ind., he embarked on a flatboat loaded with produce and floated down the creeks and rivers to New Orleans, 1,800 miles distant, where the cargo and craft were disposed of, and the young voyagers made their way homeward. He was now come to the years of manhood, was six feet four inches tall, an athlete, tough and wiry of fibre, and eminent as a worker and woodsman. The family moved once more, in 1830, this time to Illinois, where they built another log cabin, near Decatur, Macon Co. After assisting his father to build the cabin, split rails and fence and plough fifteen acres of land, Abraham Lincoln struck out for himself, hiring himself to any who needed manual labor. His father finally settled in Goose-Nest Prairie, Coles Co., Ill., where he died in 1851 at the age of seventy-three. His son cared for him up to his latest years *although their relationship was cool and distant.* In the spring of 1831 Abraham Lincoln, accompanied by his cousin John Hanks, took a flatboat, produce-laden, to New Orleans, for one Denton Offutt, a country trader, and on his return was engaged by Offutt to take charge of a small trading store in New Salem, Ill. At this post he continued until the following spring, when the business was discontinued. He took an active interest in politics, was noted as a graphic and humorous storyteller, and was regarded as one of the oracles of the neighborhood. His unflinching honesty gained him the title of "Honest Abe Lincoln". Resolving to run for the legislature, he issued a circular dated March 9, 1832, appealing to his friends and neighbors to vote for him. Before the election came on, Indian disturbances broke out in the northern part of the state, and Black Hawk, the chief of the Sacs, headed a formidable war party. Lincoln joined a party of volunteers and marched to the scene of hostilities. The conflict was soon over, and Lincoln returned to

New Salem, Sangamon Co., ten days before the election. He was defeated, but he received nearly every vote of his own town. He was a whig in politics, and was an ardent admirer of Henry Clay, then the great whig chief. Once more he made an essay in trading, and bought on credit, after the fashion of the time, a small country store and contents, associating with himself, at sundry times, partners in business. The venture was a losing one, and the principal occupation of Lincoln during this period was that of diligent study and the reading of everything on which he could lay hands, newspapers and old political pamphlets chiefly. He studied law and surveying and, in 1833, he began work as a land-surveyor, a vocation which in that region then gave one frequent employment. In that year, too, he was appointed postmaster of New Salem, an unimportant office, which he valued only because it gave him an opportunity to read the newspapers of its patrons. He was again a candidate for the legislature in 1834, was elected at the head of the poll, there being three other candidates in the field. He was now twenty-five years of age, manly, independent, well-poised and thoroughly informed in all public matters. He had formed his manner of speech on the few books which he read—the Bible, Shakespeare, Burns's poems and Bunyan's "Pilgrim's Progress." In the legislature his commanding height attracted attention, but he took very small part in the active duties of legislation, contenting himself with observation and study of all that passed. Next year, when he was again returned to the legislature, he participated actively in the affairs of the house, and distinguished himself by an unavailing protest against the "Black Laws" of the state, which forbade the entrance of free persons of color into Illinois, and by his support of the bill to remove the seat of government from Vandalia to Springfield. In 1837 Lincoln removed to Springfield, the new capital of the state, and established himself very modestly in the business of a lawyer. In this practice he remained until his election to the presidency in 1860. His first partner in business was John T. Stuart, in 1837; this partnership was changed four years later, when he associated himself with Stephen T. Logan. In 1843 the law partnership of Abraham Lincoln and William H. Herndon was formed; this firm was not dissolved until the death of Lincoln in 1865. During the "Tippecanoe and Tyler too" campaign of 1840, when the country was deeply stirred by the presidential candidacy of Gen. William Henry Harrison, Lincoln threw himself into the canvass with great ardor, and was one of the electors on the whig ticket. He was highly elated by the triumph of Harrison and the whig party, and he distinguished himself by his fearless opposition to the party that had, up to that time, been dominant and proscriptive in the country. *In 1835 he suffered a great disappointment and bout of depression* with the death of a beautiful young lady, Ann Rutledge, to whom he was tenderly attached, and this grief made upon his temperament a lifelong impression. *November 4, 1842,* he was married to Mary Todd, daughter of Robert Todd, of Kentucky. Miss Todd was visiting relations in Springfileld when circumstances brought her into intimate friendly intercourse with Lincoln, which ripened into marriage. He was now gradually acquiring a profitable law practice, and the days of grinding poverty, long endured without complaint, were passing away. In 1846, after several disappointments, he was given the whig nomination to congress from the Sangamon district, and was elected over his democratic opponent, Peter Cartwright, by a majority of 1,611, polling an unexpectedly large vote. During the preceding winter Texas had been admitted to the Union, and the bitterness with which the whigs opposed this step, and the measures that grew out of it, was shared by Lincoln, who made good use of arguments against these matters on the canvass, and

subsequently during his term in congress. Among the members of the house of representatives with Lincoln were John Quincy Adams, Robert C. Winthrop, Alexander H. Stephens, Robert Toombs, and Andrew Johnson. In the senate were Daniel Webster, Lewis Cass, John C. Calhoun, Jefferson Davis and Stephen A. Douglas. Lincoln in congress opposed the war with Mexico, but voted consistently for rewards to the soldiers who fought in it. He served only one term in congress, and did not leave any marked impression in the annals of that body. He voted with the men who favored the formation of the new territories of California and New Mexico without slavery, and he introduced a bill to abolish slavery in the District of Columbia, providing for the emancipation of slaves there by governmental purchase. He was not a candidate for re-election, and was succeeded by his intimate friend Edward D. Baker. Gen. Zachary Taylor having been elected president of the United States, Lincoln applied for the office of commissioner of the general land office, but was offered, in lieu thereof, the governorship of the territory of Oregon. This he declined, and returned to his practice of law in Springfield. The eldest son of Abraham and Mary Lincoln, Robert Todd, was born Aug. 1, 1843; the second, Edward Baker, was born March 10, 1846, and died in infancy; the third, William Wallace, was born Dec. 21, 1850, and died during his father's first year in the presidential office; Thomas, the youngest son, was born Apr. 4, 1853, and survived his father, dying at the age of nineteen years. As a lawyer, Lincoln was now engaged in several celebrated cases. One of these was that of the negro girl, Nancy, in which the question of the legality of slavery in the Northwestern territory, of which Illinois formed a part, was involved. Another, in which the seizure of a free negro from Illinois by the authorities of New Orleans was opposed, was also undertaken and conducted by him. In both these causes Lincoln succeeded. In 1850 there were many premonitions of the coming of the storm which the long-continued agitation of the slavery question had induced. Lincoln was a close but generally silent observer of the signs of the times. In 1854 the virtual repeal of the Missouri Compromise measures, in which Stephen A. Douglas took a leading part, aroused the Northern and free states to excited debate. The passage of the Kansas-Nebraska bill, by which those two territories were organized, with the question of the legality of slavery left open to be settled by a popular vote, was the signal for a great outburst of feeling against the institution of slavery in the non-slaveholding states. In October of that year Lincoln and Douglas met in debate at the great annual State Fair held in Springfield, Ill., and Lincoln made his first famous speech on the question that thenceforward began to engross the minds of the people. Lincoln opposed the repeal of the Missouri Compromise, and Douglas defended it. A few days later the two men met again at Peoria, Ill., and the debate was renewed, amidst great popular excitement. On both occasions Lincoln's speeches evoked much enthusiasm by the closeness of their logic and their perspicacity. His public speeches from this time forth were regarded throughout the western states as the most remarkable of the time. In

1856 the first republican national convention was held in Philadelphia. John C. Frémont was nominated for president of the United States and William L. Dayton for vice-president. Abraham Lincoln received 110 votes for the second place on the ticket. James Buchanan and John C. Breckenridge were nominated by the democratic party. Lincoln was a candidate for presidential elector on the republican ticket of Illinois, and took an active part in the canvass, speaking from one end of the state to the other almost continually throughout the campaign. The democratic candidates were elected, Buchanan receiving 174 electoral votes against 114 cast for Frémont. Maryland cast her eight electoral votes for Fillmore and Donelson, the whig candidates. *In 1858,* Douglas's term in the senate drawing to a close, Lincoln was put forward as a competitor for the place. The two men accordingly agreed on a joint canvass of the state, the members of the Illinois legislature then to be elected being charged with the duty of choosing a senator. The contest between Lincoln and Douglas that year was memorable and significant. The debates attracted the attention of the entire country. In their course the slavery question in all its bearings, but more especially with reference to its introduction into territory hitherto regarded as free, was debated

with great force and minuteness on both sides. The total vote of the state was in favor of Lincoln, but as some of the holding-over members of the legislature were friendly to Douglas, and the districting of the state was also in his favor, he was chosen senator by a small majority. At the republican convention, held in Decatur, Ill., in May, *1860,* Lincoln was declared to be the candidate of his state for the presidential nomination of 1860. This was the first public demonstration in his favor as a national candidate. At that convention several  rails from the Lincoln farm in Macon county were exhibited as the handiwork of Abraham Lincoln, and the title of "the rail-splitter" was given him. In the autumn *of 1859* Lincoln made political speeches in Ohio and Kentucky, arousing great enthusiasm wherever he appeared. In February, 1860, he accepted an invitation to speak in New York, and, for the first time in his life, he visited the Atlantic states. He spoke in the Cooper Union hall, New York, and his oration, which was a discussion of the great question of the day, created a profound impression throughout the country. It gave him at once a national reputation as a political speaker. The democratic national convention assembled in Charleston, S.C., Apr. 23, 1860, to nominate candidates for president and vice-president. The slavery issue divided the body, so that the pro-slavery delegates finally withdrew, and organized a separate convention in Richmond, Va., where John C. Breckinridge was nominated. The remaining delegates adjourned to Baltimore, where they nominated Stephen A. Douglas. Meanwhile the whigs and a few other conservatives met in Baltimore and nominated John Bell, of Tennessee. The republican national convention assembled in Chicago, Ill., *May 16, 1860,* and, amid unparalleled enthusiasm, nominated Abraham

Lincoln for president. Hannibal Hamlin, of Maine, was nominated for vice-president. The electoral canvass that year was one of the most intense excitement. It was universally conceded that the question of the extension or the confinement of slavery to its present limits was to be determined by the result of this election. Douglas was the only one of the four presidential candidates who took the field to speak in his own behalf. Lincoln was elected, having received 180 electoral votes; Breckinridge had seventy-two votes; Douglas twelve; and Bell thirty-nine. The popular vote was distributed as follows: Lincoln, 1,866,452; Breckinridge, 847,953; Douglas, 1,375,157; Bell, 590,631. As soon as the result of the election was known, the members of President Buchanan's cabinet who were in favor of a secession of the slave states began to make preparations for that event. The army, which mustered only 16,000 men, was scattered through the southern states, and the small navy was dispersed far and wide. United States arms had been already ordered to points in the Southern states, and active steps had been taken by the more rebellious of those states toward a formal severance of the ties that bound them to the Union. Their attitude was one of armed expectancy. The cabinet of President Buchanan was torn by the conflicting views of its members, some of them being in favor of resolutely confronting the danger of secession, and others opposing any action whatever. The Federal forts in Charleston harbor, S.C., being threatened by the secessionists, Lewis Cass advised reinforcement; he resigned when his advice was disregarded at the instance of his associates. Jeremiah S. Black, attorney-general, gave an opinion that the states could not be coerced into remaining in the Union, and shortly a general disruption of the cabinet ensued. Southern senators and representatives now began to leave Washington for their homes, declaring that they could no longer remain in the councils of the nation. Formal ordinances of secession were passed by the states in rebellion. South Carolina adopted its ordinance of secession *Dec. 20, 1860;* Mississippi, Jan. 9, 1861; Florida, Jan. 10th; Alabama, Jan. 11th; Georgia, Jan. 19, 1861; Louisiana, *Jan. 26th* and Texas Feb. 1st. Representatives of the seceding states met at Montgomery, Feb. 4, 1861, and organized a provisional government, generally resembling in form that of the United States; Jefferson Davis, of Mississippi, was chosen president, and Alexander H. Stephens, of Georgia, vice-president. Davis assumed an aggressive tone in his public speeches, and, while on his way to take the reins of government of the new Confederacy, he said: "We will carry the war where it is easy to advance, where food for the sword and the torch awaits our armies in the densely populated cities." Lincoln remained at his home in Springfield, Ill., making no speeches, and silent, so far as any public utterances were concerned. He broke this silence for the first time when, on Feb. 11, 1861, he bade his friends and neighbors farewell as he took the railway train for Washington. In that simple address he said, among other things: "I go to assume a task more difficult than that which has devolved upon any other man since the days of Washington. He never would have succeeded except for the aid of divine Providence, upon which he at all times relied. I feel that I cannot succeed without the same divine blessing which sustained him; and on the same Almighty Being I place my reliance for support." On the way to Washington the president-elect was received with great popular enthusiasm, and was frequently called from his railway carriage to speak to the people. Nearing Washington, he learned of a plot to take his life while passing through Baltimore, and by the advice of trusty friends the movements of the party were

Lincoln's Inauguration

463

changed, in order to disconcert the conspirators. Speaking at Independence Hall, Philadelphia, Feb. 22nd, during these trying hours, he referred to the fundamental principle propounded in the declaration of independence, and said: "If this country cannot be saved without giving up that principle, I was about to say I would rather be assassinated on the spot than surrender it." Lincoln was inaugurated president of the United States at noon, March 4, 1861, in front of the national capitol, Washington. His inaugural address was an earnest and plaintive appeal for peace and union. At the same time he took care to say that the union of the states is perpetual, and that to the best of his ability he would "take care that the laws of the Union be faithfully executed in all the states." He closed with these memorable words: "The mystic chords of memory, stretching from every battlefield and patriot grave to every living heart and hearthstone all over this broad land, will yet swell the chorus of the Union, when touched again, as surely they will be, by the better angels of our nature." In the South, and in such communities of the North as sympathized with the cause of rebellion, these utterances were received with coldness, and in many instances

with jeers and derision. Lincoln's cabinet, then announced, was as follows: Secretary of State, William H. Seward; secretary of war, Simon Cameron; secretary of the treasury, Salmon P. Chase; secretary of the navy, Gideon Welles; postmaster-general, Montgomery Blair; secretary of the interior, Caleb B. Smith; attorney-general, Edward Bates. Of this number, Seward, Chase, Bates, and Cameron had been candidates for the nomination of president at the convention at which Lincoln was nominated. Some of the new president's friends were troubled by the selection of these prominent and ambitious men as his counsellors. Subsequently it was found, when attempts were made to subordinate him to his cabinet, that he was the sole interior spirit of his administration. Of these cabinet ministers only Secretaries Seward and Welles remained in office during the remainder of Lincoln's lifetime. Secretary Chase resigned his place in 1864, and was succeeded by William Pitt Fessenden, of Maine, who resigned after a short term, and was succeeded by Hugh McCullough in March, 1865. Simon Cameron resigned *Jan 11, 1862,* and was succeeded by Edwin M. Stanton. Secretary Smith resigned his office to accept a judicial post *in 1863,* and was succeeded by John P. Usher. Attorney-General Bates retired from office in 1864, and was succeeded by James Speed, of Kentucky, and Montgomery Blair about the same time resigned the office of postmaster-general, and was succeeded by Ex-Gov. William Dennison, of Ohio. The Confederate congress, on March 11, 1861, passed a bill providing for the organization of an army. No notice was taken of this insurrectionary measure, which, it had been expected, would be regarded as a casus belli (an event that allegedly justifies a war or conflict) by the Federal authorities. Next, two commissioners, Messrs. *John Forsyth* and Crawford, were sent to Washington to negotiate a treaty with the government of the United

States, the assumption being that the new Confederacy was a foreign power. Mr. Lincoln refused to receive the commissioners, and sent them a copy of his inaugural address. Secretary Seward served upon them, however, a formal notice that they could have no official recognition from the United States government. Meantime, the determination of the president to send succor to the beleaguered Federal garrison in Charleston harbor, then collected in Fort Sumter, was made public. The people of South Carolina, impatient for the war to begin, threatened to fire upon Fort Sumter, and to attack any vessel that might bring succors. Every device to induce the president to commit "an overt act of war" was resorted to in vain. While he waited for the rebels to fire the first gun, there was much impatience manifested in the loyal Northern states at what was considered the

sluggishness of the administration. On Apr. 12, 1861, Gen. Beauregard, commanding the rebel forces at Charleston, sent a demand to Maj. Anderson, in command of Fort Sumter, to surrender. He refused to surrender, but he subsequently agreed to evacuate the fort Apr. 15th, unless he received instructions to the contrary, or provisions for sustenance, before that date. After due warning, Beauregard opened fire on the fort early in the morning of Apr. 12th, and, after feeble defence, the famishing

garrison of sixty-five men was forced to surrender, and the United States flag fell on the walls of Sumter. The war had begun. The effect of this overt act of the Confederates was instant and inflammatory all through the North. Patriotic meetings were held, men were ready to volunteer for the war, state authorities began to arm and equip troops, and a general note of preparation now sounded through the loyal states. The president called a special session of congress at the national capital for July 4, 1861. In a proclamation dated Apr. 15, 1861, the president asked for 75,000 men. This was responded to in the North with enthusiasm, and in the South with cries of derision. In the states bordering on the Confederacy, where the great battles of the war were afterward fought, this call was received with coldness. Patriotic excitement ran high all over the North, and for a time nothing was thought of but the war for the sake of the Union. One of the first regiments to march to the succor of the national capital, menaced on all sides and distracted with interior conspiracies, was the 6th Massachusetts. It was fired upon in the streets of Baltimore. This act inflamed the loyal North still more, and the excitement became intense. The governor of Maryland, alarmed by this collision, implored the president to invoke the mediation of the British minister at Washington to compose existing difficulties. Lincoln referred the governor to the secretary of state, who declared that "no domestic contention should be referred to any foreign arbitrament, least of all to that of a European monarchy." Gen. B. F. Butler surprised the people of Baltimore by seizing Federal Hill, a fortified position commanding the city, and troops thereafter marched unmolested through the city on their way to Washington. On the 19th of April the president issued his proclamation declaring the ports of Texas, Louisiana, Mississippi, Alabama, Georgia, Florida, and South Carolina in a state of blockade, and closed to commerce. One week later, North Carolina and Virginia, having also passed ordinances of secession, were added to this list. Another call for troops was made, thirty-nine regiments of infantry and one of cavalry being asked for; and, by direction of the president, the maximum force of the regular army was increased to 22,714 men; and 18,000 volunteer seamen were called for. An embassy from the state of Virginia having been sent to the president while the ordinance of secession was under consideration, Lincoln, in reply to application for his intentions,

again referred to his inaugural address, and added: "As I then and therein said, the power confided to me will be used to hold, occupy and possess property and places belonging to the government, and to collect duties and imposts; but beyond what is necessary for these objects, there will be no invasion, no using of force against or among the people anywhere." Furthermore, he intimated that it might be necessary to withdraw the United States mail service from the states in which disorder prevailed. He did not threaten to collect duties and imposts by force, but he would, employ force to retake the public property of the government, wherever that had been seized. By a vote of eighty-eight to fifty-five, the ordinance of secession was adopted in Virginia, and the capital of the state now became the seat of the

Confederate government. Meanwhile, the Confederates had taken possession of Harper's Ferry, Va., and the arsenal and munitions of war at that point, and of the navy-yard near Norfolk, Va., with the stores and vessels there accumulated. These seizures gave them much additional war material. The hostile camps on the northern border of Virginia were drawing nearer to each other as both increased in numbers and efficiency. When congress assembled in July, Confederate flags on the Virginia heights opposite Washington could be seen from the top of the capitol. The first serious engagement was that on the line of Bull Run creek, the culmination of which was on July 21, 1861. The Confederate forces, under Gen. Joseph E. Johnston, numbered about 18,000, and those under Gen. Irwin McDowell, the Union commander, were 17,676. The result was a defeat for the Union forces, and a panic-stricken retreat upon Washington. The effect of this disaster upon Lincoln and upon the country was depressing; but the people soon rallied, and indignation took the place of mortifying regret. Volunteering was resumed with vigor. Two naval and military expeditions were successful, and Fort Hatteras, N.C., and Port Royal, S.C. surrendered to the Union forces. Gen. McClellan had also cleared the Confederates from that part of Virginia which lies west of the Blue Ridge, afterward erected into the state of West Virginia. Congress responded to the call of the president for more men and money by voting $500,000,000 for war purposes, and authorizing him to call for 500,000 men. Great excitement was created throughout the country when James M. Mason and John Slidell, Confederate emissaries to European courts, were taken, *Nov. 8, 1861,* from the British packet-ship Trent, at sea, by Capt. Wilkes, commanding the U.S. steamer San Jacinto. The event was the cause of much congratulation with the people, and cabinet ministers and congress openly approved of the seizure. Lincoln was disturbed by this, and decided that the envoys should be given up to the demand of the British government, from whose flag they had been taken. In the face of popular indignation, he remained firm, and the envoys were released. Eventually, the wisdom and the justice of this course were generally admitted. In July, 1861, Gen. McClellan was assigned to the command of the army of the Potomac, and Gen. Frémont to that of the department of the West, with headquarters at St. Louis. Radical differences on the subject of slavery at once began to appear in the orders of these two generals. Lincoln was greatly embarrassed and disturbed when Frémont, Aug. 31st, issued a proclamation confiscating the property of Confederates within his lines, and emancipating their slaves. Congress had passed a bill to confiscate property used for insurrectionary military purposes, and slaves had been declared "contraband of war." The president wrote privately to Frémont, advising him to modify his orders, as if by his own motion, as these were in conflict with the course of the administration, and did not conform to the action of congress. Frémont refused to make these modifications, and Lincoln, in an order dated Sept. 11, 1861, did so modify Frémont's proclamation. During May of the following year Gen. David Hunter, commanding the department of the South, with headquarters at Hilton Head, S.C., issued an order resembling Frémont's: it was instantly revoked by the president. Lincoln was sticking to his determination to save the Union, if possible, without meddling with the question of slavery; and while none doubted his hostility to slavery, it was difficult for many to understand why he did not strike it in its vulnerable parts whenever he had an opportunity. The controversy arising out of the disposition of captured slaves by the army of the Potomac (which was usually a recognition of the rights of the slaveholders), and out of the orders of Hunter and McClellan, was very bitter in the North, and many who had supported Lincoln's

administration complained that his policy was "pro-slavery." March 6, 1862, the president sent to congress a message in which he intimated very distinctly that if the war ended then, or very soon, slavery would probably remain intact; but if it should continue, and if gradual and compensated emancipation were not accepted, then slavery would be destroyed by the operations of the war. *Lincoln's message urged Congress to pass a resolution offering monetary compensation to slaveholders in border states that enacted the gradual abolition of slavery.* Congress adopted a resolution approving the policy outlined by the president; but the border state representatives, although invited by the president to a free conference with him on the subject, kept aloof from the matter. Congress had now passed a bill to abolish slavery in the District of Columbia. It was signed by Lincoln, who, in 1849, had introduced a bill for that purpose. During the summer of 1862, the proposition of arming the freed negroes was begun; it was opposed by many conservative people, but was warmly advocated by Lincoln, who said: "Why should they do anything for us if we do nothing for them? If they stake their lives for us, they must be prompted by the strongest of motives, even the promise of freedom. And the promise, being made, must be kept." *This is misleading. The quotation dates from 1864, not 1862. Lincoln held back on the enlistment of black troops until 1863, when he embraced the policy with enthusiasm.* The law authorizing the arming of the ex-slaves, accordingly, contained a clause giving freedom to all slaves who served in the Union army, and to their families as well. During the summer military operations lagged, and much complaint was made of the sluggish movements of the army of the Potomac under Gen. McClellan. This impatience found expression in a letter to the president, written by Horace Greeley and published in the New York "Tribune," in which the writer severely arraigned the president for his alleged inactivity and lack of vigor in dealing with the slavery question. Lincoln wrote a letter in reply, in the course of which he said: "If I could save the Union without freeing any slave I would do it; if I could save it by freeing all the slaves, I would do it; and if I could do it by freeing some and leaving others alone, I would also do that. What I do about slavery and the colored race, I do because I believe it helps to save this Union; and what I forbear I forbear because I do not believe that it would help to save the Union." This appeared to settle for a long time the position of Lincoln on the slavery question. The Confederate army, under Gen. Robert E. Lee, invaded Maryland, crossing the Potomac in September, 1862. At that time Lincoln had under consideration a proclamation

freeing all slaves within the jurisdiction of the United States government, or thereafter to be brought under it. *Lincoln's proclamation would declare free only those slaves in states engaged in rebellion, not in the border states.* In the imminence of the danger then apparent, he resolved that if success should crown the Union arms, he would issue that proclamation. The battle of South Mountain was fought on Sept. 14th, and that of Antietam on the 17th; the Confederates were defeated on both fields, and retreated in great disorder. The proclamation of emancipation was issued Sept. 22nd, declaring freedom to all slaves in bondage on American soil *in states engaged in rebellion.* This proclamation electrified the nation and greatly excited the people of other countries. Jan. 1, 1863, the president issued a supplementary proclamation, in which the terms of the previous document were reaffirmed, and the parts of states exempted from the operation of emancipation were named. These portions were inconsiderable, and the action of congress in abolishing slavery throughout the entire territory of the United States made an end of slavery in the Republic. Lincoln's general plan for the conduct of the war, formulated after anxious consultation with his most trusted advisers, was as follows: To blockade the entire coast-line of the Confederate states; to acquire military occupation of the border states, so as to protect Union men and repel invasion; to clear the Mississippi of obstructions, thus dividing the Confederacy and relieving the West, which was deprived of its natural outlet to the sea; to destroy the Confederate army between Richmond and Washington, and to capture the Confederate capital. This vast plan had been formed in the mind of Lincoln by the necessities of the situation. Gen. Scott, who held the highest command in the army of the United States, had asked to be relieved from active duty and placed

Capitol of Springfield

on the retired list. His request was granted, and Lincoln accompanied by the members of his cabinet visited the general at his mansion in Washington and presented to him in person a most affectionate and generous farewell address. Gen. George B. McClellan was now in supreme command. Lincoln's immediate anxiety was for the speedy opening of the Mississippi river. In pursuance of his programme, Gen. U. S. Grant, then rising in popular esteem, attacked and destroyed Belmont, a military depot of the Confederates in Mississippi. Gen. Garfield defeated Humphrey Marshall at Middle Creek, Ky., and Gen. George H. Thomas defeated Gens. Zollicoffer and Crittenden at Mill Spring. This was followed up by the capture of Fort Henry on the Tennessee, and Fort Donelson on the Cumberland river. These streams, emptying into the Ohio river, were very necessary to promote military operations against the Confederates in the south-western states. *On the 6th–7th of April, 1862,* was fought the great battle of Shiloh, or Pittsburg Landing, in which the carnage on both sides was very great, and many brave and distinguished officers on both sides were killed. The defeated Confederates retreated to their fortified line at Corinth, Miss., where they were attacked by Gen. H. W. Halleck, and again compelled to retreat, leaving behind them a large accumulation of military stores. By the end of May, 1862, Missouri, Arkansas, Kentucky and Tennessee were virtually free from Confederate domination. That part of the programme which required the blockade and occupation of Atlantic ports of the seceded states was not overlooked. *Federal forces captured Roanoke Island, N.C., Feb. 8.* Next fell Newbern, N.C. and Fort Macon and Fort Pulaski on the same coast. In the spring of 1862 an expedition under Gen. B. F. Butler landed at Ship Island, in the Gulf of Mexico, about midway between New Orleans and Mobile. A fleet of armed vessels under Adm.

Farragut soon after arrived, and on the 17th of April Farragut appeared below the forts that guarded the approaches to the city of New Orleans. After some skirmishing, Farragut's fleet passed the forts, destroying the fleet above, and ascended the Mississippi and appeared before the city of New Orleans, to the amazement of its people. Baton Rouge, the capital of Louisiana, next fell, and the surrender of Natchez, May 12, 1862, opened the Mississippi as far north as Vicksburg, which

with its fortifications resisted the free navigation of the Mississippi river. McClellan meanwhile remained inactive before Washington, and popular discontent was constantly making itself manifest in consequence of his alleged tardiness, many people insisting that the government had failed to supply his necessary wants. Lincoln was in frequent and anxious consultation with McClellan and the other generals gathered at the capital. During the latter part of January, 1862, Lincoln issued an order specially intended to direct the movements of the army of the Potomac, in which, among other things, the army was commanded to seize upon and occupy a point on the railroad southwest of Manassas Junction. Details of this movement were to be left to the judgement of the general commanding. To this McClellan demurred, and in a long letter to the secretary of war detailed his objections and submitted a plan of his own. A council of war, to consist of twelve general officers, was finally called, and it was decided by a vote of eight to four that McClellan's plan should be adopted. Information of these debates having reached the Confederate generals, their forces withdrew from Manassas to the lower side of the Rappahannock, thereby rendering both plans useless. By this time two weeks had elapsed since the president's order directing a general advance of all the armies had been issued. After the enemy abandoned his line at Manassas, McClellan moved forward for a day or two, but soon after returned to his intrenched position at Alexandria, on the Potomac near Washington. On the 11th of March, 1862, Gen. McClellan was relieved from command of other departments of military activity and was placed in sole and immediate command of the army of the Potomac. A new base of operations was now established at Fortress Monroe at the entrance of Chesapeake Bay; but meanwhile a fight between the ironclad Merrimac and the

Federal Monitor had taken place near Fortress Monroe, and the ironclad had been beaten back to Norfolk, whence she did not afterward emerge. McClellan's immediate field of operations was on the peninsula formed by the York and James rivers. The enemy were behind a line of intrenchments that stretched across the peninsula, the key of the situation being at Yorktown on this line. Again there were unaccountable delays, and on the 3rd of April the president ordered the secretary of war to direct that the army of the Potomac should begin active operations; but McClellan demurred and informed the president by letter on the 5th of April that he was sure that the enemy in front of him and behind formidable works was in great force. He required more men. Lincoln was confident that McClellan exaggerated the strength of the force in front of him, and he besought Secretary Stanton to hurry forward everything that McClellan seemed to think

needful to insure the safety of an advance. The line held by the Confederate forces was about thirteen miles long. Much of the force behind that line was scattered in the defence of points in the rear. In answer to McClellan's call for more troops, the president yielded and sent him Gen. Franklin's division, which had been retained to defend the line between Richmond and Washington. On the 13th of April McClellan's army, according to official reports, had 130,378 men, of which 112,392 were effective. About this time McClellan called for Parrott guns, to the consternation of the president, who wrote him on the 1st of May: "Your call for Parrott guns from Washington alarms me, chiefly because it argues indefinite procrastination. Is anything to be done?" Nothing was done, and on the 25th he (Lincoln) telegraphed McClellan: "I think the time is near at hand when you must either attack Richmond or give up the job and come to the defence of Washington." Meanwhile, the Confederates, disconcerted by the accumulation of Federal troops, abandoned their line across the peninsula and retreated up to their second line of works. On the 21st of June McClellan wrote to the president asking permission to address him on the subject of "The present state of military affairs throughout the whole country." The president replied: "If it would not divert your time and attention from the army under your command, I should be glad to hear your views on the present state of military affairs throughout the whole country." The greater part of June, 1862, was spent by the army under McClellan, in fighting, advancing, retreating and in various manoeuvres. At one time a portion of the troops was within four miles of Richmond without meeting any considerable force of the enemy. On the 27th of June McClellan announced his intention to retreat to the James river, and in a letter to the secretary of war said: "If I save this army, I tell you plainly I owe you no thanks, nor to any one at Washington. You have done

your best to destroy this army." Lincoln was greatly disturbed by the temper of this dispatch. The army, harassed by the Confederate forces hanging on its rear, retreated to Malvern Hill, and the campaign of the peninsula was over. By this time it was generally understood that Gen. McClellan would be the presidential candidate at the next election of that portion of the democratic party which was dissatisfied with the conduct of the war and with the emancipation measures then under contemplation. In order to see for himself the condition of the army, the president visited the headquarters of Gen. McClellan at Harrison's Landing on the 7th of July. He examined the rosters of the troops and scrutinized the reports of the chiefs of divisions, and gave it as his judgement that the army should be recalled to Washington, and in this conclusion he was supported by the corps commanders; but to this McClellan was opposed. He required Burnside's army, then operating in North Carolina, and with this large reinforcement he thought he might achieve success. Lincoln found that McClellan had 160,000 men, and on his return to Washington he wrote to him remind him of this fact and calling attention to the additional fact that while he, Lincoln, was in the army with McClellan he found only 86,000 effective men on duty. In reply, McClellan said that 38,250 men were "absent by authority." Lincoln, feeling the necessity of a military adviser who should be near him in Washington and always readily accessible, called to the capital Gen. Henry W. Halleck, who on the 11th of July was given the rank and title of general-in-chief. About this time Gen. John Pope, whose successes in the valley of the Mississippi had given him fame, was called to the command of a new military organization of three army corps, commanded by Gens. Frémont, Banks and McDowell. These were known as the army of Virginia. On the 28th of June, 1862, was assembled at Altoona, Pa., a conference of the governors of loyal states, seventeen in number, to determine on the best means of supporting the president in carrying on the war. They issued an address, assuring the president of the readiness of the states to respond to calls for more troops and to support vigorous war measures. Thereupon the president issued a call for 300,000 men. Pope's army, 38,000 strong, was employed to defend Washington, against which point Lee was now advancing with a large force. It was expected that McClellan would make a bold attack on Richmond from his position on the James, Lee's attention being directed toward Pope. This was not done, and the army of the Potomac was ordered to the line of the Potomac river to support Pope; but McClellan, repeatedly ordered to make haste, delayed, and several weeks elapsed before he showed any indications of moving. Finally, on the 23rd of August, he sailed from Fortress Monroe, arriving at Alexandria on the Potomac on the 27th, nearly one month after receiving his orders. Meanwhile, Pope was being driven toward Washington, assailed in turn by the Confederate forces under Jackson, Longstreet and Lee. Pope was forced back upon Washington. Disaster and defeat, divided councils in the cabinet, virulent and heated debates in congress, agitated the country. Lincoln alone remained patient and courageous. The army of the Potomac was reorganized, and McClellan soon had under him not only that force, but the remnants of Pope's army of Virginia and the men brought from North Carolina by Gen. Burnside. To these were added other reinforcements from new levies, making the force under McClellan the largest that had been massed together in one army—more than 200,000 all told. On the 15th of September Harper's Ferry was surrendered to the Confederate forces. Lee, advancing into Maryland, brought on another battle, which was fought at Antietam Sept. 17th. The Confederates were defeated, and were obliged to retreat across the Potomac. McClellan failed to follow up his

victory, and Lincoln on the 6th of October, 1862, through Gen. Halleck, directed McClellan to "cross the Potomac and give battle to the enemy or drive him south." McClellan declined to obey. On the 10th of October Gen. J. E. B. Stuart crossed the Potomac, going as far north as Chambersburg, Pa., made the entire circuit of McClellan's army, and recrossed into Virginia. Finally, *on October 26, 1862, three weeks after the order to cross had been issued, the army began crossing the Potomac,* but it was too late. Gen. McClellan was relieved from command of the army on the 5th of November, and his military career was ended. He was succeeded by Gen. A. E. Burnside, a graduate of the U.S. Military Academy, who, until the breaking out of the war, had been engaged in civil pursuits. At the outset there was a disagreement between Burnside, Halleck and Lincoln as to the best line of attack upon the Confederate forces. The result of many consultations was that the route through Fredericksburg, on the Rappahannock, should be adopted. Owing to delays, Lee was able to seize and fortify the heights above the city of

Fredericksburg, and Burnside was speedily confronted by a concentrated army. An attack was made in the face of many difficulties *on the 13th of December 1862.* The assault failed with great disaster, and the year closed in gloom. In the West, Buell had been driven back in Kentucky, and the Confederate forces had re-entered that state and a provisional Confederate government had been organized at Frankfurt, the capital of the state. The cities of Louisville, Ky., and Cincinnati, O., were menaced, and it was found necessary to fortify them. At the end *of December* the combined Federal forces under Gens. Sherman and McClernand, *who was not present,* made a vigorous but unsuccessful assault upon the defences of Vicksburg. Lincoln was now besieged on the one hand with demands for the reinstatement of McClellan, and on the other with importunities for an armistice during which negotiations for a settlement might be carried on. He also was greatly disturbed by zealous friends who were eager for a change of generals. The press of the North was often bitter in its criticisms of the administration. In the army there were mutterings of discontent, and many of the elder officers openly expressed their belief that nothing but the reinstatement of McClellan could lead to victory. On the 26th of January, 1863, Gen. Joseph Hooker was placed in command of the army of the Potomac. The army was soon in good fighting condition, and the rosters, examined by the president during a visit to the army headquarters in April, 1863, showed 216,718 men on the rolls, of which 16,000 were on detached service; 136,720 were on active duty, 1,771 absent without authority, 26,000 sick, and the actual effective force was 146,000, which number could be increased at any time to 169,000 by calling in the men from outlying stations. Early in May began Hooker's offensive movement against the Confederate forces lying south of the Rappahannock. The battle of Chancellorsville terminated that campaign, and on May 6th the president received

a dispatch from Gen. Hooker's chief of staff, announcing that the army of the Potomac had recrossed the Rappahannock and was camped on its old ground. This disaster deeply agitated the country, and the president immediately visited headquarters, accompanied by Gen. Halleck. Soon after this, a law authorizing the conscription of citizens for fighting was enacted, and under the provision of the constitution permitting it, the president suspended the privileges of the writ of habeas corpus, by which the citizen deprived of his liberty could appeal to the courts for an examination in his case. Under the same authority the president proclaimed martial law. These acts, severely criticized at the time, were justified by the "war powers" of the president of the United States under the constitution. Another important act was the authorizing of the enlistment of negro troops. The arming of the ex-slaves was the cause of much popular discontent both North and South. From first to last, the number of negro troops enlisted in the war was 178,975. Financial measures also occupied the attention of congress, and the secretary of the treasury was authorized to borrow money to carry on the war. The total amount which he was given leave to raise on the obligations of the government of the United States was $900,000,000. Bonds were issued to bear fixed rates of interest, and, to meet the pressing necessities of the times, he was authorized to issue $100,000,000 in treasury notes. *In the war as a whole the U.S. government sold $2.2 billion of interest-bearing bonds and issued $450 million in non-interest bearing treasury notes—the famous "greenbacks."* The finances of the country were in a disordered condition. Gold and silver had disappeared from circulation, and the small change needed in everyday transactions of the people was now in small paper notes. In the western states popular discontent had resulted in the formation of secret societies for the propagation of seditious doctrines and the discouragement of the war. In July, 1863, fell Vicksburg, thus opening the Mississippi river, the operations being conducted under the command of Gen. Grant. In the early days of that month was fought the battle of Gettysburg, in which the troops under Gen. Lee, who had invaded the state of Pennsylvania, were repulsed with great slaughter. The Federal troops were commanded by Gen. Meade. The effective force under Meade in his three days' battle at Gettysburg was from 82,000 to 84,000 men, with 300 pieces of artillery. Lee's effective force was 80,000 men, with 250 guns. The total of killed, wounded and missing in this fight was about 46,000 men, each side having suffered equally. Twenty generals were lost by the Federal army, six being killed. The Confederates lost seventeen generals, three being killed, thirteen wounded and one taken prisoner. On July 4, 1863, Lincoln issued an announcement to the people of the United States, giving the result of the battle of Gettysburg, and concluding with these words: "The President especially desires that on this day He whose will, not ours, should ever more be done, be everywhere remembered and reverenced with profoundest gratitude." There was great joy throughout the loyal states. The president was serenaded at the White House, and appearing to the multitude said, among

other things: "I do most sincerely thank God for the occasion of this call." On July 15th the president issued his proclamation for a day of national thanksgiving in which he invited all the people to assemble on Aug. 6th, to "render the homage due to the Divine Majesty for the wonderful things He has done in the nation's behalf, and invoke the influences of His holy spirit to subdue the anger which has produced and so long sustained a needless and cruel rebellion," etc. On Oct. 3rd he instituted a permanent national festival, setting apart the last Thursday in November to be observed as a day of national thanksgiving to God for all His mercies. On Nov. 19, 1863, the battlefield of Gettysburg was solemnly dedicated as a burying-place for the remains of those who had given their lives on that now historic ground. The principal oration was delivered by Edward Everett, of Massachusetts, but the brief address of the president on that occasion was the most momentous utterance, and has now passed into the literature of the world as one of its great masterpieces. The year closed auspiciously, Grant being in command of a large force stationed in the military division of the Mississippi, with headquarters at Louisville, Ky. Gen. George H. Thomas was in command of the departments of the Ohio and Cumberland. Hooker, Sheridan and Sherman were subordinate

Monument Springfield.

474

commanders under Grant. The battles of Mission Ridge, Lookout Mountain and Chattanooga were Federal successes, and the Confederates were expelled from Tennessee. Burnside, besieged in Knoxville, was relieved by Sherman, and the Confederate army under Longstreet was driven back into Virginia. The session of congress during the winter of 1863–64 was largely occupied by political measures, a presidential campaign now coming on. Some of the republican leaders were opposed to Lincoln's re-nomination, considering that he was not sufficiently radical in his measures. As a rule these persons favored the nomination of Mr. Chase, the secretary of the treasury, and others expressed a preference for Gen. Frémont, whose career in Missouri had excited their sympathies. Lincoln remained silent regarding his political desires. The only expression of his opinion in reference to the political situation was found in his famous saying: "I don't believe it is wise to swap horses while crossing a stream." One of the most important military events of that winter was the appointment of Gen. Grant to the post of lieutenant-general of the army, that rank having been created by act of congress with the understanding that it was to be conferred upon him. On Feb. 22, 1864, the act was approved, and Gen. Grant was nominated to the post. He was confirmed March 3rd. Gen. Sherman was assigned to the command of the military division of the Mississippi, succeeding Grant, who, in an order dated March 17, 1864, took command of all the armies of the United States, with headquarters in the field. From this time all of the armies in the West and in the East acted in concert, and the enemy was pressed on all sides. Lincoln sent to Grant in the field these words: "You are vigilant and self-reliant. I wish not to obtrude any restraints or constraints upon you. If there be anything in my power to give, do not fail to let me know, and now, with a brave army and a just cause, may God sustain you." Gen. Grant made his headquarters with the army of the Potomac, on the banks of the Rapidan, and the campaign against the Confederate capital of Richmond opened in May, Meade in command of the army of the Potomac, reinforced by the ninth corps under Burnside. The army moved at midnight on the 3rd of the month. On the 5th and 6th were fought the bloody battles of the Wilderness. On the 11th Grant telegraphed to Lincoln: "Our losses have been heavy, as well as those of the enemy, and I propose to fight it out on this line if it takes all summer." *On Sept. 2, 1864,* Atlanta fell into the hands of Sherman, and Hood, hoping to drive Sherman to the northward, moved against the Tennessee country once more, passing to the right of Atlanta. The Federal forces under Thomas and Schofield fell upon Hood, who was ignominiously put to flight, and after a two days' fight his army was virtually destroyed. Gen. B. F. Butler took possession of City Point, on the James river, where Grant established a base of supplies. Gen. Hunter was sent to clear the Valley of the Shenandoah, but was compelled to retire, and the Confederate forces under Early pressed on toward Washington from the valley, entered Maryland and menaced the national capital. A great panic prevailed in that city for several days, but two army corps, dispatched by Gen. Grant, saved the capital, and the invading force withdrew. Later in the year Gen. Sheridan cleared the Shenandoah Valley, and by the end of September that region was free once more from Confederate forces. The republican national convention was held in Baltimore, June 8, 1864. Lincoln was re-nominated for the presidency, and Andrew Johnson was nominated for vice-president. In August of that year the democratic national convention assembled in Chicago, and Gen. McClellan was nominated for the presidency, and George H. Pendleton, of Ohio, for the vice-presidency. Meanwhile the radical republicans held a convention at Cleveland, O., and nominated Gen. Frémont for the presidency, and John Cochrane, of New York, for vice-president. In the course of time these latter nominations practically disappeared beneath the surface of American politics, and were heard of no more. Rumors of negotiations on the part of the Confederates looking toward a return of peace now grew more frequent. Clement C. Clay of Alabama, and Jacob Thompson of Mississippi, appeared on the Canadian border and put themselves in communication with Horace Greeley, who wrote to Lincoln July 7, 1864, asking for a safe conduct for these emissaries in order that they might go to Washington and discuss terms of peace. To this Lincoln replied in writing: "If you can find any person anywhere professing to have authority from Jefferson Davis, in writing, embracing the restoration of the Union, and the abandonment of slavery, whatever else it embraces, say to him he may come to me with you." Some correspondence thereupon ensued, and Mr. Greeley went to Niagara Falls to hold an interview with the Confederate emissaries. It soon became apparent that these agents had no authority to treat for peace on the part of the Richmond government, and the incident passed away. The losses of war required fresh levies of troops, and a call was now issued for 500,000 men. If the required number should not appear by Sept. 5, 1864, then a draft must be ordered. The presidential election came on in November, 1864, resulting in an overwhelming majority for Lincoln. Every state that voted that year declared for Lincoln and his policy, excepting the states of Delaware, Kentucky and New Jersey. The total number of votes cast in all the states was 4,015,902, of which Lincoln had a clear majority of 411,428. Lincoln had 212 of the 233 electoral votes, and McClellan had twenty-one electoral votes. There was renewed talk about peace and compromise during the winter of 1864–65. Francis P. Blair, Sr., a private citizen, was furnished with a safe conduct signed by the president, and went to Richmond, saw Jefferson Davis, and returned to Washington with a letter addressed to him by the president of the Confederacy, the contents of which he was authorized to communicate to Lincoln. In that document Davis expressed his willingness "to enter into conference with a view to secure peace in the two countries." Lincoln replied to Mr. Blair in a note in which he stated that he (Lincoln) was willing to treat on terms with a view to securing peace to the people of "our common country." This correspondence, although it did not result in any official conference, did bring to Hampton Roads, Va., Alexander H. Stephens, R. M. T. Hunter and John A. Campbell, who were received on board a steamer anchored in the roadstead of Fortress Monroe, by President Lincoln and Secretary Seward. The purpose of the Confederate agents was to secure an armistice, but Lincoln turned a deaf ear to all suggestions of this sort, and while the matter was yet pending wrote to Gen. Grant, saying: "Let nothing that is transpiring change, hinder or delay your military movements or plans." The president and secretary returned to Washington, and it was seen that the Hampton Roads conference resulted in nothing but defeat of the Confederate scheme to procure a cessation of hostilities. The second inauguration of Lincoln took place March 4, 1864. In his inaugural address the president briefly reviewed the political and military situation of the country, and closed with these memorable words: "With malice toward none, with charity for all, with firmness in the right as God gives us to see right, let us finish the work we are in, to bind up the nation's wounds, to care for him who shall have borne the battle, and for his widow and orphans, and to do all which may achieve and cherish a just and lasting peace among ourselves and with all nations." The spring of 1865 opened with bright prospects for a speedy ending of the rebellion. Gen. Sherman's march to the Atlantic sea-coast from Atlanta had rent the Confederacy in twain. His subsequent movements in the Carolinas compelled the abandonment of Charleston. The capture of Fort Fisher, N.C., by Gen. Terry, closed the last Atlantic port against possible supplies from abroad. The scattered remnants of the Confederate army now rallied around Gen. Lee for the defence of Richmond, and on March 27th a conference between Lincoln, Grant and Sherman was held on board a steamer lying on the James river, near Grant's headquarters. At that conference final and decisive measures of the campaign were decided upon. Closely followed by Grant, Sheridan now drew a line completely around the army of Virginia, under Gen. Lee. The Confederate lines were everywhere drawn in, their forces operating to the north of the James being now joined with the main army. On Sunday morning, Apr. 2nd, the bells of Richmond sounded the knell of the rebellion, and Jefferson Davis, seeing that all was lost, fled southward, but was subsequently captured and sent a prisoner to Fortress Monroe. On Monday morning, Apr. 3rd, the flag of the Union was hoisted over the building in Richmond which had been occupied by the Confederate congress. Lincoln was at City Point waiting for the final result of these movements. *He met with Grant in Petersburg April 3 when Grant announced that one more battle might be fought.* He entered the fallen capital of the Confederacy soon after its downfall. He was

unattended, save by a crew from a boat near at hand, and he led his little boy by the hand. The president returned to Washington, and on Apr. 7, 1865, Grant opened with Gen. Lee the correspondence which resulted in the surrender of the army of northern Virginia, Apr. 9th, in the village of Appomattox Court-House, Va. Great rejoicings took place all over the North, and on the night of Apr. 10th the city of Washington and many other cities throughout the country were illuminated. On Apr. 11th the city was again illuminated by the government, and a great official celebration took place. The war was over. At noon, Apr. 14, 1865, the president's cabinet held a meeting, at which Gen. Grant was present. That evening the president, Mrs. Lincoln, Clara Harris (a daughter of Senator Ira Harris of New York), and Maj. Rathbone of the U.S. army, occupied a box near the stage in Ford's theatre, Washington. John Wilkes Booth, an actor, who had conspired with certain other persons to take the president's life on the first convenient occasion, approached the box from the rear, and at half-past ten o'clock in the evening, while all persons were absorbed in the business of the play, crept up in the rear of the president, and, holding a pistol within a few inches of the base of the brain, fired. The ball entered the brain and Lincoln fell forward, insensible. Booth escaped from the theatre in the

confusion which followed. The president was carried to a house on the opposite side of the street, where he lingered between life and death through the hours of the night. At twenty-two minutes past seven o'clock on the morning of Apr. 15, 1865, Lincoln died. Andrew Johnson, the vice-president, now succeeded to the presidency by virtue of his office, and was sworn in during the forenoon. On Wednesday, Apr. 19th, the funeral of the president took place in the White House, in the midst of a most distinguished assemblage. His body was borne to the capitol, where it lay in state in the rotunda for one day, guarded by a company of high officers of the army and navy, and a detachment of soldiers. The funeral train left Washington for Springfield, Ill., on Apr. 21st, and traveled nearly the same route that had been passed over by the train that bore the president-elect from

St. Gaudens' Statue. Chicago.

Springfield to Washington five years before. This funeral cortège was unique and wonderful. Nearly 2,000 miles were traversed. The people lined the entire distance, almost without an interval, standing with uncovered heads, mute with grief, often in rain-storms, as the sombre procession swept by. Watch-fires blazed along the route in the darkness of the night, and by day every device that could lend picturesqueness to the scene and express the woe of the people was employed. Lincoln's body was finally laid to rest in Oak Ridge Cemetery, near Springfield, Ill., where a noble monument was subsequently erected. Washington excepted, no American bibliography equals Lincoln's; thousands of volumes have been written, while the magazine and newspaper biographies number hundreds of thousands. The most exhaustive history, and one which, in a measure, supersedes all others, is the "Life" prepared by his private secretaries, John G. Nicolay and John Hay, together with a complete edition of his writings and speeches, by the same authors.

LINCOLN, MARY TODD, wife of Abraham Lincoln, was born in Lexington, Ky., Dec. 12, 1818. Her father, Robert S. Todd, belonged to a family of pioneers foremost in the development of the commonwealth of Kentucky. Her great-uncle, John Todd, took part in the capture of Kaskaskia and Vincennes, under Gen. George R. Clark in 1778, and subsequently organized the civil government of Illinois. He was killed at the battle of Blue Licks, in which his brother, Levi, Mary's grandfather, was a young lieutenant and one of the few survivors. Mary Todd was carefully educated, and passed her early life in comparative luxury at the home of an aunt. At the age of twenty-one, while on a visit to a married sister in Springfield, she met Mr. Lincoln, a rising lawyer, and after a short engagement they were married on Nov. 4, 1842. Miss Todd had curiously predicted in her girlhood that she should be the wife of a

Mary Lincoln

president, and after her marriage her ambition kept pace with her husband's progress in public life. In 1860 she awaited with feverish anxiety the result of the republican convention at Chicago, keeping in mind her girlish prophecy. Her husband, not unmindful of her ambition, upon receiving the telegram announcing his nomination, remarked: "There is a little woman who has some interest in the matter," and walked home to tell her of it. On the 9th of March Mrs. Lincoln gave her first public reception, assisted by her sisters and nieces. Our portrait represents her as she appeared at that period. She made a pleasant impression, and it was perhaps the proudest moment of her existence. But it was also the inauguration of her deepest afflictions. She presided at the most gloomy period in the history of the capital. Her husband was bowed down by national cares; suspense and uncertainty was in every heart; her family was devoted to the cause of the South, while her hopes, with those of her husband and children, were with the North. Unable by temperament and education to cope with these critical issues, Mrs. Lincoln soon found herself the target of malice, detraction and falsehood. She gave weekly receptions at a time when the state of the country made the gaiety that she preferred out of keeping with the position she occupied, and the death of the second son, Willie, shed a gloom over the private life of both parents. But, during the whole of her occupancy of the White House, she was unremitting in her care of the sick soldiers in the hospitals of Washington. The summer of 1864 was spent by Mrs. Lincoln at the seaside. After the re-election of the president in the fall, the receptions of the season were renewed with a promise of unusual gaiety, that of New Year's day opening with exceptional brilliancy. After the inauguration, Mrs. Lincoln felt that brighter days were in store, and when the surrender of Gen. Lee on the 9th of April was announced, she shared in the happy excitement that filled the White House and the city. The fatal night of the 14th of April that ended the president's life also blighted her own. From its effects she never recovered. After a severe illness, she returned with her two boys to Springfield, where she was further afflicted by the death of Thomas, the youngest lad. In 1868, with a mind somewhat unbalanced and broken health, she sought rest in travel. Congress had already paid her the amount of the president's salary for one year, and in 1870 voted her an annual pension of $3,000, afterward increased to $5,000. Still later an additional gift of $15,000 was presented to her by congress to insure comfort in her old age. She possessed, besides, a small estate left by her husband. In 1880 she returned from wanderings in various countries, her mind still impaired, and spent her last days with her son Robert in Chicago. She died stricken with paralysis, July 16, 1882, and was laid to rest by the side of her husband and children in Springfield.

LIVERMORE, MARY ASHTON RICE, reformer, was born in Boston, Mass., *Dec. 19, 1820.* She was educated at the Hancock school, Boston, and the Charlestown female seminary, where she remained for three years after graduation as instructor in Latin, Italian, and French. Having received the necessary scholastic preparation, she with a few other young women applied for admission to Harvard, but received an unqualified refusal from President Quincy.

Mary A. Livermore

After three years spent in Virginia as a governess, she returned to the North a confirmed anti-slavery woman. She was at the head of the high school at Duxbury, Mass., until her marriage to the Rev. D. P. Livermore *in 1845. She moved to Chicago in 1857*, where Mr. Livermore was editor and proprietor of the Universalist publication, "The New Covenant." Mrs. Livermore became associate editor, and divided her time and energies for many years between her family, her editorial work, and pulpit duties. She is descended from a long line of Welsh preachers, and possesses by right of inheritance marked abilities as a public speaker, being humorous and pathetic by turns. It is, however, by her work in connection with the Sanitary commission that she is best known. With Mrs. Hoyt she was appointed, by the commission, agent of the Chicago branch association, and in 1862 she traveled widely through the northwestern states, organizing Soldiers' aid societies. She visited constantly the camps and hospitals of the Southwest, and secured proper food for the soldiers and the sick, and overcame, largely by her personal efforts and service, the opposition made to the employment of woman

nurses at the front. She was ordered to make a tour of the military posts and hospitals on the Mississippi river, which resulted in an organized attack on the scurvy that threatened to decimate the ranks of the army. At her solicitation immense quantities of fresh vegetables were sent to the post, the prompt distribution of which averted the danger. When money and supplies became more and more difficult to obtain, she organized the great Northwestern fair at Chicago in 1863, the first of the sanitary fairs held throughout the country. The Chicago fair netted nearly $100,000 to the Sanitary commission. She afterward organized ten other sanitary fairs, which furnished large sums of money for the army. When the war closed she began a most successful career as a lecturer, which brought her in contact with the best literary minds of the country, and made for her many friends. She labored incessantly for the advancement of women and their civil rights, and was a tireless worker in the cause of temperance. Her home was at Melrose, Mass. Mrs. Livermore has published several books. *She died May 23, 1905.*

LOGAN, JOHN ALEXANDER, soldier and senator, was born in Jackson county, Ill., Feb. 9, 1826, son of John and Elizabeth (Jenkins) Logan. His father came from the North of Ireland, settling first in Pennsylvania, then in Tennessee and finally in Jackson county, Ill. He received his preparatory education under a private tutor and at Shiloh (Ill.) college. During the war with Mexico he served as a lieutenant and for some time was quartermaster of the 1st Ill. volunteers. After the war he began to study law under his uncle, Alexander M. Jenkins, and in 1849 was elected clerk of Jackson county but soon resigned that office to continue his law studies at the University of Louisville, where he was graduated in 1851. He was admitted to the bar in 1852, was prosecuting attorney of the third judicial district of Illinois during 1853–57, and served in the state legislature in 1852, 1853,

1856, and 1857. In 1856 he was Democratic presidential elector from his district. In 1858 he was elected to congress from the 9th Illinois congressional district as an anti-Lecompton Democrat. He was re-elected to congress in 1860 and served until Apr. 2, 1862, when he resigned. In the presidential election of that year he supported Stephen A. Douglas, serving as a delegate to the Charleston convention. In the spring of 1861 as a member of congress, he took part in the Battle of Bull Run, fighting in the ranks. A month later he returned to his home at Murphysboro, Ill., and recruited a regiment of which he became colonel. In less than two months he led his regiment into battle at Belmont, where he distinguished himself by his gallantry and had a horse shot under him. He was with Grant's army through the campaigns in Kentucky, Tennessee, and Mississippi and led his regiment in the attack on Ft. Henry. At Ft. Donelson he received a wound that incapacitated him temporarily for active service. He was promoted to brigadier general after Ft. Donelson and to major general after Vicksburg. In the fighting around Atlanta he commanded the 15th corps of the Army of the Tennessee and after the death of McPherson on July 22, 1864, he took command of that army. He was relieved of this command because, he believed, of Sherman's prejudice against volunteer soldiers. He returned to Illinois in 1864 to take part in the presidential campaign in Lincoln's interest and after the election he rejoined his troops at Savannah. In May 1865 he was restored to the command of the Army of the Tennessee. After the declaration of peace, declining the offer of a permanent commission in the army, he resigned. For his service at Vicksburg Logan received a medal of honor from congress and after the evacuation of Atlanta he was presented with a medal by the Army of the Tennessee. President Jackson appointed him minister to Mexico but he declined the office. In 1866 he was elected to congress as representative-at-large from Illinois, and he was re-elected in 1868 and 1870. While in the house he served on various committees and was one of the managers of the impeachment trial of President Johnson. In 1871 he was chosen U.S. senator from Illinois. He lost this seat in 1877 but was again elected in 1879 and 1885. Both in the house and senate Logan worked vigorously for the relief of war veterans. In the Republican national convention of 1884 he received sixty-three-and-one-half votes for the presidency and, after the choice of James G. Blaine, he became the nominee for vice-president and fought an energetic but unsuccessful campaign. He was elected the second commander-in-chief of the Grand Army of the Republic in 1868, serving three terms, and it was at his order in 1868 that May 30th was designated a Decoration day. Logan was the author of "The Great Conspiracy: Its Origin and History" (1886), and "The Volunteer Soldier of America, With Memoir of the Author and Military Reminiscences from General Logan's Private Journal" (1887). James G. Blaine said of him: "General Logan was a man of immense force in a legislative body. His will was unbending; his courage, both moral and physical, was of the highest order. I never knew a more fearless man. He did not quail before public opinion when he had once made up his mind, any more than he did before the guns of the enemy when he headed a charge of his enthusiastic troops. In debate he was aggressive and effective. While there have been more illustrious military leaders, in legislative halls there has, I think, been no man in this country who has combined the two careers in so eminent a degree as General Logan." He was described as "clearly the most eminent and distinguished of the volunteer soldiers" and Sherman called him "perfect in combat." He was married at Shawneetown, Ill., Nov. 27, 1855, to Mary Simmerson, daughter of John M. Cunningham, register of the U.S. land office, and they had three children: John (died in infancy); Mary Elizabeth, wife of William F. Tucker, and John Alexander Logan. He died in Washington, D.C., Dec. 26, 1886.

LONGSTREET, JAMES, soldier, was born in Edgefield district, S.C., Jan. 8, 1821. His family removed to Alabama in 1831, and he was appointed from that state to the West Point military academy, where he was graduated in 1842, and assigned to the 4th infantry. He was at Jefferson Barracks, Mo., in 1842–44, on frontier duty at Natchitoches, La., in 1844–45, in Texas, 1845–46, and in Mexico at the battles of Palo Alto, Resaca de la Palma, Monterey, Vera Cruz, Cerro Gordo, San Antonio, Churubusco, and Molino del Rey. For gallant conduct in the two latter engagements he was brevetted captain and major, and had already been made first lieutenant, Feb. 23, 1847; at the storming of Chapultepec, Sept. 8, 1847, he was severely wounded. He was chief commissary of the department of Texas, 1849–51, was commissioned captain in December, 1852, and major and paymaster in July, 1858. In 1861 he resigned to join the Confederate army, of which he was immediately appointed brigadier-general, and won distinction in the first battle of Bull

Run, where he prevented a large force of Federal troops from supporting McDowell's flank attack. On May 5, 1862, he made a brave stand at Williamsburg, where he was attacked by Heintzelman, Hooker, and Kearny, and held his ground sturdily until Hancock arrived to re-enforce his opponents, when he was driven back. At the second battle of Bull Run he commanded the 1st corps of the army of northern

Virginia, which came so promptly to the relief of Jackson when he was hard pressed by Pope's army, and by a determined flank charge decided the fortunes of the day. He led the right wing of the army of northern Virginia at Gettysburg, and tried to dissuade Lee from ordering the disastrous charge on the third day. When Lee retreated to Virginia Gen. Longstreet, with five brigades, was transferred to the army of Tennessee under Bragg, and at Chickamauga held the left wing of the Confederate forces. He rejoined Lee early in 1864, and was so prominent in the battle of the Wilderness that he was wounded by the fire of his own troops. He was in the surrender at Appomattox, Apr. 9, 1865. Throughout the army he was familiarly known as "Old Pete," and was considered the hardest fighter in the Confederate service. He also had the unbounded confidence of his troops, who were devoted to him, and the whole army felt thrilled with renewed ardor in the presence of the foe, when it became known down the line that "Old Pete was up," Gen. Longstreet took up his residence in New Orleans after the war, and established the commercial house of Longstreet, Owens & Co. He was appointed surveyor of the port of New Orleans by President Grant, and was afterward supervisor of internal revenue in Louisiana, and postmaster at New Orleans; in 1880 he was sent as U.S. minister to Turkey by President Hayes, and under Garfield he was U.S. marshal for the district of Georgia. *He died Jan. 2, 1904.*

LORING, WILLIAM WING, soldier, was born in Wilmington, N.C., Dec. 4, 1818. In early childhood he became a resident of Florida, and when only fourteen years of age was in the ranks of the volunteers, fighting Indians in the swamps of that state. He was engaged in an umber of battles, including those of Wahoo swamp, Withahoochee, and Alachua. On June 16, 1837, he was promoted to second lieutenant. He then went to school at Alexandria, Va., and

Georgetown, D.C., and afterward studied law, being admitted in 1842 to practice at the bar. He returned to Florida, and was elected a member of the state assembly, where he served three years. *In 1846* he was appointed senior captain of a regiment of mounted riflemen, and in the following year was promoted to major,

and placed in command. He served under Gen. Scott in all the battles from Vera Cruz to the City of Mexico, and at the close of the conflict was brevetted lieutenant-colonel and colonel. While leading his regiment into the City of Mexico he lost his left arm. A sword was presented to him after the Mexican war by the citizens of Appalochicola, Fla., having engraved upon it a complimentary inscription. In 1849, on the outbreak of the gold fever in California, Col. Loring was ordered to cross the continent with his regiment, and take command of the department of Oregon, which position he held until 1851. On this occasion he marched a distance of 2,500 miles, with a train of 600 mule teams, which was considered the greatest military feat of the kind on record. Col. Loring was in command on the frontier for five years,

during which time he fought several engagements with the Indians. In 1858 he marched his regiment to the Utah territory, and was engaged in what was known as the "Mormon war." This closed Col. Loring's active service under the flat of his own country. He obtained leave to visit Europe, and spent one year in studying the armies of the foreign powers. On his return he was placed in command of the department of New Mexico, but resigned the same year to take a commission in the Confederate army. His great abilities as a soldier were at once recognized by the Southern government, and he was commissioned major-general. He led a division until the end of the civil war, and frequently commanded a corps. Gen. Loring served at Fort Pemberton during the investment of Vicksburg. In 1869 Gen. Loring, with other officers who had served in the Confederate army, entered the service of the Khedive of Egypt, and was appointed inspector-general. In 1870 he was made commandant of Alexandria, and given charge of the coast defences of Egypt. In 1875 and 1876, during the Abyssinian war, Gen. Loring was in command of the Egyptian army. He was raised to the dignity of pacha for his services, and decorated with Egyptian orders. In 1879 the American officers in the service of the Khedive were mustered out, and returned to the United States. Gen. Loring resided in Florida for a time, and then settled in New York city, where he wrote his book, "A Confederate Soldier in Egypt," which was published in 1883. He also wrote for magazines and for the press. At one

time Gen. Loring was a candidate for a seat in the U.S. senate from the state of Florida, in opposition to Senator Jones, who was an absentee. Gen. Loring died in New York city, Dec. 30, 1886.

LOVEJOY, OWEN, congressman, was born at Albion, Me., Jan. 6, 1811, was graduated from Bowdoin college, and entered the ministry but resigned his pastorate to take a seat in the Illinois legislature. He was a warm friend of Garrison, an earnest abolitionist, and attended the national convention at Buffalo *in 1848*. He was a representative in congress from Illinois in 1861, and on Jan. 23d of that year, in a brilliant speech, made a vigorous onslaught

against slavery. He was a friend of Abraham Lincoln, and defended him in a letter to Garrison, only a few weeks before he (Lovejoy) died. He wrote a memoir of his brother, the Rev. Elijah P. Lovejoy. Mr. Lovejoy died in Brooklyn, N.Y., March 25, 1864.

LOVELL, MANSFIELD, soldier, was born in Washington, D.C., Oct. 20, 1822, the son of

Dr. Joseph Lovell, who was surgeon-general of the U.S. army in 1818. His great-grandfather was a leading Boston patriot in the early days of the revolutionary war, a member of the Continental congress, and one of the signers of the old articles of confederation. He was also one of the original members of the Massachusetts society of the Cincinnati, to which membership Gen. Mansfield Lovell succeeded. In 1838, having received an ordinary school education, young Lovell was duly appointed cadet in the U.S. military academy at West Point, from which he was graduated in 1842, ninth in a class of fifty-six, among whom were Gens. Newton, Gustavus W. Smith, William S. Rosecrans, James Longstreet, Abner Doubleday, and others who subsequently attained to high rank and distinction in the military service on both sides. In 1842, as second lieutenant, young Lovell went on duty with the 4th regiment of the U.S. artillery, which regiment in 1845 joined the army of observation under Gen. Zachary Taylor, at Corpus Christi, Tex. Lieut. Lovell went through Taylor's campaign in Mexico in 1846, and was wounded at the battle of Monterey. He was afterward appointed aide-de-camp to Gen.

John A. Quitman and accompanied the command to Vera Cruz, and remained with it until the capture of the City of Mexico in September 1847. Lieut. Lovell was wounded at the Belen gate of the city, and was made brevet captain. After the war he took command of his own company, light battery G, 4th artillery, a position which he held for more than two years. He married Emily M., daughter of Col. Joseph Plympton, U.S. army, and in 1854 resigned his military commission, and settled in New York, where he engaged in commercial business. In 1858 he was made deputy street commissioner of the city, and resigned in 1861. He was a member of the Old City guard, which was composed of one hundred gentlemen of means and position. He obtained permission to use the guns at Fort Hamilton, and within two years made this company skillful heavy artillerists, each of them competent to teach others. After resigning his position in the street department, Lovell went South, where his three brothers resided, and was appointed major-general of the Confederate army, and assigned to command at New Orleans. In 1862, the Federal fleets having passed the forts, and being abreast of the city, the place was evacuated, Lovell moving his troops to Vicksburg. Here he was superseded by Gen. Van Dorn, was second in command in the

battle of Corinth, and commanded the rear guard in the retreat from that place. Lovell was soon afterward relieved from duty in the field, and immediately applied for a court of inquiry, which was after a long delay granted him. He was fairly vindicated by this court, but it was evident that there was a strong feeling, on the part of President Davis and other authorities in Richmond, that he had been in a great measure the cause of the capture of New Orleans. The charge was disproved by the publication of his correspondence with the war department in reference to the condition of that post while under his command; but Gen. Lovell was summarily relieved from command in the field, and was not again assigned to active duty. At the end of the war, he came to New York, and at first made arrangements for rice planting on the Savannah river, but the disastrous inundation of 1869 destroyed his prospects in that direction, and he returned to New York city, where he continued to reside, engaged as a civil engineer and surveyor until his death, June 1, 1884.

LOWRY, REIGART B., naval officer, was born in South America, July 14, 1826. He was appointed from Pennsylvania as midshipman Jan. 21, 1840; was promoted passed midshipman in 1846, and was attached to the home squadron during the Mexican war. He was present at several engagements, and was slightly wounded at Tuspan. He was promoted master in 1855, and commissioned lieutenant on Sept. 14th of that year, and was stationed on the steam frigate Powhatan. He was on the Pawnee in 1861 in the first firing on Fort Sumter, and commanded the steamer Freeborn in an engagement at Matthias point on the Potomac river, and commanded the steamer Underwriter in Albemarle sound. He was executive officer of the steam sloop Brooklyn in the battles with the forts below New Orleans, and his commanding officer, Capt. Thomas T. Craven, spoke of him as follows: "I have to congratulate myself on being so ably assisted by my executive officer, Lieut. R. B. Lowry. He was everywhere, inspiring both officers and crew with his own zeal and gallantry." He was engaged in the first attack upon Vicksburg, and commanded the steamer Scioto during the engagement at Donaldsonville between that vessel and a Confederate force of 900 men, Oct. 5, 1862. He was commissioned lieutenant-commander July 16, 1862; commanded the apprentice ship Sabine in 1864–68. He was commissioned commander July 25, 1866, and captain Nov. 2, 1871. He commanded the steam sloop Canandaigua on the north Atlantic station; was at the naval station, New London, Conn., 1875–77, and was commissioned commodore in 1880. He died March 25, 1880.

LYON, NATHANIEL, soldier, was born at Ashford, Conn., July 14, 1818. His father, Amasa, was a farmer, but the son early formed the plan of gaining admission to the U.S. military academy at West Point, N.Y., and bent his energies in that direction, poring diligently over books, and giving himself especially to the study of mathematics. His mother, Kezia (Knowlton), had much to do with determining his career, by rehearsing before the boy the story of the privations and achievements of the men of the American revolution. He was a student at the academy at Brooklyn, Conn., and passed thence to West Point in 1837, his appointment being secured by Orrin Holt, member of congress from the third district of Connecticut. He was eleventh in a class which numbered fifty-two at graduation, June 30, 1841, and was appointed second lieutenant in the 2d regiment U.S. infantry the next day. In November of that year he joined his regiment in Florida, where it was engaged in the war against the Seminole Indians. He distinguished himself in this service, which continued until the 27th of May, 1842. From that time until the summer of 1846 he was stationed at Sackett's Harbor, N.Y. After the Mexican war

opened *May, 1846,* the 2d regiment was ordered to the seat of hostilities, and left Comargo, Mexico, for the interior, Dec. 8, 1846. Thence Gen. Twigg's division, to which Lyon's regiment belonged, was ordered to take part in the attack upon Vera Cruz. Feb. 26, 1847, it reached the rendezvous of the U.S. troops at Lobos Island, 125 miles north of that stronghold. On the 9th of March it landed, with other U.S. troops, in front of the city. In the operations that followed, Lyon's troop had its appropriate part, and after the surrender (March 27th) the division to which it belonged left Vera Cruz on the march to the City of Mexico. Feb. 16, 1847, he was promoted first lieutenant. His regiment was sharply engaged at Cerro Gordo (April 17th) and the army rested at Jalapa for a month. A similar delay took place at Puebla, until Aug. 8th, when renewed advance toward the capital began. For gallant and meritorious conduct at the battles of Contreras and Churubusco, on the way, Lyon was made brevet captain Aug. 20, 1847, and captain in full by regular promotion June 11, 1851. When the Americans entered the City of Mexico (Sept. 14th), he was wounded in the leg

by a musket-ball. At the close of the war his regiment was stationed for a short time at Jefferson Barracks, St. Louis, Mo., and thence transferred to California, reaching Monterey Apr. 6, 1849. Excitement, consequent upon the discovery of gold, was at its height, and military service was called for to protect a frontier, hundreds of miles in extent, against the incursions of Indians. Apr. 16th Capt. Lyon's company sailed for San Diego, which place it was to garrison. His service in California continued for several years. In the second year after his arrival out (1850) he conducted a brilliant campaign against Indians in the neighborhood of Clear lake, and among the fastnesses of northern California. In the autumn of 1851 he took command of Fort Miller, in the valley of the San Joaquin, at the base of the Sierra Nevada mountains. In the spring and summer of 1852 he was in the East, having obtained leave of absence on account of the fatal illness of his mother, but returned to California and to his regiment in the fall, and was employed during the winter in laborious and fatiguing service. In February and March, 1853, he was at Washington D.C., his regiment having been ordered to the East. During the following summer he was posted at Fort Riley in Kansas, and his observation of events in that state, with the congressional debates in favor of, and in opposition to, the extension of slavery, to which he had listened during the previous winter, led him to espouse the cause of the Freestate party with earnestness. His biographer says that for the next few years the question of liberty or slavery engrossed his thoughts and offered a fruitful theme for his pen. In the summer of 1855 he served in an expedition under Gen. Harney against the Sioux Indians. In 1856 he was stationed at Fort Lookout, 120 miles below Fort Pierre, and 200 miles from Sioux City. He was in the East in 1857, making what proved to be his last visit to the region of his birth. Returning to duty he was stationed at Jefferson

Barracks, St. Louis, Mo., and then at Fort Randall, Nebraska territory, until July 1859, whence he proceeded, the same month, to Fort Kearney, thence to Prairie Dog Creek, in Kansas, for the protection of emigrants to the mines. He was continued on duty in Kansas for some time. Jan. 31, 1861, he was ordered to St. Louis, Mo., and when Mr. Lincoln took his seat as president of the United States, he became commandant at the St. Louis arsenal. Here he thoroughly understood his position and resources, and the characters arrayed in secret arms against him. His force of U.S. troops was small, but to make it appear the stronger he often sent out squads of soldiers in disguise during the night, while others slept, with orders to rendezvous at a distant point, and march back to the arsenal the next morning in uniform, with drums beating and flags flying. Union men in the city were organized into companies, armed and carefully drilled. Every precaution was taken to insure the security of the post, for an immense amount of public property was stored in the arsenal, and Claiborne F. Jackson, governor of the state of Missouri, had established a camp of instruction

for state militia near St. Louis, the main avenue of which bore the name of "Davis," and one of whose principal streets was called "Beauregard." May 10, 1861, Capt. Lyon surrounded this camp with troops from the U.S. arsenal, and gave Gen. D. M. Frost, its commander, thirty minutes in which to surrender his forces. At the end of that time he took possession of the camp. The night following this capture, Gen. Harney reached St. Louis, and took command of the U.S. forces of the city, but a few days later Capt. Lyon was elected brigadier-general of the 1st brigade U.S. Missouri volunteers, and on the 17th of May President Lincoln appointed him to that rank from the date named, and relieved Gen. Harney from command. Lyon organized and conducted an expedition to Potosi, Mo., where were extensive lead mines, to overcome the secessionists of that place. In a personal interview with Gen. Lyon, sought by Gov. Jackson in June, that functionary professed his desire to pledge the state of Missouri to a cause of strict neutrality in the civil war, on condition that the U.S. government should disband the home guards organized and armed throughout the state, and agree not to occupy, with its troops, any localities in the state not then occupied by them. To this proposition Lyon demurred, and in turn demanded the disbanding of the state militia, the nullification of the act of the legislature by which it was created, the admission of the right of the U.S. government to march and station its troops as it pleased, either for the protection of loyal subjects, or to repel invasion. He also refused to disband the home guard, or to withdraw the Federal troops, and asserted his determination to protect all Unionists to the extent of his power. The same evening Gov. Jackson and Gen. Price returned to Jefferson City, and the next day issued a proclamation claiming that the state of Missouri had been invaded by the U.S. forces, and calling into service 50,000 state militia to repel them. The following day (June 13th) Gen. Lyon left

St. Louis for Jefferson City with 1,500 troops. Jackson fled to Boonville, forty miles further up the Missouri river. At Jefferson City, which he occupied on the 15th, Gen. Lyon issued a counter-proclamation to offset Jackson's, and pushing on occupied Boonville, after a short struggle, succeeding which Jackson incontinently fled again. From Boonville Lyon sent out a second proclamation, defining the issues of the contest, and counseling Missourians in arms against the United States to lay them down and return to their homes. Having prepared a train at Boonville he moved thence on the 3d of July for Springfield, Mo., with 2,700 men, four pieces of artillery, and a baggage train two miles in length. Their objective point was reached on the 13th. By this time the Confederate army of Gen. Ben McCulloch, marching to Missouri from the South and West, had made a junction with the scattered Missouri militia troops, and was advancing against the Federal forces in numbers far greater than Lyon's. The Federal commander had called upon the Washington authorities for additional troops in vain, and now, as he learned that McCulloch's forces were preparing to move upon Springfield in two divisions, he determined to make a forced march and fight them separately. Aug. 4th, after moving from the city for this purpose, by the advice of a council of officers, it was decided to return to it, and on the 6th the Federal army was restationed at Springfield and on the roads emergent from it. On the 8th of August, at Wilson's Creek, Mo., ten or twelve miles southwest of Springfield, *11,600 Confederates* and Missourians were encamped, and to oppose them Lyon had but *5,400* effectives. He again determined, however, to march upon his foes by night and to surprise them, proposing to make his attack upon their camp in two places. The surprise of his movement, duly carried out, seems to have been complete, McCulloch having, by a singular coincidence, made arrangements to precipitate

his forces upon Springfield the same night, then having countermanded his orders on account of threatened rain, and drawn in his advanced pickets. In the fierce engagement that ensued *on the 10th of August* Lyon moved along the Federal lines encouraging his men by example and by words. His horse was shot, and he received three wounds—one near the ankle, one on his thigh, and another which cut his scalp to the bone. Mounting another horse, against the urgency of friends, with face pale from the loss of blood, he rode to the front and threw himself at the head of a column, which he ordered to charge upon the enemy with the bayonet. As his men rushed forward to follow him he fell, his left side pierced by a ball which passed near his heart, and escaped on his right side. His body servant received him in his arms, as he died on the field without a struggle. Maj. Sturgis, who succeeded to the command, ordered a retreat to Springfield after continuing the battle for three hours longer, and thence the Federal forces fell back to Rolla without pursuit from McCulloch. The operations which Lyon had conducted after leaving St. Louis had enabled the loyal men in Missouri to organize a state government and hold the commonwealth in the Union. His body after death remained in the possession of the

Confederates, but was given up on proper application, and was interred at Eastford, Conn., Sept. 5, 1861, after receiving appropriate honors on the way from West to East, in the various larger cities and towns of the northern states. The general assembly of Connecticut at its session in October of that year mourned his sudden death as that of "a beloved son who bore so distinguished a part in defence of the constitution and the suppression of rebellion," and the state received his sword, belt and chapeau for safe keeping. In December the U.S. senate adopted an appropriate resolution in recognition of his "eminent and patriotic services." Gen. Lyon left nearly the whole of his fortune, some $30,000, to the Federal government to assist in the prosecution of the war. "The Last Political Writings of Gen. Nathaniel Lyon" was published in New York in 1862. The "Memoir," by N. A. Woodward (Hartford, Conn., 1862), has been the basis of this sketch.

LYTLE, WILLIAM HAINES, soldier, was born at Cincinnati, O., Nov. 2, 1826, son of Robert T. Lytle, a distinguished public speaker, a member of the twenty-third congress, and surveyor of public lands in Ohio, who died in New Orleans Dec. 21, 1839; grandson of William Lytle, an early settler in Ohio, who took part in the Indian wars in that section, and great-grandson of William Lytle, a soldier in the French and Indian wars. He attended school in his native city, was graduated from the Cincinnati college, studied law and began its practice. When the war with Mexico commenced in 1846 his martial spirit, inherited from a soldier ancestry, was stirred within him, and he enlisted as a volunteer soldier. He was at once selected as captain of his company in the 2d Ohio regiment, and served with distinction throughout the campaign. Upon his return to Cincinnati he resumed the practice of his profession, and attained success. He was soon after elected to the state legislature as a

democrat, and in 1857 became the candidate of his party for the office of lieutenant-governor, but failed of an election. He was appointed major-general of the Ohio state militia, and on the outbreak of the civil war, enlisted and went to the front as colonel of the 10th Ohio regiment. He was assigned to Gen. McClellan's army, operating in West Virginia, and at Carnifex ferry, Sept. 10, 1861, while in command of a brigade, he was severely wounded. When convalescent, he assumed charge of the Bardstown camp of instruction, and upon full recovery from his wounds, he was placed in command of a brigade in Gen. Mitchell's division, which was guarding the Memphis and Chattanooga railroad. At the battle of Perryville, Oct. 8, 1862, he was again severely wounded, and taken prisoner. Upon his exchange he was promoted to brigadier-general of volunteers, and under Gen. Rosecrans he was with his brigade in all the battles and skirmishes of that army until, on the field of Chickamauga, while at the head of his brigade, he fell, mortally wounded, dying on the field Sept. 20, 1863. Gen. Lytle wrote, in 1857, the well-known poem, beginning "I am dying, Egypt, dying: ebbs the crimson life-tide fast." His poems were never printed in book form.

MACKENZIE, RANALD SLIDELL, soldier, was born in Westchester county, N.Y., July 27, 1840, son of Comr. Alexander S. Mackenzie, United States navy, and the grandson of John Slidell. He was appointed a cadet to the United States Military Academy, July 1, 1858, and was graduated in 1862, at the head of his class. He was assigned to the engineer corps as a second lieutenant, and served as assistant engineer of the 9th army corps in the northern Virginia campaign, being engaged in the action at Kelly's Ford, Aug. 20, 1862, and in the second battle of Bull Run, where he was wounded. He was brevetted first lieutenant in the corps of engineers. He was attached to the engineer battalion of the army of the Potomac, and in the Maryland campaign he was employed in constructing, repairing, and guarding bridges; during the Rappahannock campaign, he participated in the battles of Fredericksburg, Dec. 13, 1862, and Chancellorsville, May 2–4, 1863. He was in command of an engineer company in the Pennsylvania campaign, and took part in the battle of Gettysburg; received the brevets of captain for gallantry at Chancellorsville, and major for his conduct at Gettysburg. From August, 1863, to May, 1864, he served in the Rapidan campaign, being engaged in repairing and guarding bridges; in building blockhouses, roads, bridges, and rifle trenches; and in making reconnoissances. He was promoted captain, Nov. 6, 1863, and commanded an engineer company in the battles of the Wilderness and at Spottsylvania. While in command of a regiment he distinguished himself in the siege of Petersburg, June 10–22, 1864, where he was wounded, and was brevetted lieutenant-colonel, June 18, 1864. On July 10, 1864, he was appointed colonel of the 2d Connecticut heavy artillery, and was engaged in the defense of Washington, D.C. He commanded a brigade in Gen. H. G. Wright's corps in the Shenandoah campaign, and served with great distinction in the battles of Opequan, Fisher's Hill, and Cedar Creek, where he was again wounded. In the final siege of Petersburg, he was in command of a brigade in Gen. Wheaton's division of the 6th corps, and subsequently he commanded a division of cavalry in the army of the James, being engaged at the battle of Five Forks, Apr. 1, 1865; in the pursuit of the army of northern Virginia, and in the actions about Appomattox Court House. He was brevetted colonel, Oct. 19, 1864, for gallantry at Cedar Creek, and on the same day he was commissioned brigadier-general of volunteers. On Mar. 13, 1865, he was brevetted major-general of volunteers, and brigadier-general United States army, for services in the field during the war, and on Jan. 15, 1866, he was mustered out of the volunteer service. He was made colonel of the 41st infantry, Mar. 6, 1867; was transferred to the 4th cavalry, Dec. 15, 1869; was promoted brigadier-general, Oct. 26, 1882; and was retired from active service, Mar. 24, 1884, for disability in the line of duty. Gen. Mackenzie died at New Brighton, Staten Island, N.Y., Jan. 19, 1889.

MAGOFFIN, BERIAH, twenty-first governor of Kentucky (1859–62), was born at Harrodsburg, Mercer co., Ky., Apr. 18, 1815, son of Beriah and Jane (McAfee) Magoffin. His father was a native of Ireland and his mother of Kentucky. He was graduated at Center

College, Danville, Ky., in 1835, and then entered the law department of Transylvania University, taking his degree in 1838. He began practicing at Jackson, Miss., in 1839, and was elected reading clerk of the Mississippi senate, but in the same year returned to Harrodsburg, where he continued in practice until 1840, when he accepted the appointment of police judge. From the bench he was elected to the state senate in 1850. He was a presidential elector on the Democratic ticket for the election of 1844, 1848, 1852 and 1856, and was a delegate to the national Democratic conventions of 1848, 1856 and 1860. In 1855 he was an unsuccessful candidate for the office of lieutenant-governor, but at the next gubernatorial election was made governor for the term of four years. At the beginning of the secession movement in 1860, he wrote to commissioners from Alabama who were seeking Kentucky's co-operation with the other southern states, advising that the slave states agree on amendments to the United States Constitution that would meet with the approbation of southern Democrats. In his message to the state legislature in February, 1861, he recommended the speedy calling of a convention of the border states to determine their attitude in the impending crisis. When, on April 15, 1861, Pres. Lincoln called for 75,000 men to suppress insurrection, Gov. Magoffin replied that "Kentucky would furnish no troops for the wicked purpose of subduing her sister southern states." He issued a proclamation May 20, warning the citizens of the state from taking any part in hostilities on either side and forbidding either the United States or the Confederate government to undertake any occupation of state territory or to invade Kentucky soil with a hostile force; but recruiting for the Union service was carried on at Camp Dick Robinson, in Garrard county, and

at other places. He labored earnestly to stop the war and to have Kentucky act the part of mediator and peace maker between the North and South. In August, 1861, he sent letters to Pres. Lincoln and Pres. Davis, in which he declared the neutrality of Kentucky and requested the former to withdraw national troops from the state. When Gen. Leonidas Polk occupied and fortified Hickman and Columbus, the legislature passed a resolution directing the governor to demand the withdrawal of the Confederate troops. He promptly vetoed this resolution, but it was passed over his head, and he accordingly issued the proclamation. When shortly after the legislature passed resolutions inviting Gen. Robert Anderson, of Fort Sumter fame, to organize a volunteer force and expel the Confederate invaders and asking that the governor call out the state militia and place Gen. Thomas L. Crittenden in command, he again exercised the right of veto, and again without avail. Early in 1862 the legislature disfranchised those citizens who had entered the Confederate service and took other measures to commit Kentucky to the Union side. These acts, also, were vetoed by the governor and were passed over his veto. In August, 1862, he called an extra session of the legislature and tendered his resignation. Gov. Magoffin was married at Arcadia, Lincoln co., Ky., in 1840, to Ann, daughter of Isaac and Maria (Warren) Shelby, and granddaughter of Isaac Shelby, first governor of the state. They had five sons and five daughters. He died at his home in Harrodsburg, Ky., Feb. 28, 1885.

MAGRUDER, JOHN BANKHEAD, soldier, was born *in Port Royal, Va., May 1, 1807*. His parents destined him for the army, and his early education was directed with a view of entering the U.S. military academy at West Point. He

was appointed to a cadetship and admitted in 1826, graduating in the class of 1830 as second lieutenant, being assigned to the artillery. He was stationed at various posts in the West, on the coast of Maine, and at Fort McHenry, Baltimore. On the outbreak of the Mexican war, he, as captain, commanded the light battery of Pillow's division, and was brevetted major for gallantry at Cerro Gordo, and lieutenant-colonel for Chapultepec, where he was severely wounded. He was stationed on the Pacific coast, and at Fort McHenry, Md., after the close of the war, and for a time commanded Fort Adams, Newport, R.I., where he won especial favor with the frequenters of that fashionable resort by reason of the brilliant entertainments given at the fort during the gay seasons. Upon the secession of his native state, in 1861, he resigned his commission as captain of artillery, and entered the Confederate army as colonel of a corps of infantry *April 20, 1861. He never commanded a corps in the Confederate army; his largest command was a division.* He fought and won the battle of Big Bethel, the first engagement of the war, and

was, on June 17, 1861, commissioned brigadier-general having, on May 21st, been placed in command of all the forces on the Virginia peninsula, with headquarters at Yorktown. Here for several weeks he opposed the advance of the Federal army, and on Oct. 7, 1861, was promoted major-general. He distinguished himself at Malvern Hill, and in all of the seven days' battles before Richmond. On Oct. 10, 1862, he was placed in command of the trans-Mississippi department, District of Texas. Here he was particularly aggressive, recovering Galveston from the Federal forces on Jan. 1, 1863, capturing the U.S. revenue cutter Harriet-Lane, and driving the blockading squadron out of the harbor. He continued in command of this department up to Aug. 11, 1864, when he was assigned to the district of New Mexico and Arizona, where he remained until the close of the war. He afterward accepted a commission as major-general in the army of Maximilian in Mexico, serving until the execution of the emperor. Returning to the United States he lectured on Mexico in the various southern cities. In 1869 he retired to Houston, Tex., and died there *Feb. 18, 1871.*

MAHAN, ALFRED THAYER, naval commander and author, was born at West Point, N.Y., Sept. 27, 1840, son of Dennis Hart and Mary Helena (Okill) Mahan. His father, a graduate of the Military Academy at West Point, was a professor in that institution in 1830–71, and had a world-wide reputation for his text-books, especially those on engineering. Both parents were natives of New York city. Alfred Mahan was graduated at the U.S. Naval Academy, Annapolis, Md., in 1859, and was commissioned as lieutenant in 1861. During the civil war he saw service on the south Atlantic and Gulf squadrons, and was present at the battle of Port Royal. Later he served in the

south Atlantic, Pacific, Asiatic, and European squadrons, being promoted lieutenant-commander in 1865; commander in 1872; and captain in 1885. He was president of the Naval War College at Newport, R.I., in 1886–89, and again from July, 1892, to May, 1893; was in command of the Chicago in 1893–95. In May, 1898, he was appointed a member of the naval board during the war with Spain, was retired from active service on his own application in November, 1896, and made his home in New York city. In 1899 he was appointed by Pres. McKinley one of the delegates to the peace conference at the Hague. The degree of D.C.L. was conferred upon him by Oxford University in 1894, and that of LL.D. by Cambridge University, England, in 1894, by Harvard University in 1895, and by Yale University in 1897. He has published a number of works of great importance, chiefly studies of naval history, the expansion of a course of lectures delivered before the Naval War College. When planning these lectures, it is said, he could find no work which treated of the influence of navies upon the general course of history and, therefore, was obliged to bring forward its leading features and to discuss them from his own standpoint. Preceding this group, there appeared in 1883 an isolated work, "Gulf and Inland Waters," contributed to a series called "The Navy in the Civil War." In 1890 Capt. Mahan's "Influence of Sea Power on History, 1660–1783" was published. "The work," in the words of a reviewer in the New York "Critic," "is entirely original in conception, masterful in construction and scholarly in execution. The author took the broadest and most comprehensive view of his subject, looking into the primary causes which have brought navies into existence, the conditions under which they have grown in power, and their influence on national development. No other author with whom we are acquainted has ever undertaken to treat the subject in such a liberal, not to say philosophical, spirit, or to weave the story of the navy and its achievements into the affairs of state so as to bring out its value as a factor of national life." His next work (1892) was entitled "Influence of Sea Power on the French Revolution and Empire"; and in the same year his "Life of Farragut" was published. "Life of Nelson, the Embodiment of the Sea Power of Great Britain" (1897) met with even higher praise in England than in the author's own country, and is regarded as the most discriminating and comprehensive biography of the great admiral yet published. "The Interest of America in Sea Power, Present and Future" (1897) was a welcome contribution to literature bearing on problems of national importance. "Lessons of the War with Spain" appeared in 1899. A contributor to the "Library of the World's Best Literature," in a general view of his literary work, wrote: "The data cited in his works are common literary property; but the conclusions drawn are a distinct contribution to historical science. Capt. Mahan is the first writer to demonstrate the determining force which maritime strength has exercised upon the fortunes of individual nations, and consequently upon the course of general history; and in that field of work he is alone." Capt. Mahan was a member of the Church, University and Century clubs of New York city. He was married in New York city, June 11, 1872, to Ellen Lyle, daughter of Manlius Glendower and Ellen (Kuhn) Evans. They had three children. *He died in 1914.*

MAHONE, WILLIAM, soldier and senator, was born near Monroe, Southampton county, Va., Dec. 1, 1826. His paternal ancestors were Irish. Both grandfathers served with distinction in the war of 1812, and his father, Fielding Jordan Mahone, was spoken of as "intuitively a mathematician and a soldier," and commanded a militia regiment during the "Nat Turner insurrection." William's early education was acquired largely under his father's supervision,

with two years' attendance at school. He was graduated from the Virginia military institute in 1847, taught for two years at the Rappahannock military academy, studied civil engineering, and finally became chief engineer and constructor of the Norfolk and Petersburg railroad. At the outbreak of the civil war he joined the Confederate army, was commissioned lieutenant-colonel of Virginia volunteers, and soon became colonel of the 6th Virginia infantry. He was present at the capture of Norfolk navy yard in April, 1861, participated in most of the battles of the peninsula campaign, those on the Rappahannock, and those around Petersburg, where he won the sobriquet of the "hero of the Crater," for his splendid bravery at the time of the explosion of Grant's mine underneath Lee's outworks, July 30, 1864. He was known as a hardy fighter throughout the war. Gen. Lee held him in the highest esteem, and as a brigade commander considered him inferior only to "Stonewall" Jackson. He was commissioned brigadier-general in March, 1864, and major-general in August, for distinguished services around Petersburg. Afterward he commanded a division in Ambrose P. Hill's corps, and when Lee surrendered was at Bermuda Hundred. At the termination of the war he devoted himself again to railroad matters, and became president of the Norfolk and Tennessee railroad. Later he took an active interest in politics, endeavored, but failed, to secure the nomination for governor of Virginia in 1878, became the leader of the readjuster party, and was elected U.S. senator in 1880, serving till 1887, when he was defeated at the polls. Gen. Mahone married in February, 1855, Ortelia Butler, daughter of Dr. Butler. They have two sons and one daughter, and reside in Petersburg, Va. *He died Oct. 8, 1895.*

MALLORY, STEPHEN RUSSELL, secretary of the Confederate navy, was born in Trinidad,

W.I., in 1813, the second son of Chas. Mallory, a civil engineer of Reading, Conn. His parents settled at Key West, Fla., in 1820. Stephen was educated at Mobile and at Nazareth, Pa., and at the age of nineteen was appointed inspector of customs at Key West by President Jackson. During his incumbency of this office, he studied

law and was admitted to the bar in 1839, where he soon built up a large practice. He was judge for Monroe county and judge of probate, and in 1845 was appointed collector of customs at Key West. He served for several years as a volunteer in the war against the Seminoles in Florida. He declined to serve as a delegate to the Nashville commercial convention in 1850. In 1850 he successfully contested against David L. Yulee for a seat in the U.S. senate, was re-elected in 1857, and held the seat until 1861, the date of the secession of Florida, when he resigned and identified himself with the southern states. While he was in the senate he was for the greater part of the time chairman of the committee on naval affairs, and a member of the committee on claims. He refused the appointment of minister to Spain in 1858. He also declined to serve as chief justice of the admiralty court of Florida when that state seceded from the Union. On Feb. 21, 1861, Jefferson Davis offered Mr. Mallory the position of secretary of the navy, which he accepted and held until the close of the war. It was here that he manifested the wisdom of the choice of the Confederate president, for he succeeded in organizing a navy where none had previously existed. In April, 1865, when Richmond was abandoned, he left that city with Mr. Davis, and went to his home at La Grange, Ga., where he was arrested May 20, 1865, and was imprisoned ten months in Ford Lafayette, New York harbor. He was released on parole in March, 1866, returned to Pensacola shortly after, and practiced law until his death in that city, Nov. 9, 1873.

MANSFIELD, JOSEPH KING FENNO, soldier, was born in New Haven, Conn., Dec. 22, 1803. While at West Point he acted as assistant professor of natural philosophy for a short time, and was graduated in 1822, ranking second in a class of forty. He was assigned to the engineer corps, and for the next three years served in New York on the committee assembled for the planning of fortifications for the defence of the harbors and coast cities. In 1832 he was promoted first lieutenant, and on July 7, 1828, he was made captain. After serving in the Mexican war as chief engineer under Gen. Taylor, he received the brevet of major in 1846 for distinguished services in the defence of Fort Brown, which he had built. In September of the same year, after Monterey, where he was wounded seven times, he was brevetted lieutenant-colonel for gallant conduct, and in 1847, after Buena Vista, for like services he won the brevet of colonel. In May, 1853,

he was appointed inspector-general of the U.S. army, and in May 1861, he was commissioned brigadier-general of volunteers and stationed at Washington. He erected earthworks on the heights of Arlington, and fortified the city on every side. Subsequently he was sent to Hatteras, Camp Hamilton, and Newport News. After taking part in the capture of Norfolk, he was appointed military governor of Suffolk, Va. Later he was summoned to Washington to attend the Bull Run court of inquiry. On July 18, 1862, Gen. Mansfield was promoted major-general of volunteers. He commanded the corps formerly under Gen. Banks, and fell mortally wounded *on Sept. 17, 1862,* while gallantly cheering his troops to a charge at Antietam. *He died one day later on Sept. 18, 1862.*

MARMADUKE, JOHN SAPPINGTON, soldier and twenty-second governor of Missouri (1885–87), was born near Arrow Rock, Mo., Mar. 14, 1833, son of Meredith Miles and Lavinia (Sappington) Marmaduke. He obtained his early education in the neighborhood schools and studied two years at Yale and one year at Harvard. He was graduated at the United States Military Academy in 1857 with the rank of brevet second lieutenant. He was detailed as a member of Gen. A. S. Johnston's expedition, which put down the Mormon revolt in the spring of 1858, and for two years he saw service in Utah territory. He was stationed in New Mexico at the time the civil war broke out, and on Apr. 17, 1861, he resigned and raised a company of state guards in Missouri, and was soon elected colonel of a regiment. But disagreeing with the military and political course of his uncle, Gov. Claiborne F. Jackson, he again resigned his commission and joined the Confederate cause at Richmond, Va. He became lieutenant in the command of Gen. William J. Hardee in southeastern Arkansas, and in the autumn colonel of the 3d Confederate infantry, with which he made a brilliant showing at Shiloh. He was wounded during the second day and was promoted brigadier-general

while lying in the hospital. After being transferred to the department west of the Mississippi in August, 1862, he had command of the Confederate cavalry in Arkansas and Missouri for six months, making frequent raids and causing considerable damage to the Federal forces. Shortly after the defeat of Gen. Hindman at Prairie Grove, Ark., when Marmaduke commanded the cavalry division, the latter was ordered to strike the Federal line of communication and supply between Springfield and Rolla, Mo. He reached Springfield Jan. 8, 1863. His line advanced over the open prairie against a heavy fire and drove the Federal forces before him. Springfield was strongly fortified; inside were heavy earthworks flanked by rifle pits and deep ditches, and on the outskirts was a strong stockade protected by the guns of the earthworks. Porter's brigade had not come up, and he was thus compelled to make the attack with hardly more than half his force. He charged with his entire line, capturing a piece of artillery; but the Federals fired all the buildings outside the fortifications and his men had to fight with the flame and smoke in their faces and he was forced to retreat. In July, 1863, he participated in the attack upon Helena, Ark., and in an attack upon Pine Bluff he captured the Federal camp and stores. With his cavalry division he constantly and vigorously contested the advance of Gen. Frederick Steele upon Little Rock, Ark., and after the fall of that town he successfully covered Gen. Sterling Price's retreat. At this time he fought a duel with Gen. Lucien M. Walker—the outcome of the latter's refusal to be responsible for a certain order, when he was called a coward by Marmaduke. It was agreed that they were to advance at ten paces and continue firing until their revolvers were emptied. Walker fell mortally wounded at the second fire. In the spring of 1864 Gen. Steele

was marching to co-operate with Gen. Banks against Kirby Smith, when Gen. Marmaduke again offered a dogged opposition, harassing and delaying him by repeated attacks, until Kirby Smith could come up and defeat Steele's command at Jenkin's Ferry. For these services he was commissioned major-general. At Lake Village, Ark., during the summer of 1864, he encountered Gen. Andrew J. Smith, and a vigorous but undecisive engagement resulted. He took a prominent part in Price's invasion of Missouri, but during that campaign was surrounded near Fort Scott and captured Oct. 24, 1864. After imprisonment in Fort Warren until August, 1865, he made a European trip and then engaged in business in St. Louis. In 1871 he became part owner of the "Journal of Commerce" and also established the St. Louis "Evening Journal" and conducted the "Illustrated Journal of Agriculture," but in June, 1873, he retired from journalism to become secretary of the Missouri board of agriculture. In 1875 he was appointed state railroad commissioner and in the following year was regularly elected to that office for a term of four years. He was elected governor of Missouri in 1884, and during his term the bonded debt of the state was refunded at $3\frac{1}{2}$ per cent.—the last bonds of which were paid in January, 1903— and an appropriation was made for reclaiming the swamp lands of the southern part of the state, which added greatly to the value of the property in that section. He died while in office, at Jefferson City, Mo., Dec. 28, 1887. The lieutenant-governor, A. P. Morehouse, filled the office during the remainder of the term.

MARTINDALE, JOHN HENRY, soldier, was born at Sandy Hill, N.Y., March 20, 1815. He was graduated from the U.S. Military Academy in 1835, but resigned in 1836, and studied law. During the war he held several important commands. For gallantry at Malvern Hill he was brevetted major-general. He was attorney-general of the state of New York from 1866 to 1868, and discharged its duties with signal ability. He died Dec. 13, 1881.

MASON, JAMES MURRAY, senator and Confederate commissioner, was born on Mason's Island, Fairfax Co., W. Va., Nov. 3, 1798. He was a grandson of George Mason, a celebrated Virginia patriot of the American revolution, and a close friend of George Washington. James M. Mason was graduated from the University of Pennsylvania in 1818, and subsequently studied law at William and Mary College, Virginia, and after being

admitted to the bar practiced law at Winchester, Va. In 1826 he was elected to the state legislature, and continuously re-elected until 1832. He was a member of the Virginia constitutional convention in 1829, and in 1833 served as a presidential elector on the Jackson ticket, and was elected to congress as a Jackson democrat *in 1836*, and declined re-election at the end of his term, preferring to return to his law practice. The Virginia legislature elected him to fill an unexpired term in the U.S. senate in 1847, and he was re-elected twice. His term would have expired in 1863, but he resigned his seat in 1861 to cast his fortunes with the Confederacy. The fourteen years of his career as a senator were not records of brilliant speeches and measures, but were rather stamped with an ability for hard work. He served as chairman of the committee on foreign relations for ten years. He was a thorough democrat, and a strict constructionist of the state's rights school, was the author of the fugitive slave law in 1850, and throughout his career as a senator strongly opposed anti-slavery agitation. As soon as he resigned his seat in the U.S. senate he was elected to the Confederate congress, and appointed with John Slidell commissioner from the Confederate States to England and France. He sailed from Charleston, S.C., for Cuba, Oct. 12, 1861, and reached Havana safely, where he and Maj. Slidell were received with due form by the captain-general. The two commissioners engaged passage on the British mail steamer Trent, and were captured by Capt. Charles Wilkes, of the U.S. navy, as the vessel was passing through the Bahama Channel. They were brought to Boston, and incarcerated in Fort Warren, Boston harbor, but afterward, on demand of the British government, they were released, Jan. 2, 1862, and immediately proceeded in their mission to Europe, where, until the close of the civil war, they actively pushed the claims of the Confederacy for recognition. Senator Mason spent several years in Canada after the cessation of hostilities, but in 1868 returned to his home in Virginia, where his eventful life was peacefully brought to a close. He died at Alexandria, Va., Apr. 28, 1871.

MAURY, DABNEY HERNDON, soldier, was born in Fredericksburg, Va., May 20, 1822, the son of Capt. John Minor Maury, who was descended in a direct line from the old Virginia families of Brooke and Minor. These families emigrated from England with grants from Charles II. and Queen Anne. He was also descended from the Huguenot families of Fontaine and Maury, who left France on the revocation of the edict of Nantes in 1685. Dabney Herndon entered the University of Virginia in 1839, and in 1841 became a student in the law school of Judge Taylor Lomax. After being there one year he entered the U.S. military academy at West Point in 1842, and was graduated from this institution in 1846, and assigned to duty in the mounted rifles. He served in the Mexican war during the following year, and was complimented in special orders for gallant conduct at Vera Cruz, and was wounded at Cerro Gordo, and promoted first lieutenant. The legislature of Virginia, and the citizens of Fredericksburg presented him with a sword for his gallant conduct in this engagement. In 1847 he was appointed assistant professor of geography, history and ethics at West Point, and retained this position until 1850, when he was made assistant instructor of infantry tactics. He held this position until 1852, when he was assigned to frontier duty in Texas. From 1856–59 he was appointed superintendent of cavalry at Carlisle barracks. He published his "Tactics for Mounted Riflemen," about this time, and in 1860 was appointed adjutant-general of the department of New Mexico. When Virginia seceded he resigned his commission in the U.S. army, and was brevetted colonel and adjutant in the Confederate army, and assigned to duty in the trans-Mississippi department as chief of staff to Gen. Earl Van Dorn. In 1862 he was brevetted brigadier-general for conduct at Elk

Horn. He commanded the rear guard of the army of the West, at the evacuation of Corinth and Farmington, and commanded the 1st division of the army of the West at Iuka, and was rear guard in its retreat, and repulsed the pursuit of the enemy. He stormed Corinth during this year, and lost there 2,000 men during the two days' fight, and the following day checked Ord's corps at Hatchie Bridge, defeating his repeated attempts to cross the river. During these three days' fight his division was reduced from 4,600 to 1,200 men. In 1863 he checked Gen. Grant's advance into northern Mississippi. Gen. Maury went to the assistance of Gen. Stephen E. Lee, and aided him in defeating Sherman at Chickasaw Bluff. He was brevetted major-general for gallant and meritorious conduct at the battles of Corinth and Hatchie, and subsequently made department commander of the army of the Gulf, serving in this capacity until the downfall of the Confederacy. In 1868 Gen. Maury organized the Southern historical society, and two years afterward opened its archives to the War record office at Washington, and secured in exchange, free access to that office for the people of the South. He was first to organize the movement in 1879 for the improvement of the volunteer troops of the United States, and served as a member of the executive committee of the National guard association of the United States until 1890. In 1886 Mr. Cleveland appointed him the envoy extraordinary and minister plenipotentiary of the United States of America to the United States of Colombia. Gen. Maury was a versatile and forcible writer, and contributed valuable papers to the records of the civil war. *He died Jan. 11, 1900.*

MAURY, MATTHEW FONTAINE, hydrographer and meteorologist, was born in Spottsylvania county, Va., Jan. 14, 1806. At an early age he removed to Tennessee with his parents, and was placed at the Harpeth Academy, then under the charge of Rev. James H. Otey, who afterwards became bishop of Tennessee. When nineteen he entered the U.S. navy as a midshipman, making his first voyage in the frigate Brandywine, to France, with Gen. Lafayette. He accompanied the vessel to the Pacific, where he was transferred to the Vincennes, in which vessel he completed the circumnavigation of the globe. He again sailed as passed-lieutenant to the Pacific in the sloop-of-war Falmouth, when he was transferred as lieutenant to the Potomac. While at sea he devoted his leisure to mathematics, in which he found he was not proficient enough for the requirements of his profession, and to extend his knowledge of modern languages at the same time he used Spanish text-books. In pursuing his studies he was greatly inconvenienced by the number of different volumes employed, and with a view to saving others a like difficulty, he prepared, amid the annoyances and interruptions of a life at sea, a work on navigation. "Maury's Navigation" was commenced in the steerage of the Vincennes, and completed in the Potomac, and published in 1835, when it met with universal acceptance, and was adopted as a text-book in the navy. During this interval of active service he married Ann Herndon, a sister of Lieut. Herndon, of the U.S. navy, who rendered such conspicuous service upon the sinking of the Central America, which he commanded. In this same year he was appointed astronomer to the South Sea Exploring Expedition, but, upon the withdrawal of Com. Jones, he declined the appointment. In 1839, while on his way from Tennessee, to join a surveying vessel in New York harbor, the stage-coach was overturned and his leg was broken, which resulted in permanent lameness, and disabled him for active service. During his long period of imprisonment from his disabled leg, he amused himself writing a series of articles on the abuses in the navy, which were published in the "Southern Messenger" under the title of "Scraps from the Lucky Bag, by Harry Bluff." His forceful style produced an immediate impression, and resulted in great reforms, and ultimately in the establishment of the Naval Academy. His advocacy of the establishment of a navy-yard at Memphis, Tenn., resulted in an act of congress to build it. He made the first observations on the flow of the Mississippi river, and proposed a system of observations which would give every day, by telegraph, the state of the river and its tributaries to captains of steamers on the river. He made studies in regard to the enlargement of the Illinois and Michigan canals, by which war vessels might pass from the gulf to the great lakes, for which he received the thanks of the Illinois legislature. He was the first to suggest what is known as the warehouse system. His thirteen years' service at sea gave him an opportunity for extended meteorological and hydrographical

study, and soon after his retirement from the exploring expedition, he was appointed chief of the Hydrographical Bureau at Washington, and upon its union with the National Observatory in 1844 he became superintendent of the combined institutions. To him is due many of the present methods employed in the weather bureau. He devoted much study to the ocean currents, and collected from the log-books of the ships of war data upon which he determined the direction of winds and currents of the ocean, which he published in 1844 in a paper read before the National Institute, which was afterwards printed under the title of "A Scheme for Rebuilding Southern Commerce." Recognizing the need of systematizing the observations and records which were taken differently by the various nations, Lieut. Maury proposed a maritime congress, which, at the earnest advocacy of the United States, was held at Brussels in 1853, at which was recommended a uniform style of abstract log, to be kept by all vessels, in whatever service. At the close of the congress the merchants of New York presented him with $5,000 and a service of plate. The result of his studies upon the winds and currents, was his "Physical Geography of the Sea," which was of the utmost value to the maritime world, and was immediately translated into nearly every language, making its author at once famous throughout Europe. Humboldt declared that Lieut. Maury had founded a new science, and the governments of almost every nation in Europe conferred upon him orders of knighthood, and other insignia of honor. He was made a member of the Academies of Sciences of Paris, Berlin, Brussels, St. Petersburg, and Mexico. Lieut. Maury described with great carefulness the course of the gulf stream, showing the best course to be followed in crossing the Atlantic. He also instituted deep-sea sounding, and discovered the great plateau under the Atlantic. He first suggested to Cyrus W. Field the feasibility of telegraphic communication between Europe and this country by means of a cable laid on the bed of the ocean, and indicated the route upon which it was finally laid. His services to the scientific knowledge of the country have hardly been surpassed. In 1855 he was given the rank of commander, which position he held at the outbreak of the civil war in 1861. He resigned, to follow his native state, Virginia, out of the Union, at the same time refusing generous offers, made by both the Grand Duke Constantine of Russia, and his Imperial Highness Prince Napoleon, on condition of his settling in their respective countries. In 1862 he established a naval submarine battery service at Richmond, but before much progress had been made he was sent to England, after having attained the rank of captain in the Confederate service, and continued his studies, making a number of important discoveries, among them several improvements in the application of magneto-electricity to torpedoes. He was also appointed one of the navy agents for the Confederate states, and while in Europe, fitted out several armed cruisers. At the close of the war, he went to Mexico, where the Emperor Maximilian, a former friend of his, appointed him to a place in his cabinet. He also served for a time as commissioner of emigration, declining all other honors offered him, owing to a distrust of the stability of the French government there. This distrust finally became so great that he returned to England, where he was joined by his family from Virginia. While in Europe the University of Cambridge conferred upon him the degree of LL.D., and he was invited by Napoleon III to accept the superintendency of the imperial observatory at Paris. In 1868 he was offered the professorship *of meteorology* in the Military Institute at Lexington, Va., which he accepted. He returned to this country, and performed the duties of his professorship until his death, at the same time conducting a physical survey of Virginia, which was published in Richmond in 1868, under the

title of "The Physical Survey of Virginia." The results of this survey established through routes by rail, and a great free water-line, uniting the East and West. It also established a system of observations and reports of crops, which greatly promoted foreign commerce. With William M. Fountain he prepared and published "The Resources of West Virginia." In 1871 he accepted the presidency of the University of Alabama, but on account of ill health, returned to his professorship at Lexington. Besides the works mentioned, he has published a series of text-books on astronomy and political and physical geography, prepared during his English exile. But the work which has made Maury famous is his official work as head of the hydrographical board at Washington, which resulted in the Maury "Wind and Current Charts," and two large volumes of "Sailing Directions." These works, owing to their clear indications of the best ocean routes, shortened voyages to such an extent as to save several million dollars annually to the commerce of the world. The amount of labor they involved may be judged from the fact that 1,159,353 separate observations on the force and direction of the wind, and over 100,000 observations on the height of the barometer at sea, were necessary for the wind chart alone. He also published "Letters on the Amazon and the Atlantic Slopes of South America," "Relations Between Magnetism and the Circulation of the Atmosphere," "Laws for Steamers Crossing the Atlantic." Com. Maury is also the author of several addresses delivered in various parts of the country, among which may be mentioned those before the Geological and Mineralogical Society of Fredericksburg in 1836, and Southern Scientific Convention at Memphis, on the Pacific Railway. He died in Lexington, Va., Feb. 1, 1873.

Signal Service Office

McCANN, WILLIAM PENN, naval officer, was born at Paris, Bourbon co., Ky., May 4, 1830, son of James Hervey and Jean Rusk (Lowery) McCann. The original American representative of his family was his grandfather, John McKeand, a native of Withorn, in the county of Wigtown, Scotland, who was brought to Philadelphia before the revolution, and in 1797 was married to Nancy Penn, a descendant of the founder. He resided for a while in Maryland, and later at Paris, Ky., where both his sons and grandsons were born, and was the first to change the spelling of the family name to McCann. William P. McCann was educated at the Naval Academy, where he was graduated in 1854, eighth in a class of twenty-eight. Shortly after graduation he was promoted to passed midshipman, and assigned to the frigate Independence, on which he made a three years' cruise in the north and south Pacific and Polynesia. *On Sept. 16, 1856,* he was commissioned lieutenant; served on the receiving ship Allegheny in 1858, and in 1859 was lieutenant and navigator of the Sabine in the expedition to Paraguay. He was still attached to the Sabine at the opening of the civil war, and on April 14 and 15, 1861, assisted in the reinforcement of Fort Pickens, Fla., with sailors and marines, remaining off the fort 127 days. She was then engaged in blockading duty on the coast of South Carolina, and rescued the sailors and marines of the foundered steamer Governor, of the Port Royal expedition. Ordered to command temporarily the Maratanza, he was present at the siege of Yorktown, April and May, 1862, engaging batteries; and also at Gloucester point, where he landed sailors and marines and brought off flags from the batteries. Cooperating with the army on the York and Pamunkey rivers, at West Point, he drove off a force of Confederates attacking Franklin's corps. He was relieved by Comr. Stevens, remaining as executive officer. Also cooperating with the army of the Potomac on the James and Appomatox rivers, he was in the engagement at Point of Rocks on the latter and frequent actions on the former. On July 4, 1862, the Maratanza captured the gunboat Teazer, with plans of the batteries and defences of Richmond; also thirty-six officers and men who had been taken prisoners, and subsequently a number of blockade-runners in the Potomac

river. McCann was promoted to be lieutenant-commander July 16, 1862. On Oct. 1st he took command of the Hunchback, blockading the sounds of North Carolina; and at Newbern, March 14, 1863, resisted an attack by Gens. Hill and Pettigrew with an army corps and eighteen pieces of artillery with such skill and vigor that in an hour and a half they were forced to withdraw. During the siege of Washington, N.C., in April, 1862, he commanded five gunboats, and was frequently in action. In November, 1863, he was transferred to the Kennebec, of the west Gulf blockading squadron, and for thirteen months was actively engaged in blockading Mobile. For assisting at the destruction of the Ivanhoe under the guns of Fort Morgan, he was officially commended by Adm. Farragut. He also captured three blockade-runners with valuable cargoes. At the battle of Mobile bay, Aug. 5, 1864, the Kennebec was fifth in the line of battle; engaged the ram Tennessee; pursued and engaged the Morgan, which finally escaped. In 1865 he commanded the Tahoma, and in 1867 the Tallapoosa of the west Gulf squadron, later being stationed at the Philadelphia naval rendezvous, and in 1869–70 at the Philadelphia navy yard. He was promoted commander Dec. 8, 1867; captain, Sept. 21, 1876, and commodore, Jan. 26, 1887; was commandant of the Boston navy yard in 1887–90. On July 26, 1890, he was appointed rear-admiral, and ordered to the command of the south Atlantic station. With the Pensacola, his flagship, and the Essex, he participated in the ceremonies of embarking the remains of John Ericsson for Sweden on board the cruiser Baltimore, on Aug. 31st, an occasion made notable by the presence of three rear-admirals, Gherardi, Walker and himself. Setting sail for his station on the following day, he reached Rio Janeiro in time to assist at the first anniversary of the proclamation of the Brazilian republic. On the outbreak of the Chilean revolution in January, 1891, he was ordered to Valparaiso, in command of that portion of the Pacific station south of Guayaquil. Later, transferring his flag to the Baltimore, he was sent in pursuit of the filibuster steamer Itata, which had escaped from the U.S. authorities at San Diego, Cal. By arrangement with the insurgent authorities, she was finally captured at the port of Iquique, after an exciting chase of several weeks, and returned to California in convoy of the Charleston. Later he endeavored to arrange a peace between Pres. Balmaceda and the insurgent junta, but was unsuccessful, largely through difficulty in communicating with U.S. Minister Egan. On his return to the United States he was president of the naval examining and retiring board, and retained the office until his retirement, May 4, 1892. His services in Chili were acknowledged by the secretary of the navy, who wrote him in August, 1891, expressing the department's "high appreciation of the efficient manner in which you have performed the responsible and delicate duties which have devolved upon you as commander-in-chief of the south Pacific squadron, in consequence of the civil war now existing in the republic of Chili." The war with Spain in 1898 stirred in him a desire for active service, and, on his own solicitation, he was appointed president of the court of inquiry and court-martial in Brooklyn and Denver, and prize commission for the southern district of New York. On Jan. 31, 1867, he was married to Mary Elizabeth, daughter of Charles W. Vulte, of New York city. *He died in 1906.*

McCLELLAN, GEORGE BRINTON, soldier, was born in Philadelphia, Pa., Dec. 3, 1826. He was the son of George McClellan, M.D., and Elizabeth (Brinton) McClellan, the more remote ancestors having been Scotch. He received his early education at the schools of his native city, and in 1841 entered the University of

Pennsylvania, where he remained nearly two years. In 1842 he entered the U.S. military academy, being graduated second in the class of 1846, the largest that had ever left the academy, and he was first in the class in engineering. In June, 1846, he was commissioned brevet second lieutenant of engineers, and in September of the same year he accompanied the army to Mexico, being assigned to a company of sappers and miners which had just been organized. He distinguished himself under Gen. Scott in the battles of Contreras, Churubusco, Molino del Rey, and Chapultepec, and was commissioned second lieutenant, and brevetted captain for gallantry in action. The intrepid act which won him the brevet of captain occurred while Gen. Worth's division was camped on the Puebla road preparatory to an advance on the City of Mexico. McClellan went out at early dawn, accompanied only by an orderly, on a personal scouting expedition. On mounting a ridge he came suddenly upon a Mexican engineer officer who, it afterward developed, was engaged in the same work. Taking in the situation at a glance, McClellan dashed forward and with his large American horse rode down the Mexican, disarmed him, handed him over to his orderly, and then climbed to the summit, from which he discovered a body of 2,500 cavalry forming for attack. He promptly returned with his prisoner to camp, the "long-roll" was beaten, and the next night found Gen. Worth occupying Puebla. At the close of the Mexican war Capt. McClellan was assigned to the command of the engineer corps to which he was attached, and returned with it to West Point, where he acted as assistant instructor in practical engineering until 1851, when he was put in charge of the construction of Fort Delaware. In the following year he went on the Red river exploring expedition with Capt. R. B. Marcy. In the meantime he had written and published a "Manual on the Art of War." In 1853 and 1854 he was on duty in Washington Territory and Oregon, and commenced a topographical survey for the Pacific railway. His activity, courage, and presence of mind were shown in a marked degree during this expedition, when on a hunt with Capt. Marcy. Marcy had tried his fawn-bleat in hopes of calling up a doe. He called up a panther instead. He fired, and the panther rolled over, stunned, then, rallying, sprang for the hunters. McClellan fired, missed, took in the situation, used his rifle as a club, broke the animal's skull and his rifle at the same blow, but bagged the game. In 1855 he was one of three American officers sent to observe the campaign in the Crimea, the other two being Maj. Richard Delafield and Maj. Alfred Mordecai. These three American officers received the greatest courtesy and attention from the British government, but the French and Russians extended no facilities. After their experience in Crimea, the commission traveled through various European countries, examining military posts and fortresses, and acquainting themselves with the military methods in use. On returning each of the three made an official report; Capt. McClellan's being on the arms, equipment, and organization of the European armies. In January, 1857, McClellan, who had been promoted to a full captaincy, and had been transferred to the 1st cavalry, resigned his commission to accept the position of chief engineer, and afterward that of vice-president of the Illinois central railroad company. Later he was made president of the eastern division of the Ohio and Mississippi railroad company. On May 22, 1860, he married Ellen Mary Marcy, daughter of Capt. (afterward Gen.) Randolph B. Marcy, and settled in Cincinnati, O. At the outbreak of the civil war he was in an excellent business position, as regards both salary and prospects. He had a pleasant and happy home, and every temptation to refrain from offering his services in the war, had not his patriotism and his character as a soldier forced him to do so. He volunteered for the service, and on Apr. 23, 1861, was commissioned major-general of volunteers in Ohio, but by the recommendation of Gen. Scott, who knew his value, on May 3d following he was placed in command of the department of the Ohio. He issued a proclamation to the Union men of western Virginia and an address to his soldiers, and then entered upon the western Virginia campaign, and by the end of July had freed that section from secessionists and preserved it to the Union. He was then summoned to Washington, and assigned to the command of the division of the Potomac, as major-general, U.S. army, and on Nov. 1, 1861, was made commander-in-chief of the Union forces. This was after Bull Run, when the government was paralyzed, and the people

divided between fear and rage. Meanwhile, Washington was almost at the mercy of the enemy, inasmuch as no general there had thought of making the commonest provision for its defence. From this time forward the peculiar qualities with which McClellan was endowed became more and more essential to the safety and welfare of the Union, and were more and more devoted to these purposes. He was one of the few who foresaw a long war, and discerned the necessity of making a most careful preparation for it, organizing what should be a real army, like the armies he had seen in Europe, and not a mere mass of untrained, undisciplined volunteers or militia, and of erecting fortifications or some kind of defence for the enormous exposed frontier lines of the Union states. Unfortunately for McClellan, as for not a few others who fought in the war for the Union, the struggle was in many respects a political one, and the necessity for strengthening and perpetuating a party occasioned many acts which were detrimental to the Union cause, and many others which were crushing to individual patriots. President

Lincoln, when a lawyer in Illinois, had been well acquainted with McClellan, who was at that time vice-president of the Illinois central railroad, and Gen. Scott, who had known him from boyhood, appreciated his services during the Mexican war. Both men were aware of his useful career in high civil positions. The promptness with which he collected and organized the military resources of Ohio, Indiana, and Illinois, satisfied the authorities at Washington that he was at least the right man in the right place, and he may be said to have been called upon, after the disastrous retreat of the Union army at Bull Run, to save the government. The cry of "On to Richmond!" which originated with Horace Greeley, and filled the whole northern press in the latter part of 1861, would have driven any less determined man than McClellan to some foolish and unprepared effort that would have been completely disastrous to the Union forces. He, however, with absolute self-poise resisted this mad tendency, and succeeded in gaining time to make a real army; thereby laying the foundation for the final success of the Union

cause. This course, although wise resistance to the popular hue and cry, naturally created a great deal of impatience both on the part of the people and that of the government; in consequence of which Gen. McClellan was personally treated with far less confidence and respect than when he first assumed the task of directing the war. It was he, however, who created the army of the Potomac, and even the delays and apparent inertness at Yorktown, where it seemed that he was fortifying against the air, were the means by which McClellan was training his men to understand and apply the rules of war. Meanwhile he was unquestionably harassed, and his force depleted by the authorities at Washington for political reasons. *This is a partisan interpretation, first advanced by McClellan himself but not sustained by most modern historians.* His peninsular campaign in the spring of 1862 was based on the distinct understanding that the army which he then controlled should not be diminished; and had it not been for the withdrawal of Gen. McDowell's force of 40,000 men from the neighborhood of

Fredericksburg, it is highly probable that McClellan's army would have entered Richmond before the end of June. On the 28th of that very month, McClellan wrote to the secretary of war stating that if he had been sustained by the government he could have

Union gunboats were able to come into play at this point, and what threatened to be the destruction of the army of the Potomac was successfully avoided. The army succeeded in reaching Harrison's Landing, just before which an attack was made along their whole line by

captured Richmond and in enclosing this despatch to Stanton, he exhibited the deep chagrin and unhappiness which he felt in these words: "If I save this army now, I tell you plainly that I owe no thanks to you or to any persons in Washington; you have done your best to sacrifice this army." He had fought the battle of Gaines's Mills, and had entered upon his peninsular campaign, the most remarkable general retreat during the war, and in some respects the most remarkable in the history of any war, inasmuch as the result was not utter disaster to the general making the movement. The battles of White Oak Swamp and of Malvern Hill were followed by Savage's Station and the fighting at Frazier's Farm, where McClellan had a line eight miles in length, attacked at once by "Stonewall" Jackson, Magruder, Longstreet, and Hill. *The battle of Malvern Hill was the last of the Seven Days battles mentioned here.* Fortunately the

the exasperated Confederates, who, although fighting magnificently, were driven back and defeated. The hope that McDowell's force would again be restored to him was the real reason for the change of base to the James river, but his judgment was overruled by the political advisers of the president. Finally, on Aug. 30, 1862, he was relieved of his command, and superseded by Gen. Pope, whereupon followed the second disaster of Bull Run. *McClellan was not formally relieved of command. He was, however, ordered to forward the troops under his command to support Pope—orders he did not carry out with alacrity.* McClellan was then a second time called upon to save the government, and fought the battle of Antietam, one of the greatest victories for the Union cause that occurred during the war. Yet he was still in disgrace among the republican heads at Washington. It was charged upon him that he did not follow

509

Lee as he should have done, and soon after he was relieved by Gen. Burnside who was presently defeated at Fredericksburg, and was succeeded in turn by Gen. Hancock, *Burnside was succeeded by Joseph Hooker, not Hancock,* who immediately went into winter cantonment. From Antietam to Gettysburg the history of the army of the Potomac was a history of defeat and disaster. Meanwhile, McClellan had virtually been placed in retirement. As a general and a leader of armies, McClellan never sent a body of men into territory which he had not personally investigated. His reconnoissances were frequent, and filled with many incidents. On one occasion he climbed to the top of a tree and studied the situation with his field-glass, within range of the celebrated "squirrel-hunter rifles" of the enemy. Regarding his personal

Geo. B. McClellan

observation as preferable to the statement of scouts, on another he crept through briars and ravines and brush like an Indian, until he could hear the conversation of the enemy. From it he gleaned important information. Such conduct endeared him to the soldiery, and "Little Mac" became their idol. In 1864 Gen. McClellan was nominated for the presidency of the United States by the democratic party. He resigned his commission in the army on election day of 1864; but when the election took place he was defeated, receiving a popular vote of 1,800,000, while Mr. Lincoln polled 2,200,000. From that time until his death he was engaged in various important civil pursuits. He made a visit to Europe, on his return from which, in 1868, he settled on Orange Mountain, N.J. The same year he was offered the presidency of the University of California, and the year following that of Union college, but he declined both. In 1870 he was appointed by the mayor of New York city engineer-in-chief of the department of docks; and in 1871 was offered the nomination for comptroller of the city, which he declined. In the construction of the Poughkeepsie bridge across the Hudson, he was offered the position of superintendent. Nov. 6, 1877, he was elected governor of New Jersey, filling the chair until 1881. In 1864 he published "The Organization and the Campaigns of the Army of the Potomac." He also wrote a series of articles on the Russo-Turkish war for the "North American Review," and "McClellan's Own Story," published in 1887. To the latter work the reader is referred for Gen. McClellan's war record, and for a complete analysis of the multitude of engagements in which he fought and the campaigns which he directed. Later he settled in New York, where a number of friends presented him with a handsome residence and where he superintended several important enterprises. Gen. McClellan was five feet eight and a half inches in height, erect, and compactly built, possessed of an impressive face marked with the lineaments of a strong character and a firm will, yet capable of a peculiarly sweet smile, in which was to be seen an indication of his manner which, though dignified, was always courteous and agreeable. During the height of his successes he was called the "Young Napoleon of the War," and "Little Mac," an evidence of the deep attachment felt for him by the soldiers who had fought under him. He was, in fact, the idol of the army of the Potomac so long as he was at its head, and his men would follow him as they would follow no other general. While it will, for another generation at least, be a moot question whether the politicians or the people were right in their estimate of McClellan, it is likely that the future historian of the American civil war will set him right in history for all time. Gen. McClellan died at South Orange, N.J., Oct. 29, 1885. He left two children, a daughter and a son. Gov. Hill appointed the latter, George B. McClellan, Jr., on his official staff with the rank of colonel. After a period of journalistic experience, he was offered and accepted the position of treasurer of the board of trustees of the New York and Brooklyn Bridge, and in 1893 was elected president of the board of aldermen of New York city.

McCLERNAND, JOHN ALEXANDER, soldier and lawyer, was born in Breckenridge county, Ky., May 30, 1812. His father died

when he was four years of age, and his mother soon after removed to Shawneetown, Ill. His youth was passed on a farm, and in attendance at the common schools. In 1832 he was admitted to the bar, but left his practice to take part as a volunteer in the war with the Sac and Fox Indians. In 1835 he founded the Shawneetown "Democrat," engaging at the same time in the practice of his profession, and from 1836 until 1842 was a member of the Illinois legislature. In 1842 he was elected to congress, and served, by re-election, until 1851. In 1858 he was again elected to congress, but at the opening of the civil war recruited the McClernand brigade, and was appointed by President Lincoln brigadier-general of volunteers. He was present at the battle of Belmont, and in the assault on Fort Donelson commanded the right wing of the Federal army. He was promoted to be major-general of volunteers March 21, 1862, and led a division at the battle of Shiloh, in April, 1862. In January, 1863, he succeeded Gen. Sherman as commander of the expedition against

Vicksburg, and captured Arkansas Post. As commander of the 13th corps he took part in the operations at Port Gibson, Champion Hills, Big Black River, and Vicksburg. *In June, 1863, he was relieved from his command, and on Nov. 30, 1864, resigned from the army.* Gen. McClernand was latterly (1891) a member of the Utah commission. *He died Sept. 20, 1890.*

McCOOK, ALEXANDER McDOWELL, soldier, the fifth son, was born in Columbiana county, O., Apr. 22, 1831. He seemed to possess in the most marked degree the splendid fighting qualities of his sturdy father, who, though sixty-three years of age when the civil war broke out, yet joined eagerly in the defence of his country with his nine sons, and fell mortally wounded while leading the advance party to intercept Morgan's raid. His mother, too, who died in 1879, was a woman of great courage and strength of character, as well as highly intelligent. Alexander was graduated from the U.S. Military academy in 1852, and assigned to the 3d infantry. After a brief garrison service, he fought the Apaches in New Mexico for

several years, and from February, 1858, until April, 1861, he was assistant instructor in the infantry tactics at West Point. He became first lieutenant on Dec. 6, 1858. At the beginning of the civil war he was appointed colonel of the 1st Ohio regiment. He distinguished himself at the first battle of Bull Run, and for his services there was brevetted major. He became brigadier-general of volunteers, Sept. 3, 1861, and was brevetted lieutenant-general at the capture of Nashville, March 3, 1862, and colonel on the 7th of April following for meritorious conduct at Shiloh. He was appointed major-general of volunteers, July 17, 1862, and took command of the 20th army corps, which participated in the campaigns of Perryville, Stone river, Tullahoma, and Chickamauga. He served in the middle military division from November, 1864, until February, 1865, and in eastern Arkansas from February till May of the latter year. On March 13, 1865, he received the brevet of brigadier-general, U.S.A., for gallant services at Perryville, Ky., and also on the same date that of major-general, U.S.A., for services in the field. He investigated Indian affairs with a congressional committee from May till October, 1865, and at the close of the war was made lieutenant-colonel of the 26th infantry. Gen. McCook was stationed at Fort Leavenworth, Kan., as commandant of the school of instruction for infantry and cavalry. *He died June 12, 1903.*

McCOOK, EDWARD MOODY, fifth and seventh governor of Colorado (1869–73, 1874–75), was born in Steubenville, O., *June 15, 1833.* His grandfather, George McCook, was an Irishman of Scotch descent, who, being involved with the United Irishmen in 1780, fled to the United States. His father was John McCook, a physician of eminence, who married Catherine J. Sheldon of Hartford, Conn. John

Edward M. McCook.

and his brother Daniel were familiarly known as the "fighting McCooks," distinguished as the "tribe of John and the tribe of Dan." Edward was educated in the public schools, and when sixteen settled in Minnesota, but upon the breaking out of the Pike's Peak gold excitement, went to the Rocky Mountains, when the entire surrounding country was Arapahoe county, Kan. (The illustration shows the first house with glass windows ever built in the Rocky Mountains.) In 1859 he represented that district in the territorial legislature of Kansas, during which time the state of Kansas was formed, leaving the Pike's Peak country without government, when he went to Washington and secured the organization of the territory of Colorado, which has since become a state. When the first shot was fired at Fort Sumter he hastened to Washington and joined the Kansas Legion, which, with the Kentucky Legion were the only loyal commands in that city. As communication with the North had been cut off by the state troops of Maryland, McCook volunteered to carry Gen. Scott's dispatches; and, though Baltimore was in a state of insurrection, succeeded in getting through, and bringing back return dispatches, walking all the way back on the railroad ties. For this service, he was May 8, 1861 commissioned second lieutenant in the 1st cavalry, and in 1862 was promoted to the first lieutenancy. He served as senior major in the 2d Indiana cavalry until the battle of Shiloh, when he was made colonel of the regiment. He

received the brevet of first lieutenant in the regular army in 1862 for Shiloh, Tenn.; captain for Perrysville, Ky.; major, in 1863, for Chickamauga, Ga.; lieutnenant-colonel, in 1864, for cavalry operations in east Tennessee; colonel, in 1865, for capture of Montgomery, Ala., which was the capital of the Southern Confederacy. He was also brevetted brigadier-general in 1865, for services in the field, and major-general the same year for conspicuous gallantry. *It should be noted that these brevet appointments, with the exception of the final one as major-general, were in the regular army. In the U.S. volunteers, McCook was promoted from colonel of the 2d Indiana Cavalry to brigadier-general of volunteers on April 27, 1864, and was breveted major-general in 1865.* At Mossy Creek, with one division, he attacked two of Jackson's divisions, and captured eight battle-flags, 2,500 prisoners, and all of their artillery. He commanded the cavalry of the army of the Cumberland through the entire Atlanta campaign. Gen. McCook's most conspicuous service was in penetrating the enemy's line to prevent Gen. Taylor from reinforcing Gen. Hood, then shut up in Atlanta. He, with only 2,100 men, destroyed Hood's entire transportation train of 800 wagons and 3,000 horses and mules, which had been sent to the rear of Atlanta for safety, and captured three generals and over 200 field and line officers, besides a large body of men. On his return he encountered 4,000 of Wheeler's cavalry and two brigades of infantry, through which he was forced to cut his way, swimming the Chattahoochee river, rejoining the main army at Marietta, with a loss of 900 men and one-half his escort. He then proceeded South to the gulf, and received the surrender of all the troops in Georgia and Florida, amounting to over 19,000 men, and remained there as military governor of Florida until June, 1865.

Being unaware of the surrender of Lee, the 2d brigade of his command, under Col. La Grange, assaulted and captured West Point, Apr. 17, 1865, which was the last battle of the war. Upon his return to the North Gen. McCook married a granddaughter of Charles Thompson, the first secretary of the Continental congress. In 1866 he resigned his command to accept the appointment of minister to the Hawaiian islands, and during his term, negotiated a treaty of commercial reciprocity. In 1869 he was appointed by Pres. Grant governor of the territory of Colorado, which he found in great disorder. He organized a school system, and established a board of immigration, which greatly benefitted that section. Gen. McCook was instrumental in bringing the first railroad into Denver. He organized the water works, and was identified with all the large enterprises of the city, and was at one time the largest real estate owner in this section, and the largest taxpayer in Colorado. He was the first to advocate women's suffrage. His greatest service to the territory was in securing the transfer of the Ute Indians to Utah, which permitted the development of the rich mineral and agricultural lands which were opened for development and settlement, but which had been previously locked up in reservations. Gov. McCook lived to see fulfilled his prediction, which he made when assuming the gubernatorial chair, that within twenty-five years Colorado would no longer be on the frontier. At the earnest request of Pres. Grant he accepted the appointment of governor a second term, declining the postmaster-generalship. He was largely interested in the European telephone syndicate, and at one time was one of the purchasers of the celebrated Batopilos mines, the richest silver mines in Mexico. Gen. McCook's literary attainments and oratorical powers were of such a high order that, on the death of Gen. Thomas, he was selected to deliver the funeral oration. *He died Sept. 9, 1909.*

McCULLOCH, BEN, soldier, was born in Rutherford county, Tenn., Nov. 11, 1811. His father was an aide-de-camp of Gen. James Coffee, under Gen. Jackson in the Creek and British wars of 1812–15. His early life was spent in Dyer county, Tenn., where he had fair opportunities for an English education, but the teaching he loved best was that of nature; he seemed to possess an inborn faculty for every kind of wood-craft. Besides his farming labors, he served an apprenticeship as a raftsman and flat-boatman, in which occupation he developed the self-reliance so conspicuous in his later undertakings. In the fall of 1835, at very nearly the same time as his friend and neighbor, Col. David Crockett, he went to Texas, to aid that colony in its struggle for independence. He arrived in time to join the ranks of Gen Sam. Houston on the eve of the battle of San Jacinto. There, in command of a gun in the artillery, he displayed great coolness and dash; and there

he met Gen. Tom Green, Gen. W. P. Lane, and Ben C. Franklin—who became his life-long friends—as well as Gen. Houston, who had known him in his boyhood. When, in 1837, the army was disbanded, he became a citizen of Gonzales, and for ten or more years he was the chief defender of his section against Indian and Mexican inroads, and did gallant work in countless small engagements. He had no settled home, but such was his popularity among the people that a score of homes were always open to him, with provender for his squad of two or three trusty horses. In 1839 he was elected to the Texas congress by the people of Gonzales, and it was in connection with this election that a bitter feud arose between him and Col. Reuben Davis, which resulted in a duel, in which he received a severe wound in the arm, the use of which he never fully recovered. In the Indian raid of 1840 he was of the greatest service, both as a scout and in several considerable engagements. After the admission of Texas to the Union he was elected to the first state legislature, and in 1846 was appointed major-general of all the militia west of the Colorado. When the war with Mexico began he organized a company of picked scouts. He won great distinction at Monterey, where, advancing a hundred miles into the enemy's country, he discovered the exact strength of Santa Anna's forces, and gave to Gen. Taylor the suggestion which he adopted, of falling back to the easily defended La Angostura, that became the battle-field of Buena Vista. The exploits of McCulloch's rangers are to be found in "The Scouting Expeditions of McCulloch's Texas Rangers," written by Samuel C. Reid, a member of the company. At the height of the gold fever Col. McCulloch went to California, and was chosen sheriff of Sacramento. On his return to Texas in 1853 he was appointed U.S. marshal for the eastern district of the state. His great ability as a partisan soldier made him a valuable acquisition to the Confederate forces in the war which was now fast approaching. Though he refused the command of a regiment, he accepted the post of brigadier-general on the breaking out of hostilities. In 1861 he was appointed commander-in-chief of the southwestern division of the Confederate forces, and won the battle of Oak Hills, *usually called the battle of Wilson's Creek.* Afterward, joining his forces to those of Gen. Van Dorn, he made a successful attack upon Bentonville, then occupied by Gen. Sigel. On being driven from the city, Gen. Sigel joined Gen. Curtis at Elk Horn, or Pea Ridge, and it was while reconnoitring their combined forces that McCulloch met his death. He had ridden directly into a concealed company of sharpshooters, and a rifle-ball, entering his right side, pierced his heart, and he fell from his horse, mortally wounded. (See "Life and Services of Gen. Ben McCulloch," by Victor M. Rose.) He died near Elk Horn, March 7, 1862.

McDOWELL, IRWIN, soldier, was born in Ohio Oct. 18, 1818. He received his early education at the College of Troyes in France, and was graduated from West Point in 1838, becoming second lieutenant in the 1st artillery. He was recalled to the Military academy in 1841, and served for four years, first as assistant instructor in infantry tactics, and afterward as adjutant. On the outbreak of the Mexican trouble, he was appointed aide-de-camp to Gen. John E. Wool, and took a creditable part at the battle of Buena Vista in 1847, which earned for him the brevet of captain. He continued with the army of occupation for a while, and was then made assistant adjutant-general in the war department, serving in Washington, New York, and elsewhere. He

attained the rank of major March 31, 1856. In 1858 he visited Europe on leave of absence. After the civil war was declared he occupied himself in organizing volunteer companies at the capital until he was made brigadier-general May 14, 1861, and assigned to the command of the department of northeastern Virginia. On May 29th he was transferred to the army of the Potomac, placed at the head of 30,000 men, mostly raw recruits, and on July 16th was ordered to advance immediately and meet the Confederate forces under Gens. Beauregard and Johnston at Bull Run. A most able and masterly plan of campaign was doomed to be ineffectively executed, owing to undrilled troops. Three times the respective armies fought desperately for the position on the crest of the hill until late in the afternoon, when it remained in the hands of the Federalists; but Confederate reinforcements soon arrived, and the tide of battle was turned. McDowell's men, who had been on their feet since two o'clock in the morning, were now exhausted by fatigue, hunger and thirst, and physically unable to withstand the fierce attack of fresh troops; hence their disorderly retreat to Washington. As Gen. Sherman said, "it was one of the best planned battles, but one of the worst fought." Gen. McClellan was afterward assigned to the chief command of the army of the Potomac, and McDowell was given charge of the 1st corps, which later became known as the army of the Rappahannock. On March 14, 1862, he was made major-general of volunteers. He took part in the engagements of Cedar Mountain, Rappahannock Station, and the second battle of Manassas. Ill fortune, however, continued to follow him and he met with repeated defeats through no fault of his own. He was retired from active duty on the field Sept. 6, 1862. On July 1, 1864, he was assigned to the command of the department of the Pacific, and on July 27, 1865, he was transferred to the department of California, holding the latter office until March 31, 1868. Meanwhile he was mustered out of the volunteer service, and received the brevet of major-general, U.S.A., Sept. 1, 1866. In July, 1868, he was assigned to the department of the East, and on Nov. 25, 1872, he was promoted major-general. After this he had command of the division of the South until June 30, 1876, and again of the department of the Pacific until his retirement Oct. 15, 1882. Gen. McDowell never fully recovered from the shock of his discomfiture at Bull Run, for which defeat the public persisted in holding him responsible. A man of many refined tastes, he had an especial fondness for landscape gardening, and for some years was one of the park commissioners of San Francisco. In 1849 he married Helen Burden of Troy, N.Y. Mrs. McDowell died in New York city in 1891, leaving three children—Helen E., Eliza, and Henry Burden. Gen. McDowell died in San Francisco, May 4, 1885.

McLAWS, LAFAYETTE, soldier, was born at Augusta, Ga., Jan. 15, 1821. He was fitted for college at the schools of his native city, and in 1837 entered the University of Virginia. During his first year at this institution he received the appointment from his congressional district to a cadetship at the U.S. military academy. He left the university, and was admitted to West Point in 1838, and was graduated in the class of 1842. He gained his first army experience on the Indian frontier. On the outbreak of the Mexican war he was sent to the Texas frontier, and joined Gen. Zachary Taylor's army. Lieut. McLaws was at the occupation of Corpus Christi, the defence of Fort Brown, the battle

of Monterey, and the siege of Vera Cruz. The climate of Mexico undermining his health, he was detailed for recruiting duty, and returned to the United States. After peace was declared, he was made assistant adjutant-general of the department of New Mexico, holding the position for two years. In 1851 he was made captain of infantry. His army life was uneventful until 1858, when he took part in the expedition against the Mormons, and 1859–60 when he served in the campaign against the Navajo Indians. On the secession of Georgia, Capt. McLaws resigned his commission in the U.S. army, and offered his services to his state. On Sept. 25, 1861, he was commissioned as a brigadier-general in the Confederate army,

having in the meantime served as major of a corps of infantry, and as colonel of the 10th Georgia regiment. The bravery and knowledge of military discipline exhibited by him in the battle of Lee's Mill brought him into prominent notice, and his subsequent conduct in the retreat to Richmond, and at the battle of Williamsburg won for him the promotion as major-general on May 23, 1862. He commanded a division at the battles of Savage's Station and Malvern Hill, and on the retreat of the Federal army from the Virginia peninsula his division watched the operations at Harrison's Landing. After the defeat of Gen. Pope, and the withdrawal of the Federal forces to the defence of Washington, McLaws's division rejoined the army of northern Virginia in its March into Maryland. He was directed to capture Harper's Ferry and Maryland Heights. *Although McLaw's division captured Maryland Heights, "Stonewall" Jackson was the overall commander of the forces that captured Harpers Ferry.* McLaw rejoined the main army at Sharpsburg in time to restore the Confederate line, as the forces of Jackson and Hood were falling back in disorder. At Fredericksburg his division held the river bank opposite the city, and drove the Federal troops back in their efforts to storm Marye's Hill. At Chancellorsville he formed the right wing of the Confederate forces. At Gettysburg his division of Longstreet's corps assaulted and drove back Sickles's corps on the second day's fight. At Knoxville, in carrying out the orders of Longstreet against his own judgment, he assaulted Fort Sanders, and desisted from the attack when he found success impossible. *President Jefferson Davis and the War Department exonerated McLaws without a court martial.* At Salem Church he was in command, and defeated Gen. Sedgwick's assault. He was then ordered to the command of the district of Georgia, and opposed Sherman's march through the state, conducting the defence of Savannah, and opposing his march through South Carolina and North Carolina, commanding a division at the battle of Averysboro' on March 16, 1865, and of Goldsboro' on the 21st. He was ordered back to Augusta to resume command of the district of Georgia. Gen. Johnston's surrender included his command, and Gen. McLaws at once established himself in business at Augusta, and in 1875 was appointed collector of internal revenue, and in 1876 port warden of the city of Savannah. *He died July 24, 1897.*

McPHERSON, JAMES BIRDSEYE, soldier, was born *on a farm near Clyde, O., a dozen miles from Sandusky, O.,* Nov. 14, 1828. He was of Scotch descent, and but little is known of his childhood or early youth, which appears to have given no striking indications of his future distinction; although he would seem to have been, from the beginning, of a military turn of mind, yet he did not succeed in entering West

Point until he had reached the very last year in which entrance is possible, viz., twenty-one. But, once in the military academy, his remarkable qualities became immediately apparent. In the fourth class of 1850 he stood second, and in the second class of 1852, first, and he was graduated in 1853 at the head of a class of fifty-two members, among whom were Philip H. Sheridan, John B. Hood, and John M. Schofield, two of whom became generals-in-chief of the U.S. army. McPherson was brevetted second lieutenant of engineers, and was at once appointed assistant instructor of practical engineering at the military academy—a compliment never before nor since awarded to so young an officer. In 1854 he was appointed second lieutenant, and was made assistant engineer on the defences of New York harbor and in the improvements of the Hudson river below Albany. In this work he continued to be engaged until the winter of 1857, and made an impression on the citizens of Albany and that neighborhood on account of his kindness and gentleness of disposition and the modesty of his bearing. He was transferred to the Delaware river in 1857, charged with the

construction of Fort Delaware, and remained there until July of that year, when he was despatched to California, to superintend the erection of the fortifications on Alcatraz Island, in San Francisco bay; while at this post, he was also connected with the Pacific coast survey. In December 1858, McPherson was made first lieutenant. He continued in California during several years, and was on duty there when the civil war broke out. It would seem that McPherson's great military qualifications were lost in his remarkable ability as an engineer, while it is a fact, also, that at the beginning of the war the government had the idea that engineers would not be needed, and Gen. Scott was ridiculed for throwing up such elaborate defences in front of Washington. West Point education, even, was lightly esteemed by the public at large, and lawyers, merchants, and schoolmasters were honored with shoulder-straps, while McPherson was overlooked. He was, however, made a captain in 1861, and was ordered to Boston harbor to take charge of its fortifications; but when Maj.-Gen. Halleck was placed in command of the department of the West, McPherson was chosen his aide-de- camp and promoted to the rank of lieutenant-colonel, thus, as a matter of fact, placing upon Gen. Halleck's staff one who afterward became a greater soldier than himself. But even now McPherson saw but little field service, being chiefly engaged in engineering duty in Missouri until the beginning of 1862, when Grant began his movements on Forts Henry and Donelson. McPherson was then transferred to Gen. Grant's staff and made chief engineer. He remained with Grant until after the battle of Pittsburg Landing, for services in which he received honorable mention and was nominated for brevet lieutenant-colonel of engineers. McPherson superintended the engineering department while Halleck was making his approaches against Corinth, and he did everything in his power to carry out the plans of his commander. On May 15, 1862, he was appointed brigadier-general of volunteers, and on Halleck's being appointed to the chief command of all the Federal armies, and Gen. Grant to his place in the West, the latter made McPherson chief engineer over the U.S. military railroads in the department of West Tennessee. On Oct. 2d of that year he was placed in command of a brigade, and joined Gen. Rosecrans at the close of the battle of Corinth; being ordered by Rosecrans to pursue the enemy, he did so, over a broken country, hanging on the rear of the Confederate army until it broke and fled in every direction. McPherson was made major-general of volunteers, to date from Oct. 8, 1862, and on the 14th of that month he was placed in command of a division, with headquarters at Bolivia, Tenn. During the next two months he commanded the right wing of Grant's army, and was engaged in various skirmishes during the winter and until January, 1863, when he was in command of the 17th army corps. In the movements which resulted in the capture of Vicksburg, McPherson was Grant's right-hand man. After the battle of Port Gibson, in which he took part, he pushed the retreating enemy, overtaking them at Raymond, and, in one terrific charge, breaking their line into fragments. On May 14th he attacked Johnston's army at Jackson, captured the fortifications, and broke through the camp, chasing the flying foe into and through the town in confusion. He was engaged in the assaults on Vicksburg, May 19th and 22d, having the centre of Grant's army during the long siege which followed. On the 4th of July he led his columns into the conquered city, over which he was placed in command. Grant recommended McPherson for promotion in the regular army, using the strongest language, and he was accordingly promoted to brigadier-general in the regular army, the appointment to date from Aug. 1, 1863. His corps also voted Gen. McPherson a medal of honor. He continued with his headquarters at Vicksburg and in command, until February, 1864, and when Sherman succeeded Grant in command of the western

armies, McPherson took Sherman's place as commander of the army of the Tennessee. A painful episode of this part of McPherson's life was the fact that, being engaged to be married to a young lady in Baltimore, he was about taking leave of absence, in order to effect their union, when he received the latter appointment. He accordingly postponed his marriage until the great Atlanta campaign, which was being organized, should be completed. As a fact, he was destined never again to see his affianced. McPherson organized, at Mossbill, Ala., his portion of the army, *comprising the 15th corps and parts of the 16th and 17th corps.* Ordered by Sherman to turn the almost impregnable position of Johnston at Dalton, he made a circuitous march of thirty or forty miles with the hope of taking Resaca by surprise, but on reaching this point he saw this was impossible by assault, and accordingly fell back to Snake Creek Gap and reported to Sherman the state of affairs in his front. Hooker's corps was at once sent to his support, and McPherson stormed and carried the enemy's works. Johnston fought with desperate fury, striving to regain the lost position, but his efforts were in vain and he finally fell back. The Federal army moved forward, McPherson holding the right, occupying Kinston, and at Dallas, where the Confederate attack was directed wholly against McPherson's corps, he repelled it, inflicting heavy loss upon the Confederates. Johnston was superseded by Gen. John B. Hood, who had been McPherson's classmate at West Point, and a series of engagements followed, Hood endeavoring to prevent Sherman from flanking Atlanta. There was fighting from the 19th to the 21st of July. On the 22d Hood *attacked with one infantry corps plus cavalry—less than one half of his army—*against the left flank, which was in command of McPherson. The assault was made with terrible desperation, and for a time it seemed as if the Confederates would get in McPherson's rear and finish the battle with a blow. Meanwhile the magnificent figure of McPherson, mounted on his black horse, could be seen galloping through the smoke of the batteries, keeping his men well in line, until he discovered a gap between the 16th and 17th corps. It consisted of a piece of woods, through which there ran a country road, over which he had ridden a few hours before, and, having no idea that the enemy had even tried to occupy it, McPherson entered the woods, and sent the only officer remaining with him to Gen. Logan with orders to send up a brigade and close this gap. Then, accompanied by only one orderly, he dashed onward along the road, when he was suddenly confronted by the skirmish line of the Confederates, who ordered him to surrender. Startled at this unexpected meeting, McPherson drew his horse back on its haunches with a sudden pull, and then, raising his cap, made a graceful salutation, turned his horse quickly to the right and dashed to the woods, but a volley followed him, and he reeled from his saddle, pierced by several bullets, and fell dead. Soon after some Federal soldiers passing down the road saw the well-known horse riderless and wounded, and immediately searched for the general's body. He was found not fifty yards from the road, and still breathing, but in a few moments he ceased to live. When the news of McPherson's death reached Grant, he exclaimed, "The country has lost one of its best soldiers and I have lost my best friend," and is said to have burst into tears. His death carried grief into thousands of hearts, causing the death of the lady who was to have been his wife. McPherson's personal appearance was very commanding. He stood over six feet in height; his brow was lofty and noble; his eyes were clear and brilliant; and he had the appearance of a paladin of old. He was a superb rider, and the black horse which bore him to death, and which he had ridden through every battle from Shiloh, seemed to be almost equally inspired with himself amid the smoke and carnage of battle. Often McPherson would accompany in person his skirmishers, and wherever the heaviest fighting occurred, there he was to be found; always conspicuous by his commanding height and black horse, which had been made many a time the target of sharpshooters, but never hit. He was admired by his officers and beloved by all. He never used profane language, even in the heat of battle. A general capable of magnificent combinations, brave, energetic, determined, he permitted no plunder or lawless violence by his command; and his bright and noble career ended, leaving no stain upon his character or his reputation. The date of his death was July 22, 1864.

MEADE, GEORGE GORDON, soldier, was born in Cadiz, Spain, Dec. 31, 1815. He was the son of Richard Worsam Meade, a merchant of Philadelphia, who established himself in Cadiz, where he conducted a mercantile and shipping business, while, during the period between 1805 and 1816, he was United States naval agent at that port. George Gordon was born in the last year of his father's incumbency of this office, and soon after, the latter, who had become involved in litigation growing out of occurrences in the peninsular war, was imprisoned in Cadiz for two years and with difficulty was able to obtain his release through the influence of the United States minister. In the meantime, however, his family had been sent back to Philadelphia. Out of this Spanish matter there grew a very remarkable claim on the part of Mr. Meade, amounting to nearly half a million dollars and in the prosecution of

Gev. G. Meade

which the most celebrated lawyers of the country were engaged, including Webster, Clay, and Choate. Twice a bill enforcing the claim passed the senate and once it passed the house of representatives, but not going through both houses at the same session, it failed to become a law. Notwithstanding that Mr. Meade was sustained by a treaty, by documentary proofs, by a special affirmation of the Spanish cortes and by the royal sign manual, neither he nor his heirs were ever able to obtain the payment of this claim. As young Meade grew up he attended school at first in Philadelphia and subsequently, curiously enough, as a pupil in a school in Washington, D.C., which was conducted by Salmon P. Chase, afterward chief justice of the supreme court of the United States and who was secretary of the treasury when Meade was general-in-chief of the army of the Potomac. From this school he went to an institution at Mount Hope, near Baltimore, Md., and from there he proceeded to the West Point military academy, where in 1835 he was graduated with the rank of second lieutenant.

He was assigned to the 3d artillery and ordered to Florida, and there he served in the war of the United States government against the Seminole Indians. While in Florida his health failed, and he was obliged to leave that part of the country in order to save his life. He was detailed to conduct a party of Seminoles to a reservation in Arkansas, afterward being ordered to the Watertown arsenal, Mass., and was on ordnance duty there until Oct. 26, 1836, when he resigned from the army. Being offered the position of assistant civil engineer to aid in the construction of a railroad at Pensacola, Fla., Mr. Meade accepted it and remained there until the following April, when he was appointed by the war department to superintend a survey of the mouth of the Sabine river, Tex., and also to assist in the survey of the delta of the Mississippi, both of which duties he performed, being thus occupied until February, 1839. In 1840 Mr. Meade was employed in the astronomical branch of the expedition which was surveying the boundary line between the United States and Texas, and in the same year was assistant civil engineer in the survey of the northwestern boundary between the United States and British America. On Dec. 31, 1840, Mr. Meade married Margaretta, daughter of John Sergeant. He continued the survey of the northwestern boundary until the end of 1843, being appointed second lieutenant of topographical engineers May 19, 1842. From 1844 until the outbreak of the war with Mexico, he was engaged in surveying in Delaware Bay. In September, 1845, he joined the staff of Gen. Zachary Taylor at Corpus Christi, Tex., and during 1846, was engaged in the battles of Palo Alto and Resaca de la Palma, and was one of the force that occupied Matamoras. For brilliant conduct in the assault of Independence Hill at Monterey, Meade was brevetted first lieutenant. He was at the siege of Vera Cruz,

where he served as one of the aides of Gen. Robert Patterson of Pennsylvania. After the close of the war Lieut. Meade was engaged in the construction of lighthouses, from 1847 to 1856, except for a brief period when he was again fighting the Seminoles. He was commissioned first lieutenant of topographical engineers in 1851 and was made captain in 1856. At the time of the outbreak of the civil war, Capt. Meade was engaged in the northern lakes surveys, and on Aug. 31, 1861, was appointed brigadier-general of volunteers and assigned to the command of the 2d brigade Pennsylvania reserves. In the following year he was appointed major of topographical engineers. Gen. Meade was in command of a brigade in the battles of Mechanicsville, Gaines's Mills, and Newmarket Cross Roads, and at the latter engagement received a severe wound which necessitated his being taken to his home in Philadelphia. Here, after treatment, he gradually recovered, when he rejoined the army and was present at the second battle of Bull Run, 29th and 30th of August, 1862. When Lee invaded Maryland, Gen. Meade commanded the Pennsylvania reserves, and was at the battle of South Mountain. At Antietam, McClellan placed him in command of the 1st corps when Gen. Joseph Hooker was wounded, a special compliment to his admirable service in that engagement. In the autumn of 1862, at Fredericksburg, Meade's division succeeded in breaking through "Stonewall" Jackson's line, and here Meade had two horses shot under him. Finding his command in face of the enemy's reserves, and not being supported, he was obliged to fall back. His commission as major-general was dated Nov. 29, 1862, and on Dec. 25th he was given command of the 5th army corps, which command he held at the battle of Chancellorsville. Gen. Meade had loomed up so rapidly among the Federal leaders that his promotion was more than usually rapid, as the administration discovered his peculiar ability to lead large bodies of men, and his natural gift for understanding strategy and army tactics. In June, 1863, the army of the Potomac was encamped about *Frederick, Md.,* while Lee had marched up the Cumberland valley. Hooker was in command, and *on the 28th* Gen. Meade was ordered to relieve him, a surprise to him as it was to the country. Meade at once took the offensive, and though but little aware of the strength either of the enemy or of his own forces, he began to follow Lee on parallel lines, guarding he mountain passes as he moved on, in order to protect Baltimore, and by forced marches on the opposite side of South Mountain from Lee, gradually approached what was to be the field of Gettysburg. Lee concentrated his army on the east of South Mountain, while Meade moved along Pike creek, throwing out his left wing in the neighborhood of Gettysburg, and as the two armies approached each other on the morning of July 1st, the advance-guard of the Confederate column had a slight collision with national cavalry. Gen. Reynolds was in command, and he at once supported his cavalry with infantry, but these found the Confederates in great force and were obliged to fall back on the town, and Reynolds fell, mortally wounded. As soon as Meade heard of the loss of this great general, he ordered Gen. Hancock to take command at Gettysburg. The latter made the best disposition possible of the two army corps which had already been driven back by the Confederates, and being instructed by Meade to appoint the place for the battle which should seem in his judgment best disposed for the Federal forces, he sent a messenger to Meade, recommending the selection of Gettysburg as a defensive position and that the Federal army should be concentrated there. Meade agreeing to this, Hancock occupied Cemetery Ridge during the night, Lee being posted further west on Seminary Ridge. *Around midnight of July 1–2d,* Meade arrived at the front and the Confederates opened the fight by attacking the Federal left and left centre, where they soon routed the 3d corps; strong reinforcements coming up, the Federal troops seized Little Round Top, a most important position. On the morning of the 3d, Gen. Ewell being entrenched on the right of the Federal line, Meade attacked him and succeeded in driving him out, whereupon a desperate artillery fire commenced on the part of the Confederates, with 145 guns, which were replied to by eighty

Federal cannon on Cemetery Ridge. Just after this terrible artillery fire, Gen. Pickett's division of Longstreet's corps made its celebrated attack on Meade's centre, his men marching up almost to the Federal lines under a terrific fire of infantry and artillery poured in on all sides, which at length nearly annihilated the division. Meade now ordered an advance on the left of the line and drove back Hood's division, which ended the fight for the day, and in fact altogether. Both armies remained in position during the 4th, on which evening Lee retreated to the Potomac, where he threw up intrenchments. Meade followed, but so slowly that he did not come up with the Confederates until the 12th, when he would have attacked, but decided against it in deference to the conclusion of a council of war. During the night of the 13th the Confederate army crossed the river. The battle of Gettysburg was one of the most magnificent of modern times. A serious misfortune was the loss of Gen. John F. Reynolds in the beginning of the action; and another the fall of Gen. Hancock at the most critical moment, when he was desperately wounded, though he did not leave the field until victory was assured. In this terrific conflict, for three days the largest armies handled in modern warfare maintained a fierce and persistent struggle. More than 200 pieces of artillery at intervals of this dreadful drama woke the echoes of the surrounding hills. The Confederate force engaged at Gettysburg was about 69,000 men, while the effective strength of the army of the Potomac is said to have been between 82,000 and 84,000 men, a superiority however, which was greatly neutralized by the fatigue of long marches. On the Federal side, 23,210 were killed, wounded, or missing; no accurate account of the Confederate loss was ever obtained, *but modern scholarship has established casualties at*

24,000–28,000, of which number nearly 14,000 were taken prisoners. Both Meade and Hancock were the recipients of universal praise and admiration on the part of their countrymen for the magnificent handling of the army of the Potomac in this conflict. As a reward for his extraordinary success, vital at this period of the war, Gen. Meade was commissioned brigadier-general in the regular army, his commission dating July 3, 1863. During the next six months, the army of the Potomac was kept comparatively inactive until the series of actions which began with Bristoe's Station and ended at Mine Run in December 1863. Gen. Meade's experience during the two years in which he held the command of the army of the Potomac was the reverse of that of most of the other officers who filled the same position. He met with no defeat, while his successes, culminating in the splendid victory at Gettysburg, were highly creditable to his courage and generalship. Meade was in every campaign of the army of the Potomac from the time of its formation, and in every one of its battles, except two. On Aug. 8 1864, he was promoted to be major-general in the United States army, and as a special honor was given the command of the grand review which took place in Washington after the close of the war. His next service was the command of the military division of the Atlantic until August, 1866, when he was placed in command of the department of the East. Between January, 1868, and the time of his death, he commanded the military district embracing Georgia and Alabama, then the department of the South, which included the same states, with South Carolina and Florida added, and at last, again, the military division of the Atlantic. Gen. Meade was a member of the American philosophical society, of the Pennsylvania historical society, of the Philadelphia academy of natural sciences, and held the degree of LL.D from Harvard. He was also one of the commissioners of Fairmount park, where was dedicated Oct. 18, 1887, an equestrian statue of him, designed by Milne Calden. Gen. Meade died in Philadelphia Nov. 6, 1872, the immediate cause of his death being pneumonia, complicated by a condition resulting from the bad wound which he had received at the battle of Newmarket Cross Roads.

MEADE, RICHARD WORSAM, naval officer, was born in New York city, Oct. 9, 1837, a son of Capt. R. W. Meade, U.S.N., and nephew of Gen. G. G. Meade, U.S.A. He was appointed a midshipman from California (the first military or naval appointment from that state) Oct. 2, 1850. He was graduated June 21, 1856, number five in a class originally composed of sixty-two members. During his career as midshipman he served in the sloop Preble, steamer San Jacinto, sloop St. Louis and frigate Columbia, and was present at the celebrated Koszta affair in Smyrna, July, 1853. After graduation at the naval academy he served in the steam frigate Merrimac, and on her return home from Europe was promoted to be acting master and lieutenant, and served in the corvette Cumberland and sloop Dale on the west coast of Africa. He was navigating officer of the Cumberland when only nineteen years of age, and received his commission as lieutenant Jan. 23, 1858. Lieut. Meade served subsequently in the steamer Saranac and sloop Cyane, in the Pacific ocean, and on the breaking out of the civil war, applied for immediate service on the Atlantic seaboard, which was refused by Secretary Toucey. Subsequently, he was taken ill with fever at Acapulco, Mex., barely escaping with his life. He was invalided and sent East, reaching the New York hospital in August, 1861, a few days after the battle of Bull

Run. He immediately applied for active service, but his health was in such condition that the surgeons recommended shore duty (the first he had ever had), and he was detailed to instruct volunteer officers in practical gunnery on the receiving ship Ohio, lying at Boston, during the winter of 1861. Among the men in this class were acting-masters Wheeler and Tibbitts, who, on leaving, went directly to the Kearsarge, and commanded the pivot guns that in 1864 sunk the Alabama. Lieut. Meade soon went to sea as first lieutenant of the steam sloop Dacotah, but his health broke down, and he lay in hospital at Chelsea two months. As soon as he was able to resume duty he joined Dupont's squadron as first lieutenant of the steamer Conemaugh, and when promoted to be lieutenant-commander, July 17, 1862, went to the Mississippi flotilla as commander of the ironclad steamer Louisville. For a time (and before he was twenty-five years of age) he commanded a division of the squadron consisting of seven vessels (four of them iron-clads) stationed off Helena, Ark., where Gen. Curtis's army was encamped. He was very

active in co-operating with Gen. W. T. Sherman in breaking up guerrilla warfare on the Mississippi, and was highly commended by Adm. Porter in official despatches. He was disabled and sent East on crutches in January, 1863, served a time on ordnance duty, and subsequently commanded the chartered steamer United States in her cruise after the Tacony; the former was the only vessel that got on the Tacony's track, arriving in Portland harbor too late, unfortunately, to prevent the Confederate officer Reed's capture of the Cushing, which occurred the day before the arrival of the United States. Lieut.-Com. Meade commanded the naval battalion of seamen and marines during the July riots of 1863 in New York city, and for the entire week maintained almost perfect order in the limits of his own down-town district, which included the arsenal on Worth street, the custom-house, sub-treasury, and down-town banks. Later, in September, 1863, he commanded the steam gunboat Marblehead in the operations against Charleston, S.C., being stationed in the Stono river, and almost constantly engaged in operations against the enemy or on picket duty. Christmas-day, 1863, witnessed the battle on Stono inlet, S.C.; the enemy, under Gen. H. A. Wise and Col. del Kemper, were stationed behind earthworks, and with siege and light artillery, a force of sixteen guns and a full regiment of infantry attacked the little gunboat, which was disabled in one of her boilers before the fight commenced, and had, all told, only seventy men. The Marblehead maintained a most determined fight, held her position, and, the steamer Pawnee and mortar schooner Williams coming to her aid, the enemy was routed with the loss of two 8-inch siege guns and many men. The Marblehead lost three men killed and six wounded, and was struck thirty times in the hull and many times aloft. Lieut.-Com. Meade, though slightly wounded in the foot by a flying fragment of the fore-bit casting, volunteered at once to bring off the abandoned guns, and heading a force of 100 men from the three ships, removed them from the deserted earthworks Dec. 28, 1863—that being the date selected by the senior officer, Capt. Balch, for the expedition. Capt. Balch of the Pawnee, division commander, reported to the admiral as follows: "I desire to bear my testimony to the skill and bravery of Lieut.-Com. Meade, who, under a sharp fire, worked his guns with great rapidity, and handled his vessel admirably." Adm. Dahlgren issued a general order, to be read on every quarter-deck in the squadron, composed of some eighty vessels, thanking Lieut.-Com. Meade for his service in face of the enemy, and subsequently both admirals, Porter and Dahlgren, recommended him for promotion for "gallant conduct in face of the enemy"—a promotion he never received, the list stopping just short of his name, his classmate, Ramsey, who graduated just ahead of him, being the last in the advanced list. The Marblehead needing extensive repairs, Lieut.-Com. Meade was ordered to the command of the steam gunboat Chocura, in Adm. Farragut's fleet, and finished the war in the western gulf blockading squadron. The Chocura was very active on the Texas and Louisiana coasts, harassing the enemy and capturing or destroying light blockade runners, six of which were under the British flag. On the night of Jan. 22, 1865, Lieut.-Com. Meade headed an expedition of forty men, in three boats, which cut out of the Calcasieu river, and destroyed the blockade runner Delphina, for which service he was officially thanked by Com. Palmer, commanding the squadron in the absence of Adm. Farragut. After the war Meade was stationed at the naval academy, Annapolis, under his old commander, Adm. Porter, and acted as head of the department of seamanship and naval tactics, reorganizing the drill and routine of the department, and introducing the important study of naval construction as part of the academic course. He also prepared and compiled works on "Boat Exercise," and "Naval Construction," which were used in the course. During his term of service at the academy he commanded the Santee, Marblehead, and Dale during the summers of 1865–66–67. Leaving the academy in 1868, he took command of the steamer Saginaw and

served in Alaska during the winter of 1868–69. He was principally occupied in surveying, and keeping quiet refractory Indians of the Kake tribe. This tribe having murdered two white traders, Walker and Manger, Com. Meade (who had been promoted to that grade Sept. 20, 1868) took thirty soldiers on board from the garrison at Sitka and laid waste the Kake settlements, destroying their villages and forcing them to seek terms at the hands of Gen. Davis, the commander of the military department. On the return of the Saginaw to San Francisco, the vessel being a lieutenant-commander's, Com. Meade was detached, and served on special and ordnance duty until July, 1870, when he was detailed to fit out the celebrated yacht America, and sail her in the race of Aug. 8, 1870, against Mr. Ashbury's yacht Cambria, which had just beaten Mr. Bennett's yacht Dauntless in the ocean race. The America beat the Cambria over four miles in this race over a course of nearly fifty miles, coming in number four out of some twenty-three yachts entered. Shortly after this Com. Meade was ordered to the command of the steamer Narragansett, and made a long cruise in the Pacific ocean, passing 431 days underway in a cruise of twenty-four months and sailing nearly 60,000 miles—mainly under canvas. The coal bill of this steamer for this long cruise was less than $13,000, and she visited almost every quarter of the Pacific ocean, as far as Australia. It was Com. Meade who negotiated the original treaty that gave the coaling station of Pago-pago, in the island of Tutuita, Samoan group, to the United States. President Grant recommended that Com. Meade's treaty be ratified by the senate. It was not done, but the secretary of the navy commended him for "great judgment and skill" in negotiating this commercial treaty and had it been ratified, nearly all the subsequent trouble in Samoa would have been avoided. After Com. Meade's return home, in May, 1873, he was detailed as inspector of ordnance at the N.Y. navy-yard, and served on that duty nearly three years. He subsequently acted as president of a board to revise the ordnance instructions, after which he was detailed to command the steam corvette Vandalia on the West India station, and served in command of that vessel about thirty-nine months—being promoted to the grade of captain March 13, 1880. Only one death occurred on the ship in all that time, and at the most unhealthy of all the naval stations. In April, 1882, Rear-Adm. Wyman, commanding the north Atlantic station, wrote officially to the naval department: "I cannot too highly commend Capt. Meade for the zeal, energy and intelligence he has displayed. . . . As a commanding officer he has no superior." From July, 1882, to July, 1883, he served on the board of inspection and survey and aided in clearing the navy list of the obsolete wooden vessels that he had written against in the columns of the "Army and Navy Journal" as far back as 1873, under the caption, "Thoughts on Naval Administration," in which iron ships were recommended, but, unfortunately, got no hearing. Capt. Meade served as second in command of the navy-yard, New York, from July, 1883, to March, 1884, and then, securing

a long furlough, took service as assistant to the first vice-president and general manager of the Missouri Pacific railway system when it included 10,000 miles of track and 52,000 employees. In November, 1885, having previously dissolved his connection with the railway, he offered his services to Secretary Whitney, and was detailed to command the notorious Dolphin. He took her out on a cruise, and gave her a thorough trial off Cape Hatteras in a gale of wind in December, 1885, and Secretary Whitney subsequently accepted her on his report. While he proved that she *was not* structurally weak, and that her engines were reliable, he characterized her as "a species of marine crazy quilt," of little use as a naval vessel, being rather a large and very expensive yacht, unsuited to the needs of the U.S. navy. After the cruise Capt. Meade served as president of the inventory board, and his report to Secretary Whitney led to an entire and radical change in the naval methods of bookkeeping and storekeeping. In September, 1887, he was ordered as commandant of the Washington navy-yard, and during his three years' term of service the new gun-factory was built, the tools installed, including three large Morgan traveling cranes, one of which is the largest traveling crane in America. A railway was built to connect the yard with the Pennsylvania system

and all the trunk lines, and a fine electric-lighting plant installed. Better methods of work were introduced and politics eliminated from the yard, as far as the naval department would allow. After Sept. 15, 1890, Capt. Meade was on duty as the naval representative of the government board of the World's Columbian exposition at Chicago, the headquarters of the board being in Washington. Capt. Meade, during his naval career, served in twenty-four vessels of all classes, and commanded twelve. He was the author of a pamphlet on "Boat Exercise," a compilation on shipbuilding, and translated numerous professional pamphlets from the French into the English language, besides contributing to the leading magazines, etc., professional and otherwise, of the country. In June, 1865, he was married to Rebecca, daughter of Rear-Adm. Paulding, U.S. navy, and granddaughter of John Paulding, the leader of the trio that captured Maj. André in 1781. He had five children—one son (who beared his name) and four daughters. *Meade retired as rear admiral in 1895 and died in 1897.*

MEAGHER, THOMAS FRANCIS, soldier, was born in Waterford, Ireland, Aug. 3, 1823. His father, a wealthy merchant in the Newfoundland trade, was a member of parliament for several years. When nine years old, young Meagher was sent to the Jesuit college of Clongowes Wood, County Kildare, where he remained six years and then entered Stonyhurst college, near Preston, England. He was graduated from that institution in 1843, and shortly afterward espoused the Irish cause. He made his first appearance as a public speaker at the great national meeting at Kilkenny, over which Daniel O'Connell presided. In 1846 he joined the "Young Ireland" party. In 1848 he was sent to Paris with an address from the Irish confederation to the provisional government of

France. On March 21st of that year he was arrested on a charge of sedition, and after the passage of the treason felony act was arrested again, and in October was convicted of treason and sentenced to death. This sentence was finally commuted to banishment for life, and on July 9, 1849, he was transported to Van Dieman's Land. He, however, escaped in 1852, and took ship for the United States. He settled in New York, studied law, and was admitted to the bar, but when the civil war broke out, he at once joined the 69th N.Y. regiment of volunteers under Col. Corcoran. He was acting major at the first battle of Bull Run, where his horse was shot under him. Returning to New York after the expiration of the three months' term of service, he organized the "Irish brigade," was elected colonel of the 1st regiment, and was later assigned to the command of the brigade, his commission as brigadier-general dating from Feb. 3, 1862. He led his brigade with notable bravery during the seven days' battles around Richmond, Va., and at the second battle of Bull Run, Fredericksburg, and Antietam, where again a horse was shot under him. He was wounded in the leg at Fredericksburg, and after Chancellorsville his brigade was so decimated that he resigned from the service. In the spring of 1864, however, he was recommissioned brigadier-general of volunteers, and assigned to the command of the district of Etowah. In January, 1865, he was ordered to join Gen. Sherman in Savannah, but performed no further active service. He was mustered out of the army in 1865, was appointed secretary of Montana territory and in September, 1866, he became governor *pro tempore*, pending the absence of Gov. Sidney Edgerton. Subsequently the hostile attitude of the Indians compelled him to take active measures of defence. Gen. Meagher was the author of "Speeches on the Legislative Independence of Ireland" (New York, 1852), which ran through six editions. While engaged in reconnoitering on the Missouri river, he fell from the deck of a steamboat and was drowned July 1, 1867.

MEIGS, MONTGOMERY CUNNINGHAM, soldier, was born at Augusta, Ga., May 13, 1816, the son of Charles Delucena Meigs and Mary Montgomery. His father was a lineal descendent of Vincent Meigs, who emigrated to America and settled in Connecticut in 1634. His mother's ancestors settled at Eglinton, N.J., 1702. Montgomery C. Meigs was educated at the Franklyn institute and at the University of Pennsylvania until he attained the age of sixteen. He then entered the West Point military academy, from which he was graduated in the class of 1836, and was commissioned a lieutenant in the 1st artillery. The following year he was made a lieutenant in the engineer corps, and promoted a first lieutenant in 1838, and made captain in 1853. While serving in the engineer corps he was employed on the works for the improvement of the navigation of the Delaware river, and upon the Delaware

breakwater, under command of Capt. Delafield. He assisted Capt. Robert E. Lee in the surveys of the harbor of St. Louis and the rapids of the Mississippi river at Des Moines and Rock Island, built Fort Wayne on the Detroit river, and had charge of the construction of Fort Montgomery at the outlet of Lake Champlain. He was superintending engineer of these and other constructions from 1831–49. He was employed in the engineer bureau of Washington, D.C., from 1849–50. He made the surveys and plans for the Potomac aqueduct

at Washington, D.C. These plans having been adopted by congress in 1853, he constructed the work, including that triumph of engineering art, the Cabin John and the Rock Creek bridges. He was also in charge of the construction of the wings of the capitol and of its iron dome, and of the halls of the capitol. In 1860 he was ordered to Florida to take charge of the building of Fort Jefferson, but was recalled to Washington in February, 1861, and was present at the inauguration of President Lincoln. In April, 1861, he was ordered by the president to plan and organize an expedition for the relief of Fort Pickens, Pensacola, which was then threatened by the Confederate troops. This expedition saved Fort Pickens and secured to the United States the important harbor of Pensacola. Capt. Meigs was commissioned colonel of the 11th infantry on May 14, 1861; quartermaster-general, U.S. army, May 15, 1861, with rank of brigadier-general, which he held until he was retired as over sixty-two years of age, on Feb. 6, 1882. As quartermaster-general he was present at the first battle of Bull Run and during the siege and the battle of Chattanooga. He visited the armies of Gen. McClellan, Gen. Butler, and Gen. Grant during the operations on the Potomac, the James, and in front of Richmond, and for a time had personal charge of the base of supplies of the army of the Potomac. He was made a *brevet* major-general on July 5, 1864, and shortly afterward visited Savannah, where he met Gen. W. T. Sherman, and refitted his army at Goldsborough and at Raleigh. His duties in charge of the vast business of equipping and supplying the large armies kept him principally confined to the offices of the quartermaster's department at Washington. Subsequent to the civil war he remained at Washington, and in connection with his official duties inspected the workings of departments under his supervision. He went abroad on account of ill health in 1867, and again in 1875 on special service to study the construction and government of European armies. In 1876 he was a member of the commission for the reform and reorganization of the army. Gen. Meigs was also a member of the board to prepare plans and specifications for the war department building, and the National museum. He was regent of the Smithsonian institute, a member of the National academy of sciences, and various scientific societies. From 1861–82 he

published annual reports of the quartermaster's department, as well as other government reports. After he was retired in 1882, he was selected as architect, and supervised the construction of the Pension bureau at Washington, congress having made an appropriation for this building with the proviso that it should be erected under the supervision of Gen. Meigs. He died at Washington, D.C., Jan. 2, 1892.

MEMMINGER, CHRISTOPHER GUSTAVUS, statesman, was born in Wurtemburg, Ger., *Jan. 9, 1803*. His father was a captain in the service of the Elector of Swabia. His grandfather was an officer in the University of Batinhausen. His father died during his infancy, and his mother, in company with some relatives, emigrated to America and settled at Charleston, S.C., where she soon afterward died. The friendless orphan attracted the attention of Thomas Bennett, who educated him. Mr. Memminger was graduated from the South Carolina College and subsequently studied law; was admitted to practice at the bar, and began

his professional career at Charleston. He entered public life at the time of the nullification excitement, and took his position as a member of the Federal party, actively opposing the nullification movement. In 1836 he was elected to the legislature, and at once took a prominent part in legislative discussions. He was made chairman of the committee on ways and means, and was for sixteen years instrumental in directing the financial policy of the state. Mr. Memminger took a particular interest in educational affairs, and in 1834, in connection with W. J. Bennett, undertook the reformation and reorganization of the public-school system of South Carolina. After working against innumerable obstacles, combating violent prejudices and persistent obstructions, he obtained a success, the appreciation of which is sufficiently proven to posterity by the presence of his bust in the council chamber of Charleston. Upon the base is inscribed, "Christopher Gustavus Memminger, founder of the present public school system in Charleston. The city board of school commissioners erect this memorial in grateful appreciation of his services for thirty-three years." In 1859 he was appointed to appear before the Virginia legislature as special commissioner from South Carolina, and when the state seceded, was elected and represented South Carolina in the convention called to frame a constitution and organize a government for the Confederate states. He was made chairman of the committee in the convention that met at Montgomery, Ala., to draft the constitution. When the government was organized, President Davis appointed Mr. Memminger secretary of the treasury, which position he retained until the last year of the civil war. Like the majority of the Confederate leaders, he accepted in good faith the issue of the war, and refraining from taking part in politics, turned his attention

toward the peaceful adjustment of affairs. His closing years were spent in solidifying the educational structure he had reared in his native state. One of his last efforts in the legislature was in defence of higher education. The character of this great Carolinian was thus summarized by one of his contemporaries: "Mr. Memminger was a man of varied talents. To see him leading the assembly by the force of his arguments, on almost any subject before that body, one would say he was a born statesman. To observe him at the head of a finance committee, it would seem that nature intended him for a minister of the treasury. To know him in a court of equity, it seemed as if he had devoted himself entirely to that branch of jurisprudence. While, to follow him in a court of law before a jury, you would be struck with his marvelous power in dealing with the facts of a case." His prolonged popularity in South Carolina was the result of his acknowledged integrity of character, talents and great business capacity. He died on the 7th of March, 1888, and was buried in the churchyard of St. John's-in-the-Wilderness, at Flat Rock, N.C.

MEREDITH, SOLOMON, soldier, was born in Guilford county, N.C., May 29, 1810. His early education was meagre. When nineteen years old he worked at any available manual employment that offered, devoting his earnings toward securing an education. *He had moved from North Carolina to Indiana in 1829.* In 1840, at the age of thirty, he was chosen sheriff of the county in 1844 and 1846; served in the state legislature 1846–49, and in the latter year became U.S. marshal for the district of Indiana. In 1854 he again served in the legislature. At the breaking out of the civil war he was elected colonel of the 19th Indiana volunteer infantry, was ordered to Virginia, and had his first

S. Meredith

experience at Gainesville, Va., where he was wounded, and half his effective force lost or crippled. Oct. 6, 1862, he was promoted brigadier-general of volunteers, and commanded the celebrated Iron brigade. In April, 1863, he forced a crossing of the Rappahannock, and took part in the battle of Chancellorsville. On July 1, 1863, he opened the three days' battle of Gettysburg, and swinging around his iron brigade at a critical juncture, captured 800 men, including their commander. Gen. Meredith was wounded so severely as to be disabled till November, 1863. He was then ordered to the command of Cairo, Ill., and in September, 1864, to the command in Paducah, Ky., where he remained till the close of the war. He was brevetted major-general of volunteers, and retired to his home. He served as surveyor-general of Montana, in 1867–69, then went into private life, devoting himself to his estate, Oakland farm, where he engaged in raising fine stock, and dispensed a generous hospitality. Gen. Meredith had a commanding presence, standing six feet six inches in height, was strongly built, and excelled in oratory. He took an active part in securing the passage of various

state school laws, and was interested in the Indiana central railroad, being for a long time its financial agent. Three of his sons served in the army, but only one returned. *Meredith died Oct. 2, 1875.*

MERRITT, WESLEY, soldier, was born in New York City, *June 16, 1834,* son of John Willis and Julia Ann (De Forrest) Merritt. He was educated in the schools of his native city and in the West, and in 1855 received appointment to the U.S. Military Academy, West Point, where he was graduated in 1860. He was assigned at once to the cavalry service as brevet second lieutenant of dragoons. On Jan. 28, 1861, he was commissioned second lieutenant; on May 13th, first lieutenant; *and on April 5, 1863,* appointed captain in the 2d U.S. cavalry. Meantime, until September, 1862, he was attached to the army of the Potomac in the Virginia peninsular campaign on the staff of Gen. Philip St. George Cooke. Then being transferred to the headquarters of the department of defences, Washington, D.C., under command of Gen. Heintzelmann, he continued until April, 1862, when he was attached to the staff of Gen. Stoneman. He was an active participant in the raid on Richmond, Va., *May 3, 1863,* and having left the staff, commanded as captain his own regiment, the 2d cavalry, at the cavalry battle of Beverly Ford, June 9, 1863, and in July was brevetted major for bravery at the battle of Gettysburg, where he was in command of the cavalry regular brigade. He was brevetted lieutenant-colonel, May 4, 1864, for gallantry at the battle of Yellow Tavern, Va., and colonel, May 28th, having, meantime, been raised to the rank of captain in the 2d cavalry, April 5, 1862, and of brigadier-general of volunteers, June 29, 1863, for gallantry at the battle of Beverly Ford. During 1864 he was in command of a cavalry brigade in Virginia under Gen. Sheridan; was present at the battles of Opequan, Cedar Creek and Fisher's Hill; commanded a division of cavalry with Sheridan in the Shenandoah valley campaign; on Oct. 19th was brevetted major-general of volunteers, and distinguished himself at Five Forks and Sailor's Creek. At the battle of Winchester a part of Merritt's cavalry division, after repeated charges, supported by the infantry, turned Gen. Early's line at the decisive moment, throwing him into retreat. Later, he defeated Gen. Kershaw's division, infantry and cavalry, in an attempt to force a passage of the Shenandoah, near Cedarville, inflicting a heavy loss. In the remainder of the campaign, he won repeated distinction, and was one of the three Federal commissioners to arrange terms of surrender at Appomattox. On April 1, 1865, he was commissioned major-general of volunteers for gallantry at Five Forks. Later he participated in a movement against Gen. Joseph E. Johnston in North Carolina, then being transferred to the military division of the southwest and the department

of Texas in command of the cavalry forces, and was finally chief of the military division of the Gulf until Dec. 31, 1865. In the fall of 1866 he was appointed lieutenant-colonel of the 9th cavalry, and employed on inspection duty at the headquarters of the department of the Gulf until February, 1867. In 1869 he was in Texas with his regiment, and at St. Louis, Mo., where he was a member of the general tactics board until December, 1870. From that time until 1875 he was stationed again in Texas, and during the next two years was inspector of cavalry in the military division of the Missouri. He was commissioned colonel of the 5th cavalry, July 1, 1876, and took part in the expedition against the Sioux under Gen. Crook; being afterwards appointed chief of cavalry of the Big Horn and Yellowstone expeditions, then assigned to forts D. A. Russell and Laramie, W.T. He was appointed superintendent of the U.S. Military Academy at West Point, in July, 1882, and continued in that position until 1887, when he was commissioned brigadier-general and assigned to the command of the department of the Missouri. In 1895 he was promoted major-general and assigned to command of department with headquarters in Chicago, and in 1897 appointed to the command of the department of the East, with headquarters at Governor's island, New York harbor. In June, 1898, during the Spanish war, he was appointed military governor of the Philippine islands, and sailing from San Francisco with an army of 8,000 men on June 29th arrived at Manila, July 25th. On Aug. 25th a pre-arranged attack on Manila was made, the trenches being stormed by the land forces under Gen. Merritt, while a division of Adm. Dewey's fleet shelled the forts at Malate, on the south side of the city. The Spanish were forced back by the army and retreated into the walled city, and there, seeing that further

resistance was useless, capitulated. Gen. Merritt went at once to the palace, where the Spanish soldiers surrendered their arms. On Aug. 27th he issued a proclamation to the Filipinos, and on Aug. 30th sailed from Manila on board the steamer China, under orders to proceed to Paris, where the peace commission was then sitting. He left the China at Hong Kong and continued his journey *via* the Suez canal, arriving at Port Said, Sept. 28th; going thence by way of Marseilles to Paris, where he arrived on Oct. 3d. On the two following days the American peace delegates devoted their entire session to a conference with Gen. Merritt, who detailed to the commission his own opinions and those of Adm. Dewey concerning the physical, geographical, moral and political conditions prevailing in the Philippine islands. On his return home, on Dec. 30th, he was relieved of the command of the department of the Pacific, and from all further duties pertaining to the Philippine islands, and was ordered to proceed to New York and assume once more the command of the department of the East. Gen. Merritt was one of the ablest and most experienced officers in the U.S. army, and always held the esteem and respect of his associates in the many important positions he so adequately filled. He was twice married: first, in 1871, to Caroline Warren, of Cincinnati, O., who died in 1893; second, Oct. 23, 1898,

to Laura, daughter of Norman Williams, of Chicago, Ill. *He died Dec. 3, 1910.*

MILES, NELSON APPLETON, soldier, was born at Westminster, Mass., Aug. 8, 1839, son of Daniel and Mary (Curtis) Miles. His earliest American ancestor was Rev. John Miles, a Baptist minister and educator, who emigrated from Wales in 1662 and settled at Swansea, Mass.; he served in King Philip's war. Nelson A. Miles was reared on his father's farm, and received a district school and academic education. In 1856 he went to Boston, where his uncles, George and Nelson Curtis, obtained a position for him in the crockery store of John Collamore. He had mastered military science at the school conducted by N. Salignac, a French colonel, and at the outbreak of the civil war he raised a company of volunteers and offered his services to his country. In September, 1861, he was appointed a captain in the 22d Massachusetts volunteers, but was considered too young for the responsibility of that command, which he was required to resign, being given a lieutenant's commission instead. On May 31, 1862, he was commissioned by Gov. Morgan lieutenant-colonel of the 61st New York volunteers. He was promoted colonel Sept. 30, 1862; was made a brigadier-general May 12, 1864, and major-general, Oct. 21, 1865. He received the appointment of colonel of the 40th U.S. infantry, July 28, 1866; was transferred to the 5th infantry, March 16, 1869; promoted brigadier-general, U.S. army, Dec. 15, 1880, and, major-general, April 5, 1890. He saw severe active service during the seven days' fighting on the peninsula of the James river and before Richmond in the summer of 1862, and was severely wounded at Fair Oaks. During the period between the battle of Fair Oaks and the change of base to Harrison's Landing, Miles acted as adjutant-general to the 1st brigade, 1st division, 2d army corps; but at Fredericksburg he led his regiment, the 61st New York volunteers. In the battle of Chancellorsville he was so severely wounded that he was not expected to recover, and was brevetted brigadier-general "for gallant and meritorious services in the battle of Chancellorsville"; and Aug. 25, 1864, was brevetted major-general "for highly meritorious and distinguished conduct throughout the campaign, and particularly for gallantry and valuable services in the battle of Ream's Station, Va." He fought in all the battles of the army of the Potomac, with one exception, up to the surrender of Lee at Appomattox Court House, Va. He was brevetted brigadier-general and major-general, U.S. army, both dating March 2, 1867, the latter for "gallant and meritorious services in the battle of Spottsylvania." After the close of

the war Gen. Miles, in command of his regiment, was employed in Indian service, and defeated the Cheyenne and Comanche Indians on the borders of the Staked Plains in 1875, and in 1876 broke up the hostile Sioux and other tribes in Montana. His successes in warfare on the plains were so great and so continuous that Gen. Miles became known as the "Indian fighter." He drove the celebrated chief Sitting Bull across the Canadian frontiers, and dispersed extensive bands led by Crazy Horse, Lame Deer, Spotted Eagle, Broad Tail, and other chiefs well known in the far West. This was in the years 1876–77, when the Indian outbreak became general, the cause being the disaffection of the Dakota Sioux, of which Sitting Bull was the principal chief. It was in June 1876, that Gen. Custer's party was defeated and massacred on Little Big Horn river, an event which was followed by the prompt and decisive campaigns of Gen. Miles. In September, 1877, another outbreak, this time on the part of the Nez Perces Indians under Chief Joseph, was met by Miles and speedily overcome, and in 1878 he captured a party of Bannocks near the Yellowstone Park. But perhaps his most difficult campaign was that against the fierce chief Geronimo, of the hostile Apaches, doubtless the most bloodthirsty and cruel tribe of Indians in the whole of North America. After innumerable depredations and raids on the part of the Indians, Gen. Sheridan, commander-in-chief, determined to have Geronimo suppressed at any cost. An expedition under Gen. George Crook was fitted out early in 1886, but as it was unsuccessful, Gen. Crook asked to be relieved and Gen. Miles was ordered to take his place. The result was that, after one of the longest and most exhausting campaigns known to Indian warfare, the Apaches were forced to yield. Miles and his troopers gave them not an hour for rest, but followed on their trail, forcing them to keep moving until even their dogged endurance could bear it no longer. The whole band was captured, and Geronimo and his principal followers were sent to Fort Pickens, Fla., in the latter part of 1886. Following these brilliant successes, Gen. Miles received the thanks of the legislatures of Kansas, Montana, New Mexico, and Arizona for his valuable services, and on Nov. 8, 1887, the citizens of Arizona presented him, at Tucson, with a sword of honor in the presence of a large gathering of the citizens of the territory. In 1890–91 Gen. Miles suppressed a fresh outbreak of Sioux and Cheyennes. In 1894, under orders from Pres. Cleveland, he commanded the U.S. troops sent to Chicago to suppress the serious rioting and threatened rebellion which occurred there. This difficult duty he accomplished with the celerity and completeness which have always characterized his obedience to the orders of his superior officers. Gen. Miles was in command of the department of the Columbia from 1880–85; from July, 1885, to April, 1886, he commanded the department of the Missouri; in April, 1886, was assigned to the command of the department of Arizona, and in 1888 was given command of the division of the Pacific. In 1897 Gen. Miles represented the United States at the jubilee celebration of Queen Victoria in London, and also visited the seat of war between Turkey and Greece. On his return he published a volume on "Military Europe," having previously given to the public a volume of "Personal Recollections" (1897). On the retirement of Gen Schofield in 1895, Gen. Miles became commander-in-chief of the U.S. army, with headquarters in Washington, D.C. On April 8, 1898, war with Spain being imminent he recommended the equipment of 50,000 volunteers, and on April 15th recommended that an additional force of 40,000 be provided for the protection of coasts and as a reserve. In a letter to the secretary of war, April 18th, he asserted his belief that the surrender of the Spanish army in Cuba could be secured "without any great sacrifice of life," but deprecated the sending of troops thither in

American Soldiers at El Caney.

the sickly season to cope with an acclimated army. War having been officially announced, he (April 26th) addressed another letter to Sec. Alger, declaring that the volunteer troops called into service ought to be in camp in their respective states for sixty days approximately in order to be thoroughly equipped, drilled and organized. As soon as definite information came that Cervera's fleet was closed up in the harbor of Santiago, Gen. Shafter was ordered to place his troops on transports and go the assistance of the navy in capturing the fleet and harbor. Gen. Miles, then at Tampa, expressed to the secretary of war his desire to go with this army corps or to immediately organize another and go with it to join this and capture position No. 2 (Porto Rico). On the following day he was asked by telegram how soon he could have an expeditionary force ready to go to Porto Rico large enough to take and hold the island without the force under Gen. Shafter, and replied that such an expedition could be ready in ten days. On June 24th he submitted a plan of campaign for Cuba; on the 26th was ordered to organize an expedition against the enemy in Cuba and Porto Rico, to be composed of the united forces of Gens. Brooke and Shafter, and to command the same in person. He was not sent to Cuba, however, until two weeks later, arriving opposite Santiago with reinforcements for Shafter July 11th, at the time Sampson's fleet was bombarding the Spanish position. Conferences with Sampson and Shafter were then had and arrangements made to disembark the troops, and on the 13th Gen. Miles, with Gens. Gilmore, Shafter, Wheeler and others, held a conference between the lines with Gen. Toral. The Spanish commander was informed that he must surrender or take the consequences, and on the same day the secretary of war telegraphed Gen. Miles "to accept surrender, order an assault or withhold the same." On the morning of July 14th Adm.

Sampson's fleet was prepared to cover the landing at Cabanas of Gen. Henry's command on the Yale, Columbia and Duchesse, but Gen. Toral surrendered his forces to Gen. Miles that day, and aggressive action was unnecessary. Gen. Miles authorized Gen. Shafter to appoint commissioners to draw up articles of capitulation, and instructed him to isolate the troops recently arrived on healthful ground to keep them free from infection by yellow fever. On the same day Sec. Alger advised Gen. Miles to return to Washington as soon as matters at Santiago were settled, and go to Porto Rico with an expedition that was being fitted out; but after some delay Miles obtained permission to proceed from Cuba. On July 21st he sailed from Guantanamo with an effective force of only 3,314 men, whereas the Spanish regulars and volunteers in Porto Rico aggregated 17,000. The objective point was Cape San Juan; but it was finally decided to go direct to Guanica, near Ponce, on the southern coast, and there, on the 25th, a detachment of troops was landed. Ponce surrendered to Gen. Miles without resistance on the 27th, and the troops were received with enthusiasm by the citizens. A proclamation by Gen. Miles, issued on the following day, asssured the inhabitants of Porto Rico that the American forces came not to devastate or oppress, but to give them freedom from Spanish rule and the blessings of the liberal institutions of the U.S. government. Town after town was occupied, as the army proceeded northward. Gen. Brooke with his command arrived on Aug. 3d to aid in occupying the island. On the 25th Gen. Miles was instructed to send home all troops not actually needed, and soon after he returned to Washington. Gen. Miles was married, in 1868, to Mary, daughter of Judge Sherman, of Ohio. They had one son and one daughter. *He was promoted to lieutenant-general in 1901; he died May 15, 1925.*

MILROY, ROBERT HUSTON, soldier, was born in Washington county, Ind., June 11, 1816. He matriculated at Norwich university, Vt., from which he was graduated, taking degrees in both the classical and military departments. He served in the Mexican war as captain of the Indiana volunteers. He subsequently studied law, and in 1850 was graduated from the law department of Indiana university and was duly admitted to the bar and began the practice of his profession. In 1851 he was appointed judge of the eighth judicial circuit court of Indiana, having served as a member of the constitutional convention of the state in 1849–50. He offered his services to the United States government at the commencement of the civil war, and was commissioned first a captain, then a colonel and afterward brigadier-general. Gen. Milroy fought under Gens. McClellan and Rosecrans in western Virginia and afterward served under Gen. Frémont in the Shenandoah valley, having command of his central column at the battle of Cross Keys. He was appointed major-general of volunteers Nov. 29, 1862, and held Winchester, Va., when it was attacked by Ewell's forces. He resisted the enemy for three days, but their superior numbers and his short supply of ammunition and provisions finally compelled him to retreat. He held that by detaining Lee's army at Winchester, he had given Gen. Meade opportunity to fight to advantage at Gettysburg, whereas if the engagement at Winchester had not taken place the famous battle would have occurred farther north. Gen. Milroy retreated from Winchester toward the Potomac with the loss of fully one-half of his force, and was subsequently called before a court of inquiry for his conduct at Winchester, but escaped a threatened court-martial, the president not being able to find cause for serious blame on that occasion. He was assigned different commands up to the close of the civil war, the last being at Tullahoma, Tenn., in charge of the defences of the Nashville and Chattanooga railroad. In 1865, his conduct again being made the subject of investigation, he resigned from the army. He was appointed trustee of the Wabash and Erie canal in 1868, and was made superintendent of Indian affairs in Washington territory, retaining the position until 1874. The following year he was made Indian agent and successively reappointed to this office until 1885, when the democrats came into power and he lost the position. *He died March 29, 1890.*

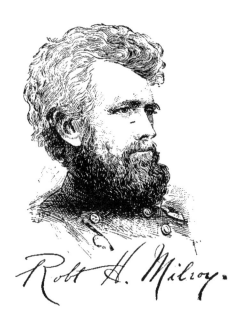

MITCHEL, ORMSBY McKNIGHT, astronomer, was born at Morganfield, Union county, Ky., Aug. 28, 1809. He received his primary instruction at Lebanon, O., having, at the age of twelve, a fair rudimentary education in English mathematics, Latin and Greek. At the age of thirteen he became a clerk in a country store at Miami, O., and afterward returned to Lebanon. In 1825 he secured an

appointment to the West Point military academy, and was graduated from there in 1829, standing fifteenth in his class, of which Robert E. Lee and Joseph E. Johnston were members. Immediately after his graduation he was made assistant professor of mathematics at the military academy, which position he retained two years, when he was assigned to duty at Fort Marion, St Augustine, Fla. He soon resigned and removed to Cincinnati, where he commenced the study of law and was admitted to the bar, at the same time serving as chief engineer of the Little Miami railroad. After practicing law for two years he abandoned it to accept the appointment of professor of mathematics, astronomy and philosophy at the Cincinnati college, which chair he occupied for ten years. While there he proposed the erection of an observatory at Cincinnati. Through his personal efforts he succeeded in raising nearly all the money required. He was made director, and went abroad in 1842 for the purpose of purchasing the apparatus and proper equipment for the observatory. Nov. 9, 1843, John Quincy

Adams laid the corner-stone of the pier which was to sustain the great refracting telescope. At first he principally directed his attention to the remeasurement of Struve's double stars south of the equator. He was then requested by foreign savants to make minute observations of the satellites of Saturn, from a point in the vicinity of Cincinnati. To these, and to "the physical association of the double, triple and multiple stars," he devoted his energies, and made interesting discoveries. Stars which Struve had marked as oblong, were divided and measured; others, double, were found to be triple. He invented the chronograph, for automatically measuring and recording right ascensions by an electro-magnetic mechanism in 1848, and in 1849 he made an apparatus for the correct measurement of great differences of declination, which, after being successfully improved, was, in 1854, attached to the equatorial. He determined the longitude of Cincinnati with reference to Washington and St. Louis, and invented an apparatus for finding the personal equation. Between 1854–59 he made in the neighborhood of 50,000 observations of faint stars, and also included in his work the discovery of the duplicity of certain stars—notably Antares, observations of double stars, comets, nebulae, solar spots, etc. His inventions and work were favorably reported upon by Prof. Pierce at the meeting of the American association for the advancement of science in 1851, which approval was endorsed by the superintendent of the coast survey, who, in his report of that year, gave a complete account of the work done by his methods of observations. He was an enthusiastic lecturer, and by his earnestness in this field was largely instrumental in aiding the establishment of some of the first observatories in the United States. In 1859 he delivered a course of lectures in the Academy of music, New York city, for the benefit of the observatory which was then proposed to be erected in Central Park. He also lectured in Boston, Mass., and in 1860 assumed the directorship of the Dudley university, Albany, N.Y., he being intrusted with the designing and construction of the building. In 1861 he entered the civil war in the cause of the Union, and was placed in command of a division of Gen. Buell's army. He served with the army of the Ohio during the campaigns of Tennessee and northern Alabama, and reached the brevet title of major-general of volunteers Apr. 11, 1862. Afterward he was placed in command of the department of the South at Hilton Head, S.C., where he was fatally stricken with yellow fever in the prime of his career. From 1846–48 he published a popular astronomical journal, entitled the "Sidereal Messenger." Among his works may be mentioned: "Stellar Worlds," "Popular Astronomy," "Astronomy of the Bible," etc. He was adjutant-general of Ohio, 1847; chief engineer of the Ohio and Mississippi railroad, 1848–53; received the degree of LL.D. from Harvard, 1851, from Washington, 1853, and from Hamilton, 1856. He was also a member of numerous scientific societies, both in Europe and America. He died at Hilton Head, S.C., Oct. 30, 1862.

MORELL, GEORGE WEBB, soldier, was born in Cooperstown, N.Y., Jan. 8, 1815, the son of George Morell, chief justice of the supreme court of Michigan, grandson of Gen. Samuel Blatchley of the revolutionary army, and nephew of Gen. James Watson Webb, at one time editor of the New York "Courier and Enquirer." Young Morell was sent to the West Point military academy, where he was graduated at the head of his class in 1835. In 1837 he resigned to become a civil engineer, and was for three years employed in railroad

construction in Michigan and in the southern coast states. In 1840 he settled at New York and entered upon the study of law. He was admitted to the bar, began practice *in 1842*; was made commissioner of the United States circuit court for the southern district of New York. At the time of the breaking-out of the civil war, he held the position of inspector-general on the staff of Maj.-Gen. Sanford, who commanded the first division of the New York state militia, and in his official capacity Gen. Morell accompanied the division to Washington. During the Shenandoah campaign, he was a colonel on the staff of Gen. Patterson. He was promoted to brigadier-general and afterward major-general, and commanded the 2d brigade, 2d division, 5th army corps, and on the promotion of Gen. Fitz John Porter to the command of a corps, Gen. Morell was placed in command of the supports of the celebrated battery of 100 guns. He was engaged at Hanover Court House, Mechanicsville, and Gaines's Mills. During the Chickahominy campaign, on account of his exposure, he contracted the germs of the disease which ultimately caused his death. Gen. Morell was married in 1864 to Catharine Schermerhorn Creighton, daughter of the late Rev. William Creighton, D.D. He left no children and was a widower during the last two years of his life. He was a member of the Society of the Cincinnati, of the Union Club, and of the "Army of the Potomac." For many years he was senior warden of Trinity Episcopal parish, Tarrytown, N.Y. He died in Scarborough, N.Y., Feb. 12, 1883.

MORGAN, CHARLES HALE, soldier, was born in Manlius, N.Y., Nov. 6, 1834. He was graduated from the U.S. military academy in 1857, assigned to the 4th artillery, and took part in the Utah expedition of 1859. He became second lieutenant Apr. 1, 1861, and after the civil war broke out was engaged in the operations in western Virginia, and in the defences of Washington from December 1861, till March 1862. He served through the peninsular campaign with the army of the Potomac, was promoted captain Aug. 5, 1862, and in October appointed chief of artillery of the 2d corps. He participated in the

Rappahannock campaign, was brevetted major after Gettysburg, lieutenant-colonel for bravery at Bristoe Station, colonel for Spottsylvania, colonel of volunteers Aug. 1, 1864, and brigadier-general of volunteers Dec. 2, 1864, for services as chief-of-staff of the 2d army corps during the battles before Richmond. He was assistant inspector-general and chief-of-staff to Gen. Hancock, commanding the middle military division from Feb. 22d till June 22, 1865. Afterward he served for two months on the board to examine candidates for commissions in colored regiments. He received the brevet of brigadier-general, U.S. army, March 13, 1865, for services in the field during the war, and became full brigadier-general of volunteers May 21, 1865. He was mustered out of the volunteer service Jan. 15, 1866. Subsequently, for a short time he was a member of the board to make recommendations for brevet promotions in the army. He then performed recruiting service, and became major of the 4th artillery Feb. 5, 1867. He was stationed later at various forts on the Atlantic coast, and finally held command at Alcatraz island, Cal., where he died Dec. 20, 1875.

MORGAN, GEORGE WASHINGTON, soldier, was born in Washington county, Pa., Sept. 20, 1820. His grandfather was the Col. George N. Morgan who gave Jefferson his first information regarding Aaron Burr's conspiracy. He entered college, but left before graduating, in 1836, to enlist with his brother, who was organizing a company to hasten to the relief of Texas, then struggling to gain independence. On his arrival he was appointed a lieutenant in the Texas army, and in a short time was promoted to the rank of captain, retiring in 1841 to enter the U.S. military academy. He left this institution, however, in 1843, and removed, for some reason, to Mount Vernon,

O., where he engaged in the practice of law. At the outbreak of the war with Mexico, he was asked to become colonel of the 2d Ohio volunteers, and subsequently was appointed colonel of the 15th U.S. infantry. Under Gen. Scott he took part in the engagements of Contreras and Churubusco. At both places he was severely wounded, and won marked distinction for his gallant conduct, for which

he received the public thanks of the Ohio legislature and the brevet of brigadier-general. He then resumed his law practice until 1856, when he was sent to Marseilles as U.S. consul, which post he held for two years until appointed minister to Portugal in 1858. Gen. Morgan returned to the United States after a successful career in diplomacy in 1861; was made brigadier-general of volunteers, and commenced active duty under Gen. Don Carlos Buell. Assuming the command of the 7th division of the army of the Ohio in March, 1862, he assailed Cumberland Gap, Ky., then held by the Confederates, and dislodged them, after hard fighting, before the end of June. He was with Gen. Sherman at Vicksburg, and later joined the 13th army corps, being in command at the capture of Ford Hindman, Ark. Failing health compelled him to resign in June, 1863. *The real reason for his resignation seems to have been friction with Sherman plus Morgan's disapproval (he was a Democrat) of the government's policy of enlisting black soldiers.* In 1865 Gen. Morgan was the democratic candidate for governor of Ohio, but was defeated. In 1866 he was elected a

representative from Ohio to the fortieth congress, serving on the committee on foreign affairs. His election was, however, contested by the republican candidate, Columbus Delano, who was seated in June, 1868, during the second session of that congress. Gen. Morgan was re-elected to the forty-first and forty-second congresses, serving on the committees on foreign affairs, military affairs, and reconstruction. His last appearance in politics was as delegate-at-large to the National democratic convention at St. Louis in 1876. Gen. Morgan, during the war, was opposed to interference with the state institution of the South. He died at Old Point Comfort, Va., July 26, 1893, the sole surviving general of the Mexican war.

MORGAN, JOHN HUNT, soldier, was born in Huntsville, Ala., *June 1, 1825.* When four years of age, he removed with his father to the vicinity of Lexington, Ky., where he was brought up on a farm and given a common-

school education. *He also attended Transylvania College for two years.* When the war with Mexico broke out he enlisted, and was afterward appointed first lieutenant in a cavalry regiment. At the beginning of the civil war, he was engaged in the manufacture of bagging, but shortly entered the Confederate service as captain of Kentucky volunteers, and joined the division of Gen. Simon B. Buckner. In 1862–63 he commanded a *brigade regiment* in Gen. Braxton Bragg's army, and rendered efficient service in annoying the outposts. At this time, too, being promoted to the rank of brigadier-general, he inaugurated his famous series of raids in Kentucky, Ohio, and Indiana, which resulted in the destruction of millions of dollars' worth of military stores, while railroad tracks were torn up, bridges burned, and culverts destroyed in the rear of the Federal army, making it necessary, at last, to garrison every important town in those states. Morgan would usually take a telegraph operator with him, and though his movements were marvelously rapid, he kept himself constantly informed of the foe's movements. *In the summer of 1863,* however, after one of his most daring raids, he was captured with nearly all of his force, and imprisoned in the Ohio penitentiary. He escaped in November, through a tunnel dug in the ground, and immediately undertook a raid in Tennessee. Some time afterward, while stationed at a farm-house, near Greenville, Tenn., he was surrounded in the night by a detachment of Federal troops under Gen. Alvan C. Gillem, and in endeavoring to make his escape, was instantly killed. The date of his death was Sept. 4, 1864.

MORRILL, JUSTIN S., senator, was born at Strafford, Vt., April 14, 1810. His early life was passed upon his father's farm and he obtained his education at common schools and academies in his neighborhood. When he grew to manhood he became a merchant and with his partner had stores in different places in the state. Though once elected justice of the peace he did not serve, as he had no aspirations for political office, but took some active part in the political discussions of the times with sympathies strongly in favor of the old whig party. In 1854 his name was suggested as a candidate for congress from the first district of Vermont. This was a surprise to him, but the nomination was unanimously made, and he was elected to the thirty-fourth congress, taking his seat Dec. 3, 1855. He belonged to the anti-slavery wing of the whig party in congress, steadily advancing in influence with his colleagues, serving on the committee of ways and means and other important committees, becoming liked by his constituents and attaining such a reputation with them that for six successive terms he was re-elected to the house where he helped to pass some of the most important measures. From the first he was an advocate of the protective tariff system and voted against the tariff bill of 1857 for the reason mainly that agricultural interests were insufficiently protected and that it was only a second edition of the Walker tariff of 1846. The next year he introduced and succeeded in having passed the first anti-polygamy measure, and in 1858 introduced the first land-grant-college bill. This passed both houses of congress, but was vetoed by President Buchanan and again passed in 1862 when it became a law with the approval of President Lincoln. During the civil war Mr. Morrill had charge of all the tariff and tax bills of 1861, which was known by his name and under which all the imports of the country were regulated, being largely framed by him. This with frequent amendments remained the law of the country until the enactment of the McKinley bill by the

fifty-first congress. The Morrill tariff bill was the first of its class changing ad valorem largely to specific duties. At the commencement of the rebellion there were added other measures for internal revenue—stamp taxes as well as direct taxes, and taxes on legacies and successions. Mr. Morrill was chairman of the ways and means committee of the thirty-ninth congress. After twelve years of faithful labor never marred by any charges of corruption or incapacity he was elected in 1867 by the legislature of Vermont U.S. senator to succeed Luke P. Poland, and was re-elected four times, at the expiration of each successive term being chosen to succeed himself. He served in the senate as chairman of the committees on finance, public buildings and grounds, and as a member of the committee on education and labor, census, revolutionary claims, select committee on additional accommodations for the library of congress, and made many speeches during his senatorial career on prominent topics. Senator Morrill never lost sight of the interests of his native state, and was

a staunch friend of its system of education, having been for years a trustee of the University of Vermont and the State Agricultural College. He was a friend of temperance and as a consequence enjoyed a vigorous and hale old age. He himself designed and built his elegant gothic residence at Strafford, Vt., which was surrounded by handsome grounds decorated with trees, shrubs, and flowers as well as with fruit and vegetable gardens. He authored a book entitled "The Self-Consciousness of Noted Persons," which was published in Boston in 1886. He was never an office-seeker and the presidential bee has never ventured to buzz about his bonnet. His highest aim was to serve his state and country in congress, and his honorable record of nearly forty years shows how well he performed his self-appointed task. He enjoyed the distinction of having served continuously in congress for a greater length of time than any other man in the history of the country at the time, and if he should serve out his present term in the senate will have been forty-two years in congress. The degree of M.A. was conferred upon Mr. Morrill by Dartmouth College in 1857 and that of LL.D. by the Vermont University and State Agricultural College in 1874 and also by the Pennsylvania University in 1884. *He died in 1898.*

MORRILL, LOT MYRICK, twenty-second governor of Maine (1858–60) was born in Belgrade, Me., May 3, 1813. He was one of a family of seven sons and seven daughters. He received his early education at the district schools, working in a saw-mill and as a clerk in a country store out of school hours. He early determined to be a lawyer, and to that end availed himself of every opportunity to study. At sixteen years of age he began to teach school, to increase his means of defraying the expenses of a college education. He entered Waterville College (now Colby) in 1833, but becoming impatient to prepare himself for his chosen profession, left college before the time he was to graduate, and entered the office of Judge Edward Fuller of Readfield. Mr. Morrill was admitted to the bar in 1837, and, entering into partnership with a fellow-student Timothy Howe, began to practice in Readfield. Desiring a wider field for professional work, he removed to Augusta in 1841, and formed a partnership with James W. Bradbury; a connection which proved very congenial to both parties, and continued many years. Mr. Morrill was a Democrat in early life, but always opposed to the extension of slavery, and was a strong temperance man. He was elected to the state legislature in 1853, and again in 1854, and received a considerable vote against William Pitt Fessenden in the U.S. senatorial contest of that year. He was a member of the state senate in 1856, and president of that body the following year. During this session, Mr. Morrill opposed the attempted repeal of the prohibitory laws, and the removal of Judge Davis from the bench, in such vigorous speeches, as gained him a state reputation; and was a warm opponent of a resolution pledging the Democratic party of Maine to further concessions on the slave question in the territories. He was, notwithstanding, made a member of the Democratic state committee, but refused to act after the Cincinnati convention in 1856, which nominated Mr. Buchanan. He wrote in a letter to E. Wilder Farky, "The candidate is a good one, but the platform is a flagrant outrage upon the country, and an insult to the North." Mr. Morrill now allied himself to the Republican party, and was elected governor on that ticket in 1857 by a large majority. He was re-elected in 1858 and 1859. He was made U.S. senator in 1861, to fill out the unexpired term of Mr. Hamlin, on his resignation to accept the vice-presidency, and in 1863 was re-elected for the full term. In 1867 he was defeated by a single vote in the memorable Hamlin-Morrill senatorial contest of that year, but was soon called to fill the vacancy in the senate, caused by the death of Mr. Fessenden in September 1869. He was again elected for the full term, but resigned in 1876 to accept the portfolio of the treasury under Gen. Grant's administration, an office he filled with distinction. So highly were his services appreciated, that Pres. Hayes gave him the choice of any position he might select, and on intimation that collector of customs for the port of Portland would be most congenial, he promptly received that appointment. Mr. Morrill was a noble man, and a faithful public servant. He was generous and warm-hearted, and in his public and private life the admiration of all who knew him. Mr. Morrill never fully recovered his health from a severe illness with nervous prostration in 1870, induced from overwork. He died in Augusta, Jan. 10, 1883.

MORTON, OLIVER HAZARD PERRY THROCK, statesman and fourteenth governor of Indiana (1861–67), was born at Saulsbury, Wayne co., Ind., Aug. 4, 1823, son of James Throck and Sarah (Miller) Morton, and a descendant of John Throckmorton, who came to this country with Roger Williams in 1631; was one of the Monmouth patentees and served as deputy in the colonial legislature of Rhode Island during 1664–73. James Morton, the governor's father, dropped the first syllable of his family name owing to a dispute he had with his brother. The son attended Wayne county seminary for one year, and after serving an apprenticeship with an older brother at the hatter's trade, he entered Miami University, Oxford, O., in 1843, but left it two years later. In 1846 he was admitted to the bar, and locating at Centreville, Ind., he practiced his profession for six years. In 1852 he was made judge of the sixth circuit by the state legislature, and filled this office until it became elective under the new constitution, eight months afterwards. He was originally an anti-slavery Democrat, and supported Pierce and Butler in the presidential campaign of 1852, but after being expelled from the Democratic state convention at Indianapolis, in May, 1854, for refusing to endorse the Kansas-Nebraska bill, he attached himself to the People's party. He was its candidate for governor of Indiana in 1856, but was defeated by Ashbel P. Willard. As a delegate to the Free-soil convention at Pittsburg, Pa., Feb. 22, 1856, he was instrumental in forming the Republican party, and in 1860 he was elected by that party lieutenant-governor on the ticket with Henry S. Lane. He was inaugurated Jan. 14, 1861. On the following day, according to a previous arrangement, Mr. Lane was elected to the U.S. senate, and the duties of chief magistrate thus devolved upon Gov. Morton. The civil war broke out very soon afterward, and the momentous events that followed offered full opportunity for the display of his great executive ability. Before the publication of Pres. Lincoln's proclamation calling for 75,000 men, he tendered to him, on Apr. 15, 1861, 10,000 men, and on April 24 he called a special session of the legislature, which passed appropriation bills to the amount of $1,740,000 to equip, organize, and support the state militia. When the Democrats carried the state in 1862, however, the governor's war measures met with determined opposition from a hostile legislature, which refused to receive his message to make the appropriations necessary for carrying on the state government. The Democratic majority had also intended to take from the governor the military command, but the prompt withdrawal of the Republican members from both houses left the legislature without a quorum, thus frustrating the plan. Gov. Morton then conducted the state government alone, refusing to convene the legislature, and on his own responsibility he assumed obligations amounting to over $1,000,000. This bold course brought upon him the severe censure of the supreme court, but it had the support of his party, and the next session of the general assembly so far indorsed his action as to order the money borrowed repaid out of the state treasury. Thus he was enabled to lend substantial aid to the Federal government at a time when it was sorely needed, and thus he earned for himself the fame of one of the greatest among the loyal war governors. During his term secret organizations were formed for the purpose of resisting the draft laws, inciting to riot and in other ways hampering the actions of the government. These organizations were known as Knights of the Golden Circle, Order of American Knights, and Sons of Liberty. They resorted to every means in order to accomplish their objects, not

even stopping at assassination. Several attempts were made to kill Gov. Morton and seize upon the state government; but the plans were discovered and the conspirators arrested. In 1864 he was again the candidate of his party for governor, and the tide this time being in favor of the Republicans, he was triumphantly re-elected. While filling the second term, he was suddenly stricken with paralysis in the lower part of his body, Oct. 10, 1865, and in November following he went to Paris, France, to consult an eminent specialist. It was in vain, for he was never able to stand again without support. Yet there was no abatement in his power as a debater or in the effectiveness of his forcible popular oratory. At that time Maximilian was on the throne in Mexico, and Gov. Morton received instructions from the president and secretary of state to urge upon the Emperor Napoleon, that a longer stay of the French troops in Mexico would be regarded by our government as an unfriendly act. It is claimed that his representations ultimately resulted in the withdrawal of the French troops and the consequent overthrow of Maximilian. On Jan. 23, 1867, he resigned the governorship, having been elected to the United States senate the previous day, and being re-elected to the same position on Nov. 26th, 1872, served until his death. In the senate he at once became the acknowledged leader of his party and he left his powerful impress on the legislation of that period. He led the opposition to the president's reconstruction policy, and to him more than to any other man was due the ratification of the constitutional amendments by the requisite number of states, *i.e., the 14th and 15th Amendments.* He opposed an increase in the currency, but changed his views on the subject after the panic of 1873; he favored the tenure-of-office law and the acquisition of Santo Domingo, and opposed civil service reform and universal amnesty. During the later years of his service in the senate he was chairman of the committee on elections and privileges, in which capacity he introduced a bill for doing away with the electoral college and electing the president by a direct vote of the people. One of his ablest speeches was in support of this measure which subsequently passed the senate but was defeated in the house. In ordinary debate he usually read and spoke while sitting, owing to his infirmity, but when dealing with questions of national importance, he addressed the senate standing, supporting himself with his two canes, and thus earned the appellation of "The Devil on Two Sticks." He was a delegate to the Republican national convention at Philadelphia, Pa., in 1872, and at Cincinnati, O., in 1876, and was one of the most trusted advisers of Pres. Grant. At the Cincinnati convention he was a candidate for the presidency and polled a strong vote, but after a few ballots he gave his support to Rutherford B. Hayes. He vigorously fought the electoral commission bill, which was designed to settle the Tilden-Hayes contest, but notwithstanding his opposition to the measure, he was chosen to head the senatorial part of the commission after it had been adopted. He earnestly advocated laws for the promotion of interstate commerce, and favored woman suffrage in discussing the admission of the proposed territory of Pembina. As chairman of the committee to investigate Chinese immigration, he went to California in 1876, and in 1877 he visited Oregon as a member of a sub-committee to investigate the election of Sen. Grover. This was his last public service, as he was taken seriously ill during the journey, and returning to his home in Indianapolis, completely broken down in health, died there shortly afterward. Gov. Morton was married May 15, 1845; to Lucinda M., daughter of Isaac and Elizabeth Burbank, of Springdale, O., by whom he had five children. The date of his death was Nov. 1, 1877. In 1899, a life-size marble statue of him, by Charles H. Niehaus, was presented to the nation by the legislature of Indiana and was placed with appropriate ceremonies in Statuary Hall in the national capitol in Washington.

MOSBY, JOHN SINGLETON, soldier, was born in Powhatan county, Va., Dec. 6, 1833. He was educated at the University of Virginia, but did not graduate, owing to a difficulty he had with a fellow student, which resulted in young Mosby seriously wounding the student, and being on consequence imprisoned. He filled up the time of his imprisonment by studying law, and when he was pardoned by the governor, and his fine remitted by the legislature, he was admitted to the bar of Virginia, and began the practice of his profession at Bristol, Va. The civil war brought out the men of Virginia in defence of their

state, and Mosby was one of the first to enlist in the cavalry service for twelve months, serving under Gen. J. E. Johnston in the early operations of the war at Bull Run, in the Shenandoah Valley, and as a picket along the banks of the Potomac. Upon the expiration of his term of service, not waiting for the furlough accorded all the twelve months' enlisted men, he with a friend re-enlisted for the war, the two solitary exceptions in his regiment. In February he was made adjutant, and two months later voluntarily returned to the ranks on account of the displacement of Col. William E. Jones from command. Gen. J. E. B. Stuart, the leader of his brigade, had observed the ability and dash of Mosby, and appointed him on his headquarters' staff as a scout. In this capacity he led the brigade in a bold raid *June 12, 1862,* gaining the rear of McClellan's army on the Chickahominy, and causing great consternation to the Federal commander. *Late in 1862* he returned to northern Virginia, then occupied by the Federal army, and recruiting an irregular cavalry force of less than 100 men he, by the aid of the sympathizing residents of the valley, harassed the enemy, and did much damage to the invading army, cutting off their supply trains, destroying communication, and opposing scouting parties and picket lines—operating upon the rear of the Federal forces. The rangers kept up communications with each other, but, except for a dash never were found together—dispersing and re-forming at the call of their leader as exigencies demanded. By this peculiar mode of warfare Mosby's men were never captured as a body, as their whereabouts could not be determined. The punishment intended to be visited on the band if captured was meted out to the residents of the valley, who were suspected of harboring and abetting the guerrilla chief and his men. Their perfected

methods of communications and means employed to gain information of the movements of the enemy made the band greatly feared, and compelled the Federal forces to strengthen their picket lines, and guard their outposts continually. His force was made up of volunteers from civil life and deserters from either army, and furloughed cavalrymen, who had lost their horses. March 8, 1863, with a party of twenty-nine men, Col. Mosby penetrated the Federal lines, and captured Gen. Stoughton at his headquarters in the midst of his troops at Fairfax Court House, Va. As a reward a commission was given him to raise a partisan battalion, with which he operated along the Potomac, and in the rear of the Federal army as it advanced into Virginia. His object was to impede its advance by destroying its communications, and to weaken it by compelling heavy details to protect its rear, and also the Capitol, which he was continually threatening. Gen. R. E. Lee once said that the only fault he ever had to find with Mosby was that he was always getting wounded. Mosby never had more than 300 or 400 men. *At a maximum he once had 800 men theoretically under his command, although they always operated in smaller bands, never more than 80 at once.* It is estimated that his small band neutralized 30,000 Federal troops, who kept watching for him. The most important service he ever rendered was in the autumn of 1864, after Sheridan had routed Early, and driven him from the Shenandoah Valley. Sheridan pursued Early's broken and demoralized army as far as Staunton. There was then nothing to oppose Sheridan in his front, and prevent his going on scattering Lee's communications with the South, and thus intercepting his supplies. Grant ordered Sheridan to push on—if he had done so the war would have ended in October, 1864, for Lee could not have spared a man from his lines at Petersburg. At that time there were no Confederate troops in northern Virginia, or in Sheridan's rear except Mosby's band. Sheridan wrote to Grant that he could not advance any further, but would be compelled to retreat in order to subsist his army—that the country was exhausted of forage for men and horses, and that it would require half his army to guard the trains and railroad that carried his supplies. He proposed therefore to retreat from Staunton down the valley to Front Royal, and that the Manassas Gap railroad from which the rails had been torn up by Jackson, be reconstructed to that point. By accumulating a large amount of supplies and transportation at that point he proposed to transport his army rapidly to Alexandria, thence by water to Grant, and to assault Lee's lines by an overwhelming force before Early's men could get there. Grant acquiesced in the plan. A large force was sent out from Washington to rebuild the railroad, but Mosby by incessant attacks so put them on the defensive that they had to suspend operations, and began to erect stockades to protect themselves. When Sherida got to Front Royal he found neither railroad or provisions. So the plan failed, and the war was prolonged.

See "Pond's Shenandoah Campaign." When Lee surrendered at Appomattox, Mosby's command was near Washington. Gen. Grant acted with great magnanimity toward Mosby and his men, and gave them the same terms that he had given Lee's army. Afterward Mosby and Grant became strong friends. In common with the Southern people, Mosby opposed the reconstruction measures of congress, but when they finally adopted them, and nominated their old enemy, Horace Greeley, for the presidency, Mosby supported Grant as the best way to restore peace between the divided sections, and to bring the influence of Southern men to direct the policy of national affairs. He was offered, but declined to accept, an office from Gen. Grant. The South got all the benefit of his friendship with Grant. He supported Hayes for the same reasons that he had supported Grant, and was appointed by him U.S. consul to Hong Kong, where he remained until removed by a democratic president (Cleveland). He instituted many reforms in the consular service. On the final settlement of his accounts it was ascertained that he had largely overpaid the government. He brought suit, and the U.S. supreme court gave a judgment in his favor. See vol. 133 U.S. Reports. Mr. Justice Blatchford, in delivering the opinion of the court, spoke in high terms of praise of the integrity that Mosby had shown in the administration of his consulate. On his return to the United States Mosby settled in San Francisco, and returned to the practice of law. *He died May 30, 1916.*

MOTT, GERSHOM, soldier, was born in Mercer county, N.J., Apr. 7, 1822, the grandson of Capt. John Mott, the revolutionary hero who piloted the army of Washington in its perilous voyage down the Delaware river to the battle of Trenton. Gershom attended the academy at

Trenton, until fourteen years of age, when he entered a store in New York city as clerk. In 1846, on the outbreak of war with Mexico, young Mott enlisted in the army, and was commissioned second lieutenant in the 10th U.S. infantry, and served until peace was declared. He was, on his return to his native state, made collector of the port of Lamberton, N.J. In 1855 he accepted a position in the Bordentown bank which he held until 1861, when, on the first call for troops, he actively engaged in recruiting and organizing the New Jersey volunteers. He accepted the lieutenant-colonelcy of the 5th New Jersey volunteers, and was afterward made colonel of the 6th New Jersey volunteers. He was severely wounded at the second battle of Bull Run, when his regiment served in the 3d brigade, 2d division, 3d army corps. This battle won for him the promotion to brigadier-general of volunteers, Sept. 7, 1862, and he led the 1st brigade of the 4th division, 2d army corps, in the battle of Chancellorsville, where he was again dangerously wounded. He continued with the army of the Potomac in command of the 4th division of the 2d army corps, having been, on

Aug. 1, 1864, made a brevet-major-general of volunteers for distinguished services. On the reorganization of the army March 31, 1865, Gen. Mott was placed in command of the 3d division, 2d army corps, and on Apr. 6, 1865, at the battle of Amelia Springs, Va., he was for the third time severely wounded while in action. After the army was disbanded Gen. Mott was given command of the provisional army corps. He was one of the general officers serving in the Wirz commission, and was made a full major-general on May 26, 1865, resigning his commission Feb. 20, 1866, to accept the position of paymaster of the Camden and Amboy railroad. He was made major-general of the New Jersey state militia, Feb. 27, 1873, and in September, 1875, he became treasurer of the state, and from 1876 to '81 was keeper of the state prison. Gen. Mott died in New York city May 29, 1884.

MOWER, JOSEPH ANTHONY, soldier, was born in Woodstock, Vt., Aug. 22, 1827. His early education was received in the district schools after which he learned carpentering.

When the Mexican war broke out he enlisted as a private in a company of engineers; he was afterward commissioned second lieutenant in the 1st United States infantry, his commission dating from June 18, 1855. When the civil war began he went promptly forward and received a captain's commission, Sept. 9, 1861. He took part in the battles in and around New Madrid, Mo., and at Corinth, Miss. At the latter place he was wounded and taken prisoner by the Confederates. He had in May, 1862, been made colonel of the 11th Missouri volunteer infantry, and for special services rendered and ability displayed at Milliken's bend, was, in November of the same year, appointed as brigadier-general. He performed prodigies of valor on several occasions, notably at Vicksburg, and afterward with Sherman on his march from Atlanta to the sea. He was made major-general in August, 1864, rose to the command of the 20th army corps by successive steps and received *the brevet appointment* of major-general in the regular army. He was transferred to the 25th infantry in 1865, then to the 29th, and at the time of his death commanded the department of Louisiana, which included also the state of Arkansas. Gen. Sherman said of him that "a better soldier or a braver man never lived." He died in New Orleans, La., Jan. 6, 1870.

N

NAGLEE, HENRY MORRIS, soldier, was born in Philadelphia, Pa., Jan. 15, 1815. He was graduated from West Point in 1835, but in the December succeeding his graduation resigned from the military service that he might become a civil engineer. At the beginning of the Mexican war he promptly rejoined the service as captain in the 1st New York volunteer infantry, his commission dating from Aug. 15, 1846. He served through the war, then engaged in banking in San Francisco, Cal. At the outbreak of the civil war he went to the front as lieutenant-colonel of the U.S. 16th infantry, his commission dating from May 14, 1861. He did not, however, join the regiment, but

became brigadier-general in the volunteer service, Feb. 4, 1862, joined the army of the Potomac, took part in the peninsular campaign, and was wounded at the battle of Fair Oaks. He served in various commands both in North Carolina and in the district of Virginia, 1863, commanding the 7th army corps. On account of his wound, he was mustered out of service Apr. 4, 1864, and retired to his home in San Francisco, where he resumed his former business of banking. Gen. Naglee also established large vineyards in San José, his principal one including more than fifty acres, from which he furnished the market with his celebrated brand of "Naglee" brandy. He died in San Francisco, Cal., March 5, 1886.

NEGLEY, JAMES SCOTT, soldier, was born in East Liberty, Alleghany county, Pa., Dec. 26, 1826. After completing his education at the Western university, in 1846, he enlisted as a private in the 1st Pennsylvania regiment. This step met with strong opposition from his parents, as he was yet a minor. He received a complimentary discharge from the secretary of war, which he declined to accept, and served with his company throughout the Mexican war, after which he devoted himself to farming until the outbreak of the civil war, when he raised a brigade of three months' volunteers. *On Feb. 6, 1862,* he was brevetted third brigadier-general *of state militia*, and placed in command of the entire western portion of Pennsylvania. He was a happy and efficient organizer, and his brigade, consisting of the 77th, 78th, and 79th Pennsylvania volunteers, was ordered to Kentucky to reinforce the U.S. army in that state. He sent them down the Ohio river on six steamboats. He also served with the army of the Ohio in Alabama and Tennessee, and commanded the troops at the battle of Lavergne, Oct. 7, 1862, and gained a victory over the

Confederates, who were commanded by Gen. Richard H. Anderson and Gen. Nathan B. Forrest. For meritorious and gallant services at Murfreesboro, he was brevetted major-general. Gen. Negley took part in the Georgia campaign. He held Owen's Gap at the battle of Chickamauga in September, 1863. At the conclusion of the civil war, he located at Pittsburg, Pa. In 1869–75 he was the republican representative of that city in congress, and was also its representative in 1885–87. He subsequently removed to New York. *He died Aug. 7, 1901.*

NELSON, WILLIAM, naval officer, was born at Maysville, Mason co., Ky., *on Sept. 27, 1824,* brother of Thomas Henry Nelson, U.S. minister to Mexico and to Chili. William Nelson entered the navy when fifteen years of age. He commanded a battery at the siege of Vera Cruz and afterward served in the Mediterranean. On Sept. 15, 1854, he became master, and on April 18, 1855, lieutenant. In 1858 Nelson commanded the Niagara, in which

the negro slaves taken from the captured slaver Echo were returned to Africa. At the outbreak of the civil war he was in Washington, D.C., on ordnance duty. He was made lieutenant-commander on July 16, 1861, and was assigned to the command of the gunboats patrolling the Ohio river, but the military service offering greater opportunities for action he exchanged from the navy to the army on Sept. 16, 1861, and was made brigadier-general of volunteers. He organized a camp between Garrardsville and Danville, Ky., and another in Washington, Mason co., Ky; participated in numerous engagements in the eastern part of Kentucky, and was untiring in the work of raising regiments. He was in command of the 2d division of Gen. Don Carlos Buell's army when it joined Gen. Grant at the battle of Shiloh. Nelson was wounded at Richmond, Ky. He was in command of the forces in Louisville when Bragg threatened that city, and on July 17, 1862, was promoted to major-general of volunteers. In an altercation with Gen.

Jefferson C. Davis at the Galt House, Louisville, Ky., he was fatally shot by that officer on Sept. 29, 1862.

NEWTON, JOHN, soldier, was born in Norfolk, Va., *Aug. 25, 1822*. His father, Thomas Newton, represented the Norfolk district in congress for thirty years, and at the time of his retirement was the oldest member in service in the United States house of representatives. Young Newton received his early instruction at the schools in his native city, and having displayed a marked talent in the direction of mathematics, when about twelve years of age he was placed under private tuition with the design of making a civil engineer of him. In July, 1838, he entered as a cadet at the military academy at West Point, and there his worth as a careful and comprehensive student became recognized by his superiors, and he received every opportunity and aid in his progress in the special direction of his intellect. He was graduated from the academy in 1842, receiving the appointment of brevet second lieutenant in the corps of engineers, standing second in his class, which included such eminent soldiers as Longstreet, Van Dorn, Rosecrans, John Pope, Seth Williams, Daniel H. Hill, Henry L. Eustis and others who held high rank during the civil war. Newton served as assistant to the board of engineers for the first two years after his graduation, and from 1843 to 1846 at the military academy, at first as assistant professor and afterward as principal assistant professor of engineering. In the latter year he was appointed assistant engineer in the construction of Fort Warren, Boston Harbor, and Fort Trumbull, New London, Conn. From this work he was transferred to be superintending engineer of construction of Forts Wayne, Michigan, and Porter, Niagara, and Ontario, New York. In 1852–53 he was employed in the

survey of bays and rivers in Maine, and then in Florida, engaged in similar work, looking to the improvement of St. John's river and the repair of the sea wall at St. Augustine, and in Georgia at Forts Pulaski and Jackson and superintending the improvement of lighthouses on the Savannah river. In 1856 he was a member of the board to examine the floating dock at the Washington navy yard, and of the special board of engineers to select sites and prepare plans for the coast defence of Alabama, Mississippi, and Texas. On July 1, 1856, he was appointed captain of engineers for fourteen years' continuous service. In 1858 he was made chief engineer of the Utah expedition, afterward superintending engineer of the construction of Fort Delaware and of the special board of engineers for modifying the plans of the fort at Sandy Hook and for selecting sites for additional batteries at Fort Hamilton. This brought him down to the period of the civil war, when he entered active service as chief engineer of the department of Pennsylvania, accompanying Gen. Patterson's column in the valley of Virginia, where he was engaged in the action of Falling Waters. In 1861 he was chief engineer of the department of the Shenandoah, and from August, 1861, till March, 1862, he acted as assistant engineer in the construction of the defences of Washington. The latter post was one of great responsibility then, and Maj. Newton did much to insure the safety of the city in case of attack, besides taking command of a brigade for the defence of the capital. He was appointed major of the corps of engineers, Aug. 6, 1861, and brigadier-general of volunteers on Sept. 23, 1861. In 1862 Gen. Newton served in the army of the Potomac in the peninsular and Maryland campaigns, and was engaged in all the battles of that period. At West Point and South Mountain, Gen. Newton distinguished himself,

and his brigade received formal commendation for its behavior at Gaines's Mills and at Glendale, and its commander was brevetted lieutenant-colonel in the regular army, Sept. 17, 1862, for gallant and meritorious services at the battle of Antietam. Gen. Newton was engaged in the battle of Fredericksburg, Dec. 13, 1862, when he was in command of a division. He was made major-general of volunteers, attached to Gen. Sedgwick's corps, and commanded the troops that stormed Marye Heights May 3, 1863. He also took part in the battle of Gettysburg, and after the death of Gen. Reynolds had temporary command of the 1st corps. For his gallant and meritorious services on that occasion he was brevetted colonel. When the march through Georgia was about to be entered upon, Gen. Newton was appointed to the command of the 2d division of the 4th army corps (Gen. Howard's), and was engaged in the operations which preceded the movement upon Atlanta. The admirable conduct of his command in resisting a sharp attack by Hood's

force at Peach Tree creek brought to Gen. Newton a brevet brigadier-generalship in the regular army under date of March, 1865. At the same time he received the brevet of major-general in the U.S. army for meritorious services in the field during the civil war. Gen. Newton's active service concluded with the occupation of Atlanta. On Dec. 28, 1865, he was made lieutenant-colonel of the corps of engineers, and on Jan. 15th next he was mustered out of the volunteer service and transferred to engineering service to have charge of the construction of the new battery near Fort Hamilton, New York harbor, and of the fort at Sandy Hook. Gen. Newton also made an examination for the improvement of the navigation of the Hudson river, and reported thereon. He also made reports on similar improvements of all the channels and harbors from Lake Champlain to the Raritan and Arthur kill. But the great work with which his name is identified is the improvement of Hell Gate channel, concerning which he submitted a report in June, 1869, for the removal of Hallett's Point by sinking shafts on the shore side and running galleries under the rock to be removed, the same project to be applied also to the Gridiron Reef, the largest instance of the use of this method. He also conceived the iron-domed scow for the removal of isolated reefs, which proved a practical success. The explosion at Hallett's Point took place Sept. 24, 1876, and was successful. That of Flood Rock took place Oct. 10, 1885. These were two of the most remarkable achievements in engineering science, of their character, known to history. The commercial value of the result could hardly be overestimated. It was a splendid compliment to Gen. Newton when in 1887 the office of superintendent of the department of public works of New York city, which has been so often filled to the detriment of the public interest, was offered to him by Mayor William R. Grace. Gen. Newton was able to accept this position by going upon the retired list of the army, to which he was entitled. The fitness of his appointment was felicitously expressed by the statement that he was the ideal man for the position. After his retirement from this office he was employed as consulting engineer in many important works. Gen. Newton was a member of the National academy of science and an honorary member of the American society of civil engineers. *He died May 1, 1895.*

NICOLAY, JOHN GEORGE, author, was born in the village of Essingen, in Rhenish Bavaria, Germany, Feb. 26, 1832, son of Jacob and Helena Nicolay. In 1838 the family emigrated to America, making their first home in Cincinnati, O. From there they followed the westward drift of emigration, successively, to Indiana, Missouri, and Illinois. During this movement the boy received about two years' tuition in elementary schools in Cincinnati and St. Louis, in which the German and English languages were taught together. By the death of his parents, he was thrown upon his own resources, and for a year, 1846–47, was clerk in a small retail store. In July, 1848, Nicolay went to learn the trade of printer in the office of the "Free Press," a county paper, published at Pittsfield, Pike co., Ill. He remained in this office about eight years, and during that time he became, successively, publisher, editor, and proprietor of the "Free Press." At the close of the Frémont and Dayton campaign of 1856, Nicolay sold his paper, and became clerk in the office of the secretary of state at Springfield, Ill., where he continued until 1860. While thus occupied, he formed a close friendship with Abraham Lincoln, who, when he was nominated for the presidency, quite without solicitation, appointed Nicolay his private

secretary. The presidential election of 1860 was no sooner over than the correspondence of the president-elect increased to such an extent that an assistant was necessary, and to aid him, Nicolay chose John Hay, a young law student, with whom he had formed an intimate friendship, and this choice was confirmed by Mr. Lincoln. They both accompanied the president-elect in his memorable journey from Springfield to Washington. During the whole presidential term they occupied a room together in the White House, performing the important and often delicate duties devolving upon them, and enjoying the closest confidence of the president. Here also they formed the design, with the knowledge and approval of Mr. Lincoln, of writing his biography, which design, in later years, they carried out in collaboration. Shortly before his assassination, the president appointed Mr. Nicolay U.S. consul to Paris, France, and at the same time appointed Col. Hay secretary of legation in the same city; but they had not yet entered upon their new duties when the president's death occurred. Mr. Nicolay held the office of consul at Paris until the spring of 1869. Returning to Washington, he was, in December, 1872, appointed marshal of the supreme court of the United States, and filled that office until December, 1887. Nicolay and Hay began the active writing of their biography of Lincoln in 1874, though the previous six years had been occupied in gathering and arranging the necessary material. Its serial publication, under the title "Abraham Lincoln: A History," was begun in the "Century Magazine" in November, 1886, and continued, without interruption, until February, 1890. In the latter year the completed work, including many important chapters not printed in the serial, was issued by the Century Co., in ten volumes, and immediately achieved a permanent place in American standard literature. Of the joint work each author wrote about one half, and concurrently also they collected, catalogued and edited "Abraham Lincoln's Complete Works," which were published by the Century Co., in two volumes uniform with the "History" in 1894. Besides this principal literary task, Mr. Nicolay wrote, in 1881, "The Outbreak of the Rebellion," it being the initial volume of the series called "Campaigns of the Civil War." Of this work Clarence King wrote in the "Century": "It contains the most accurate and valuable account yet printed of the events immediately preceding the war and of its opening scenes down to the battle of Bull Run, and shows the author to possess the indispensable qualifications of a historian—calmness of temper, unfailing candor of statement, untiring industry in the collection and arrangement of facts, and unusual clearness and decision of judgment." Mr. Nicolay also wrote the article on Pres. Lincoln in the English edition of the "Encyclopaedia Britannica," and has contributed numerous articles to American magazines. All his accomplishments and tastes were of a high order: he patented a number of inventions; was a lover of art and music, a good linguist, and a poet of considerable merit. Of the several achievements of his career he, however, derived the most satisfaction from having earned Mr. Lincoln's friendship and perfect trust, as well as of having, in collaboration with Col. Hay, successfully carried out their design of writing the biography of the great president, which is at the same time an elaborate history of his administration and of the war between the states. Mr. Nicolay resided in Washington, D.C., and was engaged in literary pursuits. He was a founder of both the Literary Society and the Columbia Historical Society of Washington, and was a life member of the American Historical Association. He was married, in June, 1865, to Therena Bates of Pittsfield, Ill., who was of Massachusetts birth and ancestry. She died in November, 1886, leaving one daughter; Helen Nicolay, an artist and writer. *John Nicolay died in 1901.*